CANADIAN STUDIES IN THE NEW MILLENNIUM

Second Edition

This popular textbook offers a thorough and accessible approach to Canadian Studies through comparative analyses of Canada and the United States, their histories, geographies, political systems, economies, and cultures. Students and professors alike acknowledge it as an ideal tool for understanding the close relationship between the two countries, their shared experiences, and their differing views on a range of issues.

Fully revised and updated, the second edition of *Canadian Studies in the New Millennium* includes new chapters on demography and immigration policy, the environment, and civil society and social policy, all written by leading scholars and educators in the field. At a time in which there is a growing mutual dependence between the United States and Canada for security, trade, and investment, *Canadian Studies in the New Millennium* will continue to be a valuable resource for students, educators, and practitioners on both sides of the border.

MARK KASOFF is an emeritus professor in the Department of Economics and former director of the Canadian Studies Center at Bowling Green State University.

PATRICK JAMES is Dornsife Dean's Professor of International Relations in the School of International Studies at the University of Southern California.

Canadian Studies in the New Millennium

Second Edition

EDITED BY MARK KASOFF
AND PATRICK JAMES

UNIVERSITY OF TORONTO PRESS
Toronto Buffalo London

© University of Toronto Press 2013
Toronto Buffalo London
www.utppublishing.com
Printed in Canada

ISBN 978-1-4426-4693-3 (cloth)
ISBN 978-1-4426-1174-0 (paper)

Printed on acid-free, 100% post-consumer recycled paper with vegetable-based inks.

Library and Archives Canada Cataloguing in Publication

Canadian studies in the new millennium / edited by Mark Kasoff
and Patrick James. – 2nd ed.

Includes bibliographical references and index.
ISBN 978-1-4426-4693-3 (bound). – ISBN 978-1-4426-1174-0 (pbk.)

1. Canada – Textbooks.   2. Canada – Civilization – Textbooks.
3. Canada – History – Textbooks.   4. United States – Civilization –
Textbooks.   5. Comparative civilization – Textbooks.   I. Kasoff,
Mark J.   II. James, Patrick, 1957–

FC155.C374 2013   971   C2013-900096-8

University of Toronto Press acknowledges the financial assistance to its
publishing program of the Canada Council for the Arts and the Ontario
Arts Council.

University of Toronto Press acknowledges the financial support of the
Government of Canada through the Canada Book Fund for its publishing
activities.

Contents

Preface

The writing of this book has been encouraged by the Association for Canadian Studies in the United States (ACSUS). Like ACSUS, it is "dedicated to improving understanding about Canada in the United States." Given the widespread comparisons between the two countries, this volume is suitable for use in Introduction to Canada courses in the United States and Introduction to American Studies courses in Canada. The need for a comprehensive introductory book about Canada was endorsed at the ACSUS biennial in 2005. As editors, we have invited both leading and up-and-coming Canadian Studies educators to shape this book and to write chapters. We have endeavoured to make the chapter transitions as seamless as possible, in order to provide an integrated text rather than a collection of essays.

We are grateful to the chapter authors: Les Alm, Sammy Basu, Roderic Beaujot, Louis Bélanger, Michael J. Broadway, Ross Burkhart, Lea Caragata, Charles F. Doran, Munroe Eagles, Andrew Holman, Mark Kasoff (thanked by Patrick James for this and many other good things), Patrice LeClerc, Michael Lusztig, Sharon A. Manna, Douglas Nord, Muhammad Raza, Mark Paul Richard, Heather Smith, Paul Storer, Robert Thacker, and John Herd Thompson. Michael Lusztig, author of chapter 8, would like to thank Mark Smith of the British Columbia Treaty Commission for helping him navigate the complex jurisprudence of Aboriginal land claims in that province.

The editors would like to express their gratitude to Christine Drennen and Cynthia Kite for their valuable contributions to the first edition.

Daniel Quinlan, our editor at the University of Toronto Press, provided excellent advice and frequent encouragement in bringing this project home. We appreciate his insight and good humour. John St

James provided superb copyediting; we would recommend him to anyone. To Paul Obringer, creative director of Unigraphics at Bowling Green State University, our thanks for designing a book cover for the first edition that lives on in the second edition and captures the spirit of Canada. David Archibald (executive director) and George Sulzner (past president) of ACSUS helped at various stages of the first edition with their goodwill and positive thoughts. We are grateful for their fellowship along the way.

We hope that Betty and Carolyn will think this has been worth the long hours devoted to it and are very pleased that we all got together, once again, as this process neared its end, in Ventura, California.

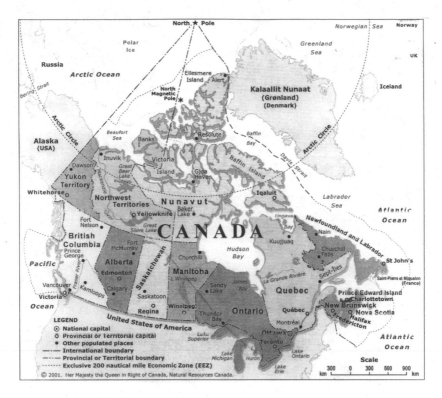

Map of Canada – Provinces and Territories. Courtesy of Listings Canada:
http://listingsca.com/maps.asp.

CANADIAN STUDIES IN THE NEW MILLENNIUM

Second Edition

Introduction

PATRICK JAMES AND MARK KASOFF

This book has been organized according to the principle that a textbook on Canadian Studies will be useful in almost any academic setting in which Canada is an important topic. It is intended either to stand alone as a basic textbook about Canada or to serve as a resource for comparative studies courses in the humanities and social sciences. Its key learning objectives are as follows:

- You will be able to identify Canada's key geographic features and political divisions.
- You will be able to describe how Canadian culture differs from American culture.
- You will be able to identify and communicate how the social welfare networks in Canada and how Canadian health care policies differ from American practices.
- You will be able to discuss the strengths and weaknesses of Canada's Westminster parliamentary system.
- You will be able to discuss the importance of French-speaking cultures in North America.
- You will be able to assess how Canada and the United States differently view shared historical events.
- You will be able to discuss Quebec's unique identity as well as issues that will affect the future of Quebec in Canada.

To our knowledge, this is the first textbook to satisfy these objectives, collectively speaking, in even a minimal way.

We start with geography. As chapter 1 emphasizes, perhaps the most fundamental feature of Canada is its geography. Geographic factors have figured into every significant aspect of the country's political, economic, and social evolution. For example, Confederation itself and attempts to renegotiate it at various times can be viewed as a cumulative reaction to the challenges to survival posed by geography. In economic terms, theorizing about Canada often begins with a review of the "staples thesis." To this day, Canada's vast territory and wealth of natural resources illuminate its trade and development. Canada's proximity to the United States has profoundly affected both its society and its view of itself. For instance, Canadians often identify themselves in terms of what they are *not* (i.e., Americans). And this is just the tip of the iceberg when it comes to understanding the importance of geography to this northern land. Thus, chapter 1 discusses the strong impact that geography has had on Canada.

Chapter 2 covers Canada's history. That history has been shaped by struggles among its earliest inhabitants – those now generally known as the First Nations, the French, and the British – as well as with the "other" – the United States. The Vikings were the earliest European settlers in North America; however, this chapter starts with the French explorers and settlers of the 1500s and the importance of the fur trade. The reader is taken through the struggle to control North America and the British victory at Quebec City in 1759. Rumblings in the thirteen colonies resulted in (1) the Royal Proclamation of 1763, which addressed relations with North American aboriginals; and (2) the Quebec Act of 1774. A remarkable document, the Quebec Act enshrined French language and culture in Quebec and permitted Roman Catholicism to flourish at a time when it was harassed in Britain. Canada became a nation in 1867, amid fears that after the American Civil War idle guns and troops would be turned North. Post-Confederation history, in turn, was shaped by the race with the Americans to settle western North America and by John A. Macdonald's National Policy, which enacted tariffs, constructed the first trans-Canada rail link, and ultimately produced three more during its continuation by the Laurier government (1896–1911). Twentieth-century Canadian history is mainly about the gradual erosion of formal and informal British control and how the two world wars made Canada a more assertive nation.

Chapter 3 examines the evolution of Canadian government and politics. While Canadian political history does include sporadic violence, military actions have never played a major role in either effecting or preventing change. Rather, Canada's political institutions have evolved through a long series of negotiations. This chapter discusses

how Canada's system of governance has evolved over the past fourteen decades since Confederation in response to internal and external
events. Students will also learn about the parliamentary system and
how it differs from the US form of government. This chapter pays particular attention to the political system as it has functioned since the
Constitution was repatriated in 1982 and the Charter of Rights and
Freedoms was enacted.

Canada's economic development is discussed in chapter 4. In the
early days, Canada's economy was based on the fur trade, fishing, forestry, farming, and mining. Macdonald's National Policy, which persisted into the first three decades of the twentieth century, is discussed
in the context of how protection can help grow a young economy, but
can lead to inefficiencies if domestic politics prevent the lifting of protectionist measures such as tariffs. Today, international trade and investment are more important to Canada than to the United States. Until
recently, around 45 per cent of Canada's economic output has been exported – a figure four times greater than for the United States. To ensure
access to the US market and to increase its own economic competitiveness, Canada signed the Free Trade Agreement with the United States
in 1989 and the North American Free Trade Agreement (NAFTA, which
included Mexico) in 1994. Canada's reasons for joining NAFTA are discussed with particular attention to how it settles trade disputes with
the United States. This chapter ends with a discussion of the economic
interdependence of Canada and the United States, which has resulted
in the largest bilateral trade relationship on the planet. It also notes the
economic impact of heightened security concerns since 11 September
2001.

Chapter 5 explores the dynamics of population growth in Canada,
emphasizing the critical importance of migration. It traces three periods, the first being from France, the second from the United Kingdom,
and more recently from Asia, Africa, and other places on the planet. In
order to sustain economic development Canada will need a steady flow
of immigrants for the foreseeable future.

Chapter 6 focuses on the persistence of the French fact in Canada
from the 1500s to present times and today's challenges to francophone
identity and cultural survival. After referencing the significance of the
Quebec Act and the historic dominance of the Roman Catholic Church,
we discuss the Quiet Revolution of the 1960s, when the Québécois rejected centuries of domination by the more affluent and powerful English-speaking minority and began to assert an independent political

voice. The election of the first Parti Québécois government in 1976 is highlighted; so are the failed first sovereignty referendum of 1980, the stillborn Meech Lake and Charlottetown Accords, and the narrowly defeated second sovereignty referendum of 1995. The chapter also addresses Quebec's changing demographics; with few new immigrants coming from France, the province finds itself having to build a linguistic cultural community rather than one based on French ancestral origins. The chapter also discusses alternative scenarios for Quebec's future.

Chapter 7 focuses on Canadian literature and popular culture. Despite economic globalization, Canada's popular culture is thriving. Present-day examples in music include Céline Dion, Nickelback, Nelly Furtado, Helix, Bryan Adams, Sum 41, Avril Lavigne, Shania Twain, and Great Big Sea. Examples of the direct style in Canadian cinema include Arcand's *Barbarian Invasions*, which was awarded the Oscar for best foreign-language film in 2004, and Egoyan's *The Sweet Hereafter*. The chapter also discusses sports in Canada, most notably hockey.

Native people are the subject of chapter 8. Few chapters are likely to rival this one for overall controversy. Aboriginal peoples in Canada have had a bleak story to tell in the centuries since the Europeans arrived. Theirs is a history of suffering, broken promises, and attempts at forced assimilation. So this chapter focuses on Native people's struggles to assert their rights and to achieve recognition as distinct peoples.

Chapter 9 considers women's issues in Canadian society. The Charter of Rights and Freedoms is hailed by advocates of human rights as an extraordinary document in terms of its recognition of women. The Charter is regarded as consistent with a global trend towards rights awareness that first took shape in the 1970s. This chapter focuses on the position of women in Canadian society in both absolute and relative terms. For example, do the periods before and after the Charter differ in kind or merely degree in terms of where women stand in Canada? Another interesting question is more relative in nature: Are women in Canada better off than those in other advanced states that normally are regarded as the country's peers? More general questions addressed in this chapter pertain to population, immigration, and women's participation in politics.

Chapter 10 reviews Canadian environmental policy in such areas as joint stewardship of the Great Lakes (with the United States), acid rain, and global climate change. Canadian provincial control of natural resources is discussed along with Canada's signing the Kyoto Accords.

The chapter evaluates Canada's performance in comparison to environmental benchmarks.

How human needs are addressed beyond the private economy and government programs are presented in chapter 11: Civil Society. Examples include voluntary, community, and charitable groups, social networks, producer and consumer cooperatives, and non-government organizations (NGOs). It shows how Canada's commitment to multiculturalism and the Charter of Rights and Freedoms has presented both opportunities and challenges for civil society.

International relations and foreign policy are discussed in chapter 12, which will tell two stories: one about Canada in the world as a whole, the other about Canada as the Americans' neighbour. Key subjects in this chapter include Canada's involvement in major world conflicts and peacekeeping, and recent controversies relating to human security and Canada's role in the War on Terrorism. The chapter emphasizes Canada's preference for multilateral approaches to solving international problems, given its status as a middle power.

Chapter 13, which concludes this book, focuses on Canada in the new millennium. It is fair to say that since 9/11 and the second Gulf War, Canada has entered a crucial period in its history. While it identifies with the American-led coalition against terrorism, it is taking part in a limited way and with much scepticism as to whether military means can bring about a lasting solution. Thus, Canada is caught between its traditional preference for multilateralism and its closest ally's generally unilateral operations. So it is appropriate to reflect on Canada as a country that may have reached a turning point in its basic orientation towards the rest of the world. Canada also faces questions about national unity and identity, and so the domestic situation also is far from tranquil. Regional disparities, alienation, and nationalism in Quebec create ongoing issues for Confederation. This final chapter draws on the insights from those preceding it to derive some ideas about where the country may be headed and how it may best meet the range of challenges from within and beyond its borders.

1 Canada: Too Much Geography?

MICHAEL J. BROADWAY

Canada is the world's second-largest country, covering nearly 3.9 million square miles and six time zones (including a separate one for Newfoundland and Labrador), yet much of it is sparsely populated. In 2011, its population of 34.4 million was less than California's (37 million). Most Canadians live in cities along their country's southern border with the United States. The country's three largest metropolitan areas, Toronto, Montreal, and Vancouver, account for over a third of the country's population, and each is within an hour's drive of the US border. Between and to the north of these areas is a vast and diverse country. In the sparsely populated Far North, glaciation and an arctic climate created the tundra – a gently undulating landscape dotted with hundreds of thousands of lakes and covered in grasses and lichen that supported a nomadic native population. By contrast, mild, moist air masses from the Pacific Ocean bring bountiful rains to British Columbia's coast and support a lush and verdant temperate rainforest that belies the popular image of Canada as a cold and snowy place. Two hundred miles inland, rainfall drops to less than 10 inches a year, semi-desert conditions prevail, and tourist brochures boast of a climate sunnier than Miami's. Across the Rocky Mountains, the prairies extend uninterrupted from Calgary to east of Winnipeg, a distance of more than 850 miles. Winnipeg's average January high temperature of 7°F conforms to the more popular stereotype about Canada's climate.

Canada's physical diversity is matched in its cultural and economic landscape. Its dependence on high immigration rates to sustain population growth has produced cosmopolitan cities like Toronto and Vancouver; in both, over 45 per cent of the population is foreign born. Yet in Saint John, New Brunswick, and Chicoutimi, Quebec, the corresponding figures are less than 3 per cent. A different type of "diversity" exists in Chicoutimi, a community of about 60,000 north of Quebec City, where 98 per cent of the people speak French as a first language. A mere 100,000 people live in the northern third of Canada; that is, less than 1 per cent of Ontario's population (see table 1.1). Unemployment in 2011 in Newfoundland and Labrador on Canada's Atlantic coast was nearly double the national average of 7.3 per cent, while weekly earnings in the rest of Atlantic Canada were well below the national average (see table 1.1). On the other side of the country, Alberta's energy-based economy produced an unemployment rate of just 5.1 per cent and the highest provincial average weekly earnings in the country (followed by Ontario and Saskatchewan).

Scholars have used the *core-periphery* concept to explain regional variations in Canada's economic development. This is a variant of the "staples thesis" (discussed at length in chapter 2). Core regions are characterized by good agricultural land, high levels of industrialization and urbanization, and close proximity to markets. Peripheral or hinterland regions emphasize resource production; they have scattered populations and weakly integrated urban systems. According to this theory, the core extracts wealth from the periphery by adding value to raw materials provided by the periphery and keeps the periphery dependent on it for markets, capital, and manufactured goods. Canada's core is the Windsor–Quebec City corridor; the rest of the country has long been viewed as the periphery. This model is not static; shifts in interregional relationships are possible owing to internal factors such as government redistributive policies and the world demand for raw materials. The rest of this chapter uses the core-periphery framework to survey Canada's geography, beginning with the Great Lakes–St Lawrence Lowlands (the core region), followed by the resource hinterlands of Atlantic Canada, the Prairies, British Columbia, and the North.

Great Lakes–St Lawrence Lowlands

Southern Ontario and southern Quebec constitute Canada's traditional heartland or core. This relatively small region is home to about 60 per cent of Canadians, half the country's large and medium-sized metropolitan areas, and half its highest-quality agricultural soils. It consists of two subregions, which are centred on the country's two largest cities, Toronto and Montreal; and it is culturally divided between mostly English speakers in Ontario and mostly French speakers in Quebec.

Table 1.1 Canadian provinces and territories, selected economic and social data

	Population (in thousands)[1]	Persons/sq. km[2]	Unemployment (%)[3]	Weekly earnings ($C)[4]
Newfoundland	510.6	1.3	12.9	837.65
Prince Edward Island	145.9	24.4	11.2	709.59
Nova Scotia	945.4	17.0	8.6	760.07
New Brunswick	755.5	10.3	9.4	761.70
Quebec	7,979.7	4.9	7.3	783.99
Ontario	13,373.0	11.7	8.1	882.38
Manitoba	1,250.6	1.8	5.2	786.35
Saskatchewan	1,057.9	1.6	4.1	846.25
Alberta	3,779.5	4.9	5.1	993.28
British Columbia	4,573.3	4.5	6.6	818.78
Yukon	34.7	0.06	–	919.32
Northwest Territories	43.7	0.03	–	1,191.63
Nunavut	33.3	0.01	–	865.46
Canada	34,482.8	3.2	7.3	853.19

Source: Statistics Canada
[1] Population estimate 1 July 2011
[2] Persons per square kilometre
[3] Unemployment rate October 2011
[4] Average weekly earnings in 2010

Notwithstanding this cultural fault line, the region has dominated Canada economically and politically since the country's very beginning.

The Rise of the Heartland

After Britain defeated France for control of North America in 1759, it acquired land north of the Great Lakes, control of the continent's fur trade, and a well-established French colony in the St Lawrence Valley between Quebec City and Montreal. Along the St Lawrence River between Montreal and Quebec City, the land was divided into long lots.

This was the seigneurial settlement system, which gave each farmer access to the river.

The Great Lakes region's rise to dominance began with an economy based on exporting staples: furs in the late eighteenth century and timber and wheat in the first half of the nineteenth. Southwestern Ontario's excellent climate and rich soils made it ideal for growing wheat. The forests of the Ottawa and Saguenay Valleys provided a wealth of timber for export to Britain. Much of this trade was controlled by Montreal's merchants, who exchanged these staples for foreign manufactured goods. These traders and their Toronto counterparts used their profits to stimulate the demand for locally produced goods, and a manufacturing sector gradually emerged. The growth in trade stimulated the development of a canal and railway network between Montreal and Toronto. Montreal's position at the confluence of the Ottawa, Richelieu, and St Lawrence Rivers, combined with its position on the Grand Trunk Railway, which linked it with Portland, Maine, and Sarnia, Ontario, gave the city an advantage over Quebec City in terms of economic development. This advantage was never relinquished, and as a result Quebec City developed more slowly.

The post-Confederation National Policy protected Canada's manufacturing sector by imposing tariffs on imported products and reinforced the primacy of manufacturing in the heartland. In late-nineteenth-century Quebec, rapid population growth and a shortage of agricultural land compelled many rural dwellers to migrate to Montreal, where they provided cheap labour for the city's shoe, textile, and clothing sectors. Southern Ontario's industrial growth during this period was based on food processing and metalworking. The region's close proximity to Appalachian coking coal gave it an advantage over Quebec, and metalworking grew into a fully fledged iron and steel industry in Hamilton. At the turn of the twentieth century, cheap hydroelectric power from Niagara Falls attracted more industries, including factories for producing electrical goods, industrial machinery, and chemicals and, in the 1920s, the automobile industry. Canada's high tariff structure meant that foreign companies that wanted access to the Canadian market had to build branch plants. US manufacturers preferred Ontario because it was Canada's largest market and was closest to the US manufacturing belt.

In 1965 the Canada-US Auto Pact removed tariffs on original equipment manufactured (OEM) parts and automobiles on both sides of the border; this led to the auto industry's expansion, primarily in southern

Ontario. Over the next thirty years, General Motors, Toyota, Ford, DaimlerChrysler, and Suzuki either built new plants or expanded old ones near the Highway 401 corridor between Windsor and Oshawa, while Honda established a plant north of Toronto along Highway 400. The most recent expansion, in the 1990s, was spurred by the declining Canadian dollar and by Canada's government-funded health care program, which gave the region significant cost savings over Michigan, the home of the US auto industry. Outside of southern Ontario, the Ottawa-Gatineau region grew to become the country's fourth-largest metropolitan area, largely on the basis of government employment and high-tech industries.

Change Comes to the Heartland

Although southern Ontario and southern Quebec are still the centre of Canadian manufacturing, globalization in the form of the 1989 Canada-US Free Trade Agreement and 1994 North American Free Trade Agreement (NAFTA) resulted in the restructuring of some industries. Eliminating tariffs on US manufactured goods coming into Canada removed the rationale for establishing branch plants, and uneconomic plants closed. Montreal's industrial decline predates the free trade era. Because it industrialized earlier, it was saddled with old and inefficient plants in labour-intensive industries such as textiles and clothing. Montreal's efforts to diversify its economy began in the 1960s. It expanded its role as a tourist destination with the 1967 World's Fair, Expo 67, the preservation of Vieux Montréal, and the 1976 Summer Olympics. Some of these *grands projets* proved extremely costly and controversial; the city finally paid off its Olympics debt in early 2006! The construction of an international airport north of the city in 1975 is symbolic of the era. Mirabel Airport was meant to be the gateway to Montreal and Ottawa, with 50 million passengers projected by 2025, but it never handled more than 3 million a year and was eventually closed to passengers in 2004. Quebec City never developed a large-scale industrial sector; today, most of its jobs are in the service sector, in government, health care, education, and tourism.

Deindustrialization between 1971 and 1986 led to the loss of more than 70,000 manufacturing jobs in Montreal. The unemployment rate soared to over 20 per cent in the city's traditional manufacturing areas. The election of separatist Parti Québécois provincial governments beginning in the late 1970s fuelled uncertainty over the province's economic future, which caused an exodus of corporate headquarters

Table 1.2 Canadian auto-sector layoffs, 2008

Date	Company and location
April 2008	GM announces 970 job cuts at Oshawa plant.
May 2008	GM announces transmission plant closure in Windsor with 1400 job losses.
June 2008	GM announces as many as 2600 will be laid off when Oshawa truck plant closes.
	Magna auto parts plant in St Thomas, Ontario, announces 400 job cuts.
	Formet auto parts in St Thomas, Ontario, announces 400 job cuts.
July 2008	Sterling Truck (DaimlerChrysler) plant in St Thomas announces 720 job cuts.
August 2008	Linamar auto parts in Guelph, Ontario, announces 500 job cuts.
October 2008	Sterling Truck (DaimlerChrysler) plant in St Thomas announces 600 job cuts.
	Ford announces 100 temporary layoffs at its Oakville, Ontario, plant.
November 2008	GM announces 500 temporary layoffs at its Oshawa, Ontario, plant.

Source: CBC News

from Montreal to Toronto and Calgary. As a result, Toronto overtook Montreal as Canada's premier city as well as its financial capital. Efforts to revitalize Montreal's manufacturing sector have focused on the pharmaceutical and transportation sectors; the city is the home of Bombardier, a global aerospace and mass transit company with more than 25,000 employees. The city remains the corporate headquarters for Quebec-based companies and is the province's major service centre. Alcan, a major aluminum producer based in Montreal merged with Rio Tinto, a global mining corporation, in 2007. Two years later, as a result of the global economic downturn, the company announced plans to shut down one of its smelters southwest of Montreal, with the loss of 220 jobs. Outside of Montreal, General Motors shut down its Sainte-Thérèse plant in 2002, with the loss of several thousand jobs.

In southern Ontario, competitive pressures resulted in layoffs in Hamilton's steel industry, while General Motors closed plants in

Scarborough (an old suburb of Toronto), Oshawa, and St Catharines. In 2006 Ford announced it would be closing facilities in Windsor and cutting a shift at its St Thomas plant. The global recession that began in 2007 had a disastrous impact on North America's auto industry. The collapse of credit markets led to a massive reduction in the demand for automobiles and companies were forced to cut back production. Ontario was particularly hard hit as the so-called Big 3 (GM, Ford, and DaimlerChrysler) announced a series of plant closures that led to job cuts and layoffs among parts suppliers (table 1.2). The shrinking auto labour markets led Ontario's jobless rate to hit a fifteen year high in April 2009 at 9.4 per cent.

In the 1970s, the City of Toronto began losing manufacturing jobs to the outlying suburbs. But unlike Montreal, it has been able to replace many of those jobs with high- and low-paying service-sector jobs, and as a result it has lower unemployment. Toronto is Ontario's provincial capital and cultural and entertainment centre; it is also Canada's financial, corporate, and media hub. Downtown Toronto is home to the head offices of hundreds of major companies; lower-paid support positions, the so-called "back office" functions, are increasingly out in the suburbs.

Metropolitan Growth and Agriculture

Since 1971 the core's highest population growth rates have occurred in and around the Toronto metropolitan area (see table 1.3). Oshawa is the eastern anchor of the Golden Horseshoe, an industrialized and highly urbanized area extending along Lake Ontario to Niagara Falls that includes Hamilton and Toronto. Oshawa's spectacular population gains over the past forty years are attributable to its relatively cheap housing and Toronto's suburban expansion. In southwestern Ontario, London, always known as a major insurance town, has experienced growth related to its role as a parts supplier to the auto industry and to the expansion of its service sector. The Kitchener-Waterloo-Cambridge area markets itself as Canada's technology triangle and is home to RIM, Research in Motion, maker of the Blackberry. High-tech industries have been attracted to the area by the University of Waterloo's technological expertise and highly skilled labour force. Older industrial areas such as Hamilton, St Catharines, and Windsor have experienced much slower population growth since 1971, as have Montreal and Quebec City.

Table 1.3 Population change in major core metropolitan areas, 1971–2011

Metropolitan area	2011 population	Change, 1971–2011
Toronto	5,838,800	+3,222,700
Montreal	3,390,700	+1,238,600
Ottawa Gatineau	1,258,900	+639,100
Quebec City	761,700	+261,700
Hamilton	750,200	+247,000
Kitchener	498,500	+259,900
London	496,900	+243,000
St Catharines	405,300	+119,500
Oshawa	370,800	+253,300
Windsor	332,500	+84,200

Source: Statistics Canada

St Catharines is growing slowly; even so, its suburbs continue to encroach on valuable agricultural land in the Niagara fruit belt. This region is one of the few in Canada with a climate and soils suitable for tender fruit crops like cherries, peaches, pears, and grapes. Low farm incomes encourage farmers to sell their land to developers; this has made the area a battleground between developers and preservationists. Continued population growth in southwestern Ontario is threatening some of Canada's highest-quality agricultural land, most of which is used for growing corn and other livestock feeds. At the southern tip of the region, almost within sight of downtown Detroit, is the greenhouse capital of North America. Leamington, Ontario, has more than one thousand acres of greenhouses devoted to vegetable production, mostly tomatoes, cucumbers, and peppers. Some of this area's vegetables are exported to the United States; many of its tomatoes find their way to the local Heinz factory for processing into ketchup.

Atlantic Canada

Atlantic Canada includes the provinces of Newfoundland and Labrador, Nova Scotia, Prince Edward Island, and New Brunswick and is

Table 1.4 Selected demographic indicators, Atlantic Canada

	Pop. change 1981–2011 (%)	Per cent rural, 2006	Per cent foreign-born, 2006
Newfoundland and Labrador	−10	42	1.6
Prince Edward Island	+14	55	3.5
Nova Scotia	+9	45	4.9
New Brunswick	+8	49	3.6
Canada	+38	20	19.6

Source: Statistics Canada

the country's poorest region. One hundred years ago its resource-based economy, built around fishing, forestry, and mining, made it a prosperous place. Today, these industries have almost disappeared and the biggest export for many rural communities is people. Because of out-migration, Newfoundland's population declined 10 per cent between 1981 and 2011; the rest of the region has experienced slower growth than Canada as a whole (see table 1.4). The region's sluggish economy means it attracts fewer immigrants than the rest of the country (see table 1.4). Job creation is largely confined to the service sector, which dominates the two largest metropolitan areas in the region: Halifax, Nova Scotia (2011 population 408,300), and St John's, Newfoundland (2011 population 199,200). To counter structural economic change and population losses, Atlantic Canada's provincial governments have attempted to diversify their economies. For any industry or business to survive and prosper in the region, it must overcome obstacles imposed by geography, most notably a small and highly dispersed internal market and long distances from major US and Canadian markets.

The region's physiography makes farming a challenge; much of it is glaciated hills, with cold winters and warm summers. Arable land is confined mostly to Prince Edward Island, the Annapolis Valley in Nova Scotia, and the Saint John River Valley in New Brunswick. Nearly half the region's 2.3 million people reside in villages scattered along the coast. Newfoundland exemplifies this pattern. The interior of the island is largely devoid of settlement except for towns along the Trans-Canada Highway, which links St John's with Port aux Basques. Settlement in

Nova Scotia and New Brunswick exhibits the same characteristic, reflecting the historic importance of the sea to the region's people.

The first permanent European settlers in the region were attracted by its enormous stocks of cod and other groundfish. Off the coast of Newfoundland on the Grand Banks, the Gulf Stream's warm waters meet the cold Labrador Current, creating ideal conditions for sustaining a large fishery. Beginning in the seventeenth century, Europeans established hundreds of small fishing communities along the coast. At the end of the twentieth century, cod and groundfish stocks collapsed, creating a crisis that threatens the sustainability of many communities throughout Atlantic Canada.

Crisis in the Fishery

Fishing is important throughout the region, but there are significant variations among the four provinces in fisheries employment and in the types of species caught. In the late 1980s the industry accounted for 21 per cent of all jobs in Newfoundland compared to just 5 per cent for New Brunswick. Newfoundlanders depended largely on cod caught on the Grand Banks; fishers in other provinces caught a wider variety of sea life, including lobsters and scallops.

Technological innovations after the Second World War supported the industry's expansion. The construction of ocean-going freezer trawlers, the use of sonar to locate fish stocks, and heavier use of gill nets all increased the catches on the Grand Banks. In an effort to manage the resource, in 1977 the federal government established the Department of Fisheries and Oceans (DFO) and declared a two-hundred-mile economic zone off the coast. By 1992 the cod stocks had fallen so dramatically that the DFO declared a moratorium on the cod fishery to allow them to recover. Many believed this would be a short-term measure, but nearly twenty years later the moratorium remains largely in place.

The cod stocks collapsed largely because the DFO overestimated their size and set the total allowable catch (TAC) too high; also, the DFO was unable to regulate foreign fishing outside the two-hundred-mile limit, specifically on the "nose" of the Grand Banks. In addition, there were political pressures to keep the TAC high, since fishing supported thousands of processing jobs in an area of high unemployment. After the moratorium, an estimated 30,000 workers lost their jobs. The federal government spent billions of dollars on retraining workers. But the reality is that there is little alternative employment in remote coastal

Table 1.5 Changing population structure of Newfoundland fishing communities

Community	2011 population	% change 1996–2011	% > 65 in 2011	Median age in 2011
Grand Bank	2,415	–27	25	52
Twillingate	2,269	–23	26	53
Trepassey	570	–47	25	56
Newfoundland	514,536	–7	16	44

Source: Statistics Canada

communities; so many Maritimers moved elsewhere, leaving behind an increasingly elderly dependent population. The village of Grand Bank, on the Burin Peninsula on Newfoundland's south shore, typifies the crisis in rural communities. Between 1996 and 2011 its population declined by 27 per cent; even more significantly for the community's future, the number of children under 15 dropped by 270 during the same period. Twillingate on the province's north shore and Trepassey on the Avalon Peninsula are facing a similar fate (see table 1.5).

Crab, shrimp, lobster, and clams have replaced cod, and thanks to high prices the value of the catch has increased. In Newfoundland shellfish accounted for 82 per cent of the $444 million worth of fish caught in 2009. In Nova Scotia the equivalent figures for 2009 were 80 per cent and $600 million respectively. Both provinces are looking to expand aquaculture, and specifically the production of salmon and shellfish, to provide employment and exports.

Other Traditional Exports

The first commercial coal mine in Canada opened at Port Morien on Cape Breton Island in 1720, launching the region's long association with the industry. Underground mining in the Sydney coalfield was never very profitable and had to be protected from competition by tariffs and subsidies. In the mid-1960s the Dominion Steel and Coal Corporation announced its intention to get out of the coal business. After a public inquiry into the future of mining in the region the federal government announced the establishment of the Cape Breton Development Corporation to operate the mines with the goal of closing them by 1981. The 1970s energy crisis saw a policy reversal, with the federal government encouraging the use of locally produced coal to replace imported oil for electricity generation. But finally, in 2001, high production costs and onerous subsidies forced the government to get out of the coal business. It closed the last mines, with the loss of thousands of jobs.

Nearly 90 per cent of Atlantic Canada is forested, forming the basis for a lumber and pulp-and-paper sector. Many of the region's pulp mills are located near river mouths, since water was long used to transport logs and is still a raw material in the pulping process. Most of the region's pulp and paper is exported, making it vulnerable to changes in demand as well as to foreign competition. To maintain a competitive industry, companies have been investing in labour-saving technology; this has reduced employment opportunities in a region already beset with high unemployment.

An iron and steel industry was established in Sydney and New Glasgow, Nova Scotia, based on local supplies of coal and imported iron ore from Newfoundland and Labrador. But despite government subsidies, continued losses have forced these plants to close. Shipbuilding in Saint John, New Brunswick, has suffered a similar fate. From the mid-1980s through the early 1990s the local shipyard employed about three thousand workers. After the last order for nine frigates for the Canadian military was fulfilled, most of the yard's workers were laid off. The yard closed for good in 2001. Today, most industries in the region are relatively small in scale and based on the processing of local materials for local consumption.

Because of the short growing season and the lack of arable land, agriculture is of minimal importance in Atlantic Canada. Most of the region's farmers raise livestock, and most farmland there is used to grow livestock feed or as pastureland. The exception to this pattern is Prince Edward Island, where more than half the land is devoted to farming. The island's chief cash crop is potatoes – which is also the principal crop in northwestern New Brunswick, home to McCain Foods, the world's largest producer of frozen French fries. The company, founded in 1956 in Florenceville, has become a multinational corporation, with operations on six continents and a worldwide labour force of more than 20,000.

New Opportunities

Atlantic Canada is a resource hinterland in transition. Its traditional resource-based industries are in decline. The challenge for the region is to diversify its economy and attract new jobs. The discovery of oil two hundred miles off the southeastern coast of Newfoundland in the 1960s led to the development of the Hibernia and Terra Nova oil fields in 1997 and 2002 respectively. Coping with icebergs, rogue waves, fog, hurricanes, and winter storms meant constructing the world's largest oil production platform. In the process, specialized manufacturing facilities were established in Newfoundland and Nova Scotia. In 2004 Newfoundland's oil and gas sector claimed to have generated more than 17,000 jobs directly and indirectly. In 1993 one of the world's largest nickel concentrations was discovered at Voisey's Bay in northern Labrador. After years of negotiations between the mining company, First Nations, and the Newfoundland government, the mine began operations in the fall of 2005; it currently employs about 450 people.

Government agencies charged with promoting economic development have focused on expanding tourism. Heritage and ecotourism show particular promise. Newfoundland boasts L'Anse aux Meadows, the eleventh-century remains of a Viking settlement, as well as Gros Morne National Park, a place of spectacular coastal scenery. Nova Scotia's Cape Breton Island is rich in historical sites from the Fortress of Louisbourg, the largest reconstructed eighteenth-century French fortified town in North America, to the Miners' Museum in Glace Bay. There are opportunities to observe wildlife and hike trails in Fundy, Cape Breton Highlands, and Terra Nova National Parks. Prince Edward Island boasts sandy beaches and the warmest waters north of the Carolinas; it is also the setting for the popular Anne of Green Gables books. But tourism's potential as a job creator is limited by the relatively short summer and distances from major markets. New England is the nearest major population centre, but the drive from Boston, Massachusetts, to Halifax, Nova Scotia, is almost seven hundred miles. Opportunities exist to expand the region's knowledge-based industries, using the scientific expertise lodged in its major universities. It remains to be seen how well these and other efforts will succeed in addressing the region's have-not status.

The Prairies

The western interior provinces of Manitoba, Saskatchewan, and Alberta share some similarities with Atlantic Canada. They are sparsely populated, have minimal manufacturing, and share a resource-based economy. But unlike Atlantic Canada, the Prairie provinces are a region of recent European settlement where agriculture is of primary importance. Even more significantly, the discovery of a major oilfield in Leduc, just south of Edmonton, in 1947 launched a boom-and-bust economy in Alberta. At the beginning of the twenty-first century, another boom is in full swing thanks to the oil sands near Fort McMurray. Across the Saskatchewan border, recent increases in commodity prices for oil, potash, and uranium have brought about another boom, and migrants are flocking to the province, with the result that in 2011 Saskatchewan had the fastest population growth rate of any Canadian province.

Settlement and the Development of an Agrarian Economy

The Hudson's Bay Company was given a royal charter in 1670 to trade in Rupert's Land, an area corresponding to the lands draining into Hudson Bay. For the next two hundred years the company enjoyed a monopoly on the region's fur trade and used it to block settlement, except for a small colony established in 1812 near Fort Garry, north of present-day Winnipeg. Little was known about the Prairies until John Palliser's 1857 expedition, which determined that the region was suitable for agriculture. Palliser reported fertile conditions across much of the region, except for an area in southern Alberta and Saskatchewan along the Montana border, which he believed to be an extension of the Great American Desert. This semi-arid area was named Palliser's Triangle.

In 1870 the government of Canada acquired Rupert's Land from the Hudson's Bay Company and began negotiating treaties with the Native peoples there. The treaties that resulted would confine Native people to reserves and ensure the availability of homesteading land. The next step in promoting settlement was the completion of Canada's first transcontinental railway, the Canadian Pacific Railway (CPR). The CPR agreed to build the line in return for $25 million and millions of acres of adjacent land for future sale to settlers. The company's selection of a southerly route greatly influenced the region's growth. Brandon, Manitoba, and Moose Jaw and Regina, Saskatchewan, were all towns created by the CPR. In Calgary, the company selected a site for its station about a mile west of the initial settlement so that it could make money from land sales around the station.

Under the National Policy, the prairie region was meant to produce food for Central Canada and Europe, as well as provide a market for Central Canada's manufactured goods. Manufacturing was protected by tariffs; prairie settlement was promoted by recruiting immigrants, constructing an extensive railway network, and subsidizing the export of grains (via the so-called Crow Rate). The CPR was completed in 1885.

A decade later the federal government launched a vigorous recruitment campaign, promoting the region as the last agricultural frontier in North America. Most newcomers to the Prairies during this period came from eastern and central Europe, with the largest single source being the Ukraine. By 1914 most of the available agricultural land had been taken and settlement was complete.

Life was not easy for the homesteaders. The land was mostly flat and the soil was rich, but a short growing season and unreliable rainfall made farming a challenge. This situation changed in 1910 with the introduction of Marquis wheat, a strain developed specifically to thrive in the region's climate. The adoption of this new strain and the development of dry-land farming techniques led to a rapid expansion of the prairie grain economy.

The Crow Rate was established in 1897. In return for a federal subsidy to construct a railway through the Crowsnest Pass in the southern Rockies, the CPR agreed to reduce freight rates on grain moving east out of the Prairies and on settlers' effects moving west. Over time, the rate was expanded to include shipments to west coast ports and to cover more than fifty commodities ranging from wheat to sunflower oil.

Changes in the Farm Economy

Agriculture's role in the region's economy has diminished over time, with farming changing from a labour- to a capital-intensive enterprise. Productivity soared when machinery began replacing labour, sparking an exodus from the land. This trend accelerated in the last quarter of the twentieth century, when commodity prices collapsed, making it difficult for farmers to make ends meet. Fewer farms has meant fewer people to support rural businesses, and this has contributed to a downward spiral in the rural population, a trend that is most pronounced in Saskatchewan. Between 1941 and 2011 that province lost over 100,000 farms (see table 1.6); during the same period, average farm size more than tripled and the number of rural dwellers fell by about 300,000.

In 1995 the Crow Rate was eliminated, in part because under NAFTA it was considered an unfair subsidy. Farmers now pay the full costs for their grain shipments. Confronted by a large supply of cheap grain, provincial governments have promoted the livestock and meatpacking sector as a means of adding value to the grain. The work of feeding

Table 1.6 Prairie Provinces, number of farms 1941–2011

	1941	2011	Change
Manitoba	58,024	15,877	−42,147
Saskatchewan	138,713	36,952	−101,761
Alberta	99,732	43,234	−56,498

Source: Statistics Canada

grain to animals, raising them, and slaughtering, processing, and shipping them has generated thousands of jobs in a region long characterized by rural out-migration. One year before the Crow's termination, NAFTA was signed, providing Canadian livestock producers and meatpackers with expanded access to the US and Mexican markets. In response, livestock production expanded throughout the region and new meatpacking plants were constructed. Between 1995 and 2005 the number of hogs produced in Manitoba rose by 5.1 million or 182 per cent. Similar, albeit smaller, increases occurred during the same period in Saskatchewan (98 per cent) and Alberta (38 per cent); the prairie region's share of Canadian hog slaughter rose from 32 to 37 per cent, with most pork being exported to the United States. But rising feed-grain prices between 2006 and 2009 have hurt the industry and curtailed production and exports.

Alberta's prominence as a livestock-producing province predates the ending of the Crow. Its natural advantages – plentiful grazing land and good soil for feed grains – promoted cattle production from the earliest days of European settlement. Until the 1980s large numbers of cattle were shipped from the Prairies to be slaughtered in southern Ontario. Then, faced by competitive pressures, meatpackers adopted a series of innovations developed in the United States that allowed plants to locate close to where cattle are fattened. As a consequence, the industry relocated to small towns in southern Alberta. The province now slaughters about three-quarters of all Canadian beef cattle. In 2002, 99.77 per cent of the province's cattle exports went to the United States; the equivalent figure for beef exports was 74.9 per cent. The total value of this trade was about $2 billion. The perils of this export dependence were demonstrated a year later when a single case of BSE or "mad cow disease" was discovered in Alberta. The United States closed its border to Canadian beef exports for four months and to cattle exports for over two years.

The loss of this market led to a collapse in cattle prices and a disastrous drop in farm incomes.

Economic Diversification

Agriculture remains a significant component for the region's economy, but the Prairies also have significant mineral and forest wealth. Saskatchewan has potash and uranium resources, while Manitoba is a major nickel producer. The northern thirds of all three provinces are home to lumber mills and pulp and paper plants. Alberta's oil and natural gas wealth differentiate that province from the other two; the province accounts for two-thirds of Canada's conventional oil production, four-fifths of its natural gas production, and all of its bitumen and synthetic crude production. Over 60 per cent of the province's oil and natural gas sales are to the United States. High oil prices and the instability of Middle East supplies have led oil companies to spend about $100 billion in the first decade of the twenty-first century to develop the tar sands near Fort McMurray, a five-hour drive north of Edmonton. Tar sands are a combination of clay, sand, water, and bitumen. The bitumen is extracted from the "sand" and upgraded into synthetic crude oil or refined directly into petroleum products. Extracting the bitumen is an extremely costly and energy-intensive process that involves adding hot water to the sands and skimming off the oil that floats to the top. Total production in 2008 amounted to 1.3 million barrels of oil a day. This process requires vast quantities of water and generates enormous quantities of waste, but thanks to geography it is largely unseen by most Canadians!

During Alberta's oil boom in the 1970s, migrants from the rest of Canada flocked to the province. The subsequent bust in the 1980s led to much slower population growth. The good times, however, have returned in the first decade of the twenty-first century. Most of the province's recent population growth is concentrated in the Calgary–Edmonton corridor. The combined metropolitan area populations of those two cities account for 62 per cent of Alberta's population. Oil companies have their headquarters in Calgary, while the oil services industry is based in Edmonton. Edmonton is also a research centre for nanotechnology and the life sciences, while high-tech manufacturing, transportation services, and financial services have expanded in Calgary.

Tourism is heavily promoted in Alberta. It is home to three famous national parks in the Rocky Mountains. Calgary offers the Stampede, a celebration of "cowboy" culture. But the province's biggest single attraction in terms of number of visitors is the West Edmonton Mall, which comes complete with the world's largest indoor wave pool and amusement park. Manitoba and Saskatchewan offer fewer tourist attractions and their economic growth is concentrated in the major urban centres of Winnipeg, Saskatoon, and Regina. At the beginning of the twentieth century, Winnipeg controlled western Canada's grain trade besides serving as the region's administrative and financial services hub. It developed a diverse manufacturing base in the twentieth century and remains a major service centre. Saskatoon and Regina have small manufacturing sectors based on processing raw materials, but primarily they are service centres. Saskatoon promotes itself as Canada's "Science City" with its Innovation Place, a research park that is home to about one hundred high-tech companies that are attempting to commercialize basic scientific research in biotechnology, life sciences, and agriculture. It is affiliated with the University of Saskatchewan.

British Columbia

British Columbia (BC) is another resource hinterland, but unlike the Prairies and Atlantic Canada, it has developed in relative isolation. The province is effectively cut off from the rest of the country by the Rocky Mountains, which rise to over 12,000 feet along the BC-Alberta border. Most of British Columbia is part of the Cordillera, a vast expanse of mountains, valleys, and plateaux, except for the Peace River country, in the northeast, which is an extension of the Prairies. Off the coast, mountains run northwards along the spine of Vancouver Island and into the Queen Charlotte Islands (Haida Gwaii). Driving from Calgary to Vancouver along the Trans-Canada Highway, a person would first cross the Rocky Mountains, then the Rocky Mountain Trench, a valley that extends almost the entire length of the province, then the Columbia Mountains, the Interior Plateau, and finally the Coast Range. The contrast in elevation between the Coast Range and the Interior Plateau has resulted in two distinct climates. The coast is characterized by mild winters and warm summers with year-round rainfall ranging from 45 inches in Vancouver to 97 inches in Prince Rupert. Inland, the Interior Plateau has a continental-type climate characterized by hot summers and cool winters with minimal rainfall due to the rain shadow effect of the Coast Range.

Settlement

Natives had been living along the coast for thousands of years when the first European explorers arrived in the mid-eighteenth century. The Russians, Spaniards, and British all had trading interests in the region, but it was the British who eventually took control, when the Northwest Company established a series of fur-trading posts in the region. In the 1840s, American settlers arrived on the Pacific coast and the United States challenged the British presence in the area by laying claim to the coast from the Columbia River to Russia's trading posts in Alaska. In 1846 Britain and the United States settled on the 49th Parallel and the channel between Vancouver Island and the Olympic Peninsula to separate the two nations.

The discovery of gold in the upper Fraser Valley in 1858 drew 25,000 people to the region, mostly from California. Faced with another challenge to its sovereignty, Britain established the mainland colony of British Columbia, later merging it with Vancouver Island in 1866. The British government encouraged its colonies to unite into a single country, with the result that Canada was established in 1867. To get British Columbia to join the eastern provinces in Confederation, the federal government promised to build a railway to the Pacific. In 1871 the province joined Canada, but it wasn't until the CPR was completed in 1885 that it became integrated with the rest of the country and its role as Canada's gateway to the Pacific began.

The impact of Europeans on British Columbia's Native peoples was catastrophic (see chapter 2). They lost their land, their cultures were suppressed, and attempts were made to assimilate them by force. As in many other parts of Canada, Aboriginal land claims in British Columbia have yet to be resolved. The provincial government finally recognized Aboriginal peoples' title to the land in the early 1990s and established an administrative procedure for resolving land claims.

European settlers' attitudes towards Asian immigrants were little better. The recruitment of Chinese to work on the railways and in the mines provoked a backlash in the late nineteenth century. The province passed a law denying Chinese the right to vote, while the federal government, under lobbying from the BC government, imposed a head tax on Chinese immigration. Most of these laws were based on US laws. Anti-Chinese sentiment reached its height with the 1923 Chinese Immigration Act, which further restricted Chinese immigration. Japanese immigrants were treated in a similar fashion. During the Second

World War they were forcibly removed from within one hundred miles of the coast and relocated to camps in the interior. Their property was confiscated and sold. In 1989 the federal government issued an official apology for its treatment of Japanese Canadians and provided compensation for those born or residing in Canada before 1948. In 2006 a similar effort began to compensate Chinese Canadians for the head tax.

A Resource Hinterland

British Columbia's early development was based on its abundant natural resources. In the southeast, silver, lead, zinc, copper, and gold have been mined, while oil, natural gas, and coal have been developed in the northeast. Minerals abound throughout the province, but high production costs, environmental regulations, and transportation costs make future mine development unlikely. Most raw materials have been exported to Britain, the United States, and (more recently) East Asia. Successive provincial governments, with federal financial assistance, have spent billions of dollars to develop an infrastructure to support the resource economy. The risks associated with this strategy are illustrated by the development of coal resources in the province's northeast. In the late 1970s, developers signed a contract with Japanese steel companies to supply them with coal for fourteen years. Governments then helped the developers by upgrading the railway line between Prince George and Prince Rupert; constructing a coal terminal at Prince Rupert and a new railway line to the mines at Tumbler Ridge; and building the community of Tumbler Ridge to house mine workers. By the time this work was completed the world price for coal had dropped below the original negotiated price and the Japanese were demanding that a lower price be negotiated. In 1999 the first mine closed, followed four years later by the second mine. Since then other mines have opened nearby which have helped to stabilize Tumbler Ridge's population.

Salmon are synonymous with British Columbia, but they are endangered. Salmon have a life cycle of up to five years. They spawn in the upper reaches of the province's rivers, then migrate out to sea before returning to spawn again. Humans have disrupted this cycle through overfishing, constructing dams on rivers (preventing fish from returning to spawn), and destroying salmon habitat by scouring river bottoms with logs. Efforts to manage the resource must involve the United States, because when salmon migrate they swim through US waters. Obtaining agreement between the two countries on catch levels has proved difficult, with the occasional "fish war" breaking out. The resource is also threatened by a rise in ocean temperatures; above 44.6°F there are no salmon. Aquaculture is now a major source of salmon. This industry started in the 1980s, and by 1997 its production had surpassed the wild salmon catch. Most salmon farming involves constructing net pens in sheltered bays. Atlantic salmon are preferred because they are easier to raise. Several environmental hazards are associated with the industry: the farms foul ocean bottoms and contaminate wild salmon with sea lice (which breed in the net pens), and escapees from the net pens breed with the wild stocks.

Forests are British Columbia's most important natural resource. As recently as the 1970s it was estimated that 50 cents of every dollar spent in the province was generated by the forest industry. Forests cover about 60 per cent of the land, with the provincial government owning 95 per cent of them. They provide a major revenue source for the province through stumpage fees on logs – a tax that varies according to species, size, quality, end use, and location. The government manages the resource by leasing lands to companies according to the principle of sustained yield; however, maintaining that principle has proved difficult. The amount of timber cut during the 1980s and 1990s was more than double the 1960s levels; this has reduced mature forest stands and left little time for logged areas to regenerate. Environmental activists were drawn to this issue when clear-cutting threatened the old-growth rainforest on Vancouver Island's Clayoquot Sound in the mid-1990s. In response to public pressure, the government introduced new restrictions on logging, increased the acreage of wilderness parks in areas of mature forests, and developed an ecologically sustainable logging plan for Clayoquot Sound in conjunction with First Nations, Greenpeace, and a forest products company.

The coastal forest was the first to be exploited because its trees were larger and it was easy to float logs to sawmills. Technological changes and the expansion of infrastructure allowed the interior forests to be developed, and by the 1970s this region had surpassed the coast in terms of volume of wood cut. Sawmills have been built in the Georgia Strait area and throughout the interior's river valleys, where they are often the only source of employment. Pulp and paper mills were added to the industry's mix in the 1950s; most of them are located close to sawmills so that the latter's by-products can be used in pulp production. Most of the harvested timber is used by the construction industry, with the United States being the principal export market. In the 1980s, Canada and the United States became involved in a lengthy dispute over this trade in softwood lumber (see chapter 4). The US industry complained that British Columbia's low stumpage fees amounted to an unfair subsidy. To protect its industry, the United States imposed a levy on Canadian softwood lumber exports, which reduced exports and led to plant layoffs in British Columbia. Canada challenged the levy under NAFTA and the World Trade Organization's rules. Even though Canada repeatedly won favourable rulings, the United States continued to keep the levy in place. The issue was finally resolved in October 2006, when Canada and its neighbour signed a seven-year trade deal. The United States agreed to return about $4 billion of the $5 billion in duties it had collected on Canadian imports, while Canada agreed not to increase its current share (34 per cent) of the US softwood market.

Because British Columbia is so mountainous, it has little arable land. Agriculture is largely confined to the Okanagan and the lower Fraser Valleys, although wheat is grown in the Peace River country and there are cattle ranches throughout the interior. Irrigation has transformed the Okanagan into a fruit-growing area and an expanding wine industry. Unfortunately, British Columbia's most productive land coincides with its areas of greatest population growth. To protect its farmland, the province established agricultural land reserves in 1972. This policy has helped conserve land, but it has also limited opportunities for farmers to "cash in" on rising land values.

A Rising Core Region?

Manufacturing is concentrated in the Vancouver region and consists primarily of processing raw materials for export. Of much greater significance in terms of employment is the province's service sector. Vancouver's port is Canada's most important one for foreign trade; it imports manufactured goods from the Pacific Rim and exports resources from the Prairies and the BC interior. Nearly two-thirds of the province's exports go to the United States, followed by Japan (12 per cent) and China (3 per cent). The Vancouver region is also the centre of the province's high-tech and film industries. Burnaby, a suburb of Vancouver, is home to Ballard Power Systems, the world leader in zero-emission fuel cells. Other major employers in the city are tourism, banking, finance, and real estate. Corporate headquarters for resource-based industries are also major employers. Tourism is a major component of the region's economy. Vancouver boosted its international image when it hosted the 1986 World's Fair (Expo 86), which drew more than 20 million visitors. In 2010 the city, along with the mountain resort of Whistler, hosted the Winter Olympics. The city used the event to make much-needed investments in infrastructure to address traffic congestion and air pollution. The United States is the leading supplier of foreign tourists to the province, but tourism is extremely sensitive to currency fluctuations. The rising value of the Canadian dollar against the US dollar has meant a steady decline in the number of US visitors since 2004, which means the province has had to increase its marketing to other locations, most notably Asia.

Vancouver's mild climate and spectacular physical setting, where the Coast Range Mountains meet the Georgia Strait, have attracted newcomers from across Canada and the world. Since 1991 the city's population has grown by more than 100,000 without any change in its boundaries; much of this growth has been accommodated by high-rise developments along its extensive waterfront. The city has earned a global reputation for innovative urban planning and routinely tops the list of the world's most liveable cities.

On Vancouver Island, the provincial capital of Victoria is experiencing similar growth problems, albeit on a smaller scale. Retirees are drawn to the area by Canada's mildest climate; in 2011, 18 per cent of the capital region's population was over the age of sixty-five, compared to 14 per cent for the province as a whole. Tourists are attracted by the city's "taste of England" – by its double-decker buses, formal gardens, and afternoon tea at the Empress Hotel overlooking the harbour. The rest of the island emphasizes ecotourism attractions, including whale watching and hiking trails.

British Columbia's population growth has outpaced Canada's in every decade since 1871. The Greater Vancouver District has emerged as BC's core region. It is home to over 50 per cent of the province's population on just 0.3 per cent of its land area. Its growth in recent decades has been based on an expanding service sector and high-tech manufacturing. The rest of the province still depends largely on exporting resources, with the United States being its principal market. This dependency means it is at the mercy of changes in external demand and the vagaries of trading rules, as evidenced by the softwood lumber dispute. The recent rise in the value of the Canadian dollar against the US dollar has made Canadian goods and services more expensive. For the province to begin to rival central Canada as a core region, it will need to diversify its economy and lessen its dependence on a single market.

The North

Canada's largest region is the North. It plays a key role in the Canadian identity; for example, in "O Canada," the national anthem, the words "True North Strong and Free" figure prominently. Yet paradoxically, the North contains the fewest number of Canadians. It consists of the three territories – the Yukon, Nunavut, and the Northwest Territories (NWT) – and the northern portions of all the provinces except New Brunswick, Nova Scotia, and Prince Edward Island. The region is sparsely populated, has virtually no agriculture (because of its cold climate and poor soil), and serves as a resource hinterland and home for many of Canada's Native people.

The Canadian Shield covers most of the region except for the western portion, where the Cordillera and interior plains extend northward. The Shield consists mainly of rolling, rugged uplands and consists of extremely old rocks. It is shaped like a saucer, with Hudson Bay at its centre and its highest elevations at its outer edges. The landscape bears the scars of glacial erosion and deposition, with thousands of lakes, little soil, and long, low hills deposited by retreating glaciers.

The region has two climates, arctic and subarctic. The arctic climate is characterized by long, cold winters, extremely cool and short summers, and low precipitation. Alert, Canada's northernmost inhabited community, at the tip of Ellesmere Island, has an average temperature of –27°F in February and 37°F in July and receives only six inches of precipitation a year. The subarctic climate is less severe and covers the largest land area of any climatic region in Canada. Yellowknife, the capital of the NWT, is typical: it has an average temperature of –15°F in its coldest month and 62°F in its warmest, and receives 11 inches of precipitation per year. The warm but short growing season supports extensive coniferous forests.

Underlying most of the Far North is permafrost – permanently frozen ground. The depth of the permafrost varies from more than 1600 feet near the Mackenzie Delta to less than 10 feet on its southern margins near James Bay. During the brief summer, the active layer melts to a depth varying from a few inches in the Far North to several feet in the subarctic zone. This thawing poses engineering challenges, since any foundations will shift. To prevent collapse, many buildings are raised on stilts sunk into the permafrost and frozen in place.

Global warming is having a strong impact on the region. The northern ice cap is warming at twice the global rate and is predicted to lose between 50 and 60 per cent of its ice over the next hundred years. Melting ice opened up the Northwest Passage, a shipping route between the Atlantic and Pacific, for the first time in modern history in 2007. Such occurrences will become more commonplace with continued melting of the ice cap. Over the past twenty years the amount of sea ice in western Hudson Bay has fallen sharply; this has lengthened the ice-free season for the port of Churchill by three weeks, but it has also forced polar bears into human settlements in search of food. The melting ice is also prompting challenges to Canadian sovereignty in the area. Canada claims the water between the arctic islands as internal waters, a position that is rejected by the United States and other countries. In 2005 a diplomatic row between Canada and Denmark erupted when the Danes occupied Hans Island, a dot of land between Greenland and Ellesmere Island. To symbolize Canadian claims to the region, Canada's prime minister in 2006 announced plans to construct a deepwater harbour on the northern end of Baffin Island at the entrance to the Northwest Passage.

Settlement and Economic Development

When Europeans first came to the region, they encountered Inuit in the Arctic and First Nations peoples in the Subarctic. These groups had adapted to the environment and developed a unique way of life. In the early nineteenth century, whaling ships from Europe and the United States arrived and some Inuit signed on with them as harpooners. In exchange they received guns, knives, and other items. Contact also brought European diseases, against which the Inuit had no immunity, and many died. Large-scale whaling ended in the 1890s and was replaced by the fur trade.

Canada took possession of most of the region with the purchase of Rupert's Land in 1870; then, in 1880, the Arctic Archipelago was transferred from Britain to Canada. The federal government left the territorial north (Yukon and the NWT) in the hands of fur traders and missionaries until the outbreak of the Second World War, when the region assumed strategic importance. During the 1940s a series of landing fields were constructed so that planes could fly overland to either Europe or Asia, and the Alaska Highway was built through the Yukon to supply an American base in Fairbanks. After the war the North became a buffer between the United States and the Soviet Union with the construction of a series of radar posts – the so-called Distant Early Warning Line – to detect any Soviet attack.

In the late 1950s, after sixty members of an Inuit group starved to death, the federal government launched a controversial relocation policy for Aboriginal groups throughout the North. Most of them moved to trading posts and were ill prepared for the social dislocation that soon followed. The pressure to obtain cash income increased, yet jobs were hard to find; while hunting and trapping now involved a journey by snowmobile rather than dogsled. On the other hand, access to food and health care improved, which reduced infant mortality and increased the population. Schools were established in which English was taught. The major employer became the government; however, most of the senior administrative and professional positions were taken by southerners who had the necessary educational qualifications. Today, most of the available jobs are in the capital cities of Whitehorse, Yellowknife, and Iqaluit.

The region has long supported two economic systems: industrial capitalism and an Aboriginal economy. The latter is based on harvesting land and sea resources, on commercializing those resources by selling fish and meat, carvings, and prints, and on earnings from ecotourism. Industrial capitalism is characterized by large, externally controlled, multinational corporations, which extract and process resources for export to the core regions. These systems reflect contrasting visions of the region's future. For Aboriginal people, the region is their home, and they wish to exert more control over its development. Beginning in the 1980s a series of land claims between the federal government and Aboriginal peoples were settled. The largest land claim settlement resulted in the founding of the territory of Nunavut (meaning "our land" in the Inuktitut language) on 1 April 1999. It is hoped that the creation of this new territory will strengthen Inuit culture and enable them to control the region's development.

From the perspective of outsiders, the region is a resource-rich hinterland in need of development. Oil was discovered in the Norman Wells district of the southern NWT in the 1920s; it supplied local markets until a pipeline linking it with the national pipeline system in Alberta was completed in the 1980s. Energy companies in the 1970s discovered oil and gas fields in the Mackenzie Delta and Beaufort Sea and proposed a pipeline down the Mackenzie Valley. The development was halted by the Berger commission, which gave a voice to

Aboriginal concerns and recommended delaying any construction for at least ten years until land claims and other matters could be resolved. Thirty years later, high energy prices resurrected the proposal and a new round of public hearings began in 2006. This time, four major oil companies were joined by several Aboriginal groups in proposing the pipeline. Among the latter are the Gwich'in, who oppose oil and gas exploration in the nearby Arctic National Wildlife Refuge. In early 2010 the pipeline was finally approved, but its $16 billion price tag has deterred investors and the oil companies are now seeking government assistance for the pipeline's construction. The region also has gold, diamond, lead, and zinc mines. This highly capital-intensive sector provides few local benefits, since most equipment and supplies come from southern Canada or foreign countries. To save costs, new mines in isolated areas establish work camps and fly workers in on a rotating basis, providing even fewer benefits to the territories. Outside of mining, most people are employed in the service sector.

The subarctic coniferous forest amounts to about four-fifths of Canada's forest land. Along its southern margins in Ontario and Quebec, pulp and paper mills have been established to supply the United States with newsprint. Hydroelectric power has also been developed. The largest development is the James Bay Project, built by Hydro-Québec to supply markets in Quebec and the US Northeast. The project proved extremely controversial because it flooded Aboriginal hunting grounds, destroyed wildlife habitats, and elevated mercury levels in fish due to decaying vegetation under the newly created reservoirs.

The North's wilderness is popular with tourists. The earliest developments occurred along the southern edge of the Shield in the Laurentians north of Montreal, where summer cottages and campsites dot the landscape. Development has spread northward with the construction of paved highways; some tourists fly in to remote areas to hunt and fish, providing Aboriginal people with employment as guides. Newly created national parks in Nunavut offer tourists the opportunity to visit the Arctic, but travelling to these remote locations is costly and time consuming.

Canada's Core and Periphery Reconsidered

Significant changes have occurred in Canada's core–periphery relationship over the past fifty years. Deindustrialization hit Montreal and other older industrial centres beginning in the 1970s. Uncertainty over

Quebec's status within Canada hampered investment in the province, and Montreal gave way to Toronto as the country's financial and cultural centre. The removal of tariffs on imported manufactured items as part of successive free trade agreements removed the rationale for branch plants, and the core underwent a second phase of plant closings in the 1990s. Plant closings have become a reality again in the twenty-first century, with GM's bankruptcy, the sale of DaimlerChrysler to Fiat, and restructuring at Ford. These latest developments illustrate the weakness of the region's industrial base: it remains largely foreign-owned and dependent on decisions made outside of Canada. In the West, Alberta's energy-based economy boosted the GDP by 53 per cent between 2004 and 2008 to almost surpass Quebec and become the country's second largest.

Declining resources have hurt the Maritime provinces, while Manitoba and Saskatchewan remain dependent on raw material exports. The wheat economy has diminished in importance and been replaced, in part, by a dependence on livestock and meat exports. British Columbia and Alberta have had greater success in diversifying their economies in their major metropolitan centres, but their hinterlands remain resource-based. Instead of shipping raw materials to central Canada, western Canada has gained access to the US market thanks to NAFTA, and a new dependent relationship has been established. The softwood lumber dispute and 2003 border closure to beef and cattle exports illustrate the weaknesses of this arrangement. The hinterland's economic future remains dependent on economic diversification and finding new markets for its products, particularly in Asia. The near collapse of the US auto industry has hurt Ontario, the country's traditional economic engine. In 2003, the province with 39 per cent of the country's population accounted for 53 per cent of Canada's manufacturing employment; by 2009 this figure had dropped to 44 per cent. Moreover, over the same period the province's median income fell relative to the rest of Canada by nearly $900.

Heartland and hinterland, core and periphery, have characterized Canada from its earliest days. But these relationships are not static; in the last quarter of the twentieth century, economic power shifted from Montreal to Toronto. In the periphery, a dependence on exporting resources still guides the development of most provinces. Vancouver and Calgary with their vibrant service-based economies have emerged as strong regional cores. It remains to be determined whether they will begin to rival their eastern counterparts in terms of economic and political power and a new set of relationships will guide the country's future.

RECOMMENDED WEBSITES

Federal Data Sources

Atlas of Canada: http://atlas.nrcan.gc.ca/site/english/index.html
Department of Fisheries and Oceans: http://www.dfo-mpo.gc.ca/index-eng.htm
Environment Canada: http://www.weatheroffice.gc.ca/canada_e.html
Statistics Canada: http://www.statcan.gc.ca/start-debut-eng.html

Provincial Data Sources

Newfoundland and Labrador: http://www.fin.gov.nl.ca/fin/statistics/
Nova Scotia: http://www.gov.ns.ca/finance/statistics/agency/default.asp
Prince Edward Island: http://www.gov.pe.ca/finance/index.php3
New Brunswick: http://www.gnb.ca/0024/economics/index.asp
Quebec: http://www.gouv.qc.ca/portail/quebec/pgs/commun/portrait/economie/?lang=en
Ontario: http://www.ontario.ca/en/communities/economy/ONT03_020921
Manitoba: http://www.gov.mb.ca/mbs/
Saskatchewan: http://www.stats.gov.sk.ca/
Alberta: http://www.finance.alberta.ca/aboutalberta/index.html
British Columbia: http://www.bcstats.gov.bc.ca/Home.aspx

Territorial Data Sources

Yukon: http://www.eco.gov.yk.ca/stats/
Northwest Territories: http://www.statsnwt.ca/
Nunavut: http://www.eia.gov.nu.ca/stats/

FURTHER READING

Bone, R. 2003. *The Geography of the Canadian North: Issues and Challenges.* 2nd ed. Don Mills, ON: Oxford University Press.

Bone, R. 2005. *The Regional Geography of Canada*. 3rd ed. Don Mills, ON: Oxford University Press.

McGillivray, B. 2010. *Canada: A Nation of Regions*. 2nd ed. Don Mills, ON: Oxford University Press.

Wallace, I. 2002. *A Geography of the Canadian Economy*. Don Mills, ON: Oxford University Press.

2 Canadian History in a North American Context

JOHN HERD THOMPSON AND MARK PAUL RICHARD

This chapter explains to American university students with little or no background on the subject how Canada came to be. Historians of Canada – Canadians writing for Canadian readers – have written textbooks that are just as long as the ones an American student reads in an American history class. We must do that same job in one chapter: present a narrative of five centuries as well as enough historical context to understand the rest of this book. To enable American students to begin to understand Canada, we have made the similarities and differences between Canadian and American history our central theme. We caution student readers, however, that a comparative approach is not the only way to interpret the history of Canada; we encourage them to look for other interpretations in the books listed at the end of this chapter.

In some respects, Canada and the United States have similar histories. Modern Canada and the United States (and Mexico) are the products of the European conquest of the Aboriginal peoples of North America. The founders of the United States and Canada led their respective countries through the same processes of nation-state building: they founded effective political institutions and a sense of national identity, they built economies that permitted citizens to prosper, they defined a place for their country in the world community, and they defended their country militarily when necessary. Both countries adopted federal systems of government, with the national government sharing power with subnational governments (called *states* in the United States and *provinces* in Canada). Both countries also attracted immigrants from every corner of the globe.

We must be careful, however, not to exaggerate the similarities. To use the two examples above, the Canadian federation has evolved very differently from the American federation, and Canadians and Americans have come to hold very different attitudes towards the cultural diversity created by immigration. Some of the historical differences between Canada and the United States are profound, while others are subtle. This chapter will help American students understand the differences.

Native Peoples and Newcomers, 1500 to 1791

The first people in North America were Aboriginal hunters and gatherers, who crossed the frozen Bering Strait from Asia on foot, or possibly paddled across the strait after the Ice Age. These "First Nations," as they call themselves today, and as contemporary non-Aboriginal Canadians refer to them, were not one people. Six different cultural groups lived in the territory that eventually became Canada. Historians often categorize these groups by their geographic environments. Moving from the Pacific east to the Atlantic, they are the peoples of the Northwest Coast, the Interior Plateau, the Plains, the Subarctic, the Arctic, and the Northeast. These six broad cultural groups had different material cultures, religious beliefs, and forms of political organization. They spoke more than fifty languages. Thus, from the very first, Canada has been culturally diverse.

Most Americans celebrate Christopher Columbus as the European "discoverer" of North America in 1492. However, Viking sagas and the archaeological evidence prove that Norsemen founded settlements on the continent between 800 and 1000. Overpopulation had forced these farmers and fishers from Scandinavia to look for new homes to the west, first in Iceland, then in Greenland, and finally in North America. But hostile relations between the Vikings and the Native peoples prevented permanent settlement, and voyages between Greenland and North America ended in the 1300s.

In the 1400s, other European mariners retraced the Norse routes to North America: Basques, Spanish, Portuguese, French, and English, all of them in search of the abundant whales and codfish stocks off North America's northeast coast. Navigators sponsored by European merchants and monarchs followed the whalers and fishers in search of precious metals and a shorter trade route between Europe and Asia – the elusive "Northwest Passage" that would lead them through or around North America. The French navigator Jacques Cartier explored the St Lawrence River during three expeditions between 1534 and 1542, erecting Christian crosses where he landed to claim the territory for France. But he found no gold or diamonds, and he described the rocky shores of the lower St Lawrence as "the land that God gave Cain." Cartier's comment exaggerates the harshness of the Canadian environment, but it illustrates an essential difference between the parts of North America that became Canada and the parts that became the United States. Compared to the latter, Canada had only one-fifth as much arable land to support settler communities, the resource that mattered most to a developing European colony in North America.

Continuous French settlement began in 1604, when another Frenchman, Samuel De Champlain, wintered in what he called Acadia (today's Nova Scotia). That was three years before the English Virginia Company founded Jamestown and sixteen years before the *Mayflower* reached Massachusetts Bay. The French colony in northern North America, *la Nouvelle France* (New France), grew more slowly than New England, however. Most of the French colonists formed subsistence farm families, but the more important commercial export enterprise in the colony became the fur trade. It was to further the trade with Native peoples for beaver pelts that Champlain in 1608 established Quebec, high on the cliffs of the St Lawrence River; the fortress that evolved there became the capital of France's North American empire. From 1608 until 1756, French fur traders followed rivers and lakes into the interior of North America, as far north as Hudson Bay, as far west as the Great Plains, and as far south as the Gulf of Mexico. The American cities of Detroit, St Paul, St Louis, and New Orleans all have French origins. Two of these place names remind us that not all the French who extended this far-flung network were traders. Some were Catholic missionaries who came to North America to attempt to convert the Native populations to Christianity.

The fur trade required the French to cooperate with the Native peoples who trapped the beaver and prepared the pelts. Aboriginal trading partners taught the French how to travel and to survive in the interior of North America. Aboriginal women served as interpreters, language instructors, and diplomatic agents; by marrying French traders in rituals that blended the traditions of Europeans and indigenous peoples, native women forged social ties with the French that proved critical to the growth of the fur trade in North America. Aboriginal people were also indispensable military allies of the French in North America, but by allying with some Native nations, the French inevitably alienated others. When Champlain joined the Huron, the Ottawa, and the Montagnais in a clash with the Iroquois in 1609, for example, the five Iroquois nations allied with France's rival – the English. Native people played a critical and independent role in the series of wars between France and Britain in North America that began in 1689 and ended with the British conquest of New France in 1760.

The French empire looks impressive on a map, but French settlers occupied only Quebec and Acadia: the St Lawrence Valley and the area around the Bay of Fundy. In the 1750s, only 13,000 colonists lived in Acadia and 60,000 in Quebec; by contrast, 1.5 million colonists lived in the thirteen British colonies. The question is not why the French eventually lost their foothold in North America, but how they were able to defend it for seventy years. The answer is that their Native allies, anxious to prevent the more numerous English colonists from moving west, helped the French keep the English colonies on the defensive. After Queen Anne's War (1702–13), however, Acadia came under British rule. The British renamed the territory Nova Scotia, and the Acadians struggled to survive as a neutral people wedged between the French and British empires.

The Seven Years' War (1756–63), known in American history as the French and Indian War, upset this delicate balance. The first truly world war, waged in Europe and in India as well as in North America, it represented a clash of rival world systems competing to establish colonies that would provide raw materials to, and purchase manufactured goods from, their parent countries. The conflict began early in North America: a British army marched into the Ohio River Valley to capture the French Fort Duquesne in 1755. Among the British troops routed by French soldiers and their Native allies was a young Virginia militia officer named George Washington, defeated in his first military campaign. But British ruthlessness and superior numbers eventually won the war. In 1755, British troops expelled 10,000 Acadians from their farms in Nova Scotia and dispersed them among the thirteen British colonies. Some Acadians eventually returned, albeit not to their former lands; others migrated to Louisiana, where they formed the Cajun population. The descendants of the Acadians have never forgotten this deportation. Soon after the British captured Quebec in 1759, they completed their conquest of New France, and France lost its empire in North America.

The British victory reshaped North America for the French and English colonists and for the Native peoples as well. The French Canadians became part of the British Empire, governed by British laws and institutions. The theme of conquest remains part of the consciousness of the French in Quebec; contemporary Quebec licence plates bear the provincial motto *Je me souviens* (I remember), as in "I remember our history." For two-and-a-half centuries, the francophones (French speakers) of Quebec have preserved their identity under British institutions and prevented a military and political conquest from becoming a cultural surrender. In the thirteen American colonies, the conquest of New France eliminated the French as a military threat to their expansion into the interior. To prevent settler conflict with Native peoples, however, Britain issued the Proclamation of 1763, which banned Anglo-American settlement west of the Appalachian Mountains. This proclamation also recognized that Native peoples were nations in their own right with title to their land, and that formal treaties were necessary if settlers were to acquire that land.

The proclamation angered British subjects in the Thirteen Colonies, and that anger increased when, without consulting the colonial assemblies, Britain imposed taxes on the colonies to pay the costs of the war that had defeated the French. The subsequent unrest in the Thirteen Colonies led the British to cultivate the loyalty of their French-Catholic subjects in their new colony Quebec. The Quebec Act of 1774 extended Quebec's frontiers into the Ohio region, overriding the Thirteen Colonies' long-standing claims to those lands. The same act also sanctioned the French language and system of civil law (although not criminal law), as well as the Roman Catholic faith of francophones. Britain did not grant Quebec an elected assembly like those in the Thirteen Colonies, however. The Quebec Act established the bilingual, bicultural character of Canada that exists to this day. In the Thirteen Colonies, by contrast, the colonists were furious over the benevolent treatment of their former French Catholic enemies and feared that Britain might deny them their elected assemblies. The Quebec Act helped bring about the colonists' armed conflict with Britain in 1775 and in 1776 the colonies' Declaration of Independence.

The American Revolution – now more commonly called the American War of Independence – was a pivotal event in both American and Canadian history. The colonial victory over the British created the United States from the Thirteen Colonies. The Continental Congress, the government of the embryonic United States, had invited four other British colonies in North America to join the revolution: Quebec, Nova Scotia, Prince Edward Island, and Newfoundland. All four rejected that invitation, for complex and different reasons. Clearly, those four colonies viewed themselves as different from their neighbours to the south, and their decision steered them towards a different national future. Some in the Thirteen Colonies also rejected the American Revolution; these people faced imprisonment, fines, and the confiscation of their property if they remained in the new United States. About 50,000 migrated to the four loyal colonies to the north, especially to Nova Scotia and Quebec. American history despises these people as Tories, but in Canadian history they are the United Empire Loyalists, the founders of anglophone (English-speaking) Canada. Their arrival led Britain in 1784 to found the colony of New Brunswick from the part of Nova Scotia west of the Bay of Fundy, where most of the Loyalists settled, and in 1791 to form Ontario from the western part of Quebec. Not surprisingly, New Brunswick and Ontario became bastions of support for the Crown and for British institutions.

Not all Loyalists were white. Tens of thousands of African Americans fled slavery in the Thirteen Colonies to join the British in the hope of freedom; three thousand of them migrated to Nova Scotia after the revolution. Most of these black Loyalists never received the land the British had promised them, and in 1792 about half of them emigrated to Sierra Leone. Two First Nations, the Mohawk and the Seneca of the Iroquois Confederacy, allied with the British during the Revolution in order to halt the westward expansion of the American colonists. But in 1783, when the British negotiated the Treaty of Paris with the new United States, they conceded Iroquois lands to the Americans without consulting their Native allies. Thus, about two thousand Iroquois from New York migrated to Ontario, where Britain gave them land and supplies to aid their settlement. The subjects of the British Empire who lived in North America after the revolution – French- and English-speaking, black, white, and red – were remarkably diverse. What united many of them was that they had good reasons to dislike and fear the United States; more than that, they had an abiding affection for Britain.

In 1791 Britain decided it needed firmer control of the North American colonies that remained in its empire. To this end, it imposed the Constitutional or "Canada" Act to divide Quebec into Upper Canada (today, Ontario) and Lower Canada (today, Quebec). Both colonies were to have elected assemblies, but unlike the departed Thirteen Colonies, the assemblies were to be under the strong executive control of an upper house, an executive council, and a governor, all of them appointed by the British government. The Thirteen Colonies had gained their independence from Britain through revolution; the British North American colonies that eventually became Canada gained self-government in small stages over the course of two centuries. The other new countries of the Americas – the former Portuguese and Spanish colonies – followed the American example, winning their independence in violent revolutions and establishing republics. Unique among the new nations of the Americas, Canada retained close ties with its colonial parent. It evolved constitutionally within the British Empire and has remained a constitutional monarchy, sharing a monarch with Great Britain.

British North America, 1791–1867

The end of the War of Independence did not halt conflict between Britain and the United States. The causes of the War of 1812 originated outside North America, but as it had in 1775–6, the United States launched pre-emptive invasions of Upper and Lower Canada to forestall British attacks on its own territory. The Americans mistakenly believed that British North America wanted to be liberated from Britain, just as they had liberated themselves. In fact, Canadian militiamen fought alongside British troops and allied Native nations to repel the invaders. The British North Americans were rejecting republicanism just as they had during the American Revolution. British attacks on the United States were no more successful, and the Treaty of Ghent (1814) left the boundaries where they had been. On both sides of the boundary, however, the War of 1812 inspired national feeling. It gave the United States a national anthem as well as a national hero: "The Star-Spangled Banner" describes a failed British attack on Baltimore, and General Andrew Jackson became a symbol for America after an army under his command defeated the British at New Orleans. In British North America, fighting off the American invaders helped British North Americans view themselves as distinct from Americans, and to develop an identity as Canadians.

In the twentieth century, politicians in both countries liked to extol the Canada-US border as "the longest undefended border in the world." Although the War of 1812 turned out to be the last major war, we know this only in hindsight. At the time, both Britain and the United States maintained defences along the border at considerable cost, and the last British garrisons did not leave Canada until 1905. The US army had a contingency plan for a war with Britain and Canada until the 1930s, just as Canada planned for a possible war with the United States. Today's military alliances that now link Canada and the United States, such as NATO, date only from the 1940s.

Britain did not force its six North American colonies – Upper and Lower Canada, New Brunswick, Nova Scotia, Prince Edward Island, and Newfoundland – to remain within the British Empire; they remained under British governance, for the most part, because they wanted to. A million people from the British Isles – England, Scotland, Wales, and Ireland – migrated to British North America between 1820 and 1860, further strengthening the colonies' ties to Britain. Economic links also bound the British Empire together. The fur trade had diminished greatly in importance, but the North American colonies sold staple primary products such as timber and wheat to Britain. After immigrants, the most important British export to the colonies was money. British investment financed the canals and later the railways (the Canadian term for railroads) that made possible trade and the overall economic development of the North American colonies. Between 1815 and 1860, the total population of the six British North American colonies grew to almost four million. But the United States, with its much greater population, continued to overshadow British North America in economic growth.

In part because of this American example, not all British North Americans were satisfied within the British Empire. In each of the six colonies, political reformers in the elected legislative assemblies protested the occasionally heavy-handed rule of British governors. They complained of the influence enjoyed by the groups of unelected favourites whom the governors appointed to advise them. In Upper and Lower Canada, this discontent led to armed rebellions in 1837–8. The rebels hoped the United States would support their cause, but the American government never seriously considered such intervention. Both rebellions were crushed, although ethnic divisions in Lower Canada – most of the rebels, the *Patriotes*, were French Canadians – made the rebellion much more difficult for British troops to suppress. Britain responded to these rebellions by uniting Upper and Lower Canada (calling them Canada West and Canada East) into one entity with a single government and legislative assembly. Britain hoped that this Act of Union would assimilate French speakers into the English-speaking majority. To speed assimilation, French was no longer to be an official language in the legislature and the courts.

This assimilation never came about. Instead, during the 1840s, French- and English-speaking politicians in the assembly worked successfully together to press the British governors for greater self-government in the colony's domestic affairs. By 1849 Britain had conceded "responsible government" in the United Canadas; similar concessions followed later in the other British North American colonies. Responsible government meant that the governor would respect the will of the leaders (a prime minister and a cabinet) who had the support of a majority of the members in the elected legislative assembly. The Canadian system of responsible government became the model for the other settlement colonies of the British Empire (Australia, New Zealand, and South Africa). It continues to this day to distinguish the Canadian political system from its American counterpart (for a more detailed comparison, see chapter 3). An American president is elected separately every four years and must often govern without a majority in one or both of the houses of the US Congress; a Canadian prime minister is an elected member of the legislature (the House of Commons) and must resign if he (or she) cannot command majority support in the legislature.

Another important difference between the American and Canadian political systems is that Canada has two official languages of government, English and French. In 1849, one of the first acts of the new responsible government of Canada was to restore French as the second official language of government. English-speaking politicians did not restore French because they believed in principle that Canada should be bilingual; they did so because their French-speaking political allies demanded recognition of their language as the price for their political support. Such pragmatic political alliances between French- and English-speaking politicians have continued in Canada ever since. No national government has survived for long without significant francophone support.

Americans have lived under the same written constitution (albeit with some amendments) since 1789; by contrast, British North Americans have experienced a series of very different constitutions. In 1867 the British North America Act created Canada in its modern political form through the union of four of the colonies, a process referred to in Canada as Confederation. New Brunswick, Nova Scotia, Ontario (the former Canada West), and Quebec (Canada East) became the first four provinces of a new political entity within the British Empire called the Dominion of Canada. The term *dominion* was a new constitutional designation chosen by the colonial politicians who planned Confederation; it was meant to imply a country rather than a colony, but a country firmly within the British Empire. Although Canadians today celebrate 1 July 1867 as their country's birthday, the British North America Act did not in fact make Canada an independent nation-state. It had no power over its relations with other countries, a power that Britain retained, and no power to amend its own constitution, the BNA Act. Nor did most Canadians in 1867 want independence. Some of the Fathers of Confederation even wanted to call the new country the "Kingdom" of Canada. Other alternatives at the time were "Laurentia," "Cabotia," and "The Canadas." Canada remained a constitutional monarchy under Queen Victoria, kept British symbols like the Union Jack, and continued its British form of government; after 1867 it referred to its national legislature as the Parliament, just as in Britain. Canada became independent from Britain only gradually over the next century; unlike in the United States, no single historical date can symbolize this lengthy process.

Confederation represented a divorce as well as a union, for it turned primarily English-speaking Ontario and primarily French-speaking Quebec into separate provinces in the new federal system. French speakers in Quebec would have their own legislative assembly and their own legal system. The division of powers between the federal government in Ottawa, chosen as Canada's capital, and the governments in the provinces, handed control over education to the provinces (unlike the United States, Canada can have no federal Department of Education). In this way, Confederation provided French speakers – those who lived in Quebec, at least – with institutions they could use to maintain their language and traditions; they could continue to be a nation within a larger nation-state. Of course, not all French Canadians lived in Quebec. Those in the English-speaking provinces faced a more arduous struggle for cultural survival. Rooted in Canada's history and reflected in its institutions, the dualism between English and French Canadians persists to this day; finding mechanisms to deal constructively with this dualism has long been Canada's greatest challenge.

A Dominion within an Empire, 1867–1919

Building a new country is an arduous process. New countries are precarious and tenuous, as the United States was in the 1790s. Every federation faces frictions between its central government and the subnational governments. Between 1861 and 1865 the United States fought a bloody Civil War to preserve the American union. The Canadian federation has a similar history of tensions between the national government and the provinces, but Canada has never come close to duplicating America's tragic Civil War. The first challenge came in 1868, when Nova Scotia threatened to secede unless it won better terms from the national government in Ottawa. Ottawa pacified Nova Scotia with money from the national treasury and by subsidizing a railway to connect the province to markets in Ontario and Quebec. In Canada, threats from the provinces and federal bribes soon became standard practice in the always turbulent political game that Canadians have come to refer to as federal–provincial relations.

Because it was the North American unit of the British Empire, Canada had an enormous advantage over other new countries. Britain wanted the new Canadian federation to succeed so that it could reduce the costs of maintaining a British presence in North America. When Nova Scotia tried to leave Canada, the British government refused to sanction the province's secession. In 1869 Britain made it possible for Canada to acquire the vast Hudson's Bay Company territory between the Great Lakes and the Rocky Mountains. Much of this territory eventually became three Canadian provinces: Manitoba, created in 1870, and Saskatchewan and Alberta, created in 1905. When British Columbia joined Confederation in 1871, Canada became a transcontinental country, stretching from sea to sea. Like Nova Scotia, British Columbia almost immediately threatened to secede; the transcontinental railway promised by Ottawa to lure it to join Canada took until 1885 to complete. Like Nova Scotia, British Columbia remained part of Confederation. Two islands became the last British colonies to join Canada. Prince Edward Island entered Confederation in 1873, attracted by Canadian subsidies and pressured to do so by Britain. Newfoundland, Britain's oldest colony in North America, did not become Canada's tenth province until 1949.

Canada's expansion to the Pacific happened in less than a decade, much faster than in the United States. It happened rapidly because Canada and Britain feared that if Canada did not occupy the West north of the 49th Parallel, which was the boundary between the two countries, the United States would seize the lands as its manifest destiny, just as it had taken much of Mexico. Canada's leaders knew that the future of their new country depended on the successful development of the Canadian West. The Conservative governments of Sir John A. Macdonald, Canada's prime minister from 1867 to 1873 and from 1879 to 1891, designed a development strategy called the National Policy around western expansion. Borrowing from the policies the United States had followed to develop economically, the National Policy established a tariff to shut off imports of foreign goods and to stimulate manufacturing in the four original provinces. The transcontinental railway, the Canadian Pacific Railway (CPR), carried immigrants from eastern Canada and Europe to settle in the western provinces on free homesteads – another idea Canada borrowed from its neighbour. The CPR would then transport the primary products these settlers produced in the west – wheat, beef, lumber, fish, and minerals – to eastern and European markets, and carry the manufactured goods of the new protected industries back to consumers in the West.

Canada was also like the United States in that it appropriated the lands, and trampled on the rights, of the Native peoples. Canada signed treaties with the First Nations on the Prairies and settled them on reserves (the Canadian term for reservations). But Canada rarely provided the promised federal assistance to help these peoples learn to grow crops to replace the vanishing buffalo herds. In general, however, relations between the Canadian government and First Nations were much less violent than in the American West. Between 1866 and 1895, the US Army fought 943 military engagements with Native Americans; Canadian troops fought seven. The later timing of western expansion in Canada partially explains this; neither the Canadian government nor the First Nations wanted to repeat the American experience. The most significant institutional difference between the two countries was that Canada established the North-West Mounted Police (after 1920, the Royal Canadian Mounted Police) to enforce the law in the Canadian West. The Mounties were neither as fair nor as fearless as legend makes them, but for domestic policing they were more effective than a military force. Canada's western expansion was not bloodless, however. In 1869 the Métis, French-speaking people of mixed Native and European ancestry who lived in what became the province of Manitoba, resisted Canada's occupation of their lands. They were the first to raise the question of minority rights in the new dominion. Under the leadership of Louis Riel, the Métis established a provisional government and negotiated a compromise with the federal government that made Manitoba a province, with both French and English as official languages. The government did not fully respect this agreement, however, and many Métis left Manitoba to move farther west. In 1885 these Métis in what later became Saskatchewan resisted again, this time with much greater violence. Canadian troops suppressed the North-West Rebellion, and sentenced Riel to death for leading it.

Although Riel was a Métis, he was also a French-speaking Catholic. The verdict and sentence touched off conflict in central Canada between English-Canadian Protestants, who viewed Riel as a traitor and demanded his execution, and French-Canadian Catholics, who demanded that the Macdonald government commute Riel's death sentence. Macdonald and his cabinet faced a dilemma that would continue to confront Canadian federal governments: how to respond when the country's two founding groups held profoundly different opinions. The Conservative government sided with the English-Canadian majority and hanged Riel. The party paid a heavy political price in Quebec for this choice. Until 1885 the Conservative party had won a majority of the Quebec seats in the federal parliament, and held the provincial government as well; after Riel's execution, the opposition Liberals became the dominant party in Quebec.

Canada's English-French dualism generated ethnolinguistic conflicts in other parts of the dominion as well. French-speaking minorities in provinces with English majorities faced a constant struggle to obtain public funds to support their Catholic schools (unlike the United States, Canada has no constitutional separation of church and state). In New Brunswick in 1875, French-speaking Acadians won the right to have publicly funded Catholic schools taught by religious orders. In Manitoba in 1890, however, the provincial government not only denied public funds to Catholic schools, but also abolished French as an official language. The Manitoba experience proved more typical than that of New Brunswick. In Alberta in 1905, Ontario in 1912, and Saskatchewan in 1918, provincial governments greatly restricted French-language Catholic education. As a result, French Canadians came to view themselves as a vulnerable minority except in the Province of Quebec and surmised that they were unlikely to maintain their language and culture beyond Quebec's borders. Accordingly, to preserve the French language within the province, Quebec became more strident in the late nineteenth century regarding issues of language and culture.

French Canadians had other reasons to feel vulnerable. Between 1896 and 1914, Canada's population increased from just over five million to almost eight million, largely through immigration. Very few of these newcomers spoke French. Canada chose immigrants from Britain and the United States first, from northern and western Europe second, and from central and eastern Europe last. Canada restricted the immigration of Asians and African Americans. Canadians today are proud that Canada has become a multicultural mosaic of immigrants from all parts of the world. Until the 1920s, however, official policy promoted what historians call Anglo-conformity: English Canadians expected immigrant groups to speak English, to give up their cultural distinctiveness, and to assimilate with English-Canadian society. In this respect, Canada during that era had an ideology very much like that of the US melting pot. In another respect, however, Canada has been very different from the United States, which received many immigrants and sent out very few emigrants. Canada took in immigrants from other countries, but it also sent out significant numbers of emigrants to the United States. In proportion to its population, Canada has sent more emigrants to the United States than has any other country. Between the 1840s and 1930, about one million French-speaking Canadians migrated to factory jobs in the industrial cities of the US Northeast, and about two million English speakers migrated south to seek economic opportunity. About one-third of the immigrants who came to Canada from Europe eventually moved on to the United States. (One of the authors of this chapter, Mark Paul Richard, is an American of French-Canadian descent; the other, John Herd Thompson, was born in Canada and emigrated to the United States.) Among the reasons for this migration/remigration were the relative lack of accessible farmland in Ontario, Quebec, and Nova Scotia, the slower pace of industrialization in Canada than in the United States, and the significantly higher wages an industrial worker could earn south of the border.

Canada urbanized and industrialized between the 1880s and the 1910s, but less rapidly than the United States. The central Canadian provinces of Ontario and Quebec led the way. Montreal and Toronto became Canada's financial capitals, and the transcontinental railway led to the growth of western cities such as Winnipeg, Manitoba, and Vancouver, BC. The 1920 US census revealed that more Americans lived in urban than rural areas; the 1921 census of Canada made the same conclusion about the dominion's population. As parts of the dominion moved from a pre-industrial to an industrial economy, people became increasingly dependent on wage labour. Problems arose in Canadian cities not unlike those in the United States: the gap between rich and poor widened, sanitation and disease became urban problems, and poor families experienced higher infant mortality. When the Canadian economy and standard of living improved in the early twentieth century, Canadians of British descent reaped most of the gains, whereas French Canadians, new immigrants, and especially Native peoples did not prosper to the same degree. Nor was prosperity distributed equally by region. People in Ontario and the four western provinces fared much better than people in the other provinces.

If Canada's development paralleled that of the United States, there were also essential differences. The United States became a world power, while the dominion remained an important part of the British Empire. For example, between 1899 and 1902 seven thousand Canadian volunteers fought in South Africa as units in the British army in the Boer War. Virtually all of them were English Canadians; French Canadians accepted Canada's British connection, but had no desire to shed their blood for it. Like the rest of the empire, Canada entered the First World War automatically in 1914 when King George V declared war on Germany and Austria-Hungary. Canada could choose, however, how it wanted to contribute to the empire's war effort. Most English Canadians demanded a maximum contribution, but most French Canadians felt no strong attachment to Britain or to Britain's ally, France. French Canada, after all, had been disconnected from France since 1760. The 600,000 Canadian men and women who served during the war made a major contribution to the Allied victory over Germany; more than 61,000 died. (The United States did not enter that war until April 1917. From a population ten times that of Canada, 51,000 American soldiers died.) In Canada, the war almost literally tore the dominion apart. Conservative Prime Minister Sir Robert Borden's government imposed military conscription – Americans would call it a draft – to raise soldiers for the Canadian forces. This led to a bitter wartime election in 1917 that split Canada largely along French-English lines. Attempts to enforce conscription in Quebec led to riots. Troops from Ontario fired on a crowd, killing four civilians. English Canadians viewed their country's contribution to the war as a nation-building endeavour. From the perspective of French Canadians, the English-speaking majority had once again imposed its will on them.

A Nation-State Emerges, 1919–1945

At the end of the First World War, Canada took its tentative first steps into the international community of nation-states. With Britain's blessing, it took its own seat at the League of Nations, the international organization founded in 1919 to attempt (unsuccessfully) to settle international disputes without war. The idea for the league came from US president Woodrow Wilson, but the US Senate refused to sanction American membership, in part because the senators thought that giving Canada its own seat would be like awarding Britain two votes! The senators were mistaken. Although Canada maintained close links with

Britain, in the 1920s the British Empire began to evolve into a Common-wealth, defined in 1926 as a group of "autonomous Communities … united by a common allegiance to the Crown." With Britain's coopera-tion, Canada took control of its own foreign policy – most notably the management of its most significant foreign relationship, that with the United States. Until 1927 the British embassy in Washington had admin-istered Canada–US relations; that year, Canada appointed its own am-bassador to Washington, and the United States established an embassy in Ottawa. In 1931 the British Statute of Westminster made Canada a completely autonomous nation-state, with two significant exceptions: the highest court of appeal for Canadian legal cases remained the Brit-ish Privy Council, and the power to amend Canada's constitution, the British North America Act, remained with the British parliament. This significant authority remained in London not because Britain refused to give it up, but because the dominion government and the provinces did not trust each other and could not agree on how to do these things in Canada.

This disagreement was symptomatic of the discord that marked Ca-nadian politics during the 1920s and 1930s. The bitter legacy of war-time conscription continued to alienate French from English Canadians along ethnolinguistic lines, but economic class also divided Canadi-ans. In 1919 in Winnipeg, Canada's third-largest city at the time, angry workers shut down the economy in a general strike to demand social and economic change. Similar working-class unrest paralysed the coal-fields of Nova Scotia in 1925. Both protests met with violent repres-sion. Class conflict also intersected with regional discontent. Men and women (most Canadian women voted for the first time in 1919, just a year before American women did) from the farms of Ontario and the Prairie provinces of Manitoba, Saskatchewan, and Alberta supported the new Progressive Party. The Progressives called for a "New Na-tional Policy" that would nationalize railways, public utilities, and coal mines, make government more democratic, and reduce the protective tariff that favoured cities over farms and central Canada over the West. The national election of 1921 reflected these ethnolinguistic, class, and regional conflicts. In Quebec, every parliamentary district – every "rid-ing," as Canadians call electoral districts – elected a Liberal, because the Conservatives had been the party of conscription. The Prairie provinces almost unanimously chose Progressives. Until that pivotal election, every national election since 1867 had returned a majority government – that is, either the Liberal Party or the Conservative Party had won a majority of the seats in the House of Commons. In 1921, because of the electoral success of a third party, the Progressives, the Liberal Party led by Prime Minister William Lyon Mackenzie King formed Canada's first minority government – a Parliament in which no party had a majority. Since 1921, Canadian voters have never elected a Parliament without a third (and sometimes a fourth and a fifth) party winning some constituencies. This multiparty system is the most obvious difference between Canadian and American electoral politics. In the United States, the Democrats and the Republicans dominate; no third party has seriously challenged either since the 1890s. By contrast, Canadians have been governed by eleven minority governments since 1921.

In the 1920s, Canada's elites worried that American mass culture – movies, radio, magazines, and professional sport – was making ordinary Canadians too much like Americans. It is interesting that this concern about an independent identity, emphasized in chapter 7 on literature and culture, has long been a basic characteristic of Canada, and one that can be understood only in relation to the United States. American mass culture has affected every nation on the planet to some degree, but Canada's situation has always been unique. Seven out of ten Canadians share the English language with Americans, and two Canadians in three live within 60 miles of the border. Canadian consumers have thus become the most important foreign market for American exports of popular culture. Canadian governments have attempted to protect Canada's cultural sovereignty by imposing tariffs on imports of American magazines; they have also attempted to promote Canadian mass culture through subsidies and by developing a cultural infrastructure. The Canadian Broadcasting Corporation (CBC) and the National Film Board (NFB) (Société Radio-Canada and l'Office National du Film, in French) are prominent in this regard: Canada has publicly owned, taxpayer-supported cultural industries, while the United States does not. It would be a mistake, though, to think that the founding of the CBC and the NFB meant that Canada in the 1920s and 1930s was somehow more socialist than its neighbour. Canadian governments established these Crown corporations (as government-owned businesses are called in Canada) not because of any widespread opposition to private enterprise, but because they believed that unless governments propped up broadcasting and filmmaking, Canadians would have only American-made programs to listen to and Hollywood movies to watch. As advocates of government-owned cultural industries put it, the choice was "the state or the United States." Similarly, when Canada's federal government created a government-owned railway and airline, the Canadian National Railway (CNR) and Trans-Canada Air Lines (now Air Canada), it did so to meet the unique transportation needs of a vast country with a small and scattered population. None of these Crown corporations was granted a monopoly of its industry; privately owned companies competed with them. In recent years, most have been privatized, with Air Canada as one noteworthy example.

Canada had no North American monopoly on using government intervention to deal with difficult circumstances. The Great Depression of the 1930s struck the United States and Canada more severely than any other countries in the world. By March 1933, in each country one-third of the workforce was unemployed. US president Franklin D. Roosevelt used the power of the American state to respond to the economic crisis. His New Deal programs, such as the Agricultural Adjustment Act and Social Security, redefined the federal government's role in the economy and in the lives of individual citizens; it created the modern welfare state in the United States. In Canada, by contrast, neither the Conservative government of Prime Minister R.B. Bennett (1930–5) nor the Liberal Government of Prime Minister William Lyon Mackenzie King that succeeded it offered comparable national action to deal with the Depression. The political result was further fragmentation of the Canadian party system. Frustration with the inaction of the Conservatives and the Liberals launched three new political parties. Two became parties of the right. The Social Credit Party expressed the regional alienation of farm families unable to sell their grain; it governed Alberta from 1935 to 1971 and British Columbia from 1952 to 1972. In Quebec, the Union Nationale gained office in 1936 and won every provincial election but one until 1960. The Co-operative Commonwealth Federation (CCF) was a social democratic party of the left, much like the Labour Party in Britain. The CCF became a factor in national politics, as well as in provincial politics in British Columbia, Manitoba, and Ontario, but it won power in only one province, Saskatchewan, where it governed between 1944 and 1964. The long-term success of these three parties in four provinces illustrates the much larger historical role that regionalism has played in Canada than in the United States. Imagine what the American political spectrum would look like if, from the 1930s until the 1960s, almost half the states had been governed by parties other than the Republicans or the Democrats.

Given the profound economic and political impact of the Great Depression on Canada, the country's extraordinary contribution to Allied victory in the Second World War seems even more remarkable. Canada was no longer constitutionally obligated to support Britain, but all except four of the 252 members of the Canadian parliament voted to join the fight against the Axis, and King George VI declared Canada at war with Germany on 10 September 1939, a week after he had done the same for Great Britain. Part of Canada's reason for declaring war was the understanding that, as a country that depended on international trade as the cornerstone of its economy, it could not barricade itself within North America. From June 1940, when Germany conquered France, until December 1941, when the United States entered the war after the Japanese attack on Pearl Harbor, Canada was Britain's most important military ally.

The wartime emergency also turned Canada and the United States into formal allies. In August 1940, while the latter country was still neutral, Prime Minister Mackenzie King and President Roosevelt met at Ogdensburg, New York, on the St Lawrence River, to create a Permanent Joint Board on Defence to prepare for a possible attack on North America. Once the Americans entered the conflict, Canada became a very junior partner in the strategic planning of the war effort. Yet 1.1 million Canadian men and women, out of a population of only 11.2 million, served in the Royal Canadian Army, Navy, or Air Force. On D-Day, 6 June 1944, Canadian troops had responsibility for Juno Beach, one of the five Normandy beaches during the Allied invasion of Europe. By the time the war ended in 1945, Canada had become the third most important military and industrial power in what came to be called the Free World. Canadians took justifiable pride in their wartime accomplishments, and soon after it ended, Canada's leaders played a significant role in creating the United Nations. The modern Canadian nation-state, many historians argue, emerged from Canada's participation in the Second World War.

Canada in an American Empire, 1945–1976

After the Second World War, a newly confident Canadian nation-state strode the international stage, increasingly distinct from the British Empire/Commonwealth. Canada's leaders sought a role for their country as a middle power that would work within the UN for international peace and prosperity. But the Cold War between the United States and the Soviet Union that developed after 1945 drew Canada (to some extent – never totally) into an American empire. The United

States never had to force Canada to follow its lead: the two countries were equally frightened by what they interpreted as a hostile Russia (in both countries, people usually said "Russia" rather than the Soviet Union) that seemed bent on imposing communism on the Free World. Canada shared the Americans' commitment to a stable international order and to providing the collective security essential to maintain it. Canadian leaders took an active role in the creation of the principal Cold War multilateral military alliance, the North Atlantic Treaty Organization (NATO). During the Korean War (1950–3) Canadian forces fought under American leadership to repel a Soviet-sponsored North Korean invasion of South Korea. Because Soviet long-range bombers could attack North American targets with nuclear weapons by flying over the North Pole, Canada and the United States reached a separate bilateral military agreement in 1957, to create the North American Air (later Aerospace) Defence Command, or NORAD. The United States financed and operated the Distant Early Warning radar network, or "DEW Line," stretched across Canada's North to detect Soviet incursions. Canada's leaders worried privately that these military links with the United States could erode Canadian sovereignty, but they accepted American direction rather than spend what it would have cost to build large enough Canadian forces to defend themselves.

Canada's economic integration with the United States also increased rapidly after 1945. The Canada–US economic relationship became the most important economic relationship for either country and the largest economic relationship that has ever existed between two countries in world history. Foreign investment, most of it American, financed the exploitation of Canada's abundant natural resources: oil and gas in Alberta, iron ore in Newfoundland and Quebec, nickel in Northern Ontario and Manitoba, aluminum smelting in Quebec and British Columbia. A trans-Canada pipeline brought Alberta natural gas to heat homes not only in central Canada but also in the United States. A joint engineering project, the St Lawrence Seaway, opened in 1959 by Canada's Queen Elizabeth II and President Dwight Eisenhower, enabled ocean-going ships to enter the Great Lakes from the Atlantic. Most Canadians no longer worked directly in resource industries like mining, oil and gas production, forestry, or agriculture. Instead they worked in service industries and lived in cities, and Canada became one of the most urbanized countries in the world. But natural resources remained vital to the Canadian economy, just as they had been centuries earlier when Canada depended on trade in fur and timber, and just as they remain today.

The prosperity of the 1950s and 1960s was widely shared among a rapidly growing Canadian population. By 1967, the centennial of Confederation, there were 20 million Canadians. The country's "baby boom" contributed to this growth, as the crude birth rate – the number of babies born each year – increased from twenty per thousand Canadians in the 1930s to thirty per thousand in the 1950s. Canada's population also increased because of heavy immigration. By the 1950s, Canada had become the most welcoming country in the world for immigrants. It had once preferred immigrants from Britain, the United States, and western and northern Europe. Canada now removed these preferences and restrictions so that immigrants arrived from Italy, Greece, and Portugal; later in the century they came from the Caribbean, Africa, China, and India. Where they had once settled in the Prairie provinces, they now migrated to the rapidly growing cities of Montreal, Toronto, and Vancouver. In 1900 all but a tiny percentage of Canadians could trace their ancestry to France or Britain; by the 1960s one Canadian in four had roots in other places. Canada officially embraced this growing diversity. Canadians' metaphor for their society became the "mosaic," and ethno-cultural groups were encouraged to retain their distinctive characteristics. Canadians contrasted their mosaic explicitly to the melting pot that they imagined existed in the United States. In 1971 Canada's federal government made multiculturalism an official policy and even established a cabinet position for it.

By the 1950s, Canada had grown militarily and economically closer to the United States, and seemed to be growing culturally closer as well. Canadians and Americans ate hamburgers at the A&W, drove the same Ford, GM, and Chrysler automobiles, played (mostly) the same sports, and listened to the same popular music. Canadians even watched the same television programs as Americans; except for *Hockey Night in Canada* (*la Soirée du hockey* in French), most of the hit shows on Canadian television were produced in the United States. In retrospect, however, it is clear that during the 1960s, the two nation-states began to diverge in several significant areas. In addition to multiculturalism, most Canadians today point with considerable pride to Canada's universal national health insurance program as the major feature distinguishing the two countries. Canada developed its program over the same period that several American attempts to enact a national program of health insurance failed. Most Canadians (and most Americans) do not know, however, that until the 1960s Canada lagged behind the United States in the development of its welfare state. The US federal government began to create a social safety net for Americans before Canada's did the same for Canadians. The New Deal legislation, most notably the Social Security Act of 1935, had significantly expanded the US welfare state. The Canadian federal government's failure to take similar steps brought the Co-operative Commonwealth Federation to power in Saskatchewan in 1944. In 1947 the Saskatchewan CCF government initiated the Hospital Services Plan, the first universal public hospital insurance program in North America. Other provinces copied it, which pressured the federal government to develop a national program of hospital insurance in 1957. In 1962 the Saskatchewan CCF government enacted Medicare, a universal public medical insurance plan. (American readers should not confuse Canada's Medicare, which covers all Canadians, with the US program of the same name that covers Americans over sixty-five.) By the end of the 1960s, the federal Medical Care Act was providing financial support so that Canadians in every province could benefit from similar health care programs. National health insurance was but one of a number of new Canadian social programs, which included the Canada Pension Plan (1965), the Post-Secondary Education Act (1965), the Canada Assistance Plan (1966), and an expanded system of Unemployment Insurance (1971) (since 1996, Employment Insurance).

Thus, although increasingly drawn into the American orbit in defence and economic matters during the Cold War, Canada charted its own course in other areas. In 1970, defence expenditures absorbed 60 per cent of the US government budget; Canada spent 18 per cent of its budget on the military, focusing instead on developing domestic social programs. Historians have argued that while the United States was evolving into a "warfare state," Canada was building its welfare state. But Canada could afford to do this only because it could count on the United States to provide some of its defence. This more extensive welfare state and much smaller military establishment does not mean, however, that Americans should understand Canada to be a socialist or pacifist country. Modern Canada does have a social democratic political party, the New Democratic Party (NDP), created in 1960 by the CCF and Canada's trade union movement. And a higher percentage of Canadian workers do belong to trade unions. Barely one American worker in ten belongs to a union today, while one in three Canadian workers do. Like the larger Canadian welfare state, however, this is a recent development historically. Until the 1960s the labour movement in the United States enrolled a higher percentage of workers than it did in Canada. Although there is some correlation between labour union membership and political support for the NDP (as there is a correlation in the United States between union membership and support for the Democratic Party), only a minority of Canada's unionized workers regularly votes for the NDP. The NDP has governed in five Canadian provinces at different times (Nova Scotia, Ontario, Manitoba, Saskatchewan, and British Columbia). These NDP provincial governments have regulated private enterprise but have never abolished it. At the federal level, the NDP has never come close to forming a national government in Canada, and became the official opposition for the first time only in 2011, though at times it has held the balance of power in a minority government.

Although Canada has greatly reduced the size of its armed forces, it has been a member of NATO from the beginning as well as a partner of the United States in NORAD. However, as one historian has suggested, it has become a more ambivalent ally more recently. Canadian and American foreign policies diverged in the late 1960s and early 1970s under Liberal prime minister Pierre Trudeau. For example, Canada rejected the US quarantine of Fidel Castro's communist regime in Cuba, not because Canadians supported communism, but because Canadians and their leaders believed (however unrealistically) that Canada could do more to change Cuba by continuing economic and diplomatic contact with the island than by rejecting it. Nor did Canada contribute troops to the Vietnam War. Canadians also provided refuge to about 50,000 young Americans who fled north to avoid military service in Southeast Asia, continuing a tradition of American dissenters seeking refuge in Canada that began with the American Revolution. Thousands of Canadians demonstrated against the Vietnam War, but so did Americans in far greater numbers. Canada's government never officially condemned the Vietnam War. It continued to sell military supplies to the United States during the conflict, and it allowed the United States to test weapons like the cruise missile in Canada. As one Canadian Member of Parliament (MP) put it in a speech in the House of Commons in Ottawa: "The Americans are our best friends, whether we like it or not."

Constructing a "Community of Communities," 1976–2012

The most obvious difference between Canada and the United States is that Canada has since its inception been a continuous negotiation between French and English. (To understand Canada, Americans must appreciate that the situation of French speakers in Canada is *not* the same as that of Spanish speakers in today's United States.) The relationship between francophones and anglophones has seldom been smooth. In 1867, francophones made up a majority of two provinces, Quebec and Manitoba, and about 40 per cent of the population of New Brunswick. Over the next century, however, although francophone minorities survived in other provinces, French Canada came to mean primarily the province of Quebec, where francophones became an increasing majority. An older rural and agricultural French-Canadian identity, based on Catholicism as well as language, was supplanted for most francophones by a secular urban identity as Québécois. Although francophones had always dominated Quebec provincial politics, and two French Canadians (Wilfrid Laurier, 1896–1911, and Louis St Laurent, 1948–57) had served with distinction as prime minister, francophones legitimately resented the disproportionate economic power that the anglophone minority in Quebec enjoyed in business and industry. In the 1960s they expressed this resentment in *la révolution tranquille* (the Quiet Revolution), during which many Québécois began to demand that francophones become *maîtres chez nous* (masters in our own house) in Quebec, economically as well as politically. The government of Prime Minister Pierre Trudeau responded with the Official Languages Act of 1969, which expanded the use of French in the federal government and improved the status of French across the country. As a consequence, the one in four Canadians who speak French today have a right to deal with the federal government in their mother tongue anywhere in Canada.

Québécois nationalists demanded much more; many of them called for an independent Quebec. The Quebec Liberation Front (FLQ), a tiny revolutionary terrorist group, resorted to bombs and political kidnappings to achieve this in the 1960s. The Parti Québécois, which represented the mainstream movement for independence, worked through electoral politics. In 1976, the PQ became Quebec's provincial government, with 41 per cent of the popular vote. (Remember that in multiparty systems like those in Canada, a party can win power with much less than a majority of the popular vote.) The new government passed the Charter of the French Language, Bill 101, which made French the only official language of Quebec and required the use of French in government services, in companies with fifty or more employees, on public signs, and in the education of the children of immigrants. In 1980 the PQ government asked voters in a referendum for a mandate to negotiate "sovereignty-association" – a new relationship with the rest of

Canada. Even with this mild label, 60 per cent of Quebec voters rejected this back-door route to independence.

Canada's federal governments tried various approaches to deal with this crisis of national unity. Under Trudeau, a Quebec-born Liberal, Canada drafted a new constitution in 1982 that "patriated" constitutional change to Canada from the British parliament. When Queen Elizabeth II signed the new act in Ottawa, Canada at last achieved full nation-statehood, with the right to amend its own constitution. The new constitution included a Charter of Rights and Freedoms, similar to the US Bill of Rights, which guaranteed free speech as well as the rights of association, conscience, and religion, and which protected the voting and legal rights of Canadians. All provinces agreed to the new constitution, except for Quebec, which meant that Canada was left in a constitutional limbo as a federal nation-state in which the second-largest province had rejected the document by which the country was supposed to be governed. A new Conservative federal government led by Prime Minister Brian Mulroney made two attempts to compromise with a new Quebec government that was not pledged to independence, but neither the 1987 Meech Lake Accord nor the 1992 Charlottetown Accord – both of which made concessions to Quebec – won ratification.

In 1995 the re-elected PQ held another referendum in Quebec to consider separation from Canada. Angered by the failure of constitutional compromise, Quebec voters made the referendum astonishingly close: 49.4 per cent of them supported separation. Canada has struggled with English-French dualism throughout its history and will continue to do so in the twenty-first century. Whether Quebec will become an independent nation-state depends in large part on the degree to which the other provinces accept its uniqueness within the nation-state of Canada. Canada's continued struggle for national unity, of course, continues to distinguish it from the United States; so does the remarkable civility with which Canadians have dealt with the sort of problem that has drawn other countries to division or even to civil war.

An important reason why constitutional compromises have failed in Canada has been the increased assertiveness of another community of "founding people," the First Nations, who are demanding to be included in the constitutional process. (Native issues are covered in detail in chapter 8.) This new forcefulness began in the 1940s, when improved public health and high birth rates created a population explosion that has made Aboriginal people almost 4 per cent of the total population, and a much higher percentage in the Western provinces.

(By comparison, Native Americans make up less than 1 per cent of the US population.) Although there are too many separate First Nations in Canada – more than five hundred – for them to ever speak with one voice, Aboriginal peoples have organized politically to demand that they be heard. The Canadian federal government, which took responsibility for Native peoples at Confederation, had pursued a futile policy of assimilation until the 1970s, when growing Aboriginal protest demonstrated that the First Nations would never become just another ethnic tile in Canada's multicultural mosaic. Now Aboriginal communities are pursuing, and some are winning, individual land-claim cases in the courts, and the Assembly of First Nations, the largest pan-Aboriginal organization, has become a political factor that no government can ignore. The Inuit of the eastern Arctic achieved the most spectacular triumph of any Aboriginal group when in 1999 the Canadian government created the largely self-governing territory of Nunavut. In 2005 a summit attended by Aboriginal leaders, provincial governments, and the federal government produced an accord that promised more than $5 billion to improve the lives of Aboriginal people. However, the Conservative government elected in January 2006 has not implemented the accord.

This evolving recognition of the collective rights of French-speaking Canadians and of First Nations communities offers further evidence of how profoundly different a country Canada has become as compared to the United States. Who could imagine an American government carving a territory like Nunavut out of North and South Dakota as a homeland for the Sioux? Yet despite these obvious differences, over the past two decades Canada has become more closely intertwined economically with the United States. The Canada-US Free Trade Agreement of 1989 and the trilateral North American Free Trade Agreement of 1994 that brought in Mexico have created a new North American market for production and investment. Continental economic integration has frightened many Canadians, who worry – as Canadians have since the eighteenth century – that their country might become culturally "Americanized," or perhaps eventually politically absorbed into the United States. There is little evidence that this "Americanization" is taking place, however. As but one of many examples, although Canada sent troops to fight in the US "War on Terror" in Afghanistan, it chose not to participate in the US-led "coalition of the willing" that invaded Iraq in 2003. An overview of their own history should reassure Canadians (and those Americans who study Canada) that any convergence is unlikely and that Canada and its neighbour will grow more distinct from each other even if they further integrate economically.

FURTHER READING AND RESOURCES ON THE HISTORY OF CANADA

Canadian Heritage. N.d. "Great Unsolved Mysteries in Canadian History." http://canadianmysteries.ca/en/index.php.

"Canadian Heritage Gallery." 2007. http://www.canadianheritage.ca.

La Direction des Archives de France; Library and Archives Canada; and the Canadian Embassy in Paris. N.d. "New France, New Horizons: On French Soil in America." http://www.archivescanadafrance.org.

Library and Archives Canada. 2008. *Dictionary of Canadian Biography Online*. http://www.biographi.ca/index.html.

Northern Blue Publishing. N.d. "Canadian History on the Web." http://canadachannel.ca/index.php.

Office national du film du Canada/National Film Board of Canada. 2010. http://www.nfb.ca.

Bukowczyk, John J., Nora Faires, David R. Smith, and Randy William Widdis. 2005. *Permeable Border: The Great Lakes Basin as Transnational Region, 1650– 1990*. Pittsburgh: University of Pittsburgh Press.

Dickinson, John, and Brian Young. 2008. *A Short History of Quebec*. 4th ed. Montreal, Kingston: McGill-Queen's University Press.

Fischer, David Hackett. 2008. *Champlain's Dream: The European Founding of North America*. New York: Simon and Schuster.

Granatstein, J.L., and J.M. Hitsman. 1977. *Broken Promises: A History of Conscription in Canada*. Toronto: Oxford University Press.

Kaufman, Joshua. 2009. *The Origins of Canadian and American Political Differences*. Cambridge, MA: Harvard University Press.

Maioni, Antonia. 1998. *Parting at the Crossroads: The Emergence of Health Insurance in the United States and Canada*. Princeton: Princeton University Press.

McRoberts, Kenneth. 1999. *Quebec: Social Change and Political Crisis*. 3rd ed. Don Mills, ON: Oxford University Press.

Miller, J.R. 2000. *Skyscrapers Hide the Heavens: A History of Indian–White Relations in Canada*. Rev. ed. Toronto: University of Toronto Press.

Morton, Desmond. 2007. *A Military History of Canada*. 5th ed. Toronto: McClelland & Stewart.

Ramirez, Bruno, with the assistance of Yves Otis. 2001. *Crossing the 49th Parallel: Migration from Canada to the United States, 1900–1930*. Ithaca: Cornell University Press.

Silver, A.I. 1997. *The French-Canadian Idea of Confederation, 1864–1900*. 2nd ed. Toronto: University of Toronto Press.

Taylor, Alan. 2002. *American Colonies*. New York: Penguin.

Taylor, Alan. 2010. *The Civil War of 1812*. New York: Knopf.

Thompson, John Herd, and Stephen J. Randall. 2007. *Canada and the United States: Ambivalent Allies*. 4th ed. Athens: University of Georgia Press.

3   Politics and Government

MUNROE EAGLES AND SHARON A. MANNA

As the chapters in this book reveal, the Canadian experience has many important similarities and differences when compared with the United States. This is certainly true in the sphere of politics and government. Both countries are advanced liberal democracies that strive to give political voice to citizens in pluralistic societies through institutionalized systems of political representation. Both political systems integrate enormous geographies and distribute power over space in federal arrangements. These and numerous other commonalities have made the two countries natural allies, sharing the world's longest undefended border, as well as partners in what is one of the most intimate and intensive bilateral relationships in the world. As Seymour Martin Lipset, one of the most prominent American scholars to turn his attention northwards to study Canada's political system, has written: "Knowledge of Canada or the United States is the best way to gain insight into the other North American country. Nations can be understood only in comparative perspective. And the more similar the units being compared, the more possible it should be to isolate the factors responsible for differences between them. Looking intensively at Canada and the United States sheds light on both of them" (1990, xiii).

Notwithstanding all the important similarities in political life in these two North American societies, there are some profoundly important political differences. Lipset's own work, for example, shows that Canadians are less fearful of governmental authority – a key difference in values that he attributes to the revolutionary origins of America and the counter-revolutionary formation of Canada. Whereas Americans charted their political course by the values of "life, liberty, and the pursuit of happiness," Canadians decided to pursue "peace, order, and good government." As several of the other chapters in this book illustrate, Canadians tolerate greater levels of government intervention in their lives than do Americans and have used political authority freely to accomplish important shared goals. To this end, they have adapted institutions of British parliamentary democracy that concentrate power and enable efficient governmental action. Put succinctly, whereas Americans set out in 1776 to create a completely new kind of political system for the new world they were settling, the Canadian challenge has been to adapt European-style political institutions and practices to the North American context (Siegfried 1906).

This chapter identifies the essential features of the Canadian political system and government, with an eye to introducing readers to the practices of an important friend and ally, but also – following Lipset's logic – to sharpen our understanding of the exceptional nature of the American political experience. We begin with a historical overview of the founding and growth of Canada, showing how the country's evolution has shaped its contemporary political life. We then discuss the institutions and operations of the parliamentary system and see how the fusion of executive and legislative branches concentrates powers in the political executive. This is followed by a discussion of the "linkage" organizations – parties, groups, and social movements – that animate Canada's parliamentary democracy and that anchor its institutions and processes firmly in Canadian society. The next section explores the evolution of Canadian federalism, chronicling the transformation of a highly centralized system into one of the world's most decentralized federations. Finally, we turn to a discussion of the judicial system in Canada and look at the very different approach Canadians have followed to protect individual rights and liberties.

From British North America to the Dominion of Canada

The Canadian genius for compromise is reflected in the existence of Canada itself.

Northrop Frye

By the middle of the nineteenth century, the existing political arrangements in place throughout the colonies of British North America (BNA), especially in the Province of Canada, began to crumble under the weight of mounting political, security, and economic pressures. The union of Upper (British) and Lower (French) Canada via the Union Act of 1840 failed in its goal of assimilating two cultures into one quasi-unitary system of government. Furthermore, as early as the aftermath of the American Revolution, Great Britain made it plain to colonial leaders that it no longer wanted to be wholly responsible for the security and economic well-being of British North America. Economically, the colonies suffered after the repeal of the British Corn Laws in 1846, which removed the certainty of established British markets in favour of the uncertainties of free trade. This forced the colonies to look more closely at a system of east–west trade. Another pressing issue was collective defence, especially with regard to the United States. American western expansion worried British North America's leaders, who feared an incursion by American settlers and businesses in the land between the Pacific colonies and the rest of BNA. It was hoped that the purchase of Rupert's Land and the Northwest Territories from the Hudson's Bay Company (which owned the lands in between British colonies), would squelch any potential land grabs ("American Expansionism"). At the close of the American Civil War, given Britain's pro-Confederacy sympathies, there was much to fear from the large, victorious Union army, which might seek to exact revenge and perhaps gain more territory by turning its attention north. Even after Confederation, there was a rather smug assumption throughout the United States that when the Canadian "experiment" went awry, America would inevitably absorb the failed dominion. Despite these concerns, the Province of Canada killed the Militia Bill of 1862, which would have provided funds for a greater self-defence capability. With the bill's defeat, Great Britain believed it should not bear the cost of protecting these colonies, and thus decided that some sort of union should be in place to substitute for the Empire (Cheffins and Johnson 1986, 36–7).

In 1864, as a result of these concerns, delegates from New Brunswick, Nova Scotia, and the Province of Canada (present at the request of John A. Macdonald) convened the first of three conferences at Charlottetown to consider the viability of a new political union. The ensuing Quebec Conference (October 1864) considered more specific details of a potential union, and from the very beginning a federal system was proposed. The failure of the quasi-unitary government of the Province of Canada indicated that a similar structure could not work for a larger political union. Seventy-two "Quebec Resolutions" were the result of the conference; they suggested the framework of a new constitutional order, the founding of a new nation to be called "Canada," and splitting the Province of Canada into the separate provinces of Ontario and Quebec. To integrate themselves more fully with the rest of the colonial economies, New Brunswick and Nova Scotia pushed hard for a railway system (ibid., 36). There was a good deal of disagreement regarding the relative strengths of federal and provincial governments in the proposed federation. Given the demands for representation by population in Upper Canada, Lower Canada's cultural demands, and the Maritimes' pre-existing political character, Macdonald believed that a federal system would be the best alternative. Such a system, in his view, would have to favour the national government (Koerner 1988, 15). He looked to the United States, which had just ended a civil war, and surmised that the conflict had been caused in part by weaknesses in the US constitution; specifically, that the document treated each state as sovereign, with federal power beginning only where state power ended. Some French-Canadian delegates felt threatened by the creation of a strong central government, their concern being that the existing local and provincial legislatures would be rendered mere figureheads. For these delegates, the current arrangement was not optimal but still presented a better existence for French Canadians. On the other hand, a federal system that remained under the Crown appealed to English Canadians, and to other French-Canadian delegates, who understood their enjoyment of rights as emanating from the Crown (ibid., 5).

During the last London Conference (1866), the British North America Act, 1867, was drafted. Confederation of a new country – to consist of Nova Scotia, New Brunswick, and the separate provinces of Ontario and Quebec – commenced by an act of the British parliament and royal assent on 1 July 1867, now commemorated as Canada Day. The BNA Act, 1867, created the Dominion of Canada, a quasi-independent nation. The new nation would still be subject to the Crown in terms of foreign policy and law (the latter through decisions of the Judicial Committee of the Privy Council [JCPC]). Similarly, the control over and resting place of the Canadian constitution would not be in Ottawa, Canada's new capital, but in Britain. Canada's constitution was in reality a piece of British parliamentary legislation. The new Canadian system mirrored Great Britain's closely; it established a parliamentary democracy that emphasized responsible government, political equality, and a role for the Crown as executive. The preamble to the BNA Act recognized its British parentage, in that it created "a constitution similar in principle to that of the United Kingdom." The BNA Act, 1867, was also a document of compromise: it created a federal system (the first known parliamentary-federal system) to share power over a set of provinces that had previously governed themselves with significant discretion.

The powers of the new federal government were enumerated in section 91, beginning with the significant power "to make laws for the Peace, Order, and good Government of Canada" in any area not specifically allotted to the provinces. This reserve or residual power of the federal parliament was contrary to the practice of the US constitution. Furthermore, the federal government, in part IV, was granted the power to disallow provincial laws. Cheffins and Johnson understand the new system of government as a deliberately crafted centralized federalism, which took from its British roots the desire to have control over its smaller units: "The power of reservation placed in the federally appointed lieutenant-governors of the provinces, and the absolute veto over provincial legislation, in the form of the disallowance power, are very strong evidence of the ability of the federal government to exercise the same powers which London exercised over its far-flung colonies" (Cheffins and Johnson 1986, 35). More specifically, section 91 also allotted the federal parliament power to regulate trade and commerce; power to raise revenue through taxation; power over banking and currency; responsibility for national defence; and the administration of criminal law. Section 92 detailed the explicit powers given to the provinces, including the ability to levy direct taxes within the province to raise revenues; the capacity to borrow money on provincial credit; and control over health care, property, and civil rights as well as the administration of justice. Lastly, section 93 allotted control of the educational system to the provinces; this included a protection for the continuation of parochial and religious schools. (Note that this constitutes a key difference in political culture; the separation of church and state is a prominent feature of the United States, where public funding for parochial schools is illegal.) Thus, while the system of government created under the BNA Act, 1867, was not the optimal political arrangement for the diverse colonies and interests, it adequately addressed the concerns common to all participants.

Several important elements were left out of the BNA Act, 1867, leaving challenges for future generations. A prime example is a domestic amending formula. Federal systems divide powers among the national and smaller units and in this way distribute sovereignty among those levels. Therefore, it is important for the levels of government to have a say in the amending of the constitution. For example, Article V of the US constitution provides just such an amending formula, requiring three-quarters of state legislatures to ratify constitutional amendments following two-thirds approval in Congress. With the constitution residing in Great Britain, a Canadian amending formula was left out of the BNA Act. Thus, as a British statute, any changes had to come from the British parliament. Second, there was no entrenched bill of rights. This omission is not much of a surprise, given the British parentage of the BNA Act. As the preamble stated, the BNA Act was to be similar in principle to the British constitution, which contained no such explicit bill of rights. Instead, through a combination of the constitution and common law, there was an "implied" bill of rights. Lastly, the BNA Act failed to make the courts anything more significant than statutory creations. While section 101 gave the federal parliament the ability to create a "general court of appeal for Canada," failing to create a constitutional Supreme Court as an institution of the government detracted from the legitimacy of the Supreme Court of Canada until 1982.

The Parliamentary System

As we have seen, the formation of a united Canada was inherently and self-consciously premised on a rejection of the American Revolution. In addition, the "Fathers of Confederation" who designed the governing system also rejected the presidential model of government, based on a separation of legislative and executive powers, in favour of a British-style parliamentary system. The preamble to the BNA Act, passed by the British House of Commons, declared that four former colonies (Ontario, Quebec, Nova Scotia, New Brunswick) were to be "federally united into One Dominion under the Crown of the United Kingdom of Great Britain and Ireland, with a Constitution similar in Principle to that of the United Kingdom." Some key differences between the United States and Canada can be traced to this fundamental institutional difference. In this section we highlight the main characteristics of the parliamentary system in Canada, leaving a discussion of the judicial system to a later section.

Liberal democracy evolved in the West through two different institutional configurations. Following the writings of Montesquieu and others, presidential systems were developed to promote liberty by enshrining the principle of the separation of powers. In the United States, the executive (president), the legislature (Senate and House of Representatives), and the judiciary are formally separate entities, each with its own constitutional allocation of powers. To further guard against a centralization of political power that might threaten individual liberty, each branch of government was given responsibilities to "check and balance" the operations of the others. Governmental action in such a complex system requires continuous negotiation and coordination across independent branches of government, making activist and interventionist governments very difficult to establish. The principal alternative to presidentialism is parliamentary government, the central defining feature of which is the *fusion* of executive and legislative powers. This is illustrated in figure 3.1: the prime minister and Cabinet (the operative parts of the political executive) overlap the Senate and the House of Commons (the legislature).

As figure 3.1 shows, in Canada's parliamentary system, the political executive has two heads, one being the formal "head of state" and the other the "head of government." Canada has remained part of the British Commonwealth and also remains a constitutional monarchy, with Queen Elizabeth II as head of state. The processes of democratization over the centuries have left the monarch with very few real powers, however, and though all legislation is enacted in her name, most of the responsibilities of the queen and her designate in Canada, the governor general, are symbolic and ceremonial. Now the governor general is appointed by the queen on the advice of the prime minister and normally serves terms of approximately five years. Over time prime ministers have used this opportunity to appoint prominent members of minority communities to the position, symbolically underscoring the inclusiveness of the political system. Past governors general have included representatives from Canada's Acadian, Ukrainian, and Asian communities, and most recently Michaëlle Jean, who served from 2005 to 2010, was a francophone immigrant born in Haiti. The current incumbent is David Johnston, former president of the University of Waterloo. Dr Johnston was born in Sault Saint Marie, Ontario, and worked in a steel mill as a young man, before embarking on a distinguished career as an academic. He assumed the office on 1 October 2010. As an unelected official, the governor general lacks the democratic legitimacy that would justify the exercise of political power, so normally he or she acts immediately and without discretion at the request of the elected government of the day.

Real political power in Canada is concentrated in the hands of the elected political executive, consisting of the prime minister and members of the cabinet (Savoie 2008). Table 3.1 lists Canada's twenty-two prime ministers to date and shows their political affiliation and term of

Figure 3.1 Canada's parliamentary system

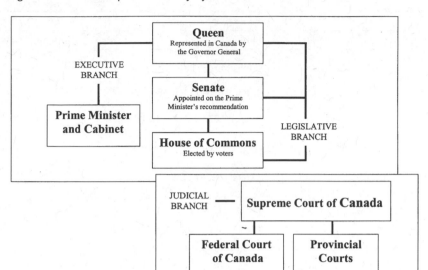

Source: Derived from http://www.parl.gc.ca/About/Parliament/GuideToHoC/index-e.
htm.

office. The prime minister is the leader of the political party that (usually) controls the largest number of seats in the elected lower house
of the legislative chamber (the House of Commons). As such, to become prime minister a person must win two separate contests – first,
he or she must be chosen (normally by election among party members)
leader of a political party, and second, that party must prevail over its
competitors in a general election. These elections are conducted using
a single-member plurality electoral system. Inherited from Britain, this
electoral system divides the entire country into distinct electoral districts (known as ridings, and currently numbering 308). (The size of the
House of Commons is set to increase by 30 seats for the next election as
a result of population growth in Ontario, Alberta, and British Columbia.)
The major parties run candidates in all ridings, with the candidate who
attracts the most (i.e., a plurality of) votes in the local riding winning
the seat. So in this system there are no nationally elected public offices –
a prime minister needs to be elected in a district like all other Members
of Parliament (MPs).

Table 3.1 Canada's prime ministers

Prime minister	Party	Term(s)	Years	Months	Days
		Time as prime minister			
John Alexander Macdonald	Cons.	1 July 1867–5 Nov. 1873	6	4	4
Alexander Mackenzie	Liberal	7 Nov. 1873–8 Oct. 1878	4	11	1
John Alexander Macdonald	Cons.	17 Oct. 1878–6 June 1891	12	7	20
John Joseph Caldwell Abbott	Cons.	16 June 1891–24 Nov. 1892	1	5	8
John Sparrow David Thompson	Cons.	5 Dec. 1892–12 Dec. 1894	2	0	7
Mackenzie Bowell	Cons.	12 Dec. 1894–27 Apr. 1896	1	4	15
Charles Tupper	Cons.	1 May 1896–8 July 1896	0	2	7
Wilfrid Laurier	Liberal	11 July 1896–6 Oct. 1911	15	2	25
Robert Laird Borden	Cons.	10 Oct. 1911–12 Oct. 1917	6	0	2
Robert Laird Borden	Unionist	12 Oct. 1917–10 July 1920	2	8	28
Arthur Meighen	Unionist	10 July 1920–29 Dec. 1921	1	5	19
William Lyon Mackenzie King	Liberal	29 Dec. 1921–28 June 1926	4	5	30
Arthur Meighen	Cons.	29 June 1926–25 Sept. 1926	0	2	27
William Lyon Mackenzie King	Liberal	25 Sept. 1926–7 Aug. 1930	3	10	13
Richard Bedford Bennett	Cons.	7 Aug. 1930–23 Oct. 1935	5	2	16
William Lyon Mackenzie King	Liberal	23 Oct. 1935–15 Nov. 1948	13	0	23
Louis Stephen St Laurent	Liberal	15 Nov. 1948–21 June 1957	8	7	6
John George Diefenbaker	P.C.	21 June 1957–22 Apr. 1963	5	10	1
Lester Bowles Pearson	Liberal	22 Apr. 1963–20 Apr. 1968	4	11	29
Pierre Elliott Trudeau	Liberal	20 Apr. 1968–3 June 1979	11	1	14
Charles Joseph Clark	P.C.	4 June 1979–2 March 1980	0	8	27

(continued)

Table 3.1 (continued)

Prime minister	Party	Term(s)	Time as prime minister		
			Years	Months	Days
Pierre Elliott Trudeau	Liberal	3 March 1980–30 June 1984	4	3	27
John Napier Turner	Liberal	30 June 1984–17 Sept. 1984	0	2	18
Martin Brian Mulroney	P.C.	17 Sept. 1984–25 June 1993	8	9	8
A. Kim Campbell	P.C.	25 June 1993–4 Nov. 1993	0	4	10
Joseph Jacques Jean Chretien	Liberal	4 Nov. 1993–12 Dec. 2003	10	1	25
Paul Edgar Phillipe Martin, Jr.	Liberal	12 Dec. 2003–6 Feb. 2006	2	1	25
Stephen Joseph Harper	Cons.	6 Feb. 2006–present			

Source: http://www.collectionscanada.gc.ca/2/4/h4-3000-e.html
Note: The abbreviations "Cons." and "P.C." refer to the Conservative Party and the Progressive Conservative Party, respectively.

In many cases, elections conducted by the rules of single-member plurality will give a single party an absolute majority of seats in the legislature. When this occurs, the prime minister leads what is called a majority government – the strongest possible form of parliamentary government. In these circumstances the prime minister can normally rely on party discipline (discussed below) to deliver a consistent majority of votes for virtually any legislation the government initiates. However, since five of the last eleven federal elections in Canada (including the one held in October 2008) failed to provide one party with a majority, we will also discuss the operation of minority governments.

According to British constitutional tradition, the prime minister is *primus inter pares*, that is, "first among equals." In reality, however, prime ministers enjoy a formidable array of formal powers. Over the years, a variety of developments have tended to enhance and augment these formal powers, and some have argued that prime ministers who lead majority governments may approach the status of being elected dictators (Bakvis 2001). While this may be an overstatement in some important respects, it is clearly true that a prime minister who is personally popular with the electorate and who is backed by a cohesive majority of supporters in the House of Commons can wield far greater constitutional power than can an American president. A quick overview of the sources and nature of prime ministerial power reveals the inadequacy of the traditional British depiction of the prime minister as merely the "first" member among equals in the House of Commons.

The most important source of prime ministerial power is the ability to appoint and remove party members from important positions in the political executive, and particularly the cabinet. Compared to "backbench" MPs, cabinet ministers enjoy much greater responsibilities for developing government policy – responsibilities that frequently include the supervision of a civil service department. With these additional powers go a number of significant perks and privileges, including a higher media profile, additional salary, and other allowances. In selecting a cabinet, the prime minister must weigh a complex array of factors, ranging from the personal qualities (career, educational background, debating and media skills, etc.) of the candidates to the need to balance the cabinet in gender, linguistic, regional, and other terms. Proceedings of cabinet meetings are secret, and since by convention the cabinet is "collectively responsible" for the government's policy and performance, public dissent by cabinet ministers is not tolerated.

As formidable as these powers are, there are additional sources of prime ministerial prominence. For example, prime ministers appoint individuals to a large number of other political and administrative posts. Unlike high-level political appointments by American presidents, these prime ministerial appointments are not usually subject to legislative review or approval. These appointed offices include the governor general, members of the Supreme Court and other federal judges, deputy ministers (top civil servants), senators, and several thousand "order-in-council" positions. As party leader, the prime minister must approve and sign the nomination papers for all the party's candidates in federal elections. In addition to these powers to reward and punish individuals, prime ministers set the general tone for all government policy and play the key role in determining the priorities of the government. They can decide when to call an election, and they typically try to do so when the political circumstances favour their re-election. In the television age, prime ministers enjoy privileged access to the media, enabling them to appeal directly to Canadians when this is advantageous. In turn, the media often personalize election campaigns, focusing on the "horse race" aspects of the competition between party leaders and thereby making the prime minister the chief campaigner for the party. All of these factors result in the prime minister being very much more than first among equals.

Following the British convention, the prime minister and cabinet (government) serve for a maximum term of five years. However, during this time governments are required to maintain the "confidence of the House" to govern. Effectively, this means that they must be able to regularly count on the support of a majority of MPs for their legislative proposals. This requirement is facilitated by the exercise of tight party discipline, which essentially means that MPs in the House of Commons are told how to vote by their political parties. Just as cabinet ministers are subjected to strict rules forbidding public dissent, ordinary MPs who dissent from their party face significant sanctions from their party leadership, including possibly being removed from the party's caucus and refused its nomination at the next election. The result is that governments that hold a majority of Commons seats are able to pass their legislative proposals efficiently and without major threat. While majority governments are considered the norm in Canada, there have been eleven governments since 1867 in which the prime minister's party did not hold a majority of seats in the House. Indeed, between 2004 and 2011, Canada had three "minority governments" in which the prime minister's party has depended on the informal support of some opposition parties for survival. Such governments are much less stable and predictable than majority governments, since a vote of non-confidence is a perpetual threat. As a result, the average life expectancy of minority governments in Canada is only about a year and a half. However, the election of 2 May 2011 ended this sequence of minority governments by returning Stephen Harper's Conservative Party to govern with a majority of seats in the House of Commons (166 of the total of 308).

As anyone who has witnessed the daily "question period" in the House of Commons is aware, the spirit that animates a parliamentary system is that of adversarial politics. Similarly to the Anglo-American legal system, where the "truth" is determined by the oppositional efforts of a public prosecutor and a defender, parliamentary government is premised on the ability of a government to propose legislation and on a loyal Opposition that opposes it. The physical layout of the House of Commons, with Her Majesty's government's MPs sitting to the right of the Speaker of the House (who serves as a kind of referee to keep proceedings as civil as possible) and facing across the centre of the chamber directly at "Her Majesty's Loyal Opposition," reflects this principle.

The leading opposition party maintains a "shadow cabinet" that stands ready to assume governmental responsibilities in the event that a sitting government loses the confidence of the House. Americans who witness the daily "question period" are often shocked by the raucous behaviour of parliamentarians. Opposition MPs seek to embarrass and discredit the government, and cabinet ministers strive to fend off these verbal attacks as deftly as possible. While all recognize that in substantive terms there is relatively little at stake in such exchanges, it seems impossible for opposition MPs to resist the opportunity to score political points with the public by making the nightly news criticizing a government member in a verbal joust on the House floor. This is a very different form of executive accountability than is practised in presidential systems. Politicians who cannot withstand the heat of this kind of scrutiny tend not to make good cabinet ministers.

The Senate constitutes the second chamber in Canada's legislative system. Senators are appointed by the prime minister from Canada's regions, roughly in proportion to population. The result is that prime ministers tend to use senate seats to reward those who have served the party well, either by holding public office themselves or by serving the party loyally as fundraisers or the like. As a result, the legitimacy of this body has diminished over the years, and while technically all legislation must pass both in the Commons and the Senate, in reality the Senate can do little more than delay legislation that has majority support in the Commons. In recent decades there have been calls, particularly from Canada's western provinces, for a "Triple E" senate – elected, equal, and effective. In fact, such a proposal was part of the ill-fated "Charlottetown Accord" that was defeated by voters in 1992. While calls for senate reform are regularly heard, these reforms would require amending the constitution, and reaching the necessary level of agreement for such a change has thus far proved to be elusive (Smith 2003). A measure of the difficulty in achieving change can be taken from the experience of Canada's current prime minister, Stephen Harper. Harper came to power in 2006 on a platform that included senate reform featuring term limits and an election process for new appointments. Harper promised not to fill vacancies in the chamber until these reforms were in place (though he did make two exceptions). However, facing a possible defeat of his government in December 2008, he quickly moved to exercise the traditional prime ministerial perquisite by making eighteen patronage appointments, a record number of such appointments for a single day.

Parties and Groups

Parliamentary systems concentrate power in relatively few hands. Ensuring that the country's political institutions are reflective of and responsive to Canada's pluralistic and diverse society is the primary function of interest groups, social movements, and the political party system. Political parties perform this role most explicitly by recruiting people to run for political office and then mobilizing support for them through the electoral process. Though political parties were not well developed in the 1860s when the country was formed – as we saw in the last section – they have become absolutely indispensable to the operations of parliamentary government. Writing a century ago, André Siegfried (1906, 123) suggested that Canadian parties and the electoral campaigns they wage were a curious mixture of "old British forms and new American free-and-easy practices." Canada's parliamentary structure and the need for party discipline together impart a leader-dominated structure similar to that found in British parties. The need for Canadian parties to mobilize support across enormously varied local contexts is one of the factors that make it difficult to develop strong and distinctive ideological appeals. As a result, Canada's major parties have tended to shift their policy positions in line with political circumstances and electoral expedience, and in this respect Canada's main parties closely resemble those of the United States. Over time, the institutional imperatives for disciplined organization and the political requirement to mobilize support from diverse and far-flung constituencies have given rise to a distinctive "franchise bargain" in which Canadian party organizations accord relative autonomy to their local organizations in the candidate nomination process in return for the imposition of strict party discipline on MPs in the House of Commons (Carty et al. 2000).

Since 1867, only two parties have formed governments in Canada: the Conservatives and the Liberals. Indeed, until 1921 these two parties monopolized Canadian politics. Canada's first prime minister, John A. Macdonald, formed the Conservative Party in 1854 by merging a number of pre-Confederation political groups in Upper (Ontario) and Lower (Quebec) Canada. Initially this was a loosely organized coalition of MPs, but gradually they galvanized into a more cohesive political force through judicious use of patronage and by uniting behind Macdonald's National Policy. Since then, and until relatively recently, the party has been viewed generally as strongly nationalistic and as guardians of Canada's British heritage. The Conservatives dominated the first decades of the country's existence, governing most of the time from 1867 to 1896. The party fell out of power between 1873 and 1878 when Macdonald was implicated in "the Pacific Scandal," which erupted when it was revealed that large amounts of money were being directed to the Conservatives from railway contractors.

In the twentieth century, Conservative electoral victories were generally of relatively short duration. Often they placed Conservatives in power at times when governing was particularly difficult (e.g., during times of war or during the Great Depression). This chequered performance has opened the party to periodic upheavals, and over the years it has reconstituted itself in response to challenges from breakaway groups or minor parties. At the end of one such period, in 1942, the party renamed itself the Progressive Conservative party. In the late 1980s support for the party was badly eroded by the emergence of the Reform Party in the former Conservative heartland in the West. However, the persistent inability of Reform (and its successor, the Canadian Alliance) to grow beyond its western and ideologically right-of-centre roots eventually led it to merge in 2003 with the Progressive Conservative Party. Having come full circle, the newly merged party went back to the old Conservative Party label. In the elections of January 2006 and October 2008 the reconstituted Conservative Party formed minority governments, but as noted above, it rallied to win a majority of seats in the most recent (2011) election and seems poised to govern for at least another four years.

It is difficult to characterize the ideology of the Conservative Party. This reflects the party's policy flexibility. For example, under Macdonald's National Policy the party campaigned for tariffs to protect Canadian industries in the first fifty years of the country's existence. However, in 1989 it was Brian Mulroney's Progressive Conservative government that implemented the Canada-US Free Trade Agreement, which removed most such barriers to trade. Moreover, there are deep ideological disagreements among Conservatives, some of whom embrace the free market principles of classical liberalism while others (so-called "Red Tories") embrace more paternalistic support for strong governmental intervention to ensure the health of the body politic.

Though currently in opposition, the Liberal Party has been more successful than the Conservatives. Liberal leaders have served as prime ministers for about two-thirds of the past hundred years. Accordingly, commentators often refer to the Liberals as the "natural governing party" in the Canadian system. The party emerged during the early years of Canada's existence, but it was under the leadership of Wilfrid Laurier, who became prime minister in 1896 and served in that capacity until 1911, that the party emerged as a cohesive organization that could win elections and govern effectively. In 1893 Laurier articulated something of a truism for Canadian party politics: "It is not enough to have great principles; we must have organization also. Principles without organization may lose, but organization without principles may often win" (quoted in Clarkson 2005, 8). In the early twentieth century, as it strengthened its organizational foundations under Laurier and his successors, the party championed free trade principles and pushed for reciprocity agreements to reduce tariffs and boost trade with the United States.

Over the years the Liberal Party practised an informal pattern of alternating between francophone and non-francophone leaders. This relative openness to French Canadians meant that, with only a few exceptions, the party was able to rely on strong support in Quebec. Liberal prime ministers presided over the adoption of official bilingualism, the rapid expansion of Canada's immigrant population and the adoption of the policy of multiculturalism, the growth of the welfare state, and the emergence of Canada as a major political supporter of the United Nations' peacekeeping efforts – all policies that have become important components of Canada's political identity. In the decade following the watershed election of 1993, and before the resurgent Conservative Party reunited the forces of the right in 2003, the Liberals were the only "national" party in the sense of being able to attract significant electoral support in all regions of the country. Following a devastating scandal that broke over the 2002–5 period and that involved kickbacks to the party from government contracts with some public relations firms in Quebec (among other things), the Liberal Party has entered a downward spiral in the eyes of the electorate. Since Jean Chrétien stepped down from his decade as Liberal leader and prime minister in 2003, the party has gone through three leaders. However, none of Chrétien's successors has been able to turn the party's fortunes around. The decline has culminated in an unprecedented third-place finish for the Liberals behind the New Democratic Party in the 2011 election. With the party gaining only 19 per cent of the vote and 34 seats in the House of Commons in that election, scholars and pundits alike are now questioning the viability and future of the once-dominant Liberals.

Compared to the United States, Canada's party politics is rendered distinctive by the presence since 1932 of a socialist, or more precisely a social democratic, party. Founded by J.S. Woodsworth during the Great Depression, the Co-operative Commonwealth Federation (CCF) united various farmer and labour groups. At the party's founding convention in Regina, Saskatchewan, in July 1933, the party endorsed a radical program of reforms. Known as the Regina Manifesto, this document advocated "a planned and socialized economy in which our natural resources and principal means of production and distribution are owned, controlled and operated by the people." After struggling electorally for more than two decades, the CCF decided in 1961 to align with the newly founded Canadian Labour Congress (CLC) and to change the party's name to the New Democratic Party (NDP). Since this time the party's fortunes have ebbed and flowed. Until 2011, its zenith at the federal level was in the 1988 election, when the party captured 43 seats in the House of Commons. However, its gains were short-lived, and the party plummeted to a record low in 1993, winning only nine seats and losing "official party" status in the House of Commons. Everything changed in 2011, however. In that election, leader Jack Layton led the NDP to an unprecedented second-place finish (103 seats) behind Stephen Harper's Conservatives. Particularly dramatic was the party's breakthrough in the province of Quebec, where it astounded election specialists by winning 59 of the province's 75 seats. It remains to be seen whether the 2011 result was an anomaly, but it can be noted that in Ontario, Manitoba, Saskatchewan, Nova Scotia, and British Columbia the NDP has formed provincial governments, and the prospect of a federal win does not any longer seem to be entirely fanciful. With the NDP's rise and the apparent demise of the centrist Liberal Party, pundits are now talking about an ideological polarization of the Canadian party system, with the Conservatives mobilizing the right of the spectrum and the NDP consolidating support on the left. The recent rise of the Green Party should be noted as another development on the ideological left in Canadian politics. Party leader Elizabeth May became the first Green MP to enter the House of Commons as a result of the 2011 election.

Since 1993 a fourth party has competed in Canadian federal elections, but only by contesting the 75 seats in Quebec. The separatist Bloc Québécois (BQ) was formed by disgruntled francophone nationalists in the aftermath of the collapse of the Meech Lake Accord in 1990. Several of its most prominent founders had been leading figures in the Conservative government of Brian Mulroney, who had negotiated that ill-fated constitutional agreement with the provincial premiers (see the section on federalism that follows). Led by former Mulroney cabinet minister

Lucien Bouchard, the BQ shocked the political establishment by winning 54 seats in the 1993 election. Ironically, this was sufficient to propel the antisystem party into the status of "Her Majesty's Official Opposition." After the narrow victory of the pro-Canada side in the referendum on separation held in Quebec in October 1995, the party's fortunes fell in line with the decline in support for sovereignty in that province. The size of the party's caucus fell to 44 after the 1997 election and to 38 in the 2000 contest. Thereafter it recovered; in the 2006 election it won 51 seats before falling back slightly in the 2008 election to a total of 49 MPs. However, the 2011 election saw the BQ decimated by what pundits referred to as the "Orange Crush" (the NDP's conventional colour is orange). Its leader of fifteen years, Gilles Duceppe, lost his own seat in the debacle, and as with the Liberal Party, academic and journalistic commentators are now speculating about the possible death of this party that has dominated federal elections in Quebec since 1993.

The competitive relationship among Canada's parties, and the ways in which these organizations have connected Canadian society with the institutions of government, have evolved significantly since 1867. Ken Carty and his colleagues (2000) argue that there have been four phases in the evolution of the party system. In the decades immediately after Confederation, and lasting through to about 1921, the Liberals and Conservatives dominated elections. These parties were in essence electoral machines, largely inactive during inter-election periods and reliant on patronage to mobilize support. The second phase, roughly between 1921 and 1957, saw the Conservatives and Liberals joined by minor parties, initially the Progressives, Labour, and United Farmers, but eventually also the CCF (and in Alberta by Social Credit, and in Quebec by the Union Nationale). During this phase Canada's major parties played a "brokerage" role for groups – and particularly regions – in Canadian society. Party leaders would negotiate alliances with these groups whereby representation and power would be given in return for electoral support. In this way, party and group elites were able to accommodate and reconcile deep regional and social differences. The onset of mass communications and media in the late 1950s and the growth of the welfare state in the late 1950s and early 1960s ushered in the third phase. Between 1957 and 1993, parties continued their brokerage role, but they did so while espousing to a greater degree a single pan-Canadian image and a national political program. Instead of appealing to group attachments, parties adopted nationally uniform messages that appealed directly to individual voters. The need for parties to promote a consistent vision of their policies and goals in all parts of the country contributed to the emergence of the party leader as the central communications vehicle for Canadian parties.

A fourth phase in the development of the party system was ushered in by the 1993 election, in which the traditional three federal parties (Conservatives, Liberals, NDP) were joined by two regional political formations, the Reform Party and the BQ. These two new parties were both expressions of the deep-seated regional differences that characterize the country, with Reform mobilizing a strong sentiment of western alienation and the BQ mining the equally deep vein of Québécois nationalism. As a result of this regional fragmentation, the Liberals dominated the 1993, 1997, and 2000 elections. However, as we have seen, the merger between the inheritors of the Reform Party (the Canadian Alliance, as the party became known) and the Conservatives in 2003 weakened this Liberal hegemony to the point where a minority Conservative administration could be elected in 2006.

Clearly the party system has been in a state of flux for the past several decades. Canadian voters have become known for being exceptionally fickle and are less and less likely to express deep and enduring loyalties to one party or another. High levels of electoral volatility, diminished feelings of partisan attachment, and growing political cynicism have all contributed to the sense that the terrain of Canada's party system, having suffered several earthquakes, is still remarkably shaky (Carty et al. 2000). This characterization was strikingly confirmed by the swings in party fortunes registered in the 2011 election.

As the attachments to parties have weakened in recent decades, voter turnout has declined precipitously. As figure 3.2 shows, turnout dropped from about 75 per cent of the eligible electorate before 1993 to a low of 58.8 per cent in 2008, before increasing slightly to 61.4 per cent in 2011). At the same time, however, political involvement in non-traditional and protest activities appears to be high – and growing – in comparative terms (Nevitte 1996, 75–111; Gidengil et al. 2004, 102–43). Citizen involvement in interest groups and other organizations in civil society has intensified. According to a 2000 survey, about 10 per cent of Canadians report belonging to an advocacy group – a level of civic engagement that exceeds what is found in Britain, Germany, and France (though lower than American rates) (Young and Everitt 2004, 28). Many of these have explicitly political objectives and agendas, and regularly lobby Canadian political and governmental officials to advance their

Figure 3.2 Voter turnout at federal elections, 1988–2011

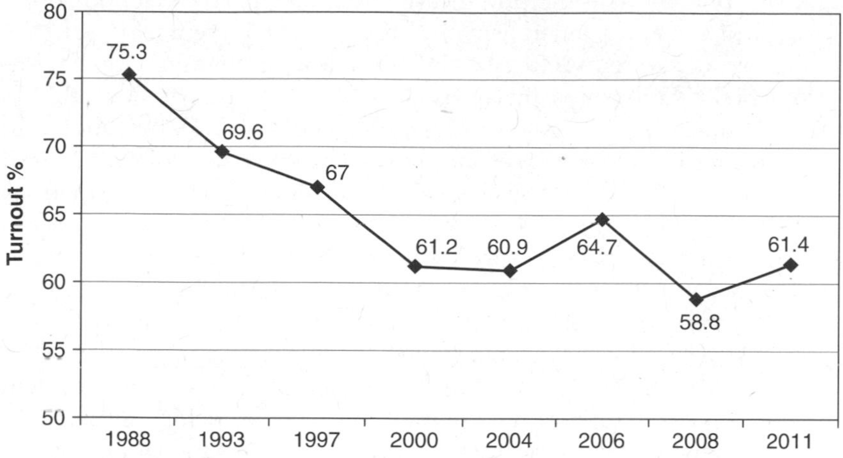

Source: www.elections.ca (Report of the Chief Electoral Officer of Canada for each election year)

common interests. In the interests of democratic accountability and transparency, since 1989 the federal government has required these groups to register their activities. There are currently more than 3500 individual lobbyists on the list maintained by Industry Canada (September 2010). More broadly, large numbers of Canadians have become active in a wide variety of social movements, the most notable of which include the women's, environmental, and gay rights movements. These movements seek to shape not only government policy but also public attitudes and private practices. As such, they represent an important means by which the institutions of political life are connected with, and ultimately rendered responsive to, Canada's civil society.

Federalism

One word emerges countless times in any review of the literature on Canadian federalism: tension. Simeon and Willis (1997, 174) call the tensions of federalism the "pre-eminent issues of governing in Canada."

These tensions relate predominantly to national unity and to Ottawa's transfer payments to the provinces. These are the two "fundamental issues" of Canadian federalism, and they create "perennial problems" (Stillborn and Asselin 2001, 3). "Canada has a fascination with federal-provincial relationships that most other nations reserve for religion or sex," noted one observer of federalism (Robert G. Evans, quoted in Thomas 2008). This section of the chapter explores the development of federalism in Canada and discusses why tensions – and preoccupations – still exist.

Federalism is a system of government based on a division of powers spelled out in a constitution. Usually the division is between a national or central government and its smaller units (usually states or provinces). As power is dispersed over the two levels, sovereignty – the right to rule – is shared. Federalism is a relatively uncommon system of government in the world. Other federal systems include India, Switzerland, Austria, Germany, Australia, and of course the United States. Federalism works well in large, diverse countries. Such a system allows for national control of certain jurisdictions and local control of others, and allows local governments to provide for the specific needs of their constituents while also allowing for national standards to be set by the central government in certain areas. Despite the many benefits of federalism, this system is not without flaws. The history of the United States presents a cogent example: the Civil War, in essence, when stripped of the moral issues surrounding slavery, can be viewed as a federal-state conflict over which level of government had the authority to make decisions in which areas. In Canada, which has never suffered a civil war, these same questions of power and control have pervaded intergovernmental politics, especially with regard to Quebec. In fact, the American Civil War was introduced by those against a federal union in Canada as a convincing argument against federalism. American federalism, having resulted in a civil war, was viewed as a failure not to be repeated in this new Canada. Still, in 1867 the new Canadian federation joined diverse areas and interests – fisherman with the fur traders, businessmen with farmers, the Maritimes with the St Lawrence, and importantly, the English with the French – and united them all into one country, albeit not without difficulty.

In Canada, the division of legislative powers is found in sections 91 and 92 of the BNA Act, 1867 (now the Constitution Act, 1982). Explicit or enumerated powers are distributed first to the federal government (s. 91) and then to the provinces (s. 92). Among the several powers given to the federal government in section 91 are the administration of criminal law, control over trade and commerce, and, most importantly, the clause "to make Laws for the Peace, Order and good Government of Canada in relation to all Matters not coming within the Classes of Subjects by this Act assigned exclusively to the Legislatures of the Provinces." This is an important clause, as it asserts two things: first, the inherent purpose of Canadian government (peace, order, and good government); and second, that the residual or unwritten powers are reserved for the federal government. Powers reserved for the provinces include education, health care, and property and civil rights.

At the drafting of the BNA Act, this division of powers was thought to be clear. It was also thought to favour the federal level, since it included provisions allowing the federal government to "declare" a provincial initiative to be of sufficient national importance, or of sufficient importance to more than one province, to be placed under federal jurisdiction. Similarly, the constitution provided the powers of reservation and disallowance of both federal and provincial legislation. The reservation power allows the governor general (via s. 55) or a lieutenant governor of a province (via s. 90) to refer a bill to the Crown to determine validity before giving "royal assent." Disallowance is the invalidation of bills passed at either level. While these powers (exercised by the governor general and lieutenant governors general, respectively) could theoretically limit the power of both levels of government, the effect was felt more heavily at the provincial level, at least until the early twentieth century. (It should be noted that while these powers were never specifically repealed, the practice of both disallowance and reservation is obsolete.) Sweeping emergency powers were also given to the federal government. The enormous constitutional preponderance that these powers assigned to the federal level led the noted scholar of federalism K.C. Wheare (1963) to argue that Canada was only "quasifederal."

Macdonald's National Policy was an example of the federal government's early push to establish itself as the pre-eminent governmental actor in the system. Over time, however, this quasi-federalism gave way to an evolving relationship between the federal government and the provinces, as a result of which the latter have become much more important political actors. Notwithstanding constitutional provisions, it would be politically unthinkable today for a federal government to have provincial legislation reserved or disallowed or to invoke its declaratory power. Despite the wording of the BNA Act, federalism is not a static arrangement. The relationship between levels of government changes over time, given national and international crises such as war and economic instability, changes in the public's political ideologies, and the like. Overlapping concerns and the growth of the nation have blurred the black-and-white distinctions of sections 91 and 92. Stillborn and Asselin (2001) acknowledge that the Canadian federation is "in a state of virtually continuous evolution." The Fathers of Confederation could never have imagined or foreseen many of the changes in society; as a consequence, the separation of provincial and federal powers, which seemed to make perfect sense in the late 1860s, is not workable in the twentieth and twenty-first centuries. Efforts to deal with the inevitability of change have led to "ad hoc and continuously negotiated arrangements" (ibid., 1).

When we look at the evolution of Canadian federalism, it is clear that what was envisioned as a strong pro-national federation has devolved into a decentralized union. The decisions of Britain's Judicial Committee of the Privy Council during the late nineteenth and early twentieth centuries served to broaden provincial power at the expense of the federal government. It did so by very narrowly interpreting the "peace, order and good government" clause, limiting Parliament's authority in this regard to national emergencies and the like (Vaughan 1999, 6). Later, when the Bennett government attempted to create national programs to ease the economic strain of the Great Depression, the JCPC constantly struck them down as infringing on provincial jurisdiction.

In response to imbalances of services across the provinces during the Great Depression, the Mackenzie King government commissioned what was to become known as the Rowell-Sirois Report. Finding a great deal of inequality in social services provided to Canadians, the report recommended a number of initiatives, including giving responsibility for unemployment insurance to the federal government. Most important, however, the report called for the creation of an equalization transfer program. The commission was initiated in 1937, with a conference called in 1941 to discuss the results and recommendations. The conference was a failure, as Ontario, Alberta, and British Columbia refused to consider the recommendations. The ongoing war delayed any implementation of programs. By the 1950s, the equalization program had finally been implemented, increasing the federal government's involvement in what was the provinces' sphere of influence and ushering in an era of fiscal federalism. Fiscal federalism refers to the transfer of money from the federal government, which enjoys much greater revenue-raising capacities than the provinces, to the latter level.

There are two key areas of transfer payments: equalization payments (to guarantee equivalent fiscal capacity across the provinces), and the Canada Health and Social Transfer (CHST) for higher education, health care, and social assistance. Postwar economic gains allowed the federal government to create family allowances as well as unemployment and hospital insurance, paid for by both levels of government. The use of equalization payments and the reliance on them by the "have not" provinces has allowed the federal government to insinuate itself in the business of the provinces. The "have nots" were generally more inclined to support the federal spending power, while those who do not rely on transfers tended to be more suspicious. At the outset, however, except in Quebec, complaints were few from the provinces, which appreciated the funding (Asselin 2001, 1–3).

The 1950s and 1960s saw the rise of "cooperative federalism," characterized by sufficient and growing resources and relative agreement between the federal government and provinces over programs and spending. This level of cooperation lessened as provinces began to question federal program priorities and as the Quebec issue rushed to the forefront of Canadian politics. Cooperative federalism morphed into "executive federalism," a more conflict-ridden and politicized set of relationships. The lessening of cooperation was exacerbated by the economic downturn of the 1970s. In the 1980s, faced with uncertainties of the economy and of Quebec's intentions, the Liberal government of Pierre Trudeau engaged in several unilateral federal actions, forsaking negotiation and compromise with the provinces. The attempt to unilaterally patriate (bring home) the constitution is an excellent example of Trudeau's position on federalism. As part of this style of federalism, the Constitution Act, 1982, included part III, section 36, which entrenched the idea of federal spending power for equalization payments. In this way, that which had been a statutory measure of the federal parliament became an element of the constitution, reinforcing the powers of the federal government.

Brian Mulroney and the Progressive Conservatives took power in 1984, having campaigned on a theme of renewed federal–provincial cooperation. The Mulroney government succeeded in demonstrating its commitment to negotiation, as exemplified by the Meech Lake Accord, which garnered initial unanimous agreement among the federal government and the provinces. The Mulroney government also tried to placate Quebec by allowing it to have control over immigration into the province – a move that highlighted the "accommodative style" of

Mulroney's form of federalism (Stillborn and Asselin 2001, 3). This early success, however, was dimmed by difficult economic circumstances, by growing discontent over federal spending cuts, and by differences of opinion between the parties controlling the federal and provincial governments. In 1990 the goodwill surrounding Meech Lake ended when the legislatures of Newfoundland and Manitoba failed to ratify the accord as required. The unsuccessful attempt to accommodate Quebec and the decrease in federal transfer moneys reinforced a suspected centrist bias inherent in Canadian federalism. With the bulk of MPs being from Ontario and Quebec, and with the Quebec issue seemingly always at the forefront, the western and Atlantic provinces showed increasing signs of becoming more alienated themselves. This feeling of being left out hurt Mulroney's "accommodative federalism," and indeed, even Meech Lake's early success apparently did little to satisfy Quebec (ibid.). This highlights an additional problem in Canadian federalism: since citizens of federal unions are subject to two sets of laws, and given a lack of a strong Canadian national identity, provincial attachments and politics can often assume greater and more immediate importance to Canadians than national issues. As a former US Speaker of the House once said, "All politics is local." This appears equally true for Canada (Carty and Eagles 2005).

The past few decades have seen a variety of actions by the federal government apparently designed to reassert the federal presence in intergovernmental relations. One of the first obvious moves was the push by the Trudeau government (under threat of unilateral federal action) to patriate the constitution. In doing so, Trudeau hoped to create a Charter of Rights and Freedoms that would establish national standards for individual rights. In addition, the entrenchment of section 36 – which made equalization transfer payments part of the constitutional regime – legitimized federal involvement in the provinces, at least to the degree that unconditional federal transfers establish standards for public services provided by the provinces. But while the Charter was Trudeau's hope for national unity, the 1995 Quebec secession referendum highlighted once again Quebec's frustration with its place in the federation. The federal government was forced to find ways to placate Quebec without slighting the rest of the provinces – a difficult task, to say the least. Given the closeness of the referendum vote (50.58 per cent to 49.42 per cent for the federalist side), the federal government decided on a number of post-referendum initiatives to try to strengthen national unity. These included a promise not to engage in shared-cost programs without majority consent from the provinces, as well as extending to all provinces the right to opt out of programs with compensation (to be used on similar programs). In addition, the Chrétien government sent three reference questions to the Supreme Court of Canada regarding the constitutional and international law legitimacy of future secession attempts by Quebec. The court ruled that the constitution does not allow for provinces to secede unilaterally. However, the court's opinion held that if Quebec engaged in a legitimate democratic process based on clear questions to encourage secession, the rest of Canada would have to agree to enter into negotiations with the province. The court's 1998 reference opinion led to the passage in 2000 of the Clarity Act, which declared that the House of Commons must approve any questions presented in future secession referendums as well as determine whether a clear majority expressed preference for separation (Asselin 2001, 4). Thus, even in terms of a successful expression of Quebec's desire for self-determination, the federal government would have a voice.

In terms of transfer payments, by the mid-1990s the CHST was being distributed as a block grant to the provinces, giving them greater discretion on spending. However, this change to a block grant system came with a reduction in the amount of the payments. These cuts remained despite federal government surpluses, and this angered the provinces. The greater discretion of the CHST also led to great variation in programs and services throughout the country, leading to federal attempts to pull back funding in order to maintain national standards and impose priorities. During subsequent premiers' and first ministers' conferences, the call came for a reworked social union, one that would establish greater provincial jurisdiction for programs. In 1999 the premiers and the federal government (with the exception of Quebec) agreed on a new framework – a new social union – under which the federal government agreed not to attempt to institute national standards without first getting majority consent of the provinces. In addition, the new social union allows for opting out with compensation should a province object to a particular set of national standards. This opting-out provision allows the provinces to still receive federal dollars, but also allows them to maintain a bit of autonomy in the construction and details of social programs, so long as general considerations are met. The opt-out ability was very much a compromise element of the social union.

The first decade of the twenty-first century finds the decades-old debates about equalization payments raging anew. The equalization formula, although tweaked over time, originally created a formula assessing the fiscal capacity of each province (a measure of a variety of provincial revenue sources) and providing payments to "have-not" provinces based upon a five-"middle-province" fiscal capacity average. Under the formula, Ontario was never eligible for equalization until 2011, Alberta qualified only in the program's infancy, British Columbia and Saskatchewan's receipt of transfers changed from year to year (a function of gas and oil revenues), while the rest of the provinces were designated as "have-nots." The impetus for instituting a new equalization formula was the presence of a "fiscal imbalance" between the federal government and the provinces. Ideally, both vertical balance – the federal government and provincial governments have enough revenues to provide services – and horizontal balance – where roughly equivalent revenue resources are available to the provinces – is the desirable outcome (Stevenson 2006). However, due to the emergence of federal budget surpluses in the late 1990s (after decades of deficits), the provinces (led by Quebec) complained that the federal government's resources created a top-heavy, vertically unbalanced system, meaning the provinces bore more of the cost of providing programs and services. Dissatisfaction with the existing system coincided with the development of the offshore oil and gas reserves in traditionally "have not" Nova Scotia and Newfoundland. This new revenue source ushered Newfoundland into "have" status (with Nova Scotia getting close) – but not without both wanting to continue receiving equalization payments, fostering complaints of "double-dipping." At a 2004 first ministers' conference, the existing system was suspended and an interim formula put in its place, with a new system to be instituted upon recommendations of an advisory panel report in 2006. Newfoundland premier Danny Williams, in a bit of political theatre, responded by lowering the Canadian flag from provincial buildings in St John's in protest. Soon after, however, both Nova Scotia and Newfoundland and Labrador, in usual Canadian fashion, were able to negotiate better "side deals." In order to appease the two provinces, the Atlantic Accords were passed in 2005, allowing for the complete exemption of oil and gas revenues from the fiscal capacity formula. In 2006, recommendations from the advisory panels led the new prime minster, Stephen Harper, to abandon the accords, announce a new equalization formula, which would use a ten-province average to set the national standard and allow only 50 per cent of non-renewable resource revenue to be exempt. However, even this new "standard" in equalization allowed for choice in calculating the "entitlements" and "offsets" for different provinces, satisfying everyone and no one at the same time.

Federalism in Canada continues to evolve: "In Canada, there are basic differences between the logic of democracy embedded in the parliamentary system, which emphasizes majority rule and parliamentary sovereignty; in federalism, which emphasizes common interests and shared sovereignty; and in the Charter, which focuses on individual rights, judicially protected. These tensions are far from fully worked out" (Simeon and Willis 1997, 173). While a degree of constitution fatigue may have set in, the rekindling of interest in the concept of "asymmetrical federalism" (Brown 2005), in which provinces need not be treated identically or equally in their relations with the federal government, suggests that intergovernmental relations will remain an important feature of the Canadian political scene for the foreseeable future. The current government's creation of "open federalism" and continuing inducements to Quebec (such as a resolution recognizing Quebec as a "nation" in 2006) only prove that the preoccupation with federalism is far from over.

The Courts and Charter Politics

When the Supreme Court of Canada issued its advisory opinion in *Reference Re: Same-Sex Marriage* (2004), concluding that the federal parliament could constitutionally allow for same-sex marriage, it set off a political firestorm. The controversy engendered by this decision centred on the usual pro- and anti-gay rights arguments, as well as the sanctity of marriage between a man and a woman. Absent were any questions as to what right the Supreme Court had in making such a pronouncement. The silence on that issue is notable, for the Supreme Court's involvement in deciding issues of individual rights and freedoms is a relatively new development in Canadian politics, one not without its own degree of controversy. Today, the Supreme Court of Canada issues decisions on a number of controversial issues and gives the final word on constitutional interpretation. This was not always so. In the not too distant past the court had no such authority to issue final decisions, nor did a written bill of rights exist.

The BNA Act, 1867, listed the powers of the judiciary in part VII, sections 96 to 101. Conspicuously absent to the modern reader is any mention of a Supreme Court of Canada. With a dominion style of government, still subordinate to Great Britain in areas of foreign policy and

law, there was no urgent need to establish a Canadian court of last resort. Instead, section 101 indicated that the federal parliament had the
power to create a "general court of appeal for Canada." Canada finally
established such a court eight years after Confederation, with the passage of the Supreme Court Act of 1875. Yet for much of its existence,
the Supreme Court had a very limited capacity to exert power. Its interpretive abilities concerning Canadian federalism were limited to deciding questions of jurisdiction in challenges over federal and provincial
laws (determining whether laws passed by either entity overstepped
the bounds of sections 91 and 92 of the BNA Act). There were no bill
of rights challenges, as such a bill did not exist in a system "similar
in principle to that of Great Britain." Furthermore, the Supreme Court
was not technically the court of last resort for Canada. Parties dissat-
isfied with its decisions, or not wanting to have the case heard before
the court, could appeal directly to the Judicial Committee of the Privy
Council, the judicial entity in Great Britain with final say on constitutional matters. Until appeals to the JCPC ended in 1949, the Supreme
Court was really, as former chief justice Bora Laskin put it, a "captive
court," with relatively little power.

In the aftermath of the Second World War, the world's attention
shifted to human rights protections through the newly established
United Nations, and many individual countries enacted bills of rights.
And while there was no political attempt to alter the BNA Act (1867)
to include an entrenched bill of rights, the Progressive Conservatives,
led by John Diefenbaker, were able to win control of Parliament in part
by promising to add some kind of rights protection to the Canadian
regime. Thus, in 1960 the Canadian Bill of Rights was adopted by the
federal parliament. This document, a legislative act, protected rights of
religion, speech, assembly, and association as well as procedural legal
rights and the right to enjoy property. However, because it was merely
a statute, the bill of rights was no more or less powerful than any other
statute enacted by Parliament. As a result, the Supreme Court was hesitant to use it forcefully and only found one law "inoperable" as being in
violation of the bill (see *R. v. Drybones (1970)*). Both the Supreme Court
and the bill of rights quickly came to be perceived as ineffective pro-
tectors of individual rights and freedoms. A remedy would need to be
found for each.

In 1931 the British parliament passed the Statute of Westminster,
declaring all of its dominion nations fully independent. At that time,
however, and for years thereafter, Canada did not ask for the patriation

of its constitution. An enormous stumbling block was the need to secure federal and provincial agreement on an amending formula, which would be necessary if the British House of Commons no longer could amend the document. Pierre Trudeau's rise to prime minister, coupled with the growing separatist movement in Quebec (and its failed referendum of 1980 on a version of political independence for the province called "sovereignty-association"), made constitutional reform a crucial political issue in the 1980s. Trudeau tried, as his predecessors had for decades, to find a proper amending formula and bring the constitution home. And like his predecessors, he had difficulty getting the provinces, especially Quebec, to agree on an amending formula. After repeated failures at compromise, Trudeau moved to patriate the constitution unilaterally – that is, without the assent of all the provinces. Trudeau saw this moment in time as a small window of opportunity to patriate the constitution and to add an entrenched charter of rights with judicial enforcement (to remedy the failures of the Canadian Bill of Rights), all to encourage national unity and thwart Quebec's separatist leanings. To make such a move without the provinces was highly controversial, and three provinces (Quebec, Manitoba, and Newfoundland) challenged the constitutionality of Trudeau's action in a Supreme Court reference. The Court's decision in *Reference Re: Resolution to Amend the Constitution* (1981) found that while Trudeau had not violated the constitution in acting unilaterally, his plan did violate constitutional convention. Because constitutional conventions are of vital importance in the British tradition, the court reasoned that provincial participation would be necessary to make patriation work. In the federal–provincial negotiations following the court's decision, a compromise constitution was crafted, and with the agreement of all the provinces except Quebec (which has still not approved), the Constitution Act, 1982, was presented to the British Parliament and the Crown. It became the supreme law of Canada on 17 April 1982.

The Canadian Charter of Rights and Freedoms is a modern and comprehensive bill of rights, similar to the US Bill of Rights but with some important differences. A prime example is section 1, which reads: "[The] Canadian Charter of Rights and Freedoms guarantees the rights and freedoms set out in it subject only to such reasonable limits prescribed by law as can be demonstrably justified in a free and democratic society." The "reasonable limits" clause of section 1 precedes all other protections, thereby placing individual rights and freedoms in a context missing in the US bill – the rights are not absolute and are to be considered in light of what is good for the rest of society. The other product of section 1 is that it has allowed the court to engage in a very broad reading and interpretation of rights. In defining the scope of rights, section 1 allows for a wide-ranging understanding of what is included in each section, with the caveat that those rights may be constrained if there are justifiable reasons for doing so.

Section 2 contains a list of fundamental freedoms, including those of expression, conscience, press, association, and assembly. Sections 3 to 5 protect democratic rights, such as the right to vote and to run for office; they also detail the five-year limits on governments, and so on. Section 6 provides for mobility rights, an aspect of the charter missing in the US Bill of Rights but one that was absolutely necessary to Trudeau's vision of a united Canada.

Sections 7 to 14 contain the legal rights protections, such as the right to "life, liberty, and security of person," as well as the protection against unreasonable searches and seizures, arbitrary detention, cruel and unusual punishment, and self-incrimination. Also included are habeas corpus, the right to information about charges, the right to legal counsel, bail, and an interpreter, and the presumption of innocence. The rights listed in sections 7 to 14 mirror those criminal procedure amendments (the Fourth through the Eighth) found in the US Bill of Rights.

Section 15 enumerates the equality rights held by all Canadians, as well as the right to be free from discrimination:

> 15(1) Every individual is equal before and under the law and has the right
> to the equal protection and equal benefit of the law without discrimination
> and, in particular, without discrimination based on race, national or ethnic
> origin, colour, religion, sex, age or mental or physical disability.
>
> (2) Subsection (1) does not preclude any law, program or activity that
> has as its object the amelioration of conditions of disadvantaged individ-
> uals or groups including those that are disadvantaged because of race,
> national or ethnic origin, colour, religion, sex, age or mental or physical
> disability.

Unlike the rest of the Charter, section 15 protections did not go into force until 1985.

Sections 16–23 entrench the commitment to language rights with the creation of official bilingualism, as well as the protection of education in minority languages – another pro-unity element of the new charter.

Of the remainder of the charter, three sections are of particular interest. The first is section 24(1), which states: "Anyone whose rights or freedoms, as guaranteed by this Charter, have been infringed may apply to a court of competent jurisdiction to obtain such remedy as the court considers appropriate and just in the circumstances." The wording in this section is intended to settle the question of the legitimacy of judicial review, an item lacking in the US constitution. As is evident below, the inclusion of section 24(1) has not reduced criticisms of the charter and courts. The second interesting element is section 33, the "notwithstanding clause." Section 33 allows for a legislative override of charter decisions; this is a sort of escape hatch through with legislatures can pass when the courts fail to decide in their favour. The section can only be invoked for sections 2 and 7 to 15, and only for five years, at which time it may be renewed. The notwithstanding clause has only been used three times (twice by Quebec, once by Saskatchewan). Quebec invoked section 33 initially to protest the patriation of the constitution, of which it refused to be a party. The last section of note is section 52, which makes the charter the supreme law of Canada. While no right in the charter is of any greater or lesser importance than any other, its protections are elevated to a stature not enjoyed by the Canadian Bill of Rights.

Almost immediately, supporters and opponents of the charter cropped up on the left (Mandel 1989, 1994) and the right (Knopf and Morton 1992. Supporters of the new document and the newly empowered Supreme Court believed it was high time that Canada entrenched individual rights and freedoms. Sceptics favoured the old way of doing things – parliamentary supremacy – and feared that the Supreme Court would become a twin to the liberal US Supreme Court of the Warren era (1950s–1960s). The power of judicial review given to the court would undo the wishes of the majority, as expressed by the passage of laws in Parliament and the provincial legislatures. This is the crux of the "antimajoritarian dilemma" – the ability of an unelected judiciary to evaluate the constitutionality of laws passed by democratically elected legislatures. The term "charter sceptic" also refers to the more conservative critics, who favour a judiciary that defers to the legislatures. Even if one begrudgingly accepts the changes brought forth by the charter, the charter sceptic would expect the courts to be more likely to rule in favour of the work of the legislatures. According to defenders of the charter, that outcome is simply an impossibility in the new system. Supporters of the charter, and of the Supreme Court's right to interpret it, argue that the very point of the charter is to entrench individual rights and for the courts to ensure that legislatures do not trample on them. Justice Ian Binnie, during a contentious debate with US Supreme Court Justice Antonin Scalia marking the twenty-fifth anniversary of the charter, offered an assured commitment to judicial review: "The ability of the courts to move with the times has served this country well. I say that if you erect a silo over our court system based on a theory of originalism, it is a very good reason to throw it out" (Makin 2007b).

Besides changing the nature of rights in Canada and the power of the courts to decide questions of those rights, the charter has also altered the nature of politics in Canada. Individuals and groups unable to gain access to the governmental process through ordinary channels – namely, Parliament – can now bypass the legislative branch to find remedy for grievances. This development has both negative and positive consequences. Negatively, it allows small groups to alter what was a system of majority rule. However, in majoritarian democracies, the possibility that rights can be trampled exists, and the courts present the sole and last place to which numerical minorities can turn. (Think of the road to school desegregation in the United States. Where would that movement be without the US Supreme Court?) Charter sceptics bemoan the emergence of the "Court Party," made up of lawyers, individuals, and "intervener groups" – those without standing to sue, but who intervene with legal briefs and arguments to insinuate interest-group agendas into the court's decision making. For example, in the same-sex marriage reference, the court heard from dozens of interveners on all sides of the issue, such as church and family groups, the Canadian Bar Association, federal and provincial human rights commissions, and civil liberties associations, just to list a few (James, Abelson, and Lusztig 2002).

In the end, if the courts go too wild in straying from the majority, Parliament and the provincial legislatures have the power to rewrite the laws while invoking section 33 – the notwithstanding clause. This clause was inserted to provide a form of "dialogue" to the interpretive process. Those who doubt the integrity of section 33 point out that it has been used rarely and that it tends to give the appearance of legislative indifference to rights.

Today, the Supreme Court of Canada is an integral part of the Canadian political landscape, as the charter has become one of the three "pillars" of Canadian political institutions, along with parliamentary government and federalism (Simeon and Willis 1997, 153). As of 2002, the court had used the charter to strike down more than seventy laws

(Saunders 2002). More current research suggests that the rate of invalidation of laws using the charter has slowed significantly since the first heady days of charter adjudication. This may be a function of a change in the membership of the court (suggesting perhaps a more deferential judiciary, or one more willing to engage in a "dialogue" with the legislature), or a dearth of new laws that require charter scrutiny (Kelly 2005, Hogg et al. 2007). Chief Justice Beverly McLachlin (one of three female justices on the current court) remarked on the substantive and philosophical change during her tenure: "The last 10 years have seen a shift in the debate. The stark, either/or alternatives of absolute legislative power and court supremacy have given way, more and more, to a recognition that in a mature democracy of rights, both institutions are vital" (Makin 2009). Furthermore, there have been gains by different groups who are otherwise under-represented in Parliament – namely, the gay and lesbian community and women. There have also been changes in police procedures to protect the rights of those suspected of or arrested for crimes. Over the charter's short history, challenges heard before the court have struck down laws criminalizing abortion (*R. v. Morgentaler*, [1988]); acknowledged gays and lesbians as classes protected against discrimination via section 15 (*Egan v. Canada* [1995]); and, via *Vriend v. Alberta* (1998), paved the way for the same-sex marriage reference. Of more recent vintage are cases challenging Canada's prosecution of the "war on terror" in cooperation with the United States (*Canada v. Khadr* [2008] and [2010]), and the extent to which Canadian authorities can limit rights of terrorist suspects (*Charkaoui v. Canada* [2007 and 2008]).

As entrenched as rights now are in the charter, so too is the charter and its interpretation by the Supreme Court of Canada well established in Canadian society. Despite the criticisms and controversy, the charter remains popular. Polls taken over the life of the charter demonstrate its consistent popularity and acceptance among Canadians: in 1987 and again in 2002, a survey of two thousand Canadians found an 82 per cent approval rating for the charter (specifically, agreeing that "the Charter is a good thing"). A 2002 Centre for Research and Information on Canada (CRIC) poll echoed that sentiment: 88 per cent of respondents agreed that the charter is good for Canada (Saunders 2002). Upon the twenty-fifth anniversary of the charter, that sentiment had been tempered some, but still majorities find that both the charter and the Supreme Court of Canada are "moving Canada in the right direction" (Makin 2007a).

Looking Ahead – Democratic Reform in Canada

This chapter has outlined the main contours of the government and politics of Canada. It describes a system in which a great deal of political power is concentrated in the hands of the prime minister. When backed by a cohesive majority of MPs, a prime minister's power is limited primarily by the constitution and by the need to be re-elected after no more than five years. The system provides efficient government, making it possible for a government to enact its programs. It also provides for a relatively clear exercise of accountability, in that the electorate is periodically given an opportunity to pass judgment on the performance of the government by re-electing it if satisfied or "throwing the rascals out" if not. The contrast with the system of separated powers in the presidential system of the United States, where one branch of government checks and balances the other and concerted action is extremely difficult to achieve, could scarcely be sharper. In terms of intergovernmental relations, we have seen how Canada has evolved from an initially highly centralized federal system to one in which the provinces are important political actors in their own right. We have seen how the charter has broadened the political terrain by opening avenues for influence to groups that have not been favoured by majoritarian parliamentary institutions. The courts are now a critically important political venue in contemporary Canada.

While Canadians remain generally proud of their country, there is also evidence of widespread concern for the health of the country's body politic that goes well beyond the customary federal-provincial wrangling and persistent regionalism so prominent in recent decades. The surprising rejection of the elite-negotiated Charlottetown Accord in a 1992 referendum clearly signalled the end of popular deference to business-as-usual procedures. Disengagement from the electoral process and declining attachment to and trust in political parties are symptomatic of, and contributors to, a kind of malaise in the country (Cross and Docherty 2005). While perceptions of the unresponsiveness of the political system seem to have peaked in the early 1990s, a significant majority of Canadians still feel that governments do not care about what they think (Gidengil et al. 2004, 107). Moreover, the taint of scandal from past controversies continues to plague both major political parties. In the case of the Liberals, this is the legacy of the "sponsorship scandal" that peaked around 2005 with revelations of criminal activity on the part of public and party officials. The Conservatives also had to weather public relations storms during 2009 related to former prime minister Brian Mulroney's receipt of several large (and previously un-disclosed) cash payments from a shady lobbyist who had advocated the purchase of jet airplanes from Airbus by Air Canada in the 1980s. The party suffered again during 2010 from the dismissal from the Conservative caucus of former cabinet minister Helena Guergis, ostensibly for misbehaviour related to the lobbying activities of her husband and former Conservative MP Rahim Jaffir.

However, the restiveness on the part of the public goes further and runs deeper. There seems to be a hunger for democratic renewal and institutional reform (Howe, Johnston, and Blais 2005). A major audit of the state of Canadian democracy involving leading scholars from across the country has turned up ample evidence of the need for a wide range of institutional reforms to ensure the continued vitality of Canada's parliamentary system (for a summary, see Cross and Docherty 2005). Such sentiments are not restricted to federal politics. In the past couple of years no fewer than five provinces have seriously explored reforming their electoral systems, and two of these (Ontario and New Brunswick) have done so in the context of a broader consideration of democratic reforms. The fact that none of the major electoral reform proposals in the provinces, and other long-standing challenges such as senate reform, have been implemented means that popular pressures for change in this important area remain unresolved. Yet public disquiet with politicians and the political process notwithstanding, there is nothing in Canada to rival the upstart "tea party" movement that is currently unsettling – and perhaps at the same time energizing – the American political landscape. Yet the large swings in fortune for the Liberals, NDP, and BQ revealed in the 2011 election give further evidence of the unease of the Canadian electorate. It is too early to say whether the country's party system is entering a new phase that will be characterized by a different – perhaps more polarized – pattern of partisan competition, or whether the shifting allegiances of Canadian voters will continue to produce electoral surprises in future elections.

WEBSITES

Canada, Parliament: http://www.parl.gc.ca
Canada Online: http://canadaonline.about.com

REFERENCES AND FURTHER READING

Asselin, Robert B. 2001. *The Canadian Social Union: Questions about the Division of Powers and Fiscal Federalism*, B00–31E: 1–20. Ottawa: Library of Parliament, Parliamentary Research Branch. PR.

Bakvis, Herman. 2001. "Prime Minister and Cabinet in Canada: An Autocracy in Need of Reform?" *Journal of Canadian Studies/Revue d'Études Canadiennes* 35 (4): 60–79.

Brown, Douglas. 2005. "Who's Afraid of Asymmetrical Federalism?" http://wwwhttp://www.queensu.ca/iigr/WorkingPapers/asymmetricfederalism/Brown2005.pdf.rsc.ca/index/php.

Carty, R.K., William Cross, and Lisa Young. 2000. *Rebuilding Canadian Party Politics*. Vancouver: UBC Press.

Carty, R.K., and Munroe Eagles. 2005. *Politics Is Local: National Politics at the Grassroots*. Toronto: Oxford University Press.

Cheffins, R.I., and P.A. Johnson. 1986. *The Revised Canadian Constitution: Politics as Law*. Toronto: McGraw-Hill Ryerson.

Clarkson, Stephen. 2005. *The Big Red Machine: How the Liberal Party Dominates Canadian Politics*. Vancouver: UBC Press.

Cross, William, and David Docherty. 2005. "Canada: A Democratic Audit." Ottawa: Canadian Study of Parliament Report (11 March). http://www.studyparliament.ca/English/pdf/ongoing/2005_Conference_Report_Eng.pdf.

Gidengil, Elizabeth, André Blais, Neil Nevitte, and Richard Nadeau. 2004. *Citizens*. Vancouver: UBC Press.

Hogg, Peter W., Allison A. Bushell, and Wade K. Wright. 2007. "A Reply on Charter Dialogue Revisited." *Osgoode Hall Law Journal* 45 (1): 193–202.

Howe, Paul, Richard Johnston, and André Blais. 2005. "Introduction: The New Landscape of Canadian Democracy." In *Strengthening Canadian Democracy*, ed. Howe, Johnston, and Blais, 3–18. Montreal: Institute for Research on Public Policy.

James, Patrick, Donald E. Abelson, and Michael Lusztig, eds. 2002. *The Myth of the Sacred: The Charter, the Courts, and the Politics of the Constitution*. Montreal: McGill-Queen's University Press.

Kelly, James B. 2005. *Governing with the Charter: Legislative and Judicial Activism and Framers' Intent*. Vancouver: UBC Press.

Knopf, Rainer, and F.L. Morton. 1992. *Charter Politics*. Scarborough, ON: Nelson Canada.

Koerner, Wolfgang. 1988. *The Foundations of Canadian Federalism*. Ottawa: Library of Parliament, Parliamentary Research Branch, Political and Social Affairs Division. BP187-E.

Lipset, Seymour Martin. 1990. *Continental Divide*. New York: Routledge, Chapman and Hall.

Makin, Kirk. 2007a. "After 25 years of Charter, most think Supreme Court on right course." *Globe and Mail*, 16 February: A8.

Makin, Kirk. 2007b. "Senior U.S., Canadian judges spar over judicial activism; Courts should move with the time, Supreme Court's Binnie says at McGill." *Globe and Mail*, 17 February: A2.

Makin, Kirk. 2009. "Chief Justice pronounces on judicial activism; McLachlin celebrates a 'rewarding' decade." *Globe and Mail*, 20 June: A9.

Mandel, Michael. 1989 (rev. 1994). *The Charter of Rights and the Legalization of Politics in Canada*. Toronto: Wall and Thompson.

Merritt, Allen S., and George W. Brown. 1983. *Canadians and Their Government*. Toronto: Fitzhenry and Whiteside.

Nevitte, Neil. 1996. *The Decline of Deference*. Peterborough, ON: Broadview Press.

Savoie, Donald. 2008. *Court Government and the Collapse of Accountability in Canada and the United Kingdom*. Toronto: University of Toronto Press.

Siegfried, André. 1906; 1966. *The Race Question in Canada*. Toronto: Macmillan.

Simeon, Richard, and Elaine Willis. 1997. "Democracy and Performance: Governance in Canada and the United States." In *Degrees of Freedom: Canada and the United States in a Changing World*, ed. Keith Banting, George Hoberg, and Richard Simeon, 150–88. Montreal: McGill-Queen's University Press.

Smith, David E. 2003. *The Canadian Senate in Bicameral Perspective*. Toronto: University of Toronto Press.

Stevenson, Garth. 2006. "Fiscal Federalism and the Burden of History." Institute of Intergovernmental Relations. Fiscal Federalism and the Future of Canada – Conference Proceedings, 28–29 Sept. 2006, folio 6.

Stillborn, Jack, and Robert B. Asselin. 2001. *Federal–Provincial Relations*, 93–10E. Ottawa: Library of Parliament, Parliamentary Research Branch, Political and Social Affairs Division. http://publications.gc.ca/collections/Collection-R/LoPBdP/CIR/9310-e.htm.

Thomas, David M. 2008. "Past Futures: The Development and Evolution of American and Canadian Federalism." In *Canada and the United States: Differences That Count*, 3rd ed., ed. D.M. Thomas and B.B. Torrey, 295–316. Toronto: Broadview Press.

Vaughan, Frederick. 1999. "Judicial Politics in Canada: Patterns and Trends." *IRPP Choices: Courts and Legislatures* 5 (1): 4–20.

Wheare, K.C. 1963. *Federal Government*. 4th ed. Oxford: Oxford University Press.

Young, Lisa, and Joanna Everitt. 2004. *Advocacy Groups*. Vancouver: UBC Press.

4   The Economy

MARK KASOFF AND PAUL STORER

The Canadian economy is vitally important to the United States. Canada is the top export market for close to three quarters of the fifty states. The trade relationship between the two is the world's largest, with over $1.5 billion of exports and imports crossing the border every day. Canada is the United States' largest foreign supplier of oil and petroleum products. Big Canadian companies such as the Bank of Montreal, Magna, and CN Rail have an American presence. Many large American companies such as Procter & Gamble, General Motors, and Dow Chemical have Canadian operations.

Now that you appreciate how important Canada is to the American economy, here's what you will learn in this chapter. First, you will understand how Canada's economy works and which aspects of it are distinctly Canadian; second, you will understand the similarities and differences between the Canadian and American economies; third, you will appreciate the great importance of international trade and investment to Canada and Canada's place in the global economy; and fourth, you will understand the benefits and challenges of Canada's economic dependence on the United States, and the consequences and policy choices that result from this dependence.

This chapter is divided into three sections. The first section describes the nature of Canada's economy, with a focus on both Canada–US economic relations and on the aspects that differ the most between the two countries' economies. Next, the most significant economic challenges facing Canada are described and discussed. Finally, the chapter concludes by examining the economic policy decisions that Canadian governments have taken in response to these challenges.

Figure 4.1 Canada's exports and imports by country

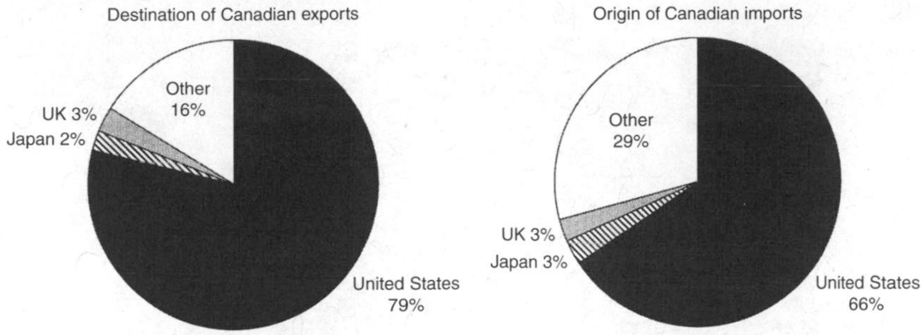

Destination of Canadian exports

UK 3%
Japan 2%
Other 16%
United States 79%

Origin of Canadian imports

Other 29%
UK 3%
Japan 3%
United States 66%

Structure of the Economy

Like all industrialized economies, the Canadian economy is a "mixed economy." It takes the exclusive private-ownership model of a pure capitalist economy as its foundation, but then adds a significant role for government to provide goods and services and to regulate economic activity. Successful private corporations that originated in Canada include Research in Motion, which developed the widely used Blackberry wireless phone and Internet access system. Many foreign companies produce manufactured goods on Canadian soil, especially in the automobile industry.

Government involvement in the economy has been greater in Canada than in the United States, but has declined in recent decades. Crown (public) corporations such as Air Canada and Canadian National Railway have been sold to private investors. Much as in the United States, the Canadian federal government and its central bank, the Bank of Canada, use macroeconomic policy to promote national economic goals. Regulation of the economy has historically been more pervasive in Canada, with some people claiming that the economic crisis of the just completed decade was much less severe in Canada because of stricter regulation of the banking and financial systems (see Knight 2012).

Canadians have one of the most successful economies in the world. Gross domestic product (GDP), the most widely used measure of prosperity, refers to the value of goods and services produced by a nation in

Figure 4.2 State trade with Canada

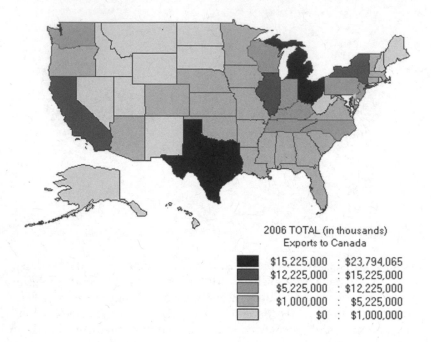

2006 TOTAL (in thousands)
Exports to Canada

$15,225,000	: $23,794,065
$12,225,000	: $15,225,000
$5,225,000	: $12,225,000
$1,000,000	: $5,225,000
$0	: $1,000,000

a given year. With a population of approximately 34 million compared to about 310 million in the United States, Canada's GDP is about one-tenth that of its neighbour. Canadian per capita GDP is about $38,000 (all numbers in US dollars and adjusted for purchasing power), which is only about 84 per cent of US per capita GDP, but higher than in countries such as Britain, Germany, and Japan, according to data from the Organization for Economic Co-operation and Development (OECD). Based on Canada's high living standards and strong social safety net (especially in health care) the United Nations in its annual Human Development Index regularly ranks Canada among the best countries in the world in which to live.

Per capita GDP is such an important measure of material well-being that economists devote a lot of time to identifying the factors that determine it. In the short run, changes in per capita GDP tend to be related to variations in the fraction of the population that is employed and/or

Table 4.1 Canadian employment and output by industry

	Employment (Thousands)	% of total	GDP $C millions	% of total
Total: All Industries	16,848.9	100	1,199,595	100
Services-producing sector	13,112.5	78	869,729	73
Retail-wholesale trade	2,639.8	16	140,488	12
Health care-social assistance	1,955.0	12	81,366	7
Education	1,192.7	7	61,792	5
Professional/technical	1,201.6	7	60,510	5
Finance/insurance/real estate	1,099.0	7	251,796	21
Accommodation/food	1,055.9	6	26,667	2
Other services	3,968.5	24	247,110	21
Goods-producing sector	3,736.4	22	329,866	27
Manufacturing	1,790.6	11	151,068	13
Construction	1,161.4	7	69,052	6
Other goods	784.4	5	109,746	9

Source: Adapted from Statistics Canada, n.d., table 282-0008, Labour Force Survey Estimates, annual; table 379-0027 Gross Domestic Product at Basic Prices, by Industry, annual. Data for GDP are for 2008 and unemployment data are for 2009. GDP expressed in chained 2002 dollars.

the average number of hours per employed worker. Over the medium to long term, the most important determinant of per capita GDP is the total amount of production per hour worked in the economy, a concept that economists call "labour productivity." When labour productivity rises, people are "working smarter," either because they have more machinery and equipment to help them work or because they are using a more advanced technology. When labour productivity rises, people can have both shorter work hours and more material goods.

Labour productivity improvements generally reflect conscious decisions to invest in the future by producing more productive machinery and equipment (known as "capital" by economists) or new knowledge or discoveries. Investment spending accounts for about 20 per cent of Canada's GDP, with examples of investment including businesses investing in buildings and equipment and governments investing in schools, roads, and public infrastructure.

Previous chapters on Canadian geography and history show how proximity to the United States has shaped the values and structures underpinning the Canadian economy. The "staples thesis" of historian Harold Innis emphasized the importance of natural resources for Canadian economic development. As already noted in chapter 1, Canada is richly endowed with natural resources. Fishing, the fur trade, farming, and forestry stimulated economic growth in the past, and agriculture and forestry are still significant. Energy and mining have grown in importance. The fur trade faded more than a century ago, while the importance of fishing has declined in recent decades.

While basic commodities are still important, Canada has moved well beyond its reliance on natural resources to become a modern manufacturing and services economy. As table 4.1 shows, goods production, including agriculture, accounts for 22 per cent of total employment. Manufacturing, especially automotive-related production, is the largest goods-producing sector. Since 2004, more motor vehicles have been produced in Ontario than in Michigan. Key service sectors in the Canadian economy include financial services, health and social services, and retail and wholesale trade.

Canada's Trade Pattern

Canada relies much more heavily than the United States on foreign trade (imports and exports). In 2008 Canada's exports were about 35 per cent of the value of total production and imports about 34 per cent. Putting it another way, about 70 per cent of the Canadian GDP is connected to foreign trade; the comparable figure for the United States is about 25 per cent. The vast majority of Canada's exports are sold in the United States, which is also Canada's key source of imports. Millions of jobs in both countries are supported by this enormous trade relationship.

The determinant factors for Canada–US trade are proximity coupled with similar consumer preferences and industry practices. The degree of integration between the United States and Canada is difficult to overstate. In 1981 about 65 per cent of exports went to the United States; in 1989 the figure was 74 per cent; by 2009 it stood at around 75 per cent. A number of factors have contributed to this trend, including the implementation of a Canada–US free-trade deal in 1989; variations in the Canada–US exchange rate which affect the cost of Canadian goods for American purchasers; and the strength or weakness of the US economy relative to other world economies.

Primary commodities still account for nearly one-quarter of Canada's exports. Examples include forest products (wood, pulp, newsprint), minerals (petroleum, copper, coal, nickel), and agricultural crops (wheat, canola, barley). The non-American share of Canadian exports consists mainly of these goods.

A little-known fact is that Canada exports more oil and petroleum products to the United States than any other country in the world. Traditional sources of oil are limited, but Canada's huge supply of petroleum in the Athabasca oil sands of northern Alberta exceeds the known reserves of Saudi Arabia. Getting this oil to market is more expensive than traditional sources, but quite profitable when prices are above $30 a barrel.

In addition to its large share of US energy imports, Canada also provides about one-third of the softwood lumber used in the United States. In recent years Canada and the United States have been involved in a dispute over allegations by US lumber producers that Canadian lumber is sold at an unfairly low price. The cause of this dispute is the difference in the way that private companies are sold the right to harvest timber on public lands, as well as the greater reliance on publicly owned timberland in Canada. The Canadian provinces charge "stumpage fees" for the right to cut down a tree, while the United States conducts auctions. US producers claim that the provinces subsidize Canadian producers by charging a stumpage fee that is below the fair market value. Over the past few decades, a variety of taxes, duties, and export restrictions have been placed on US imports of Canadian timber. These trade restrictions have benefited American lumber producers, but US consumers have paid a price, estimated to be several thousand dollars per new home, through increased construction costs. Canada has had some success in appealing these US softwood lumber restrictions before the NAFTA and WTO arbitration panels.

Canada–US trade in manufactured goods such as cars and car parts shows the depth of the economic integration achieved in North America. Automotive components cross the borders numerous times as they are incorporated into progressively more complex parts and assemblies. These components are finally assembled into finished vehicles which might be sold on either side of the Canada-US border. Much of the manufacturing trade occurs within the same industry. For example, automotive products account for large shares of both exports and imports in Canada-US trade. Furthermore, trade is often between Canadian and US affiliates of the same corporation. Given this level of integration, Canada–US trade is often described as a cooperative process of "making things together" rather than a competitive struggle to sell finished goods to the other country.

With regard to Canadian trade with Japan, exports are strongly affected by consumption and less so by Canadian costs. With the exception of autos there is very little economic integration between Canada and Japan. Canadian exports to Japan are almost entirely driven by Canada's comparative advantage in primary products.

The Tax System in Canada

Government spending is financed primarily through tax revenues. In Canada, companies pay taxes on profits while individuals pay income, sales, and property taxes. Unlike the United States, Canada levies a national sales tax of 5 per cent called the goods and services tax (GST). All the provinces except Alberta levy an additional provincial sales tax (PST), which ranges from 5 per cent in Saskatchewan to 10 per cent in Nova Scotia and Prince Edward Island. More than half of the provinces now have a single harmonized sales tax (HST) that combines the provincial and federal goods and services taxes. Combined federal and provincial sales taxes in Canada can add over 15 per cent to the final price of a good or service. In the United States, by contrast, there is no national sales tax and state sales taxes usually only apply to products. As a percentage of GDP, total Canadian tax revenue was 33.3 per cent in 2008, slightly below the Organisation for Economic Co-operation and Development (OECD) average of 35.9 per cent but above the United States' 28.0 per cent. Business taxes in Canada are about the same as in the United States, while personal taxes are higher. These higher personal taxes have encouraged some highly skilled Canadians to migrate to their neighbour.

Health Care in Canada and the United States

Health care is perhaps the sector of the economy where the mix between the private sector and the public sector differs the most between Canada and the United States. According to 2008 data from the OECD, government accounted for 70 per cent of health care spending in Canada versus 47 per cent in the United States.

All legal Canadian residents have access to hospital and physician services, although dental care and prescription drug costs are frequently covered through private insurance or out-of-pocket payments. Health care spending in Canada is funded through the tax system, and Canadians do not pay the provider any fee for health care services. Provincial governments administer the hospital system and the single-payer health insurance plan. The federal government provides additional funding to all the provinces, which in return must agree that their insurance plans will cover all medically necessary procedures, be available and accessible to all residents, be portable between locations and jobs within Canada, and be administered by a public-sector agency.

In the United States, health care for most people under age sixty-five is essentially a privately provided good funded through a mix of individual and employer contributions. Health insurance in the United States is available from a number of competing private insurers rather than through the single government insurer that operates in each Canadian province. Most Americans obtain access to health care services by participating in an employer-based health benefit plan to which they contribute. Unlike their Canadian counterparts, Americans who work less than full-time at any single employer or who are unemployed often find that they are uninsured and that they must pay for health care expenses out of pocket. Two notable exceptions to the American private system are the publicly provided Medicaid (a federal-state program primarily for low-income families with children and the disabled) and Medicare (for seniors).

Provision of health care is expensive in both countries, and costs are expected to increase with the rising average age of the population. According to the OECD, health represents a 10 per cent share of GDP in Canada, while in the United States it is relatively more expensive, at about 15 per cent of GDP. The two systems appear to be slowly converging. Canadians have made some moves towards a two-tier public and private system, with some individuals seeking to obtain private services. Meanwhile in the United States, President Obama signed legislation in 2010 to expand the availability of health insurance and to provide a larger role for government in regulating the health insurance market. Some Americans argue that a publicly funded system would result in labour cost savings and thereby make companies more internationally competitive, while others worry about government inefficiency.

The Canadian Banking System

Historically, the westward expansion of the United States was accompanied by a distrust of large out-of-state banks. In contrast, the settlement of the Canadian West was more accepting of centralized corporate power and of government regulation. The differences between the two banking systems reflect these divergent attitudes. In Canada a limited number of large banks with many branches across the country were established, while in the United States thousands of separate banks with few branches were the norm. Canadian commercial banking is a branch banking system, while the United States has a mix of branch and unit banking. The "Big Six" major Canadian banks dominate, with offices nationwide, and control of 90 per cent of bank assets and a large majority of the brokerage and investment banking business in the country. In part because Canadian bank regulators have discouraged Canadian bank mergers, the relative size of Canadian banks on the international market has decreased to the point where at present no Canadian bank is listed among the hundred largest in the world. Canadian banks are nevertheless quite active in American financial markets. In Chicago, for example, Harris Bank is owned by the Bank of Montreal. TD Ameritrade is a discount broker business owned by the Toronto-Dominion Bank.

Canadian banks operate under greater regulatory scrutiny than banks in the United States and are forced to bear a larger share of the risks involved in making loans. In large part because of these regulatory differences, Canada experienced slower growth of mortgage debt and less of an unsustainable "bubble" in the housing market in the second half of the 2000s. In addition, Canadian mortgages usually are reset every five years and foreclosure procedures are more draconian. Canada also eschews the mortgage interest deductibility that stimulated US home price inflation. As a result, Canada was spared the worst of the housing and financial sector crash seen in the United States when the housing bubble eventually (and inevitably) burst.

Canada's Economic Challenges

Living Standards and the Canada-US Productivity Gap

While Canada has a high per capita GDP by global standards, the natural point of comparison for many Canadians is the country next door. Canadians often refer to the fact that, when Canadian dollars are adjusted for their relative purchasing power, per capita GDP in Canada is only about 84 per cent of its US level. This GDP difference can be traced to a productivity gap that has at different times been linked to different levels of incentives to work or invest, lower levels of research and development in Canada, or a higher proportion of lower-productivity industries in Canada. On the other hand, the total GDP is more equally divided among the population in Canada as opposed to the United States. Some Canadians feel that a somewhat lower average GDP is a price worth paying for a reduced gap between the rich and poor.

Unemployment

Persistently elevated unemployment rates were a problem for Canada throughout much of the 1980s and 1990s. The national average unemployment rate rose to peaks of 11.3 per cent in 1984 and 11.4 per cent in 1993. The high unemployment of the early 1990s was a concern in part because it followed the decision to enter into a free-trade agreement with the United States, and some Canadians viewed this unemployment as a consequence of competition with low-cost American businesses. Relatively strong economic growth beginning in the mid-1990s lowered the Canadian unemployment rate to 6 per cent by 2007, but then the recession of the late 2000s pushed the Canadian unemployment rate back up to 8.3 per cent for 2009.

In addition to being concerned about the level of the Canadian unemployment rate, policymakers in Canada have also reacted to the fact that Canada has tended to have a higher unemployment rate than the United States, leading to fears that Canada might be under-performing. While Canada had the same unemployment rate as the United States in 1981, from 1982 through 2008 the unemployment rate was higher in Canada, on average 48 per cent higher over these 27 years. Part of the historical Canada–US unemployment differential is due to measurement differences in the two countries, accounting for nearly 1 percentage point of the gap. The remaining gap may have been due to slow productivity growth, a strong concentration in natural resources and primary industries, and generous Employment Insurance. Regional differences persist, with high rates in Atlantic Canada and lower rates in the industrial heartland and the West. The latter points cause us to recall the core-periphery model from chapter 1, which seems relevant to some aspects of Canadian development even today.

Whatever the cause of the higher Canadian unemployment rate from 1982 through 2008, by 2009 this situation had reversed itself due to the much more severe recession in the United States relative to Canada. It is unclear whether the Canadian rate will remain below its US counterpart or whether the Canadian unemployment rate will soon fall back to its pre-recession lows. In both Canada and the United States, governments have focused on preventing the unemployment rate from rising to post-Depression highs.

Looking forward, a weak American economy poses a significant economic threat to Canada, due to its heavy dependence on exports to its neighbour. For example, a slowdown in new residential construction in the United States hurts the Canadian forest products industry, which supplies about one-third of that country's softwood lumber. Likewise, a falloff in American demand for new cars and trucks leaves Canada feeling the pain.

Budget Deficits and the Public Debt

Until a few years ago, large government deficits at the federal and provincial levels (with corresponding high debt) were a serious and persistent problem confronting Canada. Accumulated deficits led to massive debts for both federal and provincial governments. By 1994 the Canadian ratio of net public debt to GDP had climbed to about 64 per cent, 25 per cent higher than in the late 1980s. The net government debt-to-GDP ratio in the United States that same year was much lower, at about 40 per cent. Canadian government debt as a percentage of GDP was second only to that of Italy among the G7 countries. Persistent Canadian federal deficits started in the 1970s, when tax cuts were instituted without coincident reductions in spending. Rising interest rates also increased interest payments on the public debt, and the recessions in the 1980s and 1990s further reduced tax receipts. Provincial and local deficits had been quite small until the 1980s, when they increased substantially, in some cases because of reduced revenues and in others because of increased spending. When the recessions hit, provincial deficits soared.

Large, persistent deficits limit the government's ability to provide a fiscal stimulus policy in the short run and can reduce a nation's income and welfare in the long run. A large debt (the accumulation of annual budget shortfalls) can cause interest rates to rise, thus crowding out private investment and reducing economic growth. The strategy of raising tax rates in an attempt to reduce the debt may be counterproductive, because it drives people and capital underground or abroad. Furthermore, there is a risk of a financial crisis if people fear that the tax base cannot support the debt. Thus, Canada's fiscal position appeared fragile during the early to mid-1990s. While budget deficits in Canada turned into surpluses in the late 1990s, deficits have returned as a consequence of the recession starting in 2008.

Costs and Benefits of Globalization

As a country with a relatively small population spread over a large geographic area, Canada faces some particular economic challenges. Productivity, one of the most important determinants of material living standards, can be raised by investing in machinery and equipment, education and training, or knowledge acquired through research and development. These types of investments require large up-front expenditures that could be difficult for a small country to finance solely through its domestic savings. In addition, modern manufacturing in sectors such as automobiles typically requires high production levels to reach the point where per-unit production costs are minimized (economists refer to this effect as "economies of scale"). In a small country the domestic market might be so small that per-unit costs remain at a relatively high level, reducing living standards and competitiveness.

Interaction with foreign countries offers Canada a potential solution to both the need to finance investment and the need to have a sufficiently large production level. Historically, Canada has attracted investment from countries such as Britain and the United States to finance the building of new factories or infrastructure such as railways. For trade, Canadian producers can surpass the limited size of the domestic market by exporting a large part of their production. Beginning with the Canada-US Automotive Pact of 1965, Canada has entered into a number of free-trade agreements designed to give Canadian producers access to larger markets in North America and elsewhere.

Access to foreign capital and foreign markets does not come without potential drawbacks, however. When foreign companies buy or build factories in Canada they obtain control over their investment and some Canadians worry about the effect of foreign control over the economy, especially in the energy and natural resource sectors. There is also debate over whether the Canadian subsidiaries of foreign firms do any R & D work in Canada or whether they simply produce using technology developed in their home country.

While trading with other countries gives Canadians access to new markets for their exports, domestic Canadian producers also have to compete with foreign producers. This new competition can cost jobs for some workers even if trade creates more jobs than are lost. There is also concern that trade could squeeze distinctive Canadian products out of the market and replace them with products that cater to the tastes of the larger foreign market. This concern is most acute in what Canadians call the "cultural industries" such as movies, television, books, and magazines. In these cultural industries there may be limited export market for movies or television programs that are distinctively Canada. While these cultural products might play a crucial role in strengthening a sense of Canadian identity, they may be unable to compete against cheaper imported (usually American) movies and television programs.

Much of Canada's experience with trade and investment policy has involved trying to balance the perceived costs and benefits of access to foreign capital and markets. For example, Canada's attitude towards foreign investment has evolved over time in response to changing assessments of the costs and benefits of inflows of foreign investment funding. When Canada was a British colony, "foreign" investors from Britain provided the funds needed to build railways and canals. After the First World War, the primary form of investment in Canada shifted from relatively passive portfolio investment to direct investment in which the investor takes an active role in running the business. Portfolio investment involves purchases of government or corporate bonds and shares issued by companies, while direct investment might involve building a new factory in Canada or purchasing a controlling interest in an existing firm. At the same time, the United States became Canada's principal foreign investor.

In the early 1950s Canadians became concerned about the growing amount of foreign direct investment (FDI) in Canada. FDI in the natural resource sector, such as petroleum, gas, and mining, raised concerns over possible loss of control over Canada's important resource wealth. In the manufacturing sector, a major concern was that foreign owners would limit innovation in Canada by conducting all R & D in their US operations and by reducing the number of upper management positions in Canada. Another concern was "extraterritoriality," the tendency of foreign companies to apply laws from their own country to their Canadian operations. For example, a US company might try to force its Canadian subsidiary to respect the US embargo on trade with Cuba.

Faced with these concerns over FDI, the Trudeau government established Canada's first investment screening body, the Foreign Investment Review Agency (FIRA) in 1974 to screen all but the smallest foreign takeovers and newly established businesses in order to ensure that these firms would provide a "significant benefit" to Canada. Canadian policy on FDI changed dramatically in 1984, however, when a newly elected Conservative government reduced restrictions on foreign investment in Canada. Prime Minister Mulroney replaced FIRA with Investment Canada in 1985 and declared that Canada was "open for business."

One explanation for Canadians' growing willingness to accept foreign investments is that Canadians are themselves big investors abroad, especially in the United States. Manulife of Ontario, for example, recently acquired the John Hancock insurance company. Magna International is an Ontario-based automotive supplier with over fifty manufacturing operations in the United States and two hundred worldwide. In the resources sector, Alcan, headquartered in Montreal, operates in fifty-five countries and has over one hundred locations in North America. Over the past decade, outward Canadian foreign investment has exceeded inward FDI levels. During the 1970s, for every dollar invested in Canada about 25 cents was invested by Canadians in the United States. This figure now stands at about 80 cents, with Canadian FDI growing faster in the US than US FDI in Canada.

An illustration of the changed attitude to FDI is that Canadians are currently expressing some concern that Canada might have too little rather than too much FDI. Over the past few decades, Canada's share of global FDI has dropped by more than half, from around 8 to 3 per cent of worldwide totals. NAFTA has not reversed this trend. Heightened border security measures taken after 9/11 may be encouraging foreign investors to locate in the much larger American market and then export to Canada rather than establishing in Canada and taking a chance on having US-bound exports delayed by increased border security. Concern about declining FDI is motivated by the fact that FDI often brings advanced technology to Canada and improved labour productivity (output per worker). Toyota's recent investment in a state-of-the-art production facility in Woodstock, Ontario, is one example of Canadian labour productivity benefiting greatly from FDI. The important links between and among FDI, productivity, and living standards explains why Canada's declining relative investment experience is worrisome.

Regional Differences

Large and persistent differences in income and standards of living exist among the Canadian regions and provinces. As table 4.2 reveals, GDP per capita is lowest on Prince Edward Island, the poorest province, and highest in Alberta, the most prosperous province. The most populous province, Ontario, has a high per capita income as well, although it is even higher in Alberta due to the recent oil boom there. Regional differences in income have persisted for decades. In the 1960s, for example, the Atlantic provinces were the poorest, with GDP per capita between 49 and 65 per cent of the Canadian average.

Wide variations in unemployment rates throughout Canada are another indication of strong regional economic differences. In the new millennium the national unemployment rate hovered around a thirty-year low. In 2009, the average annual unemployment rate varied from a low of 4.8 per cent in Saskatchewan to a high of 15.4 per cent in Newfoundland. Annual unemployment rates are higher in the Atlantic region, around the national average in the industrial heartland of Ontario and Quebec, and lower in the Prairie provinces and British Columbia. In recent decades unemployment rates have been consistently higher in the Atlantic region than in the rest of Canada, with future prospects no better. Some contend that Canada's Employment Insurance program and equalization payments are partly responsible. Because more generous benefits are targeted to depressed regions, the unemployed have less incentive to move to areas with better job prospects.

Policy Responses to Economic Challenges

Macroeconomic Policy

Macroeconomic policy refers to attempts by government to promote a high overall standard of living for its people. In Canada, the government achieves its goals by using its policy instruments to promote sustainable economic growth, a low inflation rate, and low unemployment rates. Macroeconomic policy tools fall into two broad areas: fiscal policy (taxation and government spending) and monetary policy (control of interest rates and the monetary supply).

Canadian macroeconomic policy in the 1970s and 1980s involved a combination of expansionary monetary and fiscal policy intended to create faster economic growth. These growth rates turned out to be

Table 4.2 Variations between Canada's provinces

	Personal income per person		GDP per person		
	$C	Gap (in % points)	$C	Gap (in %points)	Unemployment rate (%)
Canada	36,804	0	39,648	0	8.3
Newfoundland and Labrador	30,884	−16	39,398	−1	15.4
Nova Scotia	32,054	−13	31,193	−21	9.2
Prince Edward Island	28,899	−21	29,745	−25	12.0
New Brunswick	31,322	−15	31,254	−21	8.9
Quebec	33,333	−9	34,780	−12	8.5
Ontario	37,266	1	41,141	4	9.0
Manitoba	33,231	−10	35,160	−11	5.2
Saskatchewan	35,960	−2	41,024	3	4.8
Alberta	47,918	30	51,665	30	6.6
British Columbia	36,156	−2	37,529	−5	7.6

Source: Adapted from Statistics Canada, n.d. Table 384-0013, Selected Economic Indicators, Provincial Economic Accounts, annual; Table 051-0001, Estimates of Population, by Age Group and Sex for July 1, annual; Table 109-5304 Unemployment Rate, Canada, Provinces, Health Regions and Peer Groups, annual. Data for personal income and GDP are for 2008 and unemployment data are for 2009. GDP is expressed in chained 2002 dollars.

unsustainable and led to ballooning government budget deficits and rising inflation rates. Eliminating the undesirable consequences of these policies was costly and the experience led Canada to its current more modest focus on low inflation as a means to achieving economic prosperity.

Canada eventually eliminated the legacy of high budget deficits thanks in part to added revenues generated by a booming economy in the late 1990s. A more painful contribution to deficit reduction came from spending cuts in federal programs (in agriculture and national defence, for example), and through reductions in transfers to individuals and the provinces. Higher income taxes, reduced Employment

Insurance assistance, and a reduction in the number of federal employees helped turn things around. The provinces, too, enacted significant budget cuts that have been difficult for Canadians, particularly in the areas of health care and education. Once its budget deficit was eliminated, the federal government was able to focus its fiscal policy on increasing business productivity and innovation, expanding markets through trade, modernizing infrastructure, and promoting education, science, and technology.

The Canadian federal budget remained in surplus through most of the 2000s, in stark contrast to the American experience of record deficits. While the recession of the late 2000s increased government spending and lowered tax revenue in both countries, Canada experienced a much smaller increase in its budget deficit.

The goal of Canadian monetary policy is to foster good economic performance with price stability by controlling interest rates. Over the past few years the Bank of Canada – the country's central bank – has been quite successful at this strategy. Inflation has not been a serious problem in Canada since 1982, when the consumer price index (CPI) increased by 10.6 per cent. The Bank of Canada adopts and announces a formal target for the inflation rate and the US Federal Reserve has been evaluating the benefits of using this approach in US monetary policy.

Equalization Policy

Since the 1940s Canadian policy has provided for a federal system of transfer payments to the poorer provinces in an effort to narrow the differences in living standards throughout the country. A program of "equalization payments" exists to subsidize the poorer provinces so that public services are equivalent across Canada. For years, unemployment benefits and other social assistance payments have been higher and made available on better terms in the poorer provinces.

While the exact reasons for the wide differences in income among the provinces are not fully known, certain plausible explanations exist. In the past, economic development and growth in the different regions was based in part on staples products. The Atlantic region depended on fish and timber for growth and development, and to a large extent still does so today, but the linkages necessary to create a robust economy did not occur with these staples. Wheat, by contrast, provided Ontario and the Prairie provinces with the means to prosper because of the strong linkages that the wheat industry created to other activities such as rail transportation.

Though their intent was the opposite, government equalization payments, Employment Insurance, and other social services may have exacerbated the problem of large regional economic disparities. It is possible that federal government policies masked market forces for a long time. High unemployment rates are a signal that workers should move to areas with better job and earnings prospects, thereby raising their own incomes as well as the levels of those who remain. But generous government programs tend to restrict labour mobility by encouraging the unemployed to remain in the region, perpetuating the problem. Although the Atlantic region has had lower income levels relative to the rest of Canada for many years, it has an excellent education system with many high-quality universities and is beginning to diversify and expand its economy based on a highly skilled labour pool. In addition, the West is teeming with Maritimers who showed a willingness to relocate in spite of government subsidies to stay put.

Attempts to reform equalization and other transfers have met with little success. Prosperous provinces like Alberta are at odds with Atlantic provinces such as Newfoundland and Labrador and Nova Scotia. The latter want payments increased, while the former continues to be the only province that normally receives nothing under the equalization formula.

Trade and Investment Policies

From 1867 to 1988 Canada was replete with examples of attempts to reduce economic dependence on the United States. Macdonald's National Policy for the new nation included a protective tariff – a classic approach for infant economies. Eventually, though, Canada opened itself to freer trade with the United States and found that its economy was able to thrive in this close continental economic relationship, at least as long as the US economy remained strong. Free trade arrived first in a single industry with the 1965 Canada-US Auto Pact. This agreement allowed virtually unrestricted trade between manufacturers for new cars and parts, subject to stipulations intended to balance the quantities crossing the border. But this honeymoon was short lived.

In the 1970s, Prime Minister Trudeau's FIRA and National Energy Policy sought to reduce Canada's dependence on the United States. Policies such as the FIRA and foreign affairs minister Mitchell Sharp's famous Third Option followed. According to Sharp, Canada had three choices. Option 1: Do nothing and let relations with the United States develop as they may. Option 2: Actively pursue closer economic integration with the Americans. Option 3: Reduce dependence on the United States through aggressive action to sell Canadian goods outside North America, particularly in Asia and Japan. It was also hoped that Japan would become a bigger foreign direct investor in Canada, with greater emphasis on manufactured goods than on natural resources. But Sharp's Third Option was no more successful than earlier efforts to divert trade away from the United States. By the end of the Trudeau years, Canadian dependence on the American market had actually increased.

During the 1980s, Prime Minister Brian Mulroney pursued option 2 by establishing policies meant to bring about closer economic integration with the United States. Mulroney hoped to ensure access to American markets during a new wave of tough American protectionism; to make Canadian industry more competitive on a global basis; to create a binding and better way to settle trade disputes; and to protect Canadian culture.

A new era began in 1989 when Canada entered a free trade agreement (FTA) with the United States. The Canadians hoped to ensure access to the American market, to establish a mechanism for settling trade disputes, and to make the Canadian economy more productive and competitive. In 1994 Mexico joined the FTA in what is now known as the North American Free Trade Agreement (NAFTA).

NAFTA is a trade bloc that gives preferential treatment to its member nations for trade and direct investment. It has phased out most tariffs (import taxes) between the countries, ensured predictable market access (open markets), and instituted national treatment for investment. Two side accords on labour and the environment take into account that different standards exist in the three nations. The side accords are meant to prevent a "race to the bottom," where producers are attracted to whichever jurisdiction has the most lenient standards. These accords were a response to the concerns of environmental groups, labour unions, and anti–free trade protesters.

Under a preferred trader agreement, the signatories must have a way to verify that products have in fact been manufactured within the free trade zone. This proof of origin prevents free riders or manufacturers from outside the free trade zone from enjoying preferential status, in the NAFTA case a zero tariff rate. Rules-of-origin documentation requires customs inspections; this in turn means that NAFTA's internal borders remain important to the enforcement and integrity of the agreement. By contrast, the European Union (EU) is a customs union that sets a common external tariff and removes internal checkpoints for trade. Most NAFTA merchandise is shipped by truck and passes through a handful of very busy border crossings. The efficiency of these checkpoints is vital to the economies of all three nations. Many other goods are traded by rail, air, and pipeline.

The "national treatment" of investment is a key feature of NAFTA. Canada, the United States, and Mexico have agreed not to block private foreign direct investment based on the national origin of the investor. This does not mean that investment rules in the three countries are the same. It does mean that an American firm wishing to invest in Canada is on the same playing field as a Canadian firm. Exceptions to national treatment exist in certain industries. For example, cultural industries such as radio, television, film, and publishing remain protected from foreign ownership. When economic icons such as the Hudson's Bay Company, Alcan, and Tim Hortons are taken over by foreign investors, some Canadians express the same fears that led to FIRA in the 1970s.

The Liberal government of Prime Minister Jean Chrétien, first elected in 1993, accepted Canada's close integration with the continental economy. After the face-saving NAFTA side agreements on environmental and labour issues, the Liberals moved to take advantage of a Canada more open to trade and investment. Globalization is a term with multiple meanings and is often vilified as a cause of domestic economic decline. The world economic trading system has imperfections that provide economic nationalists with fuel for criticism. If by globalization we mean trade and foreign investment, then it is clear that most Canadian workers have jobs that depend on the international sector. Politically speaking, most Canadians seem to accept the reality of globalization and are not willing to put their economic welfare at risk through an overly aggressive nationalist economic policy. Canadians prefer a multilateral approach to trade and investment rule making; by and large, they accept the reality of increasing North American economic integration.

The Canadian economic development community points to the benefits of globalization: large merchandise trade surpluses, as well as the growing numbers of branch plants that are larger and more outward-oriented than companies that only sell to the Canadian market. These firms hire workers in greater numbers and spend more on R & D.

Economic nationalists like the Council of Canadians are vocal supporters of various policies: the protection of Canadian culture, a ban on the sale of bulk water, and limits to foreign control of key industries such as chemicals and pharmaceuticals, transportation equipment, and electronic products. For those who embrace these positions, NAFTA is an unmitigated disaster that Canada should either withdraw from or radically revise.

Some Canadian economic icons have been purchased by foreign investors. Examples include Tim Hortons by American-based Wendy's (and later spun off as an independent company), Bauer ice skates (now controlled by Nike, which purchased Canstar sports), and the merger of Coors and Molson (as noted in chapter 7, the latter ran a turn-of-the-century ad campaign styled "I Am Canadian" that was highly nationalistic in tone and that ranted on differences between Americans and Canadians). The privatization of the CNR, formerly a Crown corporation, through the issuance of common shares resulted in control by largely American investors.

Multilateralism through the WTO (formerly the General Agreements on Tariffs and Trade) is a pillar of Canada's trade policy. Regional groupings such as NAFTA complement and intensify the WTO's rule-based trading system.

In recent years there has been significant growth in emerging markets such as China and India. The 1980s was a period of dramatic economic change in Asia, and this affected that continent's trade and investment relations with the Western industrialized economies. Most notably, China embarked on economic reforms, pursuing foreign trade and accepting foreign direct investment. Rapid economic growth was sustained by high rates of savings and investment and low wages; Asia began catching up in terms of productivity and technology gaps. Canada hoped to get on the Asian trade bandwagon and get its slice of the growing economic pie. Increased business would contribute to Canadian prosperity and would also help reduce dependence on the United States. One response to the deep US recession of the late 2000s has been calls to again pursue something like Sharp's Third Option, with the argument being that Canada should seek economic ties with countries that are in relative growth rather than relative decline.

Another implication of the growth of countries such as China and India is that they have attracted foreign direct investment that might have once found its way to Canada. This trend has led some Canadian policy makers to ask what should be done to offset Canada's declining inward FDI trend. Traditional policies to attract FDI – ensuring a skilled labour pool, establishing competitive business tax rates, reducing regulations – are essential but the border policies implemented by Canada and the United States for homeland security purposes might discourage FDI despite these traditional policies. Increased staffing at borders and investments in customs information technology and roads, bridges, and inspection equipment are welcome developments in the Canada-US business community. However, these steps do not erase the fact that the United States has shown a willingness to slow or altogether close the border whenever it perceives a security threat. If "security trumps trade," as then US ambassador to Canada Paul Cellucci stated in 2003, then investors may prefer American locations over Canadian ones.

Some have called for an EU-style customs union and common perimeter approach with the United States where the current border would eventually fade away for commercial purposes. But Canadian fears about loss of national sovereignty make this a controversial proposal. A further deepening of trade and investment relations with the United States in the key automotive and energy industries could also benefit the Canadian economy. The Auto Pact of 1965, which created free trade for original equipment manufacturers in the auto industry, demonstrates the benefits of selective industry cooperation. Without such bold policies, Canada's share of global FDI will continue to decline.

The Canadian Dollar and the Debate over a Common Currency

How does the value of the Canadian dollar influence exports, foreign trade, and investment? Early in the 2000s, when the Canadian dollar grazed 60 cents against the US dollar, Canadian goods became relatively cheap when compared to their US counterparts and this change in relative prices encouraged Canadian exports to the United States. Americans became increasingly likely to take vacations in Canadian locations such as Whistler or Montreal and American film crews turned Vancouver into "Hollywood North." Just a few years later, in 2007, the Canadian dollar was worth more than a US dollar and the bargains were found on the other side of the border. With this strong Canadian dollar, it wasn't long before Canadian licence plates became a common sight in the parking lots of shopping malls in US border towns.

What factors influence the value of the Canadian "loonie"? The weak Canadian dollar of a decade ago puzzled economists. The Canadian economy was growing steadily, the balance of international merchandise trade was positive, and the federal budget was in surplus, with most provinces also putting their fiscal houses in order. These were all signs of a healthy economy. True, substantial debt overhang from the past existed (and has yet to be paid off). But overall, improving economic trends should have helped, not hurt, the loonie.

What were some of the other factors that worked against the Canadian dollar? For some time Canadian interest rates had been lower than American levels. The Bank of Canada did not want to choke off economic growth with higher rates, surmising that the falling loonie helped stimulate exports. Another factor cited was the erroneous perception that Canada's exports were primarily raw materials and agricultural products. In fact, with 80 per cent of exports to the United States and with the automotive industry dominating trade, only about one-third of Canada's exports worldwide are in primary products. Still, Canada is more export dependent than the United States.

Eventually, the Canadian dollar strengthened owing to ongoing fiscal and balance-of-payments surpluses and rising world prices for natural resources, especially oil. The huge negative imbalances in the United States served to weigh down the relative value of its dollar. Today, some Canadians fear that their strong dollar will reduce exports and discourage tourism, especially from the United States.

The recent wild ride of the Canadian dollar has convinced some Canadians that it would be better to avoid this currency volatility by adopting a euro-like common currency to be shared by Canada and the United States. Advocates of this new currency claim that trade and investment would benefit if the uncertainty associated with currency fluctuations could be removed. Opponents of a monetary union with the United States point out that Canada would have to give up control over its own monetary policy (and would probably see familiar faces removed from its currency). These opponents also point out, with some justification, that exchange-rate adjustments between Canada and the United States serve a useful purpose. As close as the two economies are, their fortunes sometimes diverge and changes in the exchange rate reflect these different forces and induce stabilization-enhancing economic flows. At present, the prospects of a common Canada-US currency seem remote.

Conclusions

Canada is home to a world-class technology-driven services economy that also turns in a strong performance in the goods-producing sector.

Automotive manufacturing and petroleum and natural gas industries are significant sources of jobs and revenue. The Canadian economy is characterized by very large regional variations that have persisted over time despite federal attempts to reduce vastly different living standards across the provinces and territories. Well over half the Canadian economy is tied to the global system through trade and investment, and most of this is connected to its chief economic partner, the United States. The two countries share the largest bilateral trade relationship in the world today.

What are the prospects for Canada lessening its dependence on the United States? Trade with Asia has been erratic from year to year and has remained at low levels. This is due to the structure of Canadian exports to the area – exports that are dominated by primary and related products. The size of the Chinese wheat harvest, for example, directly influences wheat purchases from Canada. Also, many Asian markets are only slowly opening up to manufactured goods from Canada and other industrialized countries. Canada has a negative trade balance with Asia, with imports growing more rapidly than exports. The EU share of Canadian exports will, most likely, continue to slowly decline owing to quotas, protective tariffs, and non-tariff barriers to trade. As the EU countries struggle to get their fiscal house in order, austerity measures will dampen economic growth and the demand for Canadian products. At the same time, a Canada-EU free trade agreement could partially offset these developments.

In contrast, owing to NAFTA, the North American market is relatively open and trade with the United States has grown and remains at high levels. Under NAFTA, Canadian exports to Mexico have grown but remain at very low levels. While Canada records a trade deficit with Asia, merchandise trade with the United States is in surplus. The American market will continue to be attractive to Canadian exporters owing to its close geographic proximity, similarity in demand patterns, culture and language, and so on. These factors are compelling for small and medium-sized Canadian companies. Business with Asia may grow, but so will trade with the United States. For these reasons, little change in Canada's trade dependence with the United States is expected.

Despite attempts by various Canadian governments to pursue trade elsewhere, dependence on the United States has only increased. The American market remains open for trade and investment despite border security worries and irritating disputes over softwood lumber, durum wheat, and other products. However, the FTA has ensured long-term market access for Canada. Aside from the anxiety of the "mouse sleeping with the elephant," Canadians can at least take comfort that their values and culture have not converged with those of the United States.

WEBSITES

Bank of Canada: http://www.bankofcanada.ca
Department of Finance Canada: http://www.fin.gc.ca/access/ecfisc-eng.asp
Industry Canada: http://www.ic.gc.ca
Statistics Canada: http://www.statcan.ca

FURTHER READING

Armstrong, Muriel. 1988. *The Canadian Economy and Its Problems*. 4th ed. Scarborough, ON: Prentice-Hall Canada.

Knight, Malcolm. 2012. "Surmounting the Financial Crisis: Contrasts between Canadian and American Banks." *American Review of Canadian Studies* 42 (3).

Lipsey, R.G., and C. Ragan. 2008. *Economics*. 12th Canadian ed. Toronto: Pearson Addison Wesley.

Norrie, K., and D. Owram. 2002. *A History of the Canadian Economy*. 3rd ed. Scarborough, ON: Nelson.

Organization for Economic Co-operation and Development (OECD). 2006. *Economic Survey of Canada*. Paris.

Strick, J.C. 1992. *Canadian Public Finance*. 4th ed. Toronto: Holt, Rinehart and Winston of Canada.

Wallace, I. 2002. *A Geography of the Canadian Economy*. Don Mills, ON: Oxford University Press.

5 Population and Immigration Policy

RODERIC BEAUJOT AND MUHAMMAD MUNIB RAZA

As seen in the chapters on geography and history, the story of Canada needs to include immigration. Before the constitutional arrangement of 1867 that established the county as a federation that started with four provinces, there had been the arrival of Aboriginal populations who crossed the Bering Straits from Asia, then the arrival of Europeans across the Atlantic, who were later followed by peoples from all continents of the planet. Immigration is often portrayed as a point of unity across these populations, with the concept that "we are all immigrants or descendants of immigrants." Of course, for some the immigration dates from ancestral times, while for others it is much more recent.

This chapter elaborates the role of immigration and immigration policy in the population history of Canada. We start with the broad characterization of migration in population history, and of immigration policy in Canada. Certain phases of immigration are then identified in historical and policy contexts. After characterizing the determinants of immigration, we focus on the consequences, especially in terms of population growth, age structure, and distribution over geography. The chapter concludes with the social, economic and cultural impact of immigration.

Migration in Modern Population History

In a broad article, "Human Migration in Historical Perspective," McNeill (1984) proposes that we can distinguish four forms of pre-modern migration around the world: radical displacement of one population by another, conquest leading to symbiosis of two previously diverse groups, infiltration by outsiders with some acceptance on the part of the original population, and importation of populations that have been forcibly uprooted. These migration patterns took place in pre-modern civilizations, with small ruling groups and often a division of labour along ethnic lines. McNeill further proposes that for both civilizations of the past and modern states, migration brings diversity, multi-ethnicity, and pluralism.

In modern times, the differential levels of development over space, and the population pressures associated with the demographic transition, have brought further movement of peoples. As Europe was undergoing its demographic transition, with the associated population growth, there was significant displacement within countries, principally urbanization, but also movement of the "surplus" European population to other continents (Zelinsky 1971). If we characterize the world as consisting of a North and a South, until about 1950 there was more movement from the North to the South, with Europeans not only settling in other countries of the North, like North America and Australia, but also in Africa, Asia, and South America. Over the nineteenth century, 54 million persons crossed the Atlantic (Coleman 2009: 3). From the sixteenth to the early twentieth centuries, the demographic expansion of Europe changed the face of other continents, sometimes almost replacing the indigenous populations, as in North America.

Since the 1950s, it is the continents of the South that are undergoing demographic expansion, and the associated population pressures have brought a net movement from South to North. Once again, development is bringing migration, including urbanization and movement beyond national boarders. This is occurring at a time of greater effective resistance on the part of previous populations in a world that has few "empty spaces." But there is also an interest in taking advantage of these arrivals in terms of productivity and innovation.

Over the twentieth century, the greatest international movements have occurred in two periods of globalization, first in the early part of the century, then in its later half. In between, through two world wars and a Great Depression, there was retrenchment. Both in the past and in the present, migration brings a transformation of the ethnic composition of populations. For Canada, the wave of migrations during the early twentieth century brought not only British and French, but other western, northern, then eastern and southern Europeans. While they were "white," there was visible diversity in language, dress, and customs, including differential settlement patterns. In the current period of globalization, the movement has come to be dominated by Asians, but it includes peoples from all parts of the South, with diversities that are more visible along ethnic lines. In both cases, the movements bring transformations of ethnic composition. Coleman (2006) has aptly characterized the change as another "demographic transition," resulting this time from immigration and ethnic composition rather than a change in deaths and births.

Conceptualizing Migration

Of the three demographic processes, fertility, mortality, and migration, it is migration that is hardest to conceptualize. Migration includes the complexity that some people live and die in the same place while others move several times, even back to their place of origin. Migration can be over shorter or longer distances, which can be qualified as internal migration and international migration.

In theorizing about migration, it is useful to start with what might be called a natural tendency not to move. Staying represents integration with family and friends (Goldscheider 1971). The importance of integration can be seen in the generalization that people who have moved once are more likely to move again, and that return migration is a common phenomenon. The importance of social integration is also consistent with chain migration, that is, people who know each other tend to follow from a given place of origin to a given destination. It would appear that life course and social factors are more important in determining whether or not people move, while economic factors are more important in choosing the place of destination. People move especially at stages of the life course that involve disruptions, such as leaving home, finishing school, finding a job, starting or terminating a relationship, or retirement. Whether or not people move would also be a function of how integrated they are in a given location. Once people are prone to move, economic factors, or more broadly the push and pull factors, determine the place of destination. When people are settled, especially when there is a two-income family with children, a higher salary at a different location will not be attractive. But when they are looking for a first job, a higher salary may prompt people to move, especially if they see additional opportunities at the place of destination.

Thus, at the micro level, we theorize that social and life-course questions associated with the extent of integration in family and community are more responsible for whether or not people move, and economic questions are more responsible for the choice of destination when people do migrate. At the macro level, there would be movement towards locations that provide greater potential to integrate, in both economic and social terms. Besides these push-and-pull factors, there are barriers as represented by information, communication, transportation, and distance.

For international migration, the factors to consider include the opportunities for social and economic integration at places of origin and destination, along with links and barriers between countries, including policy barriers. Clearly, levels of immigration are a function of things happening within Canada and others happening outside of the country, along with the links and barriers across countries, both in the short and longer terms (Simmons 2010).

In *The Age of Migration*, Castles and Miller (2009) argue that international migration is a constant in human history and that population movements accompany demographic growth, technological change, as well as political conflict and warfare. Over the last five centuries, they propose that mass migrations have played a major role in colonialism, industrialization, the emergence of nation-states, and the development of the capitalist world market. They also suggest that international movements have never been as significant as today, linking these high levels of movement to the greater inequality across countries, and to transnational networks and cultural interchange.

In their theoretical synthesis, Massey et al. (1994) propose that globalization creates both mobile populations following on various economic displacements and demand for labour in the largest cities. With communication links and family and other networks, migratory exchanges are perpetuated between places of origin and destination. Consequently, recent migrants are concentrated in large cities, which in Canada means Toronto, Montreal, and Vancouver.

In *Immigration and Canada: Global and Transnational Perspectives*, Simmons (2010: 39–40) proposes that international migration should be conceptualized in terms of specific streams, including their stages of initiation, growth, stabilization, and decline. There are typically multiple overlapping streams associated with large regions of origin and destination. The streams can further be characterized in terms of who is actually moving, by ethnicity, class, gender, and other attributes. Simmons proposes that transnational factors, including associated networks and institutions, are at the core of migration systems. These migration systems would emerge within specific political economic contexts, be they the colonial, trade, and cultural diffusion processes of the past or the global ideology and global financial institutions of the contemporary era. This transnational perspective is thus able to include questions of (1) why people leave, (2) the extent to which they settle and integrate, and (3) the links that are maintained across origins and destinations.

Canada and Immigration Policy

It is not surprising that states pay careful attention to international population movements. The movement of people across international boundaries can affect the relations between states, introducing links or sometimes conflicts. In addition, as Weiner (1985) notes, international migration can create interdependence either by "bringing the outside in" or because "a piece of you is now outside." The previous residents of other countries can have specific interests in the political processes of their new countries, and they can attempt to influence the political processes in their countries of origin. It is therefore not surprising that states will pay careful attention to questions of the international movement of populations, elaborating rules of entry (and sometimes of exit) in order to ensure that the process produces a maximum of benefits. Equally understandable is the deep interest that the public takes in migration questions as they affect the very society in which we live.

Immigration has always presented a certain ambivalence for policymakers. On the one hand, immigration has been viewed positively, first in nation building, then in promoting economic development, and later in building a multicultural society. On the other hand, concerns were raised about immigrants using Canada as a passage to the United States, then about immigration undermining the position of labour, and often about the different "stock of people" that prompt a broadening of the very definition of who we are as a society.

While government policy has attempted to steer a path, sometimes rather hesitantly, between these conflicting considerations, there has also been a sense that government does not completely control the process. When agriculturalists were sought to settle the West, many in fact became unskilled labourers in Canada's early industrial development. When specialized skills were sought to fuel the urban-industrial expansion of the postwar era, many sponsored immigrants arrived as unskilled labourers (McInnis 1980). It was widely reported in the mid-1950s that for every Italian admitted into Canada, another forty-nine gained legitimate access through sponsorship (Hawkins 1972, 51).

While the points system introduced in 1967 helps in selecting persons who can more easily integrate, it does not necessarily align those arriving with the existing opportunities in Canada. On the refugee side, controlling arrivals has become complex when large numbers make refugee claims from within the country, straining the refugee boards that are seeking to determine which claims are legitimate. Though Canada is geographically removed from the areas of the world that generate refugees, the policies permitting refugees to become permanent immigrants, combined with a humanitarian attitude towards refugees, make Canada an attractive destination for refugees, both political and economic.

These wide-ranging policy considerations can lead politicians, interest groups, and the public to conclude too readily that immigration is either the cause of, or the solution to, our problems, without sufficiently recognizing that there may be both positives and negatives, along with conflicts of interest. The broad policy questions at any one point in time are: (1) what should be the level of immigration? (2) what should be the composition of the immigrant stream? and (3) how is the integration of immigrants to be achieved?

Now that we have placed migration in a historical, theoretical, and policy context, the chapter seeks to identify phases of Canadian immigration, then focus on consequences, including demographic, social, economic, and cultural impacts. But first, it is useful to have an overview of the population of Canada.

The Population of Canada

It is essentially impossible to estimate the pre-contact Aboriginal population of the area now known as Canada. Mooney (1928) had proposed the figure of 200,000, while physical anthropologist Ubelaker (1976) arrived at the figure of 270,000. Returning to earlier estimates, and making adjustments for the most serious omissions, historical demographer Charbonneau (1984) proposed the figure of 300,000, a figure that suggests two important demographic observations. First, it took almost two centuries, that is, from 1608 to about 1790, for the European-origin population to reach a comparable figure. Second, the European arrivals clearly spelt disaster for the original populations of the land, which declined to just over 100,000 according to the estimates for 1871–1910 (Kerr and Beaujot 2010). The Métis rebellions, in 1869–70 in Manitoba and 1885 in Saskatchewan, are further evidence of the conflicts with the original populations.

Counting only the Maritimes, Ontario, and Quebec, the 1801 population of Canada is estimated at 332,500 persons (McInnis 2000, 373). The 1901 census, which includes all but Newfoundland, gives us the figure of 5,278,000, while the estimate for 2011 is 34.5 million. This sixfold increase, in the past 110 years, is much larger than the increase of the world population, which has seen a four-fold growth.

There are other important changes to the population of Canada, including the high growth of the Western provinces over the period 1871–1921. As late as 1931, over half of the population lived in rural areas, while in 2006 the metropolitan areas comprise 68 per cent of the population.

In terms of ethnic and language composition, it is estimated that in about 1805 the English population became larger than the French, while in 2006, some 16% were classified as visible minorities, defined as neither white nor Aboriginal. With larger numbers identifying with their Aboriginal origins, and intermarriage, 3.8% of the 2006 population, or 1,173,000 persons, declared an Aboriginal identity, including 256,365 persons who could speak an Aboriginal language. In terms of the official languages, 67.6% of the total Canadian population could speak English only, 13.3% French only, 17.4% both, and 1.7% neither.

Phases of Canadian Immigration

If one pays attention especially to changing historical contexts, the following phases of Canadian immigration can be identified: New France (1608–1760), British colony (1760–1860), net outmigration (1860–96), first wave (1897–1913), interlude (1914–45), postwar European arrivals (1946–61), diversification (1962–88), and sustained high levels (1989–present). While these demarcations are somewhat arbitrary, they pay attention to the numbers and characteristics of immigrants, places of origin and destination, and the policy context.

New France, 1608–1760

While there were previous arrivals from Europe, the first permanent settlement was at Quebec in 1608. During the period of New France, until 1760, it is estimated that at least 25,000 immigrants had spent at least one winter in the new colony, with 14,000 settling permanently, and 10,000 marrying and having descendants in the colony (Charbonneau et al. 2000, 99). While the numbers were small, the migration from France managed in effect to establish a French-speaking nation in the Americas that would continue for centuries to come.

With more favourable health conditions, natural increase soon played a larger role than net migration in building a population which numbered 70,000 in 1760. It is estimated that the British conquest brought the departure of 2000 people, including a third of the nobility (ibid., 131). Another major movement affected by the hostilities of the Seven Years' War was the deportation of some 6000 Acadians in 1755 from what is now New Brunswick, mostly to the American colonies (Beaujot and McQuillan 1982, 18).

Compared to the 70,000 in Canada, the 1760 white population of the United States is estimated at 1,267,800 (Gemery 2000, 150). That is, the then population of the United States was 18.1 times that of Canada. With the British conquest, and the much larger population in New England, it would have been hard to imagine that the French would have persisted as a significant population and language group in North America.

British Colony, 1760–1860

The British conquest in 1763 brought a stop to the immigration from France, which had never been very strong, and arrivals were now from the British Isles. These arrivals were not very numerous at first, with the number of English in Quebec increasing from 500 in 1765 to some 10,000 in 1791 (Beaujot and McQuillan 1982, 12–14). The American War of Independence brought the arrival of some 40,000 United Empire Loyalists, most arriving in 1784 (McInnis 2000, 375).

The arrivals from Britain increased after the War of 1812 and the return to peace in both Europe and North America in 1815. This movement was aided by both private interests and public authorities. The arrivals from the British Isles increased further in the 1830s, due in part to major disease epidemics, and in the 1840s, with the Irish potato famine (McInnis 2000, 378–88). However, most of the migrants from the British Isles went to the New England colonies. In addition, considerable numbers of the persons who came to Canada moved on to the faster developing New England colonies, which also attracted some of the native-born population of French descent. The emigration to New

England of the population of French descent had gained momentum in the 1830s, with some 40,000 departures over the decade, reaching 190,000 in the decade of the 1850s (Beaujot and McQuillan, 1982, 15–16). While there were large numbers of departures, and much uncertainty, the balance in total migration was positive. McInnis (2000, 387) estimates a total net immigration of 487,000 for 1821–61, which would have contributed 20 per cent of the population increase over the period (see also. While arrivals from the British Isles were the largest component, there were also significant numbers of eastern European, southern European, and Jewish immigrants (Thornton and Gauvreau 2010).

By 1860, the figures for the total population are 31,443,000 in US and 3,230,000 for Canada (Haines 2000, 306). That is, relative to the Canadian population of European origin, that of the United States was 18.1 times higher in 1760, while the total population was 9.7 times higher than that of Canada in 1860.

Net Outmigration: 1860–1896

While the estimates remain uncertain, there is agreement that the next four decades after 1860 involved net outmigration from Canada. McInnis (2000, 422) estimates a total immigration of 892,000 and emigration of 1,891,000, for a net loss of 999,000. While Canada is known as a county of immigration, the four decades from 1861 to 1901 had net outmigration (see also Beaujot and McQuillan 1982, 83). For the period 1861–1911, Lavoie (1972, 39, 70) puts the estimate of total emigration at 1.8 million persons.

The earlier industrialization of the American economy offered employment prospects that attracted both recent immigrants to Canada and persons born in Canada. In addition, dry-farming techniques suitable for the colder climate of Canada's west were not developed until the 1880s. The period surrounding Confederation was a time of depression in international trade, which undermined the markets for Canadian staple products. By 1900 the population of Canada was 5,301,000, while that of the United States was 75,994,000, or 14.3 times higher.

The net emigration from Canada was in the context of considerable efforts to enhance immigration. In 1868, one year after Confederation, the Free Grants and Homestead Act sought to increase immigration, especially to the Canadian west. In subsequent years, numerous efforts were made to encourage agriculturalists to immigrate to Canada, including aggressive recruitment in the United Kingdom and Europe.

The government entered into various agreements, especially with the railroad companies, for the recruitment, selection, transportation, and establishment of potential agriculturalists. In addition, mining, lumber, and especially railway interests desperately required sturdy labourers willing to accept difficult working conditions and prepared to move to areas where workers were needed. In effect, the period of the mid-1880s to the First World War involved a deliberate use of immigration as an instrument of industrial development and nation building, including the settlement of the wheat-growing prairies.

In other regards, policy attempted to restrict immigration, and it soon became clear that not all prospective immigrants would be considered suitable. In one of the government's earliest pieces of legislation, re-strictions were placed on immigrants through the prohibition, among other things, of "the landing of pauper or destitute immigrants in all parts of Canada, until such sums of money as may be found necessary are provided and paid into the hands of one of the Canadian immigra-tion agents" (Beaujot and McQuillan 1982, 80).

The 1885 Chinese Immigration Act imposed a "head tax" on prospec-tive Chinese immigrants. At around the same time, the United States, Canada, and Australia all decided that "the Chinese were unassimila-ble, that they were a positive hindrance to the process of nation-build-ing, and that with few exceptions their immigration should be stopped completely" (Rao et al. 1984, 15, citing Price 1974, 275). This act was up-dated several times to restrict the arrival of Chinese workers after the railroads had been built, and was only set aside in 1947.

First Wave of Post-Confederation Immigration, 1897–1913

While the net numbers were negative for the decade 1891–1901, in ef-fect, the turnaround came in 1897, with the numbers of immigrants climbing from 17,000 in 1896 to 400,000 in 1913. The years 1911–13 had record numbers that have never since been surpassed. While depar-tures remained important, the gains of the decade 1901–11 more than balanced the net loss of the four previous decades. This followed the improved attractiveness of the Canadian west and the onset of indus-trialization. Immigrants from the British Isles continued to be the larg-est stream, but there were others not only from western and northern Europe, but also from southern, central and eastern Europe. The settle-ment of the Prairie provinces brought a majority whose ethnic origins were neither British nor French. Specific rural areas and towns of the

Prairies tended to attract people of a specific origin who established churches and community institutions along ethnic lines.

The appointment of Clifford Sifton as minister of the interior in 1896 had brought much energy to the immigration portfolio. His goal was to promote the arrival of farmers and farm labourers. However, there were also policies that attempted to restrict immigration. In 1907 and 1908 measures were taken to limit immigration from Japan and India. The Immigration Acts of 1906 and 1910 placed diseased persons as well as those advocating violent political change on the restricted categories. The 1910 act allowed the government to introduce regulations on the volume, ethnic origin, and occupational composition of the immigrant flow.

Interlude, 1914–1945

The onset of the First World War interrupted this period of globalization and brought this wave of immigration to an abrupt end. While immigration picked up somewhat in the 1920s, the depression of the 1930s and the period of the Second World War make the whole period 1914–45 somewhat of an "interlude" in immigration. The 1930s saw once again more departures than arrivals. Annual arrivals were under 20,000 for the period 1933–44. The places of origin were similar to that of the previous period, with the British being by far the largest, followed by the German and Austrian, Scandinavian, and Ukrainian.

In terms of policy, the 1922 Empire Settlement Act offered assistance in settlement to British subjects. The 1925 railway agreement was especially conducive to the arrival of Central Europeans. There were also exclusions. Amendments to the Immigration Act in 1919 made it possible for non-Canadian strike leaders to be deported, and the prohibited classes were extended to include alcoholics, conspirators, and illiterates (Manpower and Immigration Canada 1974, 12). These amendments were mostly aimed at excluding persons who had been "enemy aliens," but there were also provisions to exclude Doukhobors, Mennonites, and Hutterites on the grounds that their "peculiar customs, habits, modes of life and methods of holding property" made them unlikely "to become readily assimilated" (as cited in Simmons 2010, 56).

While some restrictions were lifted in the 1920s, in 1933 various categories of immigration were deleted, and even British subjects were discouraged (Corbett 1957, 7). The act was used in the 1930s to deport persons belonging to the Communist Party of Canada or other persons who had run into trouble with the law, often simply accused of being "public charges" (Avery 1979, 115). The period of the Second World War was also a time of restrictions. Canada did not play a role in admitting refugees fleeing from Nazi Germany. In 1939, the *St Louis*, an ocean liner carrying 907 desperate German Jews, was refused entry into Canada and was forced to return to Europe (Abella and Troper 1982).

In general, the period 1867–1945 can be seen as involving both the encouragement of immigration and attempts to restrict its flow. Encouragement was strongest in times of economic growth, particularly in 1896–1913 and in the 1920s, while restrictions were strongest in the periods of war and the 1930s. Encouragements tended to focus on British and northern European immigrants, while non-white arrivals were severely restricted. In the 1920s, there was active opposition to the admission of Ukrainians and others from eastern Europe on the grounds that this would lead to the balkanization of the country (Simmons 2010, 56). At the same time, immigrants from Britain were offered inexpensive fares for crossing the Atlantic.

Postwar European Immigration, 1946–1961

The period since 1946 can be thought of as a second wave of post-Confederation immigration. While annual arrivals fluctuated considerably, from a low of 64,000 in 1947 to a high of 282,000 in 1957, the total arrivals between 1941 and 1961 amount to 2.1 million. Although the rate of immigration compared with the total size of the Canadian population was lower than in the period 1897–1913, and while no single postwar year saw the arrival of as many as had come in each of the years from 1911 to 1913, the net migration of 1.25 million persons from 1941–61 was higher than the comparable figure of 1.12 million net migrants for the period 1901–21 (see table 5.1).

On a year-to-year basis, historical fluctuations in immigration levels followed the path of events both inside and outside of the country. There was a spurt right after the war with the arrival of war brides and refugees. After new regulations were in place and the Department of Citizenship and Immigration was established in 1950, immigration was high for the rest of the decade. The high point in 1956–7 reflects the entry of British subjects escaping the Suez crisis and refugees from the Hungarian revolt. The dip in 1961 coincided with a downturn in the economy.

Table 5.1 Population growth and components of growth, 1821–2011, Canada

Period	Pop. at the end of period	Total Pop. growth	Births	Deaths	Immigrants	Emigrants	Net migration / total growth	Annual immigrants per 100 population	Net migration per 100 births
(Thousands)									
1821	722								
1821–31	1,076	354	–	–	147	41	0.30	1.64	–
1831–41	1,630	554	–	–	211	27	0.33	1.56	–
1841–51	2,523	737	–	–	242	131	0.15	1.17	–
1851–61	3,230	793	1,281	670	352	170	0.23	1.22	14.2
1861–71	3,689	459	1,370	760	260	410	-0.33	0.75	-10.9
1871–81	4,325	636	1,480	790	350	404	-0.08	0.87	-3.6
1881–91	4,833	508	1,524	870	680	826	-0.29	1.49	-9.6
1891–01	5,371	538	1,548	880	250	380	-0.24	0.49	-8.4
1901–11	7,207	1,836	1,925	900	1,550	740	0.44	2.46	42.1
1911–21	8,788	1,581	2,340	1,070	1,400	1,089	0.20	1.75	13.3
1921–31	10,377	1,589	2,415	1,055	1,200	970	0.14	1.25	9.5
1931–41	11,507	1,130	2,294	1,072	149	241	-0.08	0.14	-4.0
1941–51	13,648	2,141	3,186	1,214	548	379	0.08	0.44	5.3
1951–56	16,081	2,433	2,106	633	783	185	0.25	1.05	28.4

(continued)

Table 5.1 (continued)

Period	Pop. at the end of period	Total Pop. growth	Births	Deaths	Immigrants	Emigrants	Net migration / total growth	Annual immigrants per 100 population	Net migration per 100 births
(Thousands)									
1956–61	18,238	2,157	2,362	687	760	278	0.22	0.89	20.4
1961–66	20,015	1,777	2,249	731	539	280	0.15	0.56	11.5
1966–71	21,568	1,553	1,856	766	890	427	0.30	0.86	24.9
1971–76	23,450	1,488	1,760	824	1,053	358	0.47	0.93	39.5
1976–81	24,820	1,371	1,820	843	771	278	0.36	0.64	27.1
1981–86	26,101	1,281	1,872	885	678	278	0.31	0.53	21.4
1986–91	28,031	1,930	1,933	946	1,164	213	0.49	0.86	49.2
1991–96	29,611	1,580	1,936	1,024	1,118	338	0.49	0.78	40.3
1996–01	31,021	1,410	1,705	1,089	1,217	376	0.60	0.80	49.3
2001–06	32,576	1,557	1,682	1,129	1,194	203	0.64	0.75	58.9
2006–11	34,484	1,908	1,872	1,196	1,263	259	0.60	0.75	53.6

Sources: 1821–41: McInnis (2000, 387)

1851–2001: Statistics Canada: http://www.statcan.gc.ca/tables-tableaux/sum-som/l01/cst01/demo03-eng.htm

2001–2006: Statistics Canada 2009, tables 2.1, 3.1

2006–11: Statistics Canada 2012, CANSIM Table 051.004. The total includes net returning emigrants and net non-permanent residents.

In policy terms, the end of the Second World War brought considerable uncertainty regarding the appropriate direction for future immigration. In 1944, the Quebec legislative assembly had indicated its opposition to mass immigration. Throughout the country, many argued that priorities should concentrate on the integration of returning soldiers. Others were concerned that Canada might return to the economic situation of the 1930s, for which immigration would be inappropriate. On the other hand, arguments were made that Canada could raise its international stature by helping to rescue persons displaced by the war in Europe (Angus 1946). In addition, a report to the deputy minister responsible for immigration concluded that a larger population made sense from an economic point of view (Timlin 1951).

In 1947, then prime minister Mackenzie King set out the government's policy on immigration in a frequently quoted statement that involved a careful compromise between these divergent concerns. King called for immigration as a support for higher population growth, but cautioned that such immigration should not be in excess of the number that could be advantageously absorbed. While he recognized the obligation to humanity to help those in distress, he clearly indicated that he would not support a massive arrival that would alter the "character of our population." The "character of our population" could mean various things, but it obviously included a desire to continue receiving immigrants mainly from the traditional sources. An important administrative procedure for admissions at this time was the widening of eligibility for "sponsored relatives." This was an interesting political solution, since those who had argued for restricted entries could hardly oppose the arrival of relatives. This also assured that immigrants would largely be from the traditional, "preferred" sources – those who already had relatives in Canada. At the same time, gone was the earlier objective of bringing agriculturalists.

This 1947 statement by Mackenzie King is an important point of demarcation, including making reference to the independent and family classes of immigrants. Immigration was to serve economic development, build the labour force, strengthen demographic resources, and it was also a humanitarian matter. It is noteworthy that his priority not to change the basic "character of our population" did not generate any debate in the House of Commons.

The 1953 Immigration Act allowed the government to prohibit the entry of immigrants for a variety of reasons, including nationality, ethnic group, and "peculiar customs, habits, modes of life or methods of holding property." Preference was given to persons of British birth, together with those from France and the United States. Second preference went to persons from western European countries – if they had the required economic qualifications. Persons from other countries could not enter unless sponsored by a close relative. A small exception involved an arrangement, in force between 1951 and 1962, that allowed for selected arrivals from Asian Commonwealth countries (Hawkins 1972, 99). However, very low limits were set: a combined total of three hundred people per year from India, Pakistan, and Sri Lanka.

Diversification of Origins, 1962–1988

In his chapter "Immigration and Nation-Building," Simmons (2010, 54) proposes that the period 1867–1960 can be entitled "a European nation in the Americas." In the early 1960s, there were rising concerns regarding discrimination on the basis of racial origins. In 1962 the national-origin restrictions to immigration were officially lifted. In 1967 a "points system" for the selection of independent immigrants was established. This reinforced the non-discriminatory aspects of immigration policy by clearly outlining the "education, training, skills and other special qualifications" under which immigrants were to be selected. The policy of multiculturalism, promulgated in 1971, underlined an open attitude to the arrival of immigrants from various parts of the world.

There have also been important shifts in the government attitude to immigration. For instance, the 1966 white paper was very positive towards immigration: "Without a substantial continuing flow of immigrants, it is doubtful that we could sustain the higher rate of economic growth and the associated cultural development which are essential to the maintenance and development of our national identity" (cited in Taylor 1987, 3). Just eight years later, the 1974 green paper was much more reserved: "When all the arguments are sifted, it would probably be a not unfair assessment of our understanding of the economic consequences of higher against lower population growth rates ... to conclude that the evidence in favour of higher rates is uncertain" (Manpower and Immigration Canada 1974, 6).

Immigration policy was subjected to a thorough review in the period from 1973 to 1975, culminating in the 1976 Immigration Act (ibid.). The main change introduced by the new act was the introduction of a target level for immigration, to be set by the minister responsible for immigration. This level is to be determined after consultation with the provinces

concerning regional demographic needs and labour market considerations, and after consultation with such other persons, organizations,
and institutions as the minister deems appropriate. It is an indication
of the importance placed on immigration that the act requires an annual "Statement to Parliament" on the government's goals with respect
to immigration. The 1976 act also incorporated the 1951 UN Convention on Refugees. Canada had signed the convention in 1969 and was
already obligated to protect people arriving who were found to be refugees, but at the time few were actually arriving, reaching some 500 per
year by 1976.

The 1976 act in many regards involved continuity in policy, explicitly
affirming the fundamental objectives of Canadian immigration laws,
including family reunification, non-discrimination, concerns for refugees, and the promotion of Canada's demographic, economic, and cultural goals. In effect, immigration has been administered through three
"classes." The independent class is admitted through the points system;
the family class gains admission based on a close family connection; the
refugee class is administered on the basis of humanitarian concerns.

On an annual basis, the immigrant arrivals increased in the latter half
of the 1960s after the establishment of the Department of Manpower
and Immigration and the strong economic growth of the period. The
peak in 1974 is somewhat artificial since it results from an amnesty program whereby persons in the country without landed immigration status were admitted even if they did not meet the criteria. The dip in
1983–5 coincided with a downturn in the economy. The increase of the
period 1986–90 followed on a deliberate program of "moderate controlled growth" in immigration levels. The total arrivals for the period
1961–86 amount to 3.9 million, or an average of 157,000 per year – about
0.7 immigrants per 100 population.

Sustained High Immigration, 1989–present

There are several bases through which to consider 1989 as the beginning of a new era in immigration. First, the 1988 Canada–United
States Trade Agreement (CUSTA) and the 1992 North American Free
Trade Agreement (NAFTA) place Canada in a new relationship with
the United States and Mexico, including a more open and competitive
economy. Second, as seen in the early 1990s, there is no longer a reduction of immigrants when unemployment is high. Up to and including
the economic recession of the early 1980s, there had been reductions in

Figure 5.1 Permanent resident admissions by immigration class, Canada, 1980–2011

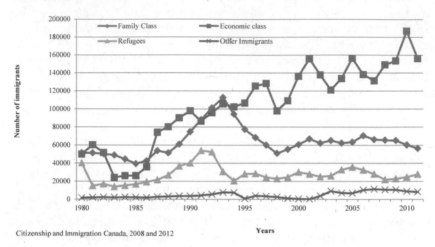

Citizenship and Immigration Canada, 2008 and 2012

Source 1 covers period before 1987
Source 2 covers period from 1987–2011
Source: Citizenship and Immigration Canada (2008): Facts and Figures, http://www.cic.gc/english/resources/statistics/facts2008/permanent/01.asp
Citizenship and Immigration Canada (2012): Facts and Figures, http://www.cic.gc.ca/english/resources/statistics/facts2011/permanent/02.asp. retrieve on October 19, 2012

immigrant levels during difficult economic times (Veugelers and Klassen 1994). Third, the immigrant arrivals have been sustained at levels that are high compared to all historical periods except 1910–13. Fourth, there is increasing emphasis on the economic class of immigrants, and also on the admission of temporary workers. In the period since 2004, the number of temporary residents has increased substantially, including foreign workers, foreign students, and refugee claimants, all of whom have access to temporary work permits.

In terms of numbers, the period before the First World War had only the four consecutive years 1910–13 with levels above 200,000, while all but two of the twenty-two years between 1990 and 2011 have seen these levels. The total numbers over the period 1986–2011 amount to 5.9 million, or an average annual arrival of 237,000, representing 0.8 immigrants per 100 population. This has also been a period during which immigration has come to constitute a significantly larger proportion of population growth. While in the period 1951–91 net migration accounted for about a quarter of population growth, it accounted for more than 60 per cent of growth in the period 1996–2011.

Immigration policies have sought to attract highly skilled immigrants, but there are also migrant worker programs bringing increasing numbers of temporary workers for unskilled work and for short-term skilled work. In particular, there is continued emphasis on the business class and independent immigrants, while the family and refugee classes have remained stable (figure 5.1). The changes in the 1990s have focused on cost recovery in the administration of immigrant arrivals, more refined selection within each class, and a higher proportion of the independent class. The adaptations that have been made to the points system in the early part of the new century have focused less on specific occupational qualifications, with more emphasis on education, skilled trades, work experience, and knowledge of the official languages, in attempts to bring workers who have transferrable skills. A big change has been a larger involvement of the provinces in the selection of immigrants and in the arrival of temporary workers.

Immigration and Population: Growth, Distribution, and Age Structure

Immigration has played a significant role in Canadian population growth. For the period 1901–2011 net migration accounted for 32% of population growth. The contribution was high during 1901–11, at 44% of total growth, and in 1996–2011, at 60% of growth (table 5.1). As a percentage of the receiving population, the immigrants of a given year have comprised as much as 2.46% in the period 1901–11, compared to 0.59 for the period 1976–86.

While the United States was 14.3 times the size of Canada in 1900, the relative size of Canada increased over the following century (table 5.2). Thus, by 2010, the United States was 11.0 times the size of Canada. The total foreign-born in a country at a given time provides another indicator of the demographic impact of immigration. For the world as a whole, the population living in a country other than their country of birth represents only 3.1% of the 2010 world population. In Europe 9.5% of the population is foreign born, compared to 13.5% in United States, 21.3% in Canada, and 21.9% in Australia (United Nations, Population Division, 2009).

Table 5.2 Populations of Canada and United States of America, 1760–2010

Date	Canada	United States	United States/ Canada
		(Thousands)	
1760*	70	1,268	18.1
1790*	260	3,172	12.2
1860	3,230	31,443	9.7
1870	3,625	39,819	11.0
1880	4,255	50,156	11.8
1890	4,779	62,948	13.2
1900	5,301	75,994	14.3
1910	6,988	91,972	13.2
1920	8,556	106,711	12.5
1930	10,208	122,755	12.0
1940	11,381	131,669	11.6
1950	13,712	150,697	11.0
1960	17,870	179,823	10.1
1970	21,297	203,302	9.5
1980	24,516	226,546	9.2
1990	27,697	254,865	9.0
2000	30,689	287,842	˙9.3
2010	34,017	310,384	11.0

* White population only.
Sources: United States – 1760: Gemery 2000, table 5.1; 1790–1990: Haines 2000, table 8.1; 1990–2010: United Nations, Population Division, 2011
Canada – 1760–1860: Beaujot and McQuillan 1982, 5, 13; 1870–1970: Statistics Canada 1985, 28–9; 1980–2000: Statistics Canada, Annual demographic statistics, 2005, 21; 2010: United Nations, Population Division, 2011

Another way to appreciate the impact of immigration is to compare immigrants to births as the two forms of additions to population. As seen in table 5.1, the net immigration per 100 births was in the range of 33 to 36 net immigrants per 100 births in the period 1971–91, but it has since risen to 54 in the 2006–11 period. This is higher than the figures for

Figure 5.2 Percent foreign born, Canada and provinces, 2006

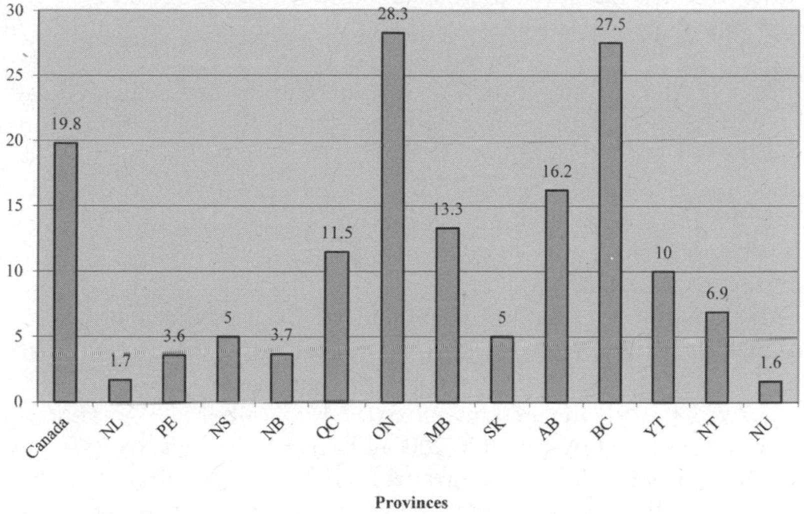

Provinces

Source: Statistics Canada, 2007: http://www12.statcan.gc.ca/census-recensement/
2006/dp-pd/hlt/97-557/T403-eng.cfm?SR=1

the United States, at 23, and Australia, at 37 net migrants per 100 births in 2005–10 (United Nations, Population Division, 2009).

Within Canada, immigration has played a significant role in the distribution of population. The first wave of immigration, in 1897–1913, brought especially a growth of the Prairie provinces and British Columbia, while postwar immigration has made for a relative growth of the metropolitan areas, especially those west of Quebec, plus Montreal. In the 1980s and 1990s the three largest metropolitan areas, Toronto, Vancouver, and Montreal, have received a high proportion of immigrants, with arrivals of the early new century also going to other metropolitan areas, especially Calgary and Edmonton. In effect, immigration has accentuated the uneven distribution of population. While the foreign-born amount to 19.8% of the 2006 population of Canada, this varies considerably by province, with the highest proportions being in Ontario and British Columbia, at 28%, compared to 12% for Quebec and for the Atlantic provinces in the range of 2% to 5% (figure 5.2).

While immigration has a considerable impact on the size and distribution of the population, there is less impact on the age structure. Immigrants at arrival are on average slightly younger than the receiving population, but they are spread out in ages and thus there is not a large impact on the age structure. For instance, it has been calculated that the immigration of the period 1951–2001 made the population younger only by 0.8 years (Denton et al. 2001). This can also be seen in population projections, where the 135,000 more immigrants in the high as compared to the low assumption produces a population which is 9 per cent larger in size, but only 0.8 years younger in average age by 2036 (Statistics Canada 2010a).

The foreign-born are of course older than the Canadian-born, because all births to the foreign-born are counted among the Canadian-born. Looking only at the labour force, the median age of the Canadian-born is 43.7 years, while the median age of the foreign-born is 47.6 years, and the immigrants who arrived in 2000–4 had an average age of 37.8 years (table 5.3). That is, while immigrants increase the size of the population and of the labour force, there is not a large impact on the age structure of the labour force.

Sociocultural and Socio-economic Impact of Immigration

Immigration clearly has an impact on the ethnic composition of the population. By continents of origin, the arrivals of 1946–61 were 90.0% from Europe and 7.5% from United States or Australia, but by 2006–11 the largest component were from Asia and Pacific (48.1%), followed by Africa and the Middle East at 22.0%, Europe and the United States at 19.4%, and South America, with 10.5% (figure 5.3). The major change occurred in the 1960s and 1970s, with Asia displacing Europe as the major source area. This change has made for a relative growth of the visible-minority or non-white and non-Aboriginal population. When this population was first measured in 1981, the visible minority amounted to 4.7% of the population, but by 2006 it represented 16.2% of the population (Statistics Canada, 2010b). Due essentially to immigration, this proportion is expected to increase to some 30% of the 2031 population. In comparison, at the time of the 1961 census, only 2.0% of ethnic origins were neither European nor Aboriginal, including 0.3% Chinese, 0.2% Japanese, 0.2% other Asian, 0.2% Black, and 1.2% "other and not stated."

Table 5.3 Measures of age structure, education, and labour force, by place of birth and immigration cohort, Canada, 2006

	Median age	Per cent 65+	Median age of labour force	Persons 25–64			Persons 45–54	
				Per cent employed	Per cent in labour force	Post-secondary and above	Index of income Males	Index of income Females
Canadian-born	36.9	11.4	43.7	76.2	81.0	58.9	1.00	1.00
All foreign-born	45.8	18.8	47.6	72.9	78.1	64.3	0.84	0.87
Before 1950	80.0	85.2	60.9	52.6	54.4	53.8	–	–
1950–4	73.0	69.9	58.4	62.1	64.6	58.0	1.46	1.18
1955–9	69.4	65.8	55.5	68.5	70.6	53.6	1.17	1.23
1960–4	65.2	51.9	52.9	65.5	68.0	49.7	1.19	1.11
1965–9	61.4	35.3	52.9	68.3	71.1	58.6	1.06	1.15
1970–4	56.6	20.0	52.5	73.8	77.0	61.7	1.02	0.99
1975–9	52.8	15.9	49.1	78.1	81.4	62.5	0.91	1.01
1980–4	49.0	16.3	46.0	78.3	82.5	58.9	0.87	0.92
1985–9	44.4	10.0	44.3	77.1	81.7	58.9	0.84	0.86
1990–4	41.6	10.2	42.5	74.4	79.5	59.5	0.72	0.74
1995–9	36.3	5.7	40.7	72.8	78.4	67.6	0.66	0.66
2000–4	32.0	3.5	37.8	67.9	75.1	74.5	0.53	0.50

Note: Index of income = average total income of a given group compared to Canadian-born.
Source: Public use microdata file, 2006 census

Figure 5.3 Continents of birth of immigrant arrivals, 1946–2011, Canada

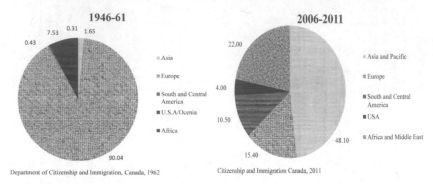

Source: 1946–61: Department of Citizenship and Immigration, Statistics Section Immigration, Ottawa 1962, p.25
2006–2011: Citizenship and Immigration Canada (2011)–http://www.cic.gc.ca/english/resources/statistics/facts2011/permanent/07.asp

More broadly, immigration makes for a more multicultural and pluralist society. In the first wave of immigration, this meant a population that was less dominated by French and British origins, especially in the west of Canada, and since the 1960s it has meant a population that is less European in origins, especially in the metropolitan areas of the country. Immigration has also brought a diversity of languages, with 20 per cent of the population having a mother tongue that is neither English nor French, but the official languages remain dominant, with only 1.7 per cent of the population being unable to converse in either English or French.

In socio-economic terms, the immigration of the postwar period has increased the relative level of education of the population. This was especially the case in the 1950s, when post-secondary education was poorly developed in Canada. The points system in the selection of immigrants in the economic class has furthered the selectivity. As seen in figure 5.1, the relative size of the economic class, where the points system applies, has increased since the mid-1980s. In the period 1996–2011, the family and refugee classes of immigrants have been relatively stable at some 65,000 and 25,000 arrivals per year respectively. In comparison, the economic class has increased from 125,000 to 155,000 and in 2011 this represented 63 per cent of arrivals.

At ages 25–64, 58.9% of the Canadian-born population has a post-secondary certificate, diploma, or degree, while 64.3% of the foreign-born have this certification (table 5.3). By immigration cohort, the proportion with post-secondary education was about 60% in the arrival cohort of 1970–94, but it has increased to 75% for the 2000–4 cohort.

In the postwar cohort of 1946–60, the 1961 census had found that their average incomes by age and sex were below that of the Canadian-born, but by 1971 most age-sex groups of this postwar arrival cohort had exceeded the average of the Canadian-born. This pattern of starting below average but coming to exceed the average Canadian-born income has applied to cohorts arriving until 1970–4 for men and 1975–9 for women, but later cohorts have not done so well. For instance, in the 2006 census, at ages 45–54, the average income of persons who had arrived in 1995–9 was only 66 per cent of this average for the Canadian-born of the same age and sex (table 5.3). The average income represents a marked contrast to the average level of education, with a high proportion of immigrants of the 1995–2004 cohort having post-secondary certification, but with the proportion in the labour force being lower than for the Canadian-born, and the average income significantly lower. For instance, in 1980, the low income (or poverty) rate of immigrants who had been in Canada for five years or less was 40 per cent higher than that of the Canadian-born, while in 2005 it was 2.7 times as high as that of the Canadian-born (Picot et al., 2009, 14; see also Picot and Sweetman 2012).

There is much research on the economic integration of immigrants, and particularly on the slower progress of the more recent cohorts. In "The Deteriorating Economic Welfare of Immigrants and Possible Causes," Picot and Sweetman (2005) observe that the conditions seem opportune to maximize the opportunity of immigrants: the economic class has become the largest category, a high proportion of immigrants have university degrees, Canada has an expanding knowledge-based economy, and there are public statements to the effect that immigrants are needed for economic reasons. Yet, there are declining entry-level earnings among immigrants, with a gap that has been increasing with successive cohorts, and the cohort of the late 1970s appearing to be the last to show signs of eliminating the earnings gap. Over the period 1980–90, the rates of low income increased for recent immigrants, while they went down for the Canadian-born, including lone parents.

In seeking to explain this deteriorating situation from cohort to cohort, Picot and Sweetman (2005) propose that perhaps a third of the decline would be a function of the changed characteristics of immigrants, including different source regions, rising level of education, fewer with English or French home language, and possibly a lower quality of education given the source regions. The next important factor would be the declining returns to foreign labour-market experience; this discounting of experience would affect older workers whose experience may be judged to be less relevant to the Canadian labour market. The third factor would be the declining labour-market outcomes of new entrants to the labour market, including competition with well-educated persons from the Canadian education system (see Picot 2008).

Another significant question is that of discrimination, given that a large proportion of immigrants can be identified as visible minorities. While discrimination is surely a factor, there are some results suggesting that the questions remain complex. For instance, in the 1981 census, the average total income, adjusting for age, was higher than that of the Canadian-born for male immigrants from Africa and South Asia, and for female immigrants from Africa and Southeast Asia, while the immigrants from southern Europe were below the average of the Canadian-born (Beaujot et al. 1988, 54). As another example, there has been a reduction of the proportion with low income, over cohorts, for immigrants from the United States and western Europe, but also for those from Southeast Asia, the Caribbean, and South and Central America (Picot and Sweetman 2005, 12). Conversely, there is an increase in the levels of low income over cohorts for immigrants from South Asia, East Asia, Western Asia, and Africa, but also from northern Europe, eastern, and southern Europe. That is, these comparative results by source regions do not map exactly with the proposition that the differences can be explained through discrimination towards visible minorities.

In an extensive study of the first four years in Canada, Schellenberg and Maheux (2007) find that the immigrants of 2000–1 remained largely optimistic regarding their decision to come to Canada, with 84% saying they would have made the same decision at the time of the third interview, four years after arrival. Asked about the most important reason for immigrating and for staying, 32% referred to quality of life, 20% the desire to be close to family and friends, 18% a positive future for their family, but only 4% gave employment-related reasons (ibid., 21). Asked what they disliked the most about Canada, 19% said there was nothing that they disliked, but 27% indicated the climate/physical environment, followed by 19% indicating lack of employment opportunities or poor economic conditions, and 7% "people's attitudes or cultural aspects" (5).

In a study of occupations where professional associations regulate entry of members into the occupation, it was found that only 24 per cent of persons who had studied abroad were in the occupation for which they had studied, compared to 62 per cent for the Canadian-born (Zietsma 2010). In terms of quality of employment, immigrants are found to earn less, have higher rates of involuntary part-time work, and be more often over-qualified compared to the Canadian-born (Gilmore 2009). On the other hand, immigrants from non-European origins who had arrived before age fifteen, as well as the second generation, compare favourably to the Canadian-born of the third generation in terms of education and occupational status (Boyd 2009). For the Canadian-born, the average earnings of visible minorities are found to be comparable to those of other Canadian-born when they are working in the public sector, but there are important gaps in the private sector, especially for Black men (Hou and Coulombe 2010).

Conclusion

The history of immigration indicates considerable shifts in trends, to the point that the lessons of one period do not easily apply to the next. From the early settlement of Canada to pre-Confederation, there was first the encouragement of French migration to New France, but the numbers were never very large, as France was often more concerned with populating other colonies whose economies were more dependent on larger populations. With British rule, the arrivals from the British Isles were supported, but the New England states had advantages that even attracted the native-born of French descent in Canada. The relative attractiveness of the United States continued into the late 1890s.

Since the early 1900s, Canada has managed to attract a stronger share of immigrants coming to the Americas. The first wave of post-Confederation immigrants, and the settlement of Western Canada, took place in a period of globalization that ended in 1914 with a world war. While there were a few years of economic growth and associated immigration in the 1920s, the whole period from 1914–45 can be described as an interlude in both globalization and immigrant arrivals. It is noteworthy that, while Canada is seen as a country of immigration, four of the eight decades between 1861 and 1941 had seen net emigration. In this context, it is not surprising that the population projections made after the 1941 census had assumed zero international migration (Charles et al. 1946).

The postwar period cautiously accepted more immigrants, with a strong interest not to change the "character" of the population. While there had been arrivals from China especially to help in railway construction, and the United Empire Loyalists included Black Americans, as did the underground railway before Emancipation, the whole period until 1961 can be described as an attempt to build a European nation in the Americas, first a French-speaking nation, then an English-speaking one, or at least one with European origins.

The lifting of racial criteria in immigration in 1962, formalized with the points system for admissions of the economic class in 1967, slowly brought a radical change in the source areas, with Asia displacing Europe as the highest region of origin, but including much diversity of origins from countries and regions around the world. The diversification continues in the most recent period since 1989, including immigration levels that are high in historical context. For instance, Citizenship and Immigration Canada (2009) lists 167 countries of origin that had sent immigrants to Canada in 2008.

There has been an interest to regulate arrivals, and to select those seen as best suited to evolving conditions. However, the selection does not always produce the intended results, since the actual economic activities of immigrants, once in Canada, often diverged considerably from their intended occupations (McInnis 1980). When agriculturalists on the Prairies were sought, many joined the unskilled labour force in the mines and factories of eastern Canada. Similarly, many chosen on the basis of their occupational skills have not managed to have their credentials recognized and have worked in other occupations.

In hindsight, it would appear that the postwar immigrants of 1946–61 benefited not only from the growing economy in which they arrived, but also from a previous period where immigration levels were low. This hiatus meant that the postwar immigrants were not competing with others who had arrived earlier. As of the mid-1970s, the economic conditions were not as strong, with higher unemployment, including periods of recession in the early 1980s and early 1990s. During the mid-1980s the levels were reduced to accommodate the high unemployment. But the period since 1989 has seen relatively high levels that continued through the recession and slow recovery of 1990–6. It may be that these levels of immigration are partly responsible for the increased difficulty of immigrants' economic integration, in spite of having high education. For instance, university-educated immigrants in Canada saw their entry wages decline relative to the domestic-born with university education, while in the United States the wages of new immigrants increased relative to the domestic-born over the period 1990–2000 (Bonikowska et al. 2011). These differences between Canada and the United States are partly due to the higher level of immigration in Canada. During the period 1990–2005, the total net immigration to Canada amounted to 8.9% of the 1990 population, compared to 7.6% in the United States (United Nations 2011). In addition, the share of new adult immigrants with university degrees increased in the 1990s from 25% to 47% in Canada, compared to an increase from 30% to 34% in the United States. Laplante and his colleagues (2011: 1) indicate a concern that "the current level of immigration cannot be sustained if the economic integration of immigrants remains an objective."

This period since 1989 can be qualified as neoliberal, where the focus is more on self-sufficiency and responsibility for one's own well-being, rather than on social policy support. It may be that open immigration is contradictory to a welfare state (Grubel, 2005). For instance, in Scandinavian countries that have a more extensive welfare state, policy seeks to enhance the labour-force participation of women, rather than relying on immigration. In a neoliberal and open economy, the large numbers of highly skilled immigrants serve the interest of employers, with more competition for jobs and the potential to take advantage of an over-skilled applicant pool. When the points system is not attracting the labour pool that is needed, the numbers of temporary migrants are increased, providing these workers with even fewer social-policy benefits. While this neoliberal approach with relatively high immigration serves the interests of employers, it is less clear that it serves the interests of immigrants themselves, let alone the Canadian educated youth who are also struggling to enter the labour force.

At the macro level, immigration clearly increases the size of the population, including the size of the labour force and that of the overall economy. However, in per capita terms, most authors conclude that immigration has a very small influence on average incomes (Sweetman 2008; Economic Council of Canada 1991). If one takes environmental questions into consideration, matters of size of the population and size of the economy may be judged rather differently.

International comparisons show that Canada has demographic advantages compared to other OECD countries. For instance, McDonald and Kippen (2001) find that Canada is well placed to have a continued growth of its labour force. Bongaarts (2004) finds that the Canadian public pension programs are more sustainable than those of some other comparable countries like Italy, France, and Germany.

All told, policy needs to balance a number of considerations, ranging from the functioning of a multicultural and pluralist society, including its humanitarian goals, to questions of discrimination and the economic integration of immigrants, and the functioning of a knowledge economy in a more open globalizing world. In effect, the question of "why Canada has immigration" needs continued assessment in research and political discussions.

REFERENCES

Abella, Irving, and Harold Troper. 1982. *None Is Too Many: Canada and the Jews of Europe, 1933–1948*. Toronto: Lester and Orpen Dennys.

Angus, H.F. 1946. "The Future of Immigration into Canada." *Canadian Journal of Economics and Political Science* 12 (3): 379–86. http://dx.doi.org/10.2307/137291.

Avery, Don. 1979. *Dangerous Foreigners: European Immigrant Workers and Labour Radicalism in Canada, 1896–1932*. Toronto: McClelland & Stewart.

Beaujot, Roderic, K.G. Basavarajappa, and R.B.P. Verma. 1988. *Income of Immigrants in Canada: A Census Data Analysis*. Ottawa: Statistics Canada, Cat. no. 91-527.

Beaujot, Roderic, and Kevin McQuillan. 1982. *Growth and Dualism: The Demographic Development of Canadian Society*. Toronto: Gage.

Bongaarts, John. 2004. "Population Aging and the Rising Cost of Public Pensions." *Population and Development Review* 30 (1): 1–23. http://dx.doi.org/10.1111/j.1728-4457.2004.00001.x.

Boyd, Monica. 2009. "Social Origins and the Educational and Occupational Achievements of the 1.5 and Second Generations." *Canadian Review of Sociology* 46 (4): 339–69. http://dx.doi.org/10.1111/j.1755-618X.2009.01218.x.

Castles, Stephen, and Mark Miller. 2009. *The Age of Migration: International Population Movements in the Modern World*. 4th ed. New York: Guilford Press. http://dx.doi.org/10.1080/10803920500434037.

Charbonneau, Hubert. 1984. "Trois siècles de dépopulation amérindienne." In *Les populations amérindienne et Inuit du Canada*, ed. L. Normandeau and V. Piché, 28–48. Montreal: Les presses de l'Université de Montréal.

Charbonneau, Hubert, Bertrand Desjardins, Jacques Légaré, and Hubert
    Denis. 2000. "The Population of the St. Lawrence Valley, 1608–1760." In *A
    Population History of North America*, ed. M.R. Haines and R.H. Steckel, 99–
    142. Cambridge: Cambridge University Press.
Charles, Enid, Nathan Keyfitz, and H. Roseborough. 1946. *The Future Popula-
    tion of Canada*. Ottawa: Dominion Bureau of Statistics, Bulletin no. FB4.
Citizenship and Immigration Canada. 2008. *Facts and Figures 2008: Permanent
    and Temporary Residents*. Ottawa: Citizenship and Immigration.
Citizenship and Immigration Canada. 2012. *Facts and Figures 2011: Permanent
    and Temporary Residents*. Ottawa: Citizenship and Immigration.
Coleman, David. 2006. "Immigration and Ethnic Change in Low-Fertility
    Countries: A Third Demographic Transition." *Population and Development
    Review* 32 (3): 401–46. http://dx.doi.org/10.1111/j.1728-4457.2006.00131.x.
Coleman, David. 2009. "Migration and Its Consequences in 21st Century Eu-
    rope." *Vienna Yearbook of Population Research* 2009:1–18.
Corbett, D.C. 1957. *Canada's Immigration Policy: A Critique*. Toronto: University
    of Toronto Press.
Denton, Frank T., Christine H. Feaver, and Byron G. Spencer. 2001. "Alterna-
    tive Pasts, Possible Futures: A 'What If' Study of the Effects of Fertility on
    the Canadian Population and Labour Force." Paper presented at the meet-
    ings of the Federation of Canadian Demographers, December, Ottawa.
Department of Citizenship and Immigration. 1962. *1961 Immigration Statistics*.
    Ottawa: Department of Citizenship and Immigration.
Economic Council of Canada. 1991. *Economic and Social Impacts of Immigration*
    Ottawa: Economic Council of Canada.
Gemery, Henry. 2000. "The White Population of the Colonial United States,
    1607–1790." In *A Population History of North America*, ed. M.R. Haines and
    R.H. Steckel, 143–90. Cambridge: Cambridge University Press.
Gilmore, Jason. 2009. "The 2008 Canadian Immigrant Labour Market: Analy-
    sis of Quality Of Employment." Statistics Canada Immigrant Labour Force
    Analysis Series no. 1.
Goldscheider, Calvin. 1971. *Population, Modernization and Social Structure*. Bos-
    ton: Little, Brown.
Grubel, Herbert. 2005. *Immigration and the Welfare State in Canada: Growing
    Conflicts, Constructive Solutions*. Vancouver: The Fraser Institute, Public Pol-
    icy Series no. 84.
Haines, Michael R. 2000. "The White Population of the United States, 1790–
    1920." In *A Population History of North America*, ed. M.R. Haines and R.H.
    Steckel, 305–69. Cambridge: Cambridge University Press.

Hawkins, Freda. 1972. *Canada and Immigration: Public Policy and Public Concern.* Montreal, Kingston: McGill-Queen's University Press.

Hou, Feng, and Simon Coulombe. 2010. "Earnings Gaps for Canadian-born Visibile Minorities in the Public and Private Sectors." *Canadian Public Policy* 36 (1): 29–43. http://dx.doi.org/10.3138/cpp.36.1.29.

Kerr, Don, and Roderic Beaujot. 2010. "Aboriginal Demography." In *Visions of the Heart: Canadian Aboriginal Issues*, 3rd ed., ed. D. Long and O.P. Dickason. Toronto: Oxford University Press.

Laplante, Benoît, Jean-Dominique Morency, and Maria Constanza Street. 2011. "Policy and Fertility: An Empirical Study of Childbearing Behavior in Canada." Manuscript.

Lavoie, Yolande. 1972. *L'Émigration des Canadiens aux États-Unis avant 1930.* Montreal: Presses de l'Université de Montréal.

Manpower and Immigration Canada. 1974. *Immigration Policy Perspectives.* Ottawa: Information Canada.

Massey, Douglas S., Joaquin Arango, Graeme Hugo, Ali Kouaouci, Adela Pellegrino, and J. Edward Taylor. 1994. "An Evaluation of International Migration Theory: The North American Case." *Population and Development Review* 20 (4): 699–751. http://dx.doi.org/10.2307/2137660.

McDonald, Peter, and Rebecca Kippen. 2001. "Labor Supply Prospects in 16 Developed Countries: 2000–2050." *Population and Development Review* 27 (1): 1–32. http://dx.doi.org/10.1111/j.1728-4457.2001.00001.x.

McInnis, Marvin. 1980. "A Functional View of Canadian Immigration." Paper presented at the Annual Meetings of the Population Association of America, April, Denver.

McInnis, Marvin. 2000. "The Population of Canada in the Nineteenth Century." In *A Population History of North America*, ed. M.R. Haines and R.H. Steckel, 371–432. Cambridge: Cambridge University Press.

McNeill, William. 1984. "Human Migration in Historical Perspective." *Population and Development Review* 10 (1): 1–18. http://dx.doi.org/10.2307/1973159.

Mooney, J. 1928. "The Aboriginal Population of America North of Mexico." *Smithsonian Miscellaneous Collections* (Washington) 80:1–40.

Picot, Garnett. 2008. "Immigrant Economic and Social Outcomes in Canada: Research and Data Development at Statistics Canada." Statistics Canada Analytical Studies Branch, Research Paper Series no. 319.

Picot, Garnet, Yuqian Lu, and Feng Hou. 2009. "Immigrant Low-Income Rates: The Role of Market Income and Government Transfers." *Perspectives on Labour and Income*, December: 13–27.

Picot, Garnett, and Arthur Sweetman. 2005. "The Deteriorating Economic Welfare of Immigrants and Possible Cuases: Update 2005." Statistics Canada Analytical Studies Branch, Research Paper Series no. 262.

Pocot, Garnett, and Arthur Sweetman. 2012. *Making It in Canada: Immigration Outcomes and Policies*. Ottawa: Institute for Research in Public Policy, Study no. 29.

Price, C.A. 1974. *The Great White Walls Are Built: Restrictive Immigration to North America and Australia*. Canberra: Australian Institute of International Affairs in association with Australian National University Press.

Rao, G. Lakshmana, Anthony H. Richmond, and Jerzy Zubrzycki. 1984. "Immigrants in Canada and Australia." In *Demographic Aspects and Education*, vol. 1. Downsview, ON: Institute for Behavioural Research, York University.

Schellenberg, Grant, and Hélène Maheux. 2007. *Immigrants' Perspectives on Their First Four Years in Canada: Highlights from Three Waves of the Longitudinal Survey of Immigrants to Canada*. Statistics Canada, Canadian Social Trends, special edition.

Simmons, Alan B. 2010. *Immigration and Canada: Global and Transnational Perspectives*. Toronto: Canadian Scholars' Press.

Statistics Canada. 1985. *Postcensal Annual Estimates of Population by Marital Status, Age, Sex and Components of Growth for Canada, Provinces and Territories*. Ottawa: Statistics Canada cat. no. 91-210.

Statistics Canada. 2005. *Annual Demographic Statistics 2005*. Ottawa: Statistics Canada cat. no. 91-213-XPB.

Statistics Canada. 2007. *Population by Immigration Status and Period of Immigration*. Ottawa: Statistics Canada cat. no. 97-557-XWE2006002.

Statistics Canada. 2008. *Canadian Demographics at a Glance*. Ottawa: Statistics Canada cat. no. 91-003-X.

Statistics Canada. 2009. *Annual Demographic Estimates: Canada, Provinces and Territories 2009*. Ottawa: Statistics Canada cat. no. 91-215-X.

Statistics Canada. 2010a. *Population Projections for Canada, Provinces and Territories 2009 to 2036*. Ottawa: Statistics Canada cat. no. 91-520-X.

Statistics Canada. 2010b. *Projections of the Diversity of the Canadian Population 2006 to 2031*. Ottawa: Statistics Canada cat. no. 91-551-X.

Statistics Canada. 2012. "Components of population growth, Canada, provinces and territories." Statistics Canada CANSIM table 051-0004.

Sweetman, Arthur. 2008. "The Other Economic Question: Immigration's Impact on the Economy." Paper presented at Metropolis CSPS webinar, December 2008.

Taylor, Christopher. 1987. *Demography and Immigration in Canada: Challenge and Opportunity*. Ottawa: Employment and Immigration Canada.

Thornton, Patricia, and Danielle Gauvreau. 2010. "A Geography of Encounter: Immigration and Cultural Diversity within Quebec, 1881–1911." Paper presented at the meetings of the Federation of Canadian Demographers, Montreal, 1–2 June.

Timlin, M.F. 1951. *Does Canada Need More People?* Toronto: Oxford University Press.

Ubelaker, D.H. 1976. "Prehistoric New World Population Size: Historical Review and Current Appraisal of North American Estimates." *American Journal of Physical Anthropology* 45 (3): 661–5. http://dx.doi.org/10.1002/ajpa.1330450332.

United Nations, Department of Economic and Social Affairs, Population Division. 2009. *Trends in International Migrant Stock: The 2008 Revision*. United Nations database: POP/DB/MIG/Stock/Rev.2008.

United Nations, Department of Economic and Social Affairs, Population Division. 2011. *World Population Prospects: The 2010 Revision*. United Nations database: www.un.org/esa/population.

Veugelers, John, and Thomas Klassen. 1994. "Continuity and Change in Canada's Unemployment-Immigration Linkage (1946–1993)." *Canadian Journal of Sociology* 19 (3): 351–77. http://dx.doi.org/10.2307/3340722. Medline:12320211.

Weiner, Myron. 1985. "International Migration and International Relations." *Population and Development Review* 11 (3): 441–57. http://dx.doi.org/10.2307/1973247.

Zelinsky, Wilbur. 1971. "The Hypothesis of the Mobility Transition." *Geographical Review* 61 (2): 219–49. http://dx.doi.org/10.2307/213996.

Zietsma, Danielle. 2010. "Immigrants Working in Regulated Occupations." *Perspectives on Labour and Income* 22 (1): 51–9.

6   Quebec's Destiny

LOUIS BÉLANGER AND CHARLES F. DORAN

Americans need to understand the power that the sense of identity holds for today's Quebec. Quebec is a Canadian province. But for a majority of its inhabitants, Quebec, with its predominantly French-speaking population, is also a nation. Long resisted by the Canadian government until Prime Minister Stephen Harper asked Parliament to officially recognize that "the Québécois form a nation within a united Canada" on 26 November 2006,[1] this identification with the idea of nation is unfamiliar to most Americans.

For Quebec, the use of the province's name to designate the national character of its inhabitants is, likewise in historical terms, a fairly new development. Descendants of French settlers often simply referred to themselves as "la nation canadienne" (the Canadian nation), "Canada" being originally the name given to the area of New France surrounding the St Lawrence and Great Lakes waterways. "Province of Quebec" was the name first given by the British Empire to the former French colony following the Conquest in 1763. Spreading from the Mississippi River to the coast of Newfoundland, it was administered from the city of Quebec. The appellation disappeared in 1791, when the colony was divided into two regions according to their respective linguistic majorities. The predominantly French-speaking eastern part of the British colony became Lower Canada. The predominantly English-speaking western part became Upper Canada. The Province of Quebec as we know it today was created in 1867, by the British North America Act, out of Lower Canada. Because important minorities of French descent lived outside of the province's boundaries, in Canada as well as in the Eastern United Sates, Quebec somewhat idealistically regarded itself until recently as the nation's homeland.

During the second half of the twentieth century, this sense of national identity was challenged and transformed. As a provincial welfare state rapidly emerged in Quebec, its citizens gradually ceased to express their nationalism in ethnic and religious terms to espouse a more civic sense of self. The Quiet Revolution, a period of rapid secularization and elite augmentation accelerated this process during the 1960s. The Quebec state, with its democratic institutions, large constitutional powers, and modern administrative apparatus, was now seen as the prime vehicle for the development of a culturally distinct society in North America. This evolution ignited a fundamental debate on the nation's destiny.

Should this newly conceived nation state remain a province inside the Canadian federation, or would it be preferable for Quebec to separate and face the future as an independent sovereign state? The Parti Québécois (PQ), a sovereignist social-democrat political party, won the provincial election in 1976, and organized a first referendum on the issue in 1980. A significant majority of Quebecers (60 per cent) then refused to give the government a mandate to negotiate with Ottawa a political secession accompanied by some kind of economic association. When successive constitutional negotiations failed afterward to accommodate Quebec's demand to redefine the terms of its participation in the Canadian federation, a second referendum was organized. In 1995, Quebec voters were clearly asked if they agreed to secede, unilaterally if necessary. Again, they answered "No," but this time by a very close margin (50.58 to 49.42 per cent).

Since then, apart from some episodes like the 2006 symbolic recognition of the "Québécois" as a nation by the House of Commons, the Quebec issue has been placed on the back burner. The approximately 40 per cent support for sovereignty in Quebec declined to a lower level.[2] But another referendum is still envisioned by the PQ, which now forms Quebec's government, a minority, after winning a September 2012 election. The issue of Quebec's destiny, as a political entity and as a national collectivity, is thus still an open one. A fundamental dimension of this issue is precisely the intimate connection Quebecers have built up between their cultural and their political identity.

History shows us that francophone Quebec struggled against great odds to survive in a wilderness that was not always welcoming and in an international political setting that was often hostile. As noted in chapter 2, on history, after the British under Wolfe defeated the French under Montcalm in 1759, Quebec faced new threats to its existence as the French governing elite for the most part withdrew to Paris. Quebec withstood challenges to its cultural unity and integrity such as the Durham Report (1839), which proposed assimilation to English Canada. Although the Quiet Revolution of the 1960s gave economic development thrust and direction, especially through the establishment of Hydro-Québec and the revenues it generated, substantial economic development had occurred long before then. Moreover, Quebec's cultural renaissance, celebrated through novels, poetry, art, dance, and movies, paralleled the surging wealth of the province and its strong commitment to the universal education of all its citizens.

The causes of Quebec's growth are open to debate. But the fact that Quebec has attained much in all these sectors cannot be questioned. The province was discussed at length in chapters 1, 2, and 3. Chapter 1 on geography revealed the importance of Quebec's sheer size and natural resources in shaping its destiny. The Quebec Act, which permitted the practice of Roman Catholicism and use of the French language in the province, was noted as a key piece of legislation in chapter 2. The ongoing tensions between Ottawa and Quebec City were prominent in chapter 3's discussion of politics and government. Here, in chapter 6, Quebec's quest for cultural survival will emerge as a major theme. Taken together, these points establish Quebec's key role in Canadian development.

This chapter challenges two myths at the centre of much contemporary debate within Quebec and in some Canadian circles about the province's past, and therefore, as well, about its future. The first myth is that Quebec was "saved" from a historically unique clerical, conservative, antidevelopmental mentality and from a hostile environment by the prescient efforts of the modern state. The second is that Quebec is somehow different from other societies in that the usual rules of economic development do not apply to it.

Here we argue that *survivance* (i.e., survival) is truly ensured both economically and culturally by much more commonplace forces: the many individuals, families, firms, and institutions that are building modern Quebec society. Economic and political integration is not a threat to Quebec society. As well, pluralism and diversity guarantee that Quebec will remain vital, vibrant, and supremely productive in the twenty-first century.

Looking Back, Looking Forward

Survival, *la survivance*, is the quintessential political issue in Quebec. With seven million francophones surrounded by 350 million

English-speaking Canadians and Americans, how could it be otherwise? At stake, though, is not only the demo-linguistic question of the
survival of a French presence in North America, but perhaps more important, the social and political quality of that presence. A good recent
illustration of this enduring debate was the uproar triggered by novelist and filmmaker Jacques Godbout's assertion that Quebec could disappear by 2076 (Vastel 2006). Nowhere in the original interview given
by Godbout did he even mention French or the language issue as part
of his pessimistic view. Linguistic assimilation is not what threatens
Quebec as a society, according to the renowned author of *Salut Galar-
neau!* Rather, it is a growing lack of national cohesiveness brought
about by scattered cultural reference points and the new communitari-
anism. Likewise, *For a Clear-Eyed Vision of Quebec*, an alerting manifesto
published by former premier Lucien Bouchard in 2005, was all about
innovation and the economic performance of the "Quebec model."
Quebecers share an obsession with their survival as a distinct society,
but have long elevated the debate well beyond the simple linguistic or
ethnic dimension.

The question of the survival of a vibrant francophone community
on the North American continent, these days more or less confined to
Quebec, is politically significant. Important debates are currently under
way that revisit the relations among culture, modernity, and economic
prosperity in an international context. This debate is of unmistakable
relevance for discussions about the historical trajectory of Quebec. For
its part, the political debate on the future of the Quebec state as a Canadian province or as a separate country continues to mobilize Quebecers. There may well be one day a third referendum on the province's
secession. So it is difficult to reflect on how cultural, economic, and political factors interplay in forging modern Quebec without considering
their implications for the future, and we will not try to evade this task.

Qualifying the Survival Issue

One cannot look at the survival of Quebec in purely quantitative terms.
We must not merely acknowledge the presence or the absence of francophones or of a French-speaking community on North American soil.
It is the specific form taken by this community and its quality that attract our attention. As a cultural minority inside Canada, do Quebecers
survive as a reclusive and xenophobic society or as an open and tolerant one, as democratic and progressive or as authoritarian and rigid,

as liberal or reactionary, as prosperous or economically backward? Examination of these qualitative dimensions of "survival" is inescapable because they are linked to the crucial issue of how the community fits into its environment and has maintained its identity and cohesiveness. These dimensions are key elements of the debate on the province's political future.

Today's Quebec is a liberal, democratic, and pluralist society. Of course the actual degree of tolerance practised by a society is best measured not by the majority response but by the perceptions of its own minorities regarding the degree of tolerance they experience. Considering that Quebec faces strong linguistic pressures and has endured centuries of political battles over its status within Canada, it is amazing to see how Quebec has developed a mainstream nationalism that has been purified of ethnic intolerance and has been able to debate its political future in model democratic fashion. Following a useful critique of many myths and stereotypic interpretations of Quebec, Daniel Latouche notes the importance of this new civic nationalism. According to him, "ethnocultural nationalism, even of the strategic variety, is not without 'dangers'": "Quebec nationalism has evolved into a more civic form of nationalism with its pro-inclusion 'We are Quebeckers' rather than the original more exclusive 'Le Québec aux Québécois' ('Quebec for Quebeckers'). Few are actually duped by this civic posturing, but theatre is also part of democracy and without make-believe the latter would certainly collapse under the weight of its own contradictions" (Latouche 2006b, 27).

The key assessment is how inclusive Quebec nationalism actually is, as opposed to how inclusive some of its architects would like that nationalism to be. Yet the basic point is the same. As a vibrant prosperous society, Quebec projects a civic nationalism that posits itself as inclusive of a diversity of ethnic and cultural groups, each of which is at home in the French language and feels full membership in the community. Diversity becomes an instrumental variable in the transition towards modernization. That most members of Quebec's intellectual elite have embraced democratic pluralism, and practise it, is another measure of Quebec's modernity (Doran 2001, 225–52).

Quebec has also developed a strong and diversified economy. With a per capita GDP regularly around 90 per cent of Canada's, Quebec finds itself around the average for all Canadian provinces. But compared to provinces with a similar industrial base – such as Ontario and British Columbia – Quebec's economy lags behind. Nevertheless, since 1960

Quebec has reduced by half its historical lag with Ontario (Fortin 2000). According to Pierre Fortin, the "rate of catching up" with Ontario and the rest of Canada in per capita income terms has been slow, about 1.5 per cent per year over the past fifty years. What explains this? Some cultural factors such as educational emphasis, a preference for hierarchy, government intervention in the economy, and minimal mobility within Canada may be among the reasons why entrepreneurship has lagged behind in Quebec and consequently why catch-up has not been faster. But again, considering the economic costs associated with being a linguistic minority (e.g., reduced geographical mobility, lower immigrant attraction; see Vaillancourt 1998), the overall record remains positive. How was this achieved? Is the survival and modernity of Quebec the product of an accommodating environment or the expression of an inner cultural and political resistance?

Being Saved: From What? By Whom?

The dominant view on *la survivance* in Quebec as well as in some English-Canadian intellectual circles is unambiguous and has acquired a quasi-mythical character. (For a review of the anglophone contributions to this mythology, see Cardinal 2003.) According to the *grand récit* of Quebec's passage to modernity (Létourneau 1992), before 1960 the combination of an archaic Catholic culture and economic domination condemned Quebec to stagnation (*la grande noirceur*). Then Quebecers woke up and, through heroic political actions and social engineering, were able to achieve their Quiet Revolution (*la révolution tranquille*) and reinvent themselves, their polity, and their economy. One of the latest recitations of this heroic story can be found in political scientist Daniel Latouche's contribution to a transnational research project on culture and development (Latouche 2006a; 2006b, 445–64). Pre-1960 Quebec society was locked in a "culture of backwardness," comprising an array of elements at the heart of which reigned Catholicism and the French heritage of Jacobinism and feudalism. These circumstances offered little hope for economic development, democracy, or intellectual creativity. "With such a heavy baggage," writes Latouche, "it is surprising that change could occur at all" (2006a, 9). But in the 1960s, Quebecers used their provincial government to carry out a massive "cultural adjustment program": support for artists has allowed the government to "single-handedly transform the symbolic and political landscape of

Québec" (ibid., 23); interventions in the economy have created a new entrepreneurial culture; nationalism has been strategically reinvented to engender a new, positive sense of citizenship and purpose. Political and intellectual leaders have reversed the odds and ensured Quebec's survival through a "cultural reconstruction process" (Harrison 2006, 169).

The state and the political elite, this account goes, have not only saved Quebec from itself but also saved it from externally imposed economic underdevelopment. During the 1950s, the Quebec economy was in the process of passing into foreign hands, condemning Quebec to traditional commodity-based industries while Ontario was developing a new industrial base. Quebec lacked what was needed in terms of financial resources and entrepreneurship. Only state interventionism could save the day, by containing foreign takeovers and nurturing the development of a new, more competent and competitive economic elite (Bélanger 1994). This was the rationale for creating new public corporations such as Hydro-Québec, the Caisse de Dépôt et de Placement, and the Société Générale de Financement, which have been profoundly changing the province's economic landscape. Quebecers have survived and achieved their passage to modernity not only against unfavourable economic conditions, themselves rooted in a Catholic and conservative culture not conducive to economic development, but also against a hostile economic environment.

Over the past several years this state-centric and heroic version of Quebec's coming of age has been sharply criticized. A new generation of historians, quickly accused of "revisionism" by some, has documented a more "normal" path towards modernity for Quebec (Rouillard 1998). The new historians have cast doubts on the revolutionary character of the social changes attributed to the Quiet Revolution and argue that, in different spheres, these changes were well under way before the 1960s. They have also contested the backwardness thesis by demonstrating that for most of the twentieth century, Quebecers enjoyed levels of industrialization and urbanization well in line with what was happening in Ontario and the US Northeast. This reality has led some authors on the political right to argue that the economic interventionism of the Quiet Revolution in fact dampened rather than fuelled the economy (Migué 1999; Paquet 1999). For example, this may have caused some companies to move operations, in whole or in part, from Quebec to Ontario.

Modern Quebec is not solely the product of a state-planned rescue. Still, many questions remain unanswered. In particular, saying that Quebec has developed "normally" (i.e., like other communities) evades what remains a key point to make about Quebec: that it has survived as a distinct society. The view that Quebec was backward before the 1960s has some basis. However, throughout the twentieth century, a strong liberal presence served as a counterweight against the power of the Catholic Church and conservative elites in the province. Support for liberal views, including the separation of church and state, was especially strong among francophone business organizations such as the Chambre de Commerce du District de Montréal and the Liberal Party (both provincial and federal). These views were disseminated in the pages of widely read newspapers such as *La Presse*, *Le Soleil*, and *La Patrie* and supported by the local chapters of international labour unions (Rouillard 1998). The question is this: Why did this liberal way of envisioning the future of Quebec finally triumph over the ethnically and religiously obsessed version supposedly defended by the clergy and other conservative elements? Why has Quebec nationalism followed a democratic and pluralist path rather than the intolerant and "ethnicist" path that has flourished elsewhere? This is not to say that there is no political or social intolerance in Quebec. The point is that intolerance is by no means a dominant strain of thought in Quebec society.

Conditions of Prosperity and Modernity

Recent works on economic development and its linkages with culture point towards an alternative explanation to the state-centric one that has dominated political debates over Quebec's destiny for more than a generation. This explanation suggests that certain causal relationships have been overlooked. First, economic conditions for Quebecers before 1960 were not as bad as the "backwardness" mythology pretends and in fact were a key factor explaining the victory of liberalism over clericalism and the emergence of Quebec's modern national identity. Second, Quebec's culture and its integration into the North American economy were not stumbling blocks that could only be overcome by state interventionism; they were in fact prime conductors of its prosperity. In a nutshell, the answer to the question What did Quebec rely on to spur its development? does not depend solely on heroic political actions that saved it from itself and from its environment.

From Prosperity to Modernity

Benjamin Friedman has argued that a given society's moral attitudes towards tolerance, democracy, and openness are strongly determined by its economic performance (Friedman 2005). According to him, peoples' attitudes towards themselves and others, which are the foundation of the moral character of a society, are a function of how they assess their material condition compared to others and to the past. And only economic growth (versus stagnation), "by continually giving most people a sense of living better than they or their families have in the not very distant past ... reduces the intensity of their desire to live better than the other" (2005, 92). Moreover, as historical comparisons show, the relationship between economic growth and democratic openness cannot be considered merely circular: "While the evidence suggests that economic growth usually fosters democracy and all this entails; it is less clear that open societies necessarily experience superior economic growth by virtue of their democratic practice" (ibid., 16).

As mentioned above, far from being stuck in economic stagnation, Quebec's economy before the Quiet Revolution was enjoying unprecedented growth. This growth was not significantly less "industrial" in Quebec than in neighbouring Ontario, and francophones were part of it. From 1940 to 1960, Quebecers' purchasing power increased substantially (personal income increased by more than 5 per cent annually between 1946 and 1958; Migué 1999, 23), while wages and benefits steadily improved (Rouillard 1998). As for catching up with Ontario in per capita GDP, this began in 1945, not in 1960 (Fortin 2000). That being said, as for the rest of Canada, this period of growth was in large part induced by massive American investment. (US direct investments in Canada tripled between the end of the Second World War and 1957. According to Migué [1999, 25], Quebec during this period was the destination of 25 per cent of these investments – a peak never reached since.) The flow of foreign capital engulfed the local business class; and, because managers and engineers followed that capital, it benefited more immediately anglophones and only later francophones. Nevertheless, well before the Quiet Revolution, the average Quebecer could assess his prosperity, compare it to that of his parents, and feel that his or her future was pretty much guaranteed.

Of course, the postwar boom was not experienced by Quebecers alone; it was felt by almost all North Americans. In the United States, once individuals took the measure of their new economic security, movements towards openness, tolerance, and democracy began to shape the political agenda. Accordingly, Americans' attitudes towards racial equality, immigration, and poverty changed dramatically during the 1950s and the 1960s, which led to desegregation policies, new and less restrictive immigration laws, and social programs such as Medicare and Medicaid. As Friedman concedes, rising incomes alone cannot explain this progressive trend; independent political forces were also at play. It would nevertheless be difficult to imagine such an era of democratization and fairness without the widespread confidence brought about by economic prosperity (Friedman 2005, 180–215). The same is true for Quebec: the political leadership and governmental activism of the 1960s certainly helped to shape Quebec nationalism, but it could hardly have happened without this climate of economically induced self-confidence.

Integration, Size, and Modernity

Would Quebec have enjoyed the same levels of prosperity and the same kind of sustainability had it not been integrated with the North American economy? It is, of course, impossible and irrelevant to imagine what would have happened to Quebec's economy had it not been embedded in its regional context. Even so, it is useful to ask whether more integration or less integration is good or bad for Quebec, considering its size. It is also legitimate to ask whether, considering its size, Quebec has benefited from integration with a larger political community.

In principle, the question of the prosperity of the small polity is researchable. The question is not whether the small state can prosper, but whether it can prosper more fully as a member of a larger federation or state. The real issue concerns relative long-term prosperity, not whether a small state can survive economically, for that is likely to be answered more readily in the affirmative.

At issue is the very heart of the notion of regional integration. If a small state can prosper as greatly as the large state, then why integrate regionally? Making the too easy assumption that the small state will maintain borders as open as if it were part of a larger polity mandating such openness (and even this mandated openness is not a matter of certainty, as the MacDonald commission discovered in trying to break down barriers across the provinces), will economies of scale and other managerial economies be such as to adequately guarantee equal prosperity, let alone superior prosperity and growth for the smaller, more autarkic actor?

Small states integrate to increase the size of their markets so that they can better exploit scale and material economies. Among the benefits, presumably, is increased economic welfare through improved productivity and rates of economic growth to exploit those welfare economies. Canadian membership in free trade agreements with the United States and Mexico is helpful to Quebec as well as to the rest of the country.

The logic here is that when a smaller entity separates from a larger state, the smaller entity – say Quebec, with fewer than eight million people – will experience a lower growth rate than the average for the larger state from which the entity has just separated and be a less desirable location for foreign direct investment. There will be short term adjustment costs. The long-term costs, measured in terms of economic growth rates forgone, are large and real for a "statelet" contemplating separation from a larger economic union, all else being equal. A related question is why these differences in economic growth rates arise between small and large states and whether free trade can be sufficient to offset the loss of a national market for the small actor that secedes. Would entry into NAFTA be enough to safeguard the economic growth rates of an independent Quebec?

The answer is that entry into NAFTA for an independent Quebec would be necessary but not sufficient. Quebec could always try to resort to bilateral trade deals with other partners. But for reasons of proximity, size, and wealth of market, no other trade arrangement could equal the attractiveness of entry into NAFTA for an independent Quebec. But would such entry into NAFTA be sufficient to eliminate the disparity in per capita income growth rates between the smaller and the larger country?

According to the empirical results examined for the Organization for Economic Cooperation and Development (OECD) countries across a decade, the answer is that the disparity in growth rates probably would not be eliminated by membership in NAFTA, however necessary that membership would be. Regional integration is not a sufficient boost to per capita growth rates because such international arrangements are not "integrative" enough. Membership does not eliminate the lower per capita income growth rates for countries below a threshold size (Doran 2001, 162–89).

Three distinct levels of integration exist today: (1) that of the state; (2) that of regional units such as the European Union and NAFTA; and (3) that of the highly differentiated international market. Highest is the degree of integration of the state. The greatest trade (exchange and speculation) occurs within large states. Small states need economies of scale as well as other efficiencies only obtainable within a larger state market above about 20 million people.

Tolerance, Diversity, and Prosperity

Even if we agree with Friedman that the causal relationship between economic growth and political openness is not perfectly circular, there are nevertheless good reasons to suggest that political openness often reinforces prosperity. For example, civic and tolerant forms of nationalism encourage diversity, or at least they do not try to suppress it. And recent empirical findings indicate that social diversity is a key to growth (Ottaviano and Peri 2004; Zachary 2000; Aldrich and Waldinger 1990; Chatman et al. 1998).

Recent findings also show that ethno-linguistic diversity in a country such as Canada contributes to the capacity for openness, innovation, and probably entrepreneurship as well (Aleksy 2006). This does not mean that a single predominant language such as French in Quebec or English elsewhere in Canada is problematic. Cultural and ethnic subnational differences need not present barriers to economic development. Far from it. But polities with an overall capacity for considerable ethno-cultural diversity, however distributed within the polity, have a growth advantage in terms of commercially relevant variables such as openness, innovation, and entrepreneurship. Together, these variables have a highly positive impact on economic growth. In past research on organizational behaviour, this result has been found at the level of the firm. More recently, in research on the international political economy, this result has also been found at the level of the state. But a critical qualifier is that diversity must occur in the "right context" of societal inputs. That context requires a growth-focused and an innovation-focused strategy. It is the innovation-focused strategy that unlocks individual and institutional creativity in a way that is useful to the market. That variable is "Research and Development as a per cent of GDP" (Aleksy 2006, 208; Helliwell and Putnam 2004; Hartenian and Gudmundson 2000).

In the Quebec context, political openness towards diversity has expressed itself both internally and in relations with the rest of Canada. Internally, the immigration policy of the Quebec government has long been to encourage diversification by attempting to attract French-speaking citizens who accept the norms and culture of Quebec, whatever their background or place of origin. In its relationships with the anglophone minority and with immigrants, Quebec has also been able to accommodate its project of imposing French as the province's official language with their historic and collective rights. Externally, Quebecers have through constitutional reforms and referendums attempted to negotiate their place in the Canadian state and society. Even though Quebec governments since 1982 have refused to ratify the current constitution, and even though Quebecers voted no (by a hair) in the 1995 sovereignty referendum, Canada as a whole has become more diverse and reciprocal openness has developed between Quebec and the other provinces.

In that sense, being part of Canada has certainly contributed to Quebec's political modernity. It is difficult to imagine that Quebecers would have ended up with the current form of nationalism had they not been obligated to negotiate their identity within the Canadian reality. This is not to suggest that the outcome would have been characterized by less openness and pluralism, but to simply admit that things would have been different. Had Quebec seceded from Canada, it would have been less integrated than it is now with its environment. In one sense, integration and secession are absolute opposites. Integration involves cohesion in terms of the economic, commercial, financial, political, social, and cultural ties and interactions that hold a society together. Secession involves the disruption or unravelling of those ties and interactions along territorial and population lines. Integration does not imply that a society is homogeneous on all parameters, or even most parameters; it does mean that a society is homogeneous with regard to its organizing principles. A society may be heterogeneous on many attributes and still remain integrated. Moreover, homogeneity is *relative* – that is, relative to the degree of homogeneity that exists in other societies or that could exist in an alternative society.

Of course, one can argue that being separate or being part of Canada would not affect the levels of integration and diversity that have contributed to making Quebec what it is today, simply because an independent Quebec would substitute international contacts for domestic ones. But even if the absolute number of contacts with a diverse international society outside an independent Quebec remained the same after separation as before, the absolute and hence relative number of such contacts with Ottawa and the rest of Canada would surely decline.

Moreover, the quality (intensity) of those contacts with the rest of Canada would likewise decline. It follows that the diversity that is Canada would not benefit Quebec as much after independence as before. Of course, the opposite is also true: the diversity offered by Quebec to the rest of Canada would be lost to Canada after independence. According to recent research on the impact of diversity on economic development, both an independent Quebec and a severed Canada would suffer from the loss of much of the present benefits of diversity because of the loss of contact with each other, and because of the loss of *intensity* of contact with each other.

An additional concern is whether an increase in absolute contacts by an independent Quebec with the outside world beyond Canada would be sufficient to offset the decrease in absolute contacts between an independent Quebec and the rest of Canada. The answer is no. At present, Quebec can and does use the bargaining power of Canada as a whole to achieve its objectives, such as airline routes through Montreal, with the world outside Canada. An isolated, independent Quebec would have to fight these battles alone. Airlines would be tempted to base themselves in the larger markets and more central locations afforded by Toronto or Chicago rather than in a separate country of only eight million people. The more the absolute contacts with the outside world for an independent Quebec, the more such battles it would face alone.

When viewed in this way, Quebec might well find itself after secession more integrated internally and not as diverse, but far less integrated externally, despite membership in one or more regional organizations. This breakdown of external ties and interactions could become quite problematic for development and growth. Clearly, the degree of integration between Quebec and the rest of Canada today is far greater than would be the degree of integration between an independent Quebec and the rest of the world, whether inside NAFTA or outside. That is the economic burden that greater political independence would entail.

Catholicism, Social Capital, and Prosperity

How is Quebec's current economic prosperity compatible with the "backward" thesis? Was that prosperity exogenously induced? One of the oldest clichés about economic development in Quebec has been that its Catholicism, with its focus on the afterlife rather than the mundane present, prevented it from embracing fully the capitalist ethic. Supported by a solid tradition in sociological thought going back to Max

Weber, the assertion that Protestant societies thrive in world economic competition has become a truism. The reality, however, may be a little more complex. First, although Weber was essentially right to historically associate the birth and rise of European capitalism with Christianity, the pivotal role he makes Protestantism play in this process is increasingly contested (Stark 1998, xi–xiii). Furthermore, Rodney Stark has recently argued that capitalism developed first in southern Catholic centres such as Florence and Genoa and only then spread to northern Europe's Protestant countries. Furthermore, he adds, it is not Catholicism but political tyranny that later impeded capitalism in Catholic countries such as France, Spain, and Italy. In the case of France, which is most pertinent for us here, this thesis is in tune with Francis Fukuyama's observations. Indeed, he notes that Catholicism cannot be considered accountable for France's low levels of trust, which he closely associates with prosperity, since the pre-absolutist French society was richly endowed with intermediate organizations of the sort that presuppose a proclivity for free association (Fukuyama 1995, 115). What, then, about Quebec?

We cannot deny that economically, before 1960, francophones in Quebec were lagging behind anglophones. Even in 1970, the average unilingual anglophone worker was still earning 20 per cent more than a unilingual francophone and 11 per cent more than a bilingual francophone. This gap no longer exists today (Latouche 2006a, 10–11). According to Yves Bélanger, in 1959, although the francophone population of Quebec was much larger than the anglophone population, the latter provided some 78 per cent of the entrepreneurs. For development to occur, this deficit had to be erased. Much of it has been. But can we seriously attribute the original gap to Quebecers' culture and religion? Quebecers may have been relatively excluded from management positions in foreign-owned booming industries, but it would be incorrect to suggest that Quebecers were not entrepreneurial. According to Bélanger (1994), 22 per cent of all businesses in Quebec were, in 1959, under the exclusive control of francophones (ibid., 2). While there were some 35,000 francophone business owners or administrators in 1941, there were 90,000 in 1961 (ibid., 3). Some of them were extremely successful; for example, the Lévesque family owned a small empire in the industrial, financial, and retail sectors. Other big families – the Simards, the Brillants, the Bienvenues, and the Bombardiers – were also running successful enterprises.

The concept of social capital – that is, "the ability of people to work together for common purposes in groups or organizations" (Fukuyama

1995, 10) – has been widely used over the past decade to establish and measure the connections between the culture of a given society and its economic performance. In Catholic societies, it is often argued, the trust in others that makes spontaneous sociability possible is particularly low (Harrison 2006, 106). Familism, a culture that supports family and kinship as the principal locus of sociability, has also been linked by Fukuyama with low levels of social capital. This is a pertinent observation for us, considering the emphasis in traditional Quebec on the family and the church as pillars of the struggle for survival. Here, the picture can be puzzling. According to certain data, social capital in Quebec is significantly lower than in the rest of Canada. A survey shows that participation in community groups or associations is significantly lower among francophones than among anglophones in Canada (Forgues 2005). For example, 35 per cent of anglophones are members of a sporting association, versus 22 per cent of francophones. Even membership in cultural organizations is more frequent in English Canada (21 per cent versus 12 per cent; ibid., 8). (Interestingly, the same survey indicates that francophones trust other people significantly less than anglophones – 35 per cent versus 61 per cent – but that there is no difference between the two linguistic groups when it comes to trust in family members; ibid., 19.) On the other hand, another recent in-depth survey of the state of non-profit and voluntary organizations in Canada indicates that Quebec is the province with the largest number of them (46,326), with a per capita ratio much higher (617 per 100,000) than in Ontario (369 per 100,000) (Statistics Canada 1998, 20). How can we explain this apparent contradiction? Perhaps Quebec's community sector comprises numerous but very small organizations. Or perhaps, more simply, many of the organizations covered by the second survey do not correspond to the categories used in the first.

One possible explanation for this apparent contradiction is that much social involvement in Quebec is carried out through organizations that do not fit the classic model of the non-profit voluntary sector generally used in North America to measure social capital (Vaillancourt 2006). More precisely, measures of social capital in Canada often miss the important sector that Quebecers call "social economy" (économie sociale), which is made up of cooperatives and non-profit enterprises that pursue social ends using business and entrepreneurial means and which operate within the marketplace instead of outside it (Goldenberg 2004, 12). It is estimated that the province counts 7200 of these entities, which are active mainly in the financial services, forestry, and food industries, home care and child care services, and housing (ibid., 13). These organizations have deep historical roots. For instance, mutual societies providing life and fire insurance policies were active in Quebec from the beginning of the nineteenth century. In 1900 the saving and loan cooperative *Mouvement des Caisses Populaires Desjardins*, now Quebec's largest "bank," was founded. Cooperatives have long been present, of course, in the agriculture sector, but beginning in the 1940s they have expanded in other sectors such as house construction, fishing, funeral services, retail grocery, and electricity distribution. Furthermore, the Catholic Church, in accordance with the *Rerum novarum* encyclical, has strongly supported this movement (Girard 1999).

Conclusion

This chapter challenges two myths of Quebec development: first that the Quiet Revolution "saved" Quebec from dissolution and subordination by strong governmental intervention. Second, that Quebec in its economic and political experience is somehow different from other sectors of North American development. Quebec development has been far more complex, market-based, and founded on individual initiative than the first myth suggests, and of far greater similarity to economic development throughout North America then the second myth contends.

Governmental actions, electoral politics, and historic figures have all undeniably had an impact on modern Quebec, and they will in the future. However, Quebec has not been *saved*, or perhaps instead preserved, from threats to its identity. Not from its culture, not from its backwardness, not from its integration to the North American economy, not from its lack of size per se, but because of much more normal processes of economic development found in all polities. All things considered, because of its size and its status as a cultural minority in North America, Quebec has benefited in many ways from its integration with larger entities and its unique character has survived intact. Because small economic entities tend to possess less capacity for diversity than very large ones, a small entity generally cannot grow as fast as a larger one. This conclusion is fully congruent with those of regional integration theory, which has long driven the formation of such regional associations as the European Union and NAFTA. Growth is generated in part by integration; it is also favoured by diversity. Here, Quebec offers Canada the same opportunity that Canada offers Quebec

– a diversity of the sort that empirical work shows drives the creativity of universities and corporations in the twenty-first century. Increasing diversity may also be a factor contributing to a decline in the sense of "perceived inequality" across individuals and regions, a decline observed by Friedman as a moral attribute of economic growth.

Our main conclusion is that modernity, economic as well as political, is not simply a creation of political will. What Quebec is today, the stylized way in which it has survived, is also a function of important factors such as size, integration, diversity, culture, social capital, and moral attitudes, which are interconnected in often surprising ways. The political economy of Quebec's destiny is a complex one. The lessons for the future are many and will of course be appreciated differently by federalists and sovereignists. Let's return to Friedman and *The Moral Consequences of Economic Growth*. According to Friedman, as individuals and households grow wealthier, they become less concerned about matters of economic and social equality. When assessing the economic situation, they compare themselves to their past status and to the status of their neighbours. Since inequality is a relative notion, comparisons are constantly being updated (recalibrated). Friedman tells us that individuals and households have a much stronger propensity to accept risk regarding the improvement of their relative status than they do regarding the risk of loss of status. They are downwardly risk averse. Are there lessons here for the way Quebecers view themselves, and view Quebec as a community? Surely lessons exist with respect to the matter of Quebec independence and of how Quebecers view their and future economic success.

As they have become richer, more educated as a population, and more urban, Quebecers have become less suspicious of outsiders, more confident of themselves and of their achievements, and less concerned that English Canada is exploiting or outperforming them. Perceived inequality has surely declined in both the ways that Friedman has defined it: (a) relative to their own historical situation; and (b) relative to the situation of the rest of Canada. For many Quebecers, the Quiet Revolution was a giant equalizer in both a material and a socio-psychological sense. Recalibration of Quebec attitudes occurs in every election. Indeed, every referendum on Quebec independence is a kind of recalibration of the attitudes of each voting Quebecer towards his or her own status vis-à-vis the past and vis-à-vis how they think they would do under independence as opposed to continuing to belong to the

Canadian federation. Attitudes could change, but they will be strongly influenced by levels of economic prosperity.

Regarding what the future holds under membership in the Canadian federation versus independence, most Quebecers are quite cautious. They may be willing to risk the promise of improvement, or different degrees of improvement, in a referendum on independence. Hence the shifting attitudes and seeming willingness to take risks on the prospect that independence might improve their relative position and status. But by the same token, Quebecers are extremely wary of any proposal for independence that might leave them worse off in terms of relative status (either compared to their own past or relative to neighbours elsewhere in Canada), and considerable long-term downside economic risk unavoidably exists in proposals for political separation. The upside is something they would be willing to weigh and debate. The downside is not open for discussion or something they would be willing to consider (risk) in deciding how to vote with respect to altering Quebec's situation inside Canada. When examining empirical findings that bear on the future economic status of Quebec inside or outside Canadian federation, these conclusions about downside risk versus upside opportunity are very important.

NOTES

1 The motion was adopted by a 266 to 16 vote. CBC News, "House Passes Vote Recognizing Québécois as Nation," 27 November 2006. http://www.cbc.ca/news/canada/story/2006/11/27/nation-vote.html.
2 Robert Dutrissac, "Sondage Léger Marketing–Le Devoir. L'appui à la souveraineté ne fléchit pas," Le Devoir, 14 May 2011. http://www.ledevoir.com/politique/quebec/323376/sondage-leger-marketing-le-devoir-l-appui-a-la-souverainete-ne-flechit-pas.

WEBSITES

Alliance de recherche universités-communautés en économie sociale: http://www.aruc-es.uqam.ca
Association internationale des études québécoises: http://www.aieq.qc.ca
Centre de recherche sur les innovations sociales: http://www.crises.uqam.ca

"For a Clear-Eyed Vision of Quebec": http://www.pourunquebeclucide.info/
cgi-cs/cs.waframe00a8.html
Institut de la statistique du Québec: http://www.stat.gouv.qc.ca/default_
an.htm

REFERENCES AND FURTHER READING

Aldrich, H.E., and R. Waldinger. 1990. "Ethnicity and Entrepreneurship." *An-nual Review of Sociology* 16 (1): 111–35. http://dx.doi.org/10.1146/annurev.
so.16.080190.000551.
Aleksy, Agnieska. 2006. "Ethnolinguistic Diversity as a Potential Economic
Benefit for Countries: Implications for International Political Economy."
PhD dissertation, Johns Hopkins University, School of Advanced Interna-tional Studies.
Bélanger, Yves. 1994. *Québec Inc.: La dérive d'un modèle?* Cahiers du Centre de
recherche sur les innovations sociales. Montreal: CRISES.
Cardinal, Linda. 2003. "In Search of a New Framework: Debating Identity in
Quebec." Research seminar of the Department of French and the Centre
for the Study of Human Settlement and Historical Change, National Uni-versity of Ireland, Galway, 27 March.
Chatman, J., J. Polzer, S. Barsade, and M. Neale. 1998. "Being Different Yet
Feeling Similar: The Influence of Demographic Composition and Organi-zational Culture on Work Processes and Outcomes." *Administrative Science
Quarterly* 43 (4): 749–80. http://dx.doi.org/10.2307/2393615.
Doran, Charles F. 2001. *Why Canadian Unity Matters and Why Americans Care:
Democratic Pluralism at Risk.* Toronto: University of Toronto Press.
Forgues, Eric. 2005. *Indicateurs du capital social des groupes de langue offici-elle au Canada.* Moncton: Institut canadien de recherche sur les minorités
linguistiques.
Fortin, Pierre. 2000. *L'économie du Québec depuis 1960: La moitié du retard sur
l'Ontario a été comblé.* Institut de recherche en économie contemporaine.
Friedman, Benjamin M. 2005. *The Moral Consequences of Economic Growth.* New
York: Knopf.
Fukuyama, Francis. 1995. *Trust: The Social Virtues and the Creation of Prosperity.*
New York: Free Press.
Girard, Jean-Pierre. 1999. *Une identité à affirmer, un espace à occupier: Aperçu his-torique de mouvement cooperative au Canada français.* Montreal: Université du
Québec à Montréal.

Goldenberg, Mark. 2004. *Social Innovation in Canada: How the Non-profit Sector Serves Canadians ... And How It Can Serve Them Better*. Ottawa: Canadian Policy Research Networks.

Harrison, Lawrence E. 2006. *The Central Liberal Truth: How Politics Can Change a Culture and Save It from Itself*. New York: Oxford University Press.

Hartenian, L.S., and D.E. Gudmundson. 2000. "Cultural Diversity in Small Business: Implications for Firm Performance." *Journal of Developmental Entrepreneurship* 5 (3): 209–19.

Helliwell, John F., and Robert D. Putnam. 2004. "The Social Context of Well-being." *Philosophical Transactions of the Royal Society* (London) B (359): 1435–46.

Latouche, Daniel. 2006a. "Culture and the Pursuit of Success: The Case of Québec in the Twentieth Century." In *Developing Cultures: Case Studies*, 145 61, ed. Lawrence E. Harrison and Peter L. Berger. New York: Routledge.

– 2006b. *The Pursuit of Prosperity in a Transition Society: The Case of Quebec in the XXth Century*. Montreal: INRS Urbanization, Culture, et Société. "Inédits," March.

Létourneau, Jocelyn. 1992. "Le Québec moderne: Un chapitre dans le grand récit collectif des Québécois." *Revue Francaise de Science Politique* 42 (5): 765–85.

McLeod, P.L., S.A. Lobel, and T.H. Cox, Jr. 1996. "Ethnic Diversity and Creativity in Small Groups." *Small Group Research* 27:246–64.

McMahon, Fred. 2003. *Quebec Prosperity: Taking the Next Step*. Vancouver: Fraser Institute, Studies in Economic Prosperity. November.

Migué, Jean-Luc. 1999. *Étatisme et declin du Québec: Bilan de la révolution tranquille*. Montreal: Éditions Varia.

Ottaviano, G., and G. Peri. 2004. "The Economic Value of Cultural Diversity." *FEEM Working Papers* 34. http://ssrn.com/abstract=499702.

Paquet, Gilles. 1999. *Oublier la Révolution tranquille: Pour une nouvelle socialité*. Montreal: Liber.

Rouillard, Jacques. 1998. "La Révolution tranquille, rupture ou tournant?" *Journal of Canadian Studies/Revue d'études canadiennes* 32 (4, Winter): 23–51.

Stark, Rodney. 1998. *The Victory of Reason: How Christianity Led to Freedom, Capitalism, and Western Success*. New York: Random House.

Statistics Canada. 1998. *Cornerstones of Community: Highlights of the National Survey of Nonprofit and Voluntary Organizations*. Ottawa: Minister of Industry.

Vaillancourt, François. 1998. "The Economics of Constitutional Options for Quebec and Canada." *Canadian Business Economics* 6 (Winter): 3–14.

Vaillancourt, Yves. 2006. "Le tiers secteur au Canada, un lieu de rencontre entre la tradition américaine et la tradition européenne." Paper presented at the First Conference of the International Society for Third-Sector Research and the EMES European Research Network, 27–9 April.

Vastel, Michel. 2006. "2076: La fin du Québec." *L'Actualité*, 1 September.

Zachary, G.P. 2000. *The Global Me: New Cosmopolitans and the Competitive Edge: Picking Globalism's Winners and Losers*. New York: Public Affairs.

7 Literary and Popular Culture

ANDREW HOLMAN AND ROBERT THACKER

This chapter examines aspects of Canadian literary and popular culture. It is a curious subject: popular culture is among the most empirically accessible expressions of what it means to be Canadian, but at the same time is the most evasive and difficult to capture in any neat analytical depiction. Though even the newest student of Canada could likely cite at least one example or manifestation of "Canadian culture" – ice hockey, good beer, the Group of Seven or Emily Carr, the music of Michael Bublé and Justin Bieber, the writing of Douglas Coupland and Margaret Atwood, or films of Sarah Polley – actually describing what this concept fully means is quite like nailing jelly to a wall. At first glance, Canadian culture exists as a loose grab bag of seemingly distinctive activities, only vaguely connected. Defining and assessing Canadian literary and popular culture more clearly (and so more usefully) is the main goal of this chapter.

Popular culture is the reflection of the everyday in the lives of ordinary people. It is expressed in literature, drama, dance, sports, art, comedy, and many other forms of human activity. It is manifest both in intricate "high art" productions, such as poetry, fiction, and film, and in more ephemeral ways, such as cartoons and television shows, popular music, and online blogs. Popular culture is what we do and consume in forms that range from the genteel, the learned, and the elaborate to those that are common, primitive, and simple. For Canada, all of these vehicles for expressing culture are meaningful. In equally profound measures, they relate the ways in which Canadians *see* themselves and *represent* themselves both to one another and to the rest of the world. These cultural manifestations encapsulate how Canadians *are* Canadian, every day. And with the driving animus of American culture so close by – and in many ways so very similar – Canadian popular and literary culture is often best understood as "the distinction of small differences." Beginning one of the best essays on cultural differences between Canadians and Americans, "Sharing the Continent," the late critic Northrop Frye wrote that when he taught in the United States, "nine-tenths of the time the responses of my American students are identical with those of Canadian students, but the tenth time I know that I'm in a foreign country and have no idea what the next move is" (Frye 1982, 57–8).

As we proceed through the twenty-first century, the differences between forms of popular culture matter much less than they used to. If in the late nineteenth and early twentieth centuries one could describe culture as deeply divided between "highbrow" and "lowbrow" forms, that assertion no longer rings true. Since the prosperous 1950s, culture as we know it has been compressed: all of its forms, from opera to professional football, have become almost universally accessible to cultural consumers. The globalization of trade and widespread use of the Internet, with its capacity for instantaneous messaging and cultural creation, have compounded this development worldwide. Culture is no longer performed for and pitched to small, localized constituencies, and it has lost its ability to delineate its consumers as "rough" or "respectable." In Canada that division was never very distinct. Canadians are a New World, frontier people who have had comparatively few resources to dedicate to cultural production, and for that reason the distance between high and low brow has been relatively short. "It's possible," Canadians Geoff Pevere and Greig Dymond assert in their comprehensive compendium of Canadian popular culture, *Mondo Canuck*, "to see as much of ourselves (if not more) in Mike Myers as it is in Margaret Atwood" (1996, x). Canadians are a "middlebrow" people.

So, how *do* Canadians see themselves? Popular culture is a particularly useful and direct means for answering this question. As Elspeth Cameron has written, what Canadians choose "to write or sing about, paint or study" reflects the ways in which Canadians have *invented* Canada – that is, how they have bestowed meaning on their daily lives (Cameron 1997, 8). Here, the idea of *iteration* is important. Canadian culture is not merely some abstract and detached idea or myth that can be "consumed," or called upon occasionally to explain to Canadians who they are. For many Canadians, popular culture is more practical: Canadians *perform* their culture. It is something that they act out, or do.

If seeing is doing, how, then, do Canadians perform *Canadianness*? Perhaps more than others, Canadians perform their culture with a palpable sense of self-awareness that stems from an inability to clearly define themselves. Canadian culture has never been one thing; it has always been many, sometimes conflicting, things – French, English, Native; eastern, western, northern; Catholic and Protestant; British and American. Moreover, Canadian culture has always been marked with the dominant impression that it, like the country it represents, was and is in transition; it is *on the road* to cultural certitude but in no danger of arriving there anytime soon. "To be Canadian," write Pevere and Dymond (1996, viii), "is to live in the space between certainties … in other words … to exist in a state of constant becoming." Canadian culture involves a large measure of obsessive self-examination. Canadians seem always to be taking stock. The act of performing culture is one of regular declaration: Canadians telling themselves and others who they think they are. *Canadianness* is a process, and the trip is more valuable than reaching the destination ever could be.

Indeterminacy is the principal hallmark of Canadian culture, and that fact has informed and imprinted itself repeatedly on literary and popular culture. This search for identity has created a literary and popular culture in Canada manifested in at least four central (and overlapping) characteristics that give it shape. First, *Canadian literary and popular culture is a historical construct*. As historian Jonathan Vance has shown in his sweeping 2009 volume *A History of Canadian Culture*, cultural expressions in Canada have continually evolved and been the subject of struggle and challenge. Canadian literary and popular culture is comparatively new and is always changing. The ways in which Canadian writers, filmmakers, artists, and athletes expressed themselves in the 1920s, for example, differ necessarily from the ways in which they do so in 2013. Second, *Canadian literary and popular culture is fragmentary*. In a nation that has always been divided – by language, by ethnicity and religion, by social class and region – it stands to reason that its popular culture will be fragmented, too. Canadian literary and popular culture, to use an old (and now hackneyed) metaphor, is a *mosaic*. Third, *Canadian literary and popular culture has always been influenced by the presence (and often threat) of an external "other."* From the late nineteenth century into the twentieth, as Canada moved from colony to nation, British influences on Canadian popular culture dissipated. Since the 1920s, American cultural influence has presented simultaneously the biggest threat to Canadian culture and its most useful foil. An external "other" provided the most fruitful muse (or inspiration) for producers of Canadian culture and made one theme central to Canadian cultural production: "survival." Fourth, *Canadian culture and cultural industries have become notably reliant on the state for survival*. Since the creation of the Canadian Radio Broadcasting League in the 1930s, and the Massey commission report in 1951, Canadians have developed a sense of comfort in relying on governments (both federal and provincial) to subsidize and protect (and sometimes deliver and market) the products of Canadian culture. State intervention and subsidies are inherent elements of Canadian popular culture. Canadian literature, for example, is thriving now in ways never seen before government involvement and subsidization.

These four characteristics give structure to the rest of this chapter. They provide context for the huge body of work that makes up Canadian literary and popular culture. To these categories, we add a fifth: *the French fact*. The literary and popular culture of French Canada warrants a separate treatment because it is qualitatively different. Francophone culture has a distinct trajectory and richness that comes from its unique situation as an island of difference in a sea of anglophone culture. Though distinct, francophone popular culture is remarkable also because it is a subset, or microcosm, of Canadian literary and popular culture writ large. For all its ostensible peculiarity, francophone literary and popular culture is a historical construct, marked by fragmentation, Americanization, and state intervention. This treatment of Canadian literary and popular culture will necessarily be cursory and selective, but it provides both an overview and an argument. The culture that Canadians have invented reveals a country in the making. Canada, even 146 years after its founding, is a work in progress.

A Historical Construct

Literary and popular culture is a historical construct, stamped indelibly by the place and time in which it was created. Canadian literary and popular culture bears the marks of the arduous historical journey of Canada and Canadians "from colony to nation" (Lower 1946; Creighton 1957; Lumsden 1970). To demonstrate this assertion is to oversimplify a complex and conflicted history. Canadian history is a big tent in which multiple stories, or versions of the past, reside (Shore 2002). The story of Canada's transition from a series of colonial outposts of Europe to a self-governed, sovereign, *American* nation remains the country's primary narrative and source of national identity. Much of Canadian literary and popular culture stems from its place in and reference to this narrative. For example, the creation and deployment of the North-West Mounted Police in 1873–4 was a means of asserting Canadian sovereignty over its west at a time of considerable trouble along the 49th Parallel, the border with the United States. The creation of the Mounties was, for Sir John A. Macdonald, Canada's first prime minister, a practical solution to a difficult problem; yet that police force emerged from those years as a defining embodiment of Canadian difference – its myth, begun in newspapers, continued in popular fiction, reached its zenith in early Hollywood films, and defines Canada to this day (Francis, Jones, and Smith 2000; Brown 2002; on the Mounties, see Thacker 1980; Berton 1975; LaDow, 2001).

Like the Mounties, Canadian sport and art clearly demonstrate cultural differences within the national narrative. Canadians see themselves in their sports, and they have done so for a long time. Sport is a part of weekly and seasonal routines for many Canadians as well as a source of nostalgic recollection and excitement. "Sport is pervasive in Canadian society" (Morrow and Wamsley 2005, 1, 6). It is a form of culture that Canadians both consume (as spectators) and perform. In Canada, the variety of sport that is watched and played is vast and reflects the country's multicultural character. Examples include cricket, soccer, rugby, gymnastics, wrestling, and boxing; bocce, Highland Games, baseball, golf, tennis, and basketball. Despite this, in Canada, not all sports are created equal. Above most, a few rest higher in public estimation and participation: the quintessential *Canadian* games, lacrosse, Canadian football, and curling; and the national *passion*, ice hockey (on lacrosse, see Metcalfe 1987, 181–218; Fisher 2005; on Canadian football, see Cosentino 1995; on curling, see Maxwell 2002). While each of these sports expresses Canadian cultural identity in profound ways, hockey stands out as the most prominent emblem of Canadian popular culture.

Ice Hockey

The history of ice hockey is, at some level, the history of Canada. As poet Richard Harrison has argued eloquently, "hockey invented Canadians as much as Canadians invented hockey" (Harrison 2004, 160). Though ball-and-stick games had been played on ice in Europe for centuries, the modern game of ice hockey was created by McGill University students in Montreal in 1875, less than a decade after Canada became a self-governing dominion. The Montreal game was branded with regular rules published in the *Montreal Gazette* in 1877 and popularized by the Montreal Winter Carnival in the 1880s. It impressed the governor general of Canada, Lord Stanley, to such a degree that in 1893 he donated a trophy to go to the amateur hockey champions of the dominion (see McKinley 2000; Whalen 1994). Within a few short years, hockey had become, truly, a national phenomenon. Canadian novelist J. Macdonald Oxley observed in 1895: "The game of rink hockey … as played in Canadian cities to-day, is, without question, a distinctly home product." By 1905, historian Alan Metcalfe writes, "hockey pervaded the whole country" (Oxley 1895, 340; Metcalfe 1987, 73). Throughout the twentieth century, the equation of hockey with Canadian popular culture has been commonplace and assumed. Canadians have prided themselves on being the first and best hockey-playing nation in the world. And this assumption has pervaded all cultural forms from coffee-table books, serious literature, and art to more ephemeral forms – beer commercials, television documentaries, and fashion (especially T-shirt) designs. In 2012, Canadians celebrated the fortieth anniversary of Canada's narrow victory over the Soviet Union in the Cold War–era "Summit Series" (on Paul Henderson's last-minute goal). The event produced a raft of misty public sentiment and reminiscence. Likewise, Canada's winning of the gold medals in both men's and women's hockey on home ice at the 2010 Vancouver Olympics resulted in an effusion of national pride and a flood of memorabilia – books, videos, lapel pins, caps, T-shirts, jackets, and team sweaters.

But hockey is a Canadian story beyond mere popular assertion, jingoist bluster, and national chauvinism. The story of hockey parallels the Canadian historical narrative "from colony to nation" (to colony). Born in post-Confederation Canada, hockey embodied the rejection and replacement of British cultural forms in the late nineteenth century. Hockey was new, northern, rugged, and independent – just what late-Victorian Canadians fancied themselves to be. According to Michael Robidoux (2002), the replacement (or subjugation) of soccer, cricket, and other "garrison games" with hockey represented, at some level, nothing less than a sporting declaration of independence. Violent, aggressive, and decidedly non-bourgeois, the game was "an identifiable image" for Canadians and a "vehicle of resistance against British … hegemony" (ibid., 220, 221). Hockey was a symbol of Canada's coming of age at the turn of the twentieth century, and, ever since, that equation (Canada = hockey) has been so regularly drawn as to become orthodoxy. Still, history is unkind to orthodoxies. Since the 1920s, hockey has become subject to the same *historical* forces that have challenged Canadian sovereignty and identity in politics and economics: Americanization and globalization. Canada's game, and its players, are regularly exported to the United States via the National Hockey League (formed in 1917) and through the minor-league professional and amateur collegiate ranks. As early as 1929, six of the NHL's ten teams were located in the United States (in 2013, only seven of the NHL's thirty teams are Canadian), and the trend of American ownership in the sport has grown ever since. A Toronto sportswriter asked in 1925, "Will U.S. cash cripple hockey?" The answer for many Canadian nationalists ever since (among them, the fans of the displaced Winnipeg Jets and the Quebec Nordiques) has been yes (Thompson and Seager 1985, 186–90; Kidd 1996, chap. 5). "What this country needs is a sport it can call its own," Bob Bossin wrote in 1970 in *Maclean's* magazine (1970). "We used to have one. Hockey." Canada has "shared" too well its enthusiasm for the game. Fewer and fewer of the game's best players and teams are Canadian. "This is our fundamental dilemma," Hall of Fame goaltender, hockey philosopher, and politician Ken Dryden wrote in *The Game*, in 1983: hockey "is part of our national heritage, and pride, part of us; but we can't control it." In their manual *How to Be a Canadian*, humorists Will and Ian Ferguson (2001) wrote wryly, "Hockey matters to Canadians. Canadians care *deeply*. Anaheim vs. Nashville. San Jose vs. Phoenix. Who will win? Who will lose? Who could possibly care one way or another? Canadians, that's who." The depth and resilience of Canadians' identity with hockey as a signature form of popular culture is remarkable. Hockey still has the ability to crystallize fellow feeling among Canadians, and this seems to have grown deeper as the game has become more universally accessible. When asked in 2004 what her weekly performance on the hockey rink meant to her, one Newfoundland woman had a common but telling reply: "This is being Canadian" (Loeffler and Beausoleil 2004).

Art

In similar ways, Canadian art has provided a historical reflection on what it has meant to be Canadian. "Canadian art" describes a body of work so broad and diverse as to defy being subsumed into a single category; it is a veritable dog's breakfast of genres, images, and styles, most impressive for its breadth of experimentation. Canadian artists have worked in many different media, including sculpture, painting, printmaking, photography, quiltmaking (and other textiles), and ceramics. Canadian art encompasses productions as diverse as modern oil portraiture, Haida totem poles, Inuit carvings, watercolour landscapes, Abstract Expressionism, cartoons, and sculpture in marble, copper, and brass. A visit to the National Gallery of Canada in Ottawa, the country's largest collection of Canadian art, shows this quickly and clearly (go to the National Gallery of Canada's website at http://www.gallery.ca/en).

In their own ways, Canadian artists *perform* Canada, sometimes in literal depictions of their lives and environments, sometimes in symbolic representations of the political, environmental, and social forces that have informed and shaped their worlds. In either way, a sense of history can be traced through much of their work. Canadian art reflects, to some degree, the broad trajectory of the dominant Canadian historical narrative: from colony to nation (and perhaps back to colony). The history of Canadian art, at one level, parallels the challenges and triumphs of a new, young, and diverse nation "coming of age."

Of course, Canadian art predates "Canada." Though not defined in the same way as modern Canadians see and use "art," Canada's First Nations have created meaningful artistic symbols about their lives for tens of thousands of years, and they continue to do so today, albeit in different economic contexts (Nemiroff et al. 1992; Hawker 2003). Contact with European culture, Vance shows us in his recent history, obliterated some Native Canadian art forms, and altered and shifted the meanings of others, including pictographs and oral tradition (Vance 2009). In the colonial era, under the French (1608–1760) and the British (1760–1867), Canadian artists mimicked – in art as in all their fledgling cultural endeavours – European trends and sensibilities, merely sprinkling in, occasionally, Canadian subjects (Paikowsky 1988, 369–81). But as with sport, Canada began to establish its own identity through art in the years after Confederation. "In Canada," Christine Boyanoski (1989) has written, "this nationalism reflected a desire … to achieve artistic maturity and a unique national expression" (3). In the twentieth century, this imperative was expressed in every genre and in a variety of ways, but the clearest expressions of Canadian "coming of age" were in the Expressionist paintings of Emily Carr (1871–1945), the sculptures of R. Tait Mackenzie (1867–1938), the surrealist works of the Automatists (1940–55), the modernist experiments in landscape painting by the

Group of Seven (1920–33), and by another artist associated with the group though not a member, Tom Thomson.

The Group of Seven and Emily Carr warrant particular attention because of their artistic accomplishments but also because of their profound impact to this day on Canadian popular culture. They have achieved an iconic status in the Canadian imagination. Their principal works are as recognizable to most Canadians today as the faces of movie stars and hockey players. The Group of Seven's symbolic status is encapsulated in the title of the exhibition catalogue for its most recent major retrospective at the National Gallery of Canada (1995–6): *The Group of Seven: Art for a Nation*. The same must be said of Emily Carr: her recent exhibit mounted at the National Gallery (2006–8) admitted her iconic status: *Emily Carr: New Perspectives on a Canadian Icon*. In between, the National Gallery mounted a major Tom Thomson retrospective (2002–3), called simply *Tom Thomson* (Hill et al. 1995; Hill 2006; Reid 2002).

At its inception, the Group of Seven included Franklin Carmichael, Lawren Harris, A.Y. Jackson, Frank Johnston, Arthur Lismer, J.E.H. MacDonald, and Frederick Varley. These men had known one another since 1911, but formed themselves into a loose collaboration only in 1920, three years after Thomson's mysterious death in Ontario's Algonquin Park. Their purpose was clear from the start: in Thomas Thorner's words, it was "a mystical and romantic crusade to create a uniquely Canadian style that captured the essence" of Canada (Thorner 2003, 238); as Ann Davis has noted, it was "to discover a sense of place and to create a series of symbols for a nation" (Davis 1997, 225; 1992). Doing so as Modernists, the Group of Seven rejected safely representational and mere photographic likenesses in favour of intuitive, subjective images that bordered on the abstract. They painted many different things, but principally the Canadian wilderness; theirs was a collective decision to elevate the artistic worth of the new country by making its landscape the focus of their labours. Even so, their subjects were hardly "national." Predominantly, they painted landscapes from Northern Ontario (the Canadian Shield, mainly north of Lakes Huron and Superior). Using broad strokes and a multicoloured palate, they painted the details that harsh, rugged landscape has to offer: pristine lakes and rivers, twisted and wind-blown trees, leaves, and ice and snow.

The group's insistence that Canadian art must derive from the landscape of Canada and the experiences of Canadians was a significant

departure from common practice in Canada, which was still, culturally, very much a colonial society before 1920. The First World War did
much to change this. But at the time, these seven painters drew immediate and harsh criticism from their contemporaries, especially from
other artists and their followers, but also from newspaper reviewers of
their exhibitions. Many thought that what the members of the group
were offering was not what art should be. When the group displayed
their works at exhibitions in Britain and the United States, and at home,
few critics were impressed. A reviewer for *Saturday Night* magazine dismissed the paintings as those of a "cult of ugliness" and as the "blood
and thunder school," confirming the belief among the British that "Canadians are crude and commonplace in taste and ideals" (Thorner 2003,
245, 244). But by 1930, these attitudes had changed. By then, across
Canada, intellectuals and others were meditating on the cultural implications of the First World War and on the future of a growing country
whose ties to Great Britain were becoming weaker.

In the 1930s, Canadians began to embrace the Group of Seven's work
as their own "national art." An editorial in *Canadian Forum* magazine
used the group's new prominence as a *cri-de-coeur* for Canadians to take
pride in their cultural coming of age. "Canadians should awake to the
fact that they have great artists interpreting their country and its soul,
and they should also be told the truth about those self-styled critics
who have only contempt for what is best and finest in the field of art in
Canada" (Thorner 2003, 249). Since then, the Group of Seven's art has
achieved a currency well beyond collectors and art professionals and
their students. Their work went into silk-screened commercial reproduction in the 1940s, and those prints have hung in Canadian school-
rooms, offices, and other public spaces for decades. In their time, they
defied the denigration of "colonial" art and, according to the National
Gallery curator Charles Hill, "attracted an audience for Canadian art
greater than at any previous time in our history" (1995, 187). Ever since,
they have served as an emblem of Canada's maturation.

Perhaps the most colonial place in Canada during the late nineteenth
and early twentieth century was Victoria, British Columbia, where
Emily Carr was born. As a young man her father had travelled throughout the British Empire, trying various pursuits, before marrying another Briton and settling down as a merchant in Victoria, an outpost
of empire, far removed from both London and even nascent Canada. A
headstrong young woman, Emily Carr was orphaned while still a teen-
ager and left to the care of a much older sister and a family guardian.

Driven to paint, she studied first in the United States, then England, and finally France, before returning to Victoria, where she lived, but for brief interludes, for the rest of her life. As part of her development, Carr roamed the coasts of Vancouver Island and the mainland, staying in Native villages and painting what she saw. This progress – chronicled by a vast output of sketches, drawings, and paintings – reveals Carr developing from a raw talent to an Expressionist of real genius, a painter who seized the scenes, totems, and landscapes of the Native villages she visited to produce an art unlike any seen before. Throughout, she lived alone, eventually becoming seen as something of a local kook in staid Victoria. She was often seen walking about town with animals of various sorts in a baby carriage, among them a pet monkey, Woo, to which she was deeply attached.

During the late 1920s Carr connected with the Group of Seven, and in 1927 her work was included in the "Exhibition of Canadian West Coast Art: Native and Modern" at the National Gallery of Canada. She travelled east for the exhibition, meeting members of the group and developing a friendship with Lawren Harris that became enormously important to her. As a result of these contacts and others, her painting was transformed during the subsequent decades with a new-found power and an almost mystical ability to paint scenes from British Columbia's landscape, particularly its forests. Throughout, Carr embodied the figure of the isolated artist, a genius true to her vision. Her iconic status emerged steadily through the latter years of her life – there is no doubt that she helped create it herself – and has continued to grow since her death. Carr and her works are now seen as the apotheosis of serious Canadian art. Towards the end of her life she turned to writing; her first book, *Klee Wyck*, won the Governor General's Award in 1941 (see also Moray 2006; Thacker 1999, 182–90).

Limited Identities: A Culture of Fragments

Two years after Canada's centennial, in 1969, the venerable historian from the University of Toronto J.M.S. Careless popularized a term to describe the conundrum of Canadian national identity, one that has received a good deal of play ever since. In those years, Canadian politicians made it fashionable to view Canadians' social, cultural, and linguistic differences as a virtue. The unofficial slogan of Canadian nationalism in that decade reflected this strange sense of being: "unity in diversity." Careless (1969, 1–10) gave this idea a historical perspective:

Canada had never had one unified, common sense of nation. Instead, it had always had a series of "limited identities." This was an important point and is true to this day. It confirmed a sense that Canadians had had of themselves for some time, but had perhaps been afraid to admit. Canada and Canadian culture is a collection of separated parts. A fragmented culture – a culture of limited identities – is, for Canada, a normal state of being. This fact can be seen best, perhaps, in Canadian literature and music.

Literature

Canadian literature is one area of popular culture that has received acclaim and a healthy following both inside the country and abroad. It is a relatively new phenomenon. Except for a handful of writers, such as Stephen Leacock (1869–1944) and Mazo de la Roche (1879–1961), both of whom achieved considerable international success as writers, Canadian literature ("CanLit") dates back only to the late 1960s. Its growth can be linked to the founding of the Canada Council in the late 1950s to subsidize Canadian artists and also to the nationalist fervour that surrounded the 1967 centennial celebrations. "Read Canadian" became a frequently heard imperative, and in the years since, Canadians have done just that. Canadian publishing has long been a precarious enterprise – one hampered, like all Canadian cultural industries, by the presence of competitive products from the United States – yet even the most casual observer cannot help but see the strength and vitality of Canadian writing today. The Governor General's Awards for literature, founded in 1936, have been surpassed (at least for fiction) by the more glitzy Giller Prize (founded in 1994). The latter is presented at a gala event that is televised across the country.

Canadian writers have long earned acclaim abroad. Morley Callaghan's short stories began appearing in *The New Yorker* not long after that magazine was founded in 1925, and Hugh MacLennan's 1945 novel of French–English relations, *Two Solitudes*, enjoyed marked success in the United States. Since then, a number of Canadian writers have achieved an international following. Any list of recent Canadian writers who have gained real notice abroad must include Mavis Gallant (a regular in *The New Yorker* since the early 1950s); Mordecai Richler (whose fiction and non-fiction were widely known in both Britain and the United States); Robertson Davies (whose novels found a loyal following abroad); Margaret Atwood (who became a major force among American feminists with *Surfacing* [1972]); Alice Munro (also a mainstay in *The New Yorker*, a "writer's writer" who gleans an excess of praise whenever she publishes); Carol Shields (whose *The Stone Diaries* [1993] won both the Governor General's Award and, owing to her Illinois birthplace, the Pulitzer Prize); and Michael Ondaatje (whose *The English Patient* was made into a successful Hollywood film). Many other writers enjoyed broad acclaim outside Canada, as when Rohinton Mistry's *A Fine Balance* (1995) was selected for Oprah's Book Club. Many more Canadian authors have built significant reputations. In chronological order, it is worth noting Thomas Chandler Haliburton, Susanna Moodie and her sister Catherine Parr Traill, E.J. Pratt, F.R. Scott, Sinclair Ross, W.O. Mitchell, Leonard Cohen, Margaret Laurence, Robert Kroetsch, Timothy Findley, Thomas King, Tomson Highway, W.P. Kinsella, Alistair MacLeod, Guy Vanderhaeghe, Ann-Marie MacDonald, Joseph Boyden, and Lynn Coady. Canada has produced a literary tradition out of proportion with its population and resources; in the literary ring, Canadian writers are remarkable for their ability to "punch above their weight."

Considering only Atwood, Davies, Munro, and Ondaatje, this prominence has been evident and growing since the 1970s. Atwood, in particular, is more than just a prolific writer; she is a public intellectual whose prescient writings have helped define the cultural moment of her generation. Her dystopic novels – *Surfacing* (1972), *The Handmaid's Tale* (1985), and *Oryx and Crake* (2003) – have been influential warnings of what faces us as a culture. Along with her other writings, these have made her the most prominent Canadian writer of the latter half of the twentieth century. How, then, is Canadian literature fragmented? The first point here is elementary: Canadian literature is fragmented by language, the very vehicle through which it is delivered. A linguistic fault line runs down the middle of the Canadian "canon," separating Canadian writers and readers, English and French – a great divide that good translation has mended, but only minimally.

Canadian literature is fragmented, moreover, by region – a theme that returns us to a basic truth unveiled earlier regarding the country's geography. English literature in Canada has reflected the great geographical and, by extension, socio-economic divisions that have separated Canadians since Confederation. "Defining the regions of Canada is a game that Canadians like to play," Elspeth Cameron writes. But, she adds: "No one can win" (1997, 17). What she means is that Canadian regional identities are changeable and shifting. For example, we can speak of central Canada or the Prairie provinces as economic and political regions, but Canadian writers have been more specific in their selections of setting and context, more limited in their focus on place. This narrowness has resulted in richer depictions of the *local* in Canadian culture. Examples are Michael Crummey's use of Newfoundland dialect; David Adams Richard's relation of class and local mentalities in the Miramichi Valley, New Brunswick; Michael Ondaatje's feel for immigrant Toronto in the Depression era; Mordecai Richler's droll renderings of Jewish Montreal; Margaret Laurence's and W.O Mitchell's miniature cosmos of prairie Canada; and John Bemrose's images of small-town industrial Ontario in decline (Crummey 2005; Richards 2000; Ondaatje 1987; Richler 1959; Laurence 1998; Mitchell 1997; Bemrose 2003). Only a handful of Canadian authors have ventured to draw meaningful connections across regions; that is, to capture a pan-Canadian meaning in the themes, settings, and characters they employ (MacLeod 2001).

More recently, Canadian literature has become fragmented (perhaps like most national literatures) by ideology, or more accurately, *perspective*. "Canada" has meant so many different things to Canadian writers that, when their works are taken together, they seem hardly to be writing from the same place. This was not always the case. In the middle decades of the twentieth century, contributors to and readers of CanLit developed a sense of common venture, or synthesis. In his influential book *The Bush Garden* (1971), literary theorist Northrop Frye recognized that CanLit in the 1950s, 1960s, and 1970s was characterized by a focus on the uneasy relationship between human beings and the land. Canadians, in their literature and in their lives, built a "garrison mentality" to protect themselves against nature's challenges to their values and norms, which asserted a sense of placelessness. "Where is Here?" was a central question motivating Canadian writers. In 1972, Atwood revised and augmented Frye's earlier formulation, asserting in her "thematic guide to Canadian literature" that the dominant theme was "survival" – Canadian writing was shot through with the challenges of physical, cultural, and spiritual survival in inhospitable environments (Atwood 1972). For a time, CanLit, it seemed, had a potential canonical blueprint. By the 1980s that potential began to dissipate as Canadians explored more and other themes. The fragmentation of perspective was visible, for example, in the works of new feminist writers, the resurgence and popularization of First Nations literature, and especially the mercurial rise of immigrant voices in Canadian writing. For these writers, questions about the Canadian landscape, "garrison mentality," and survival meant very little; in fact, there is not much in these recent works that demonstrate a concern for or preoccupation with the project of Canada as a nation at all. One late 2011 commentary published in Toronto's *Globe and Mail* made the point with a blunt question: "Are Canadian Writers Canadian?" (Barber 2011).

The best illustration of this fragmentation of perspective involves First Nations and immigrant voices in recent CanLit. Among the best and most prominent First Nations writers are Thomas King and Tomson Highway, who use the Native voice as a counternarrative to the dominant mythology of (white) Canadian identity. King's "Borders" is a brilliant short story about a Native woman who is held up at the Canada-US border and prevented from visiting her daughter in Salt Lake City when she refuses to reply to a border guard's question about her citizenship with any answer other than "Blackfoot." For her, the border (such an important symbol in traditional Canadian nation-building narrative) is meaningless; so is being "Canadian" (or "American"). (See chapter 8 for further development of themes relating to discrimination and conflict.) But "home" as she understands it is meaningful. As she points out to her daughter subtly, Salt Lake City has nothing on Standoff (her hometown in Alberta) (King 1993, 133–47; Highway 1993). Finally, the fragmentation of perspective is visible in the works of Canadian writers who either are immigrants to Canada themselves or come from families who were part of late-twentieth-century migrations to the country. Scholars, critics, and readers have embraced the works of writers such as Mistry, Wayson Choy, Nino Ricci, Ondaatje, Neil Bissoondath, M.G. Vassanji, and Vincent Lam. Their works, though often set outside Canada, are *Canadian* writings and expressions of *a* (if no longer *the*) Canadian voice. One must be careful of overgeneralization here, but one point is clear. This new pattern in Canadian literature eschews old formulas and preoccupations with "survival" and questions of nation. Many of these writers pursue parallel questions of identity – how one stays connected to one's country of origin and to far-strewn family members, lovers, and friends even as one longs for a meaningful life in Canada. The struggles of Ondaatje's Nicholas Temelcoff in *In the Skin of a Lion*, Mistry's Sarosh in "Squatter," Choy's Sek-Lung in *The Jade Peony*, and Piscine Molitor Patel in Yann Martel's *Life of Pi*, to name only a few examples, reflect variations on this theme (Ondaatje 1987; Mistry 1997; Choy 1995; Martel 2002). Ironically, the emergence of the immigrant voice in Canadian literature is not really new; it shadows and echoes a dominant theme in some of the earliest CanLit works, such as Catherine Parr Traill's *The Backwoods of Canada* (1836) and Susanna Moodie's *Roughing It in the Bush* (1852) (Traill 1966; Moodie 1967). What is old is new again: if this literary trend reveals anything, it may be that Canadian writers and readers are attracted to the concept of Canada as a nation of immigrants, perpetually in a state of being "away." The Canadian "self" is itself a series of fragments.

Music

One can see – no, hear – this sort of cultural fragmentation in other ways in the realm of Canadian music. The breadth and variety of music in the Canadian "soundscape" belies any effort by Canadian cultural nationalists to assert a Canadian sound, or a common Canadian musical voice. Charles Foran, the author of the chapter on Canadian music in *The Rough Guide to World Music*, states this clearly: "If Canada was once a series of solitudes, it is now a cacophony." But that fact, he argues, is healthy. "In such a state, some art forms become restricted by language or convention, and they suffer. Not music, though" (Foran 2000). A recent issue of *Canadian Geographic* dedicated to mapping Canadian music demonstrates both its variety and its vibrancy, from community choirs on the Atlantic coast to Punjabi hip hop in Vancouver (*Canadian Geographic*, January–February 2006). Canadian music is fragmented by genre and rooted by region. Though Canadian music has been influenced heavily by European tradition in classical forms of music – in symphony and opera, for example – and by American patterns in popular music – in blues and jazz, for example – "as a region of North America and as a culture in its own right," Michael Taft argues, "Canada has produced its own syncretistic musical traditions" (1993, 205). In other words, Canadian music is part of a larger North American whole; but it is also unique in its attachment to its regional geography and to the multicultural nature of its people. There are many Canadian sounds. As with other cultural forms, all musicians in Canada perform Canada when they sing and play, though only some of them deal overtly with Canadian themes in their titles, lyrics, and compositions. In terms of genre, there are several Canadian music constituencies. Pop and folk are the largest categories and the ones in which Canadian performers have had the most commercial success. Canada has thriving scenes in classical and industrial music, and in First Nations and gospel music as well. In pop music, many Canadians have made it big in both Canada and the United States. The Guess Who, Neil Young, The Band, Céline Dion, Rush, Shania Twain, Alanis Morissette, Dream Warriors, Avril Lavigne, Sum 41, Bryan Adams, Anne Murray, Lee Aaron, Diana Krall, Gordon Lightfoot, Joni Mitchell, Sarah McLachlan, kd lang, Ron Sexsmith, Nelly Furtado, the Tragically Hip, Nickelback, and Barenaked Ladies are just some of the popular Canadian musical acts that have achieved commercial success. More recently, throwback crooner Michael Bublé and teen pop sensation Justin Bieber have extended this list. Canadian voices all, their music (to the extent that one can generalize about such a diverse group of talents) is not preoccupied with Canadianness; in fact, for some that concept is not overtly present at all. But it is there, in The Guess Who's boldly antiwar "American Woman" (1970), in Gordon Lightfoot's "Canadian Railroad Trilogy" (1975), and in the homages to Canadian places: a Northern Ontario town in Neil Young's "Helpless," an "Old Apartment" in Toronto for Barenaked Ladies (1996), or, simply, Canada in Joni Mitchell's "A Case of You":

I drew a map of Canada
Oh Canada
With your face sketched on it twice ...
Oh I could drink a case of you darling
And still I'd be on my feet.

The regional flavour of Canadian folk music – a sense of closeness to its roots, its ethnic and immigrant origins, and its constituencies – somehow makes practitioners of this form of music more recognizably "Canadian." For Foran, folk music in Canada is best understood in five compartments: French Canada, Maritime Canada, Newfoundland, Western Canada, and the music of the First Nations. All of these forms of Canadian folk music are vibrant, but perhaps none more than Maritime music. Rooted in its Celtic and French Acadian origins, Maritime folk was the music of sea shanties, fishermen, and lumber workers, and employed simple instruments, but especially fiddle and guitar. Maritime music, like all folk music, is a storytelling vehicle, and the words and messages of songs told Maritimers who they were; the lyrics were as important as the melodies. This is borne out in the music of Hank Snow, Natalie MacMaster, the Barra MacNeils, the Rankin family, Ashley MacIsaac, Great Big Sea, and especially the late Stan Rogers, whose ballads about Nova Scotia privateers in the Revolutionary War ("Barrett's Privateers"), a crew's love for their sunken vessel ("The Mary Ellen Carter"), and the emblematic schooner *Bluenose* (1993) prod identity, memory, allegiance, and myth among Maritimers (and other Canadians):

> ... That proud, fast Queen of the Grand Banks Fleet
> Portrayed on every dime
> Knew hard work in her time ... hard work in every line
> The rich men's toys of the Gloucester boys
> With their token bit of cod
> They snapped their spars and strained to pass her by
> But she left them all behind
> Now her namesake daughter remains to show what she has been
> What every schoolboy remembers will not come again
> To think she's the last of the Grand Banks Schooners
> That fed so many men
> And who will know the Bluenose in the sun?

"The more I study Canadian music," University of Ottawa ethnomusicologist Elaine Keillor notes, "the more I feel there is a strong link with our geography" (Harris 2006, 15; see also Keillor 2003). If she is right, Canadian music is as contoured and complex – and as fragmented – as the Canadian landscape described in chapter 1.

The External Other

No artefact of Canadian popular culture reflects the fear and utility of the external "other" better than "The Rant," a 2000 television commercial advertising Molson Canadian beer (Seiler 2002). It begins with an apparently shy young man, Joe, who approaches an open microphone on a stage and gradually works himself into a discursive lather over the subject of his national identity and the shameful ignorance that (he assumes) most Americans have about Canada:

> Hey. I'm not a lumberjack or a fur trader. And I don't live in an igloo, or eat blubber, or own a dogsled. And I don't know Jimmy, Sally, or Suzy from Canada, although I'm certain they're really, really nice. I have a Prime Minister, not a President.

I speak English and French, not American. And I pronounce it "about,"
not "aboot."

I can proudly sew my country's flag on my backpack. I believe in peacekeeping, not policing; diversity, not assimilation. And that the beaver is a
truly proud and noble animal. A toque is a hat, a chesterfield is a couch,
and it is pronounced "zed" not "zee."

Canada is the second largest land mass, the first nation of hockey, and
the best part of North America! My name is Joe, and I *am* Canadian! Thank
you.

As Joe proceeds, the rant gets louder, and he is joined by background
music and a few cheers from an invisible crowd. He completes his speech
in full throat and in full conviction – a mock declaration of national love
of country delivered to the Canadian malt beverage constituency. Slyly
ironic, "The Rant" is important for two reasons. First, it is clearly intended (like virtually all anti-American references in Canadian popular
culture) for a knowing, Canadian audience. Second, it reflects a much
broader theme that runs through and colours much of Canadian popular
culture: the fear of *and need for* an external other against which Canadian
identity can be cast and measured (see CBC 2012; Seiler 2002).

Canada has never been without an "other," and arguably, the country relies on the existence of such a concept. Canada has had two successive "significant others": Britain and the United States. Unlike the
United States, Canada never rejected its British imperial parent; instead
of seizing self-government and sovereignty through revolution and
bloodshed, Canada was granted its independence from Britain peacefully and incrementally: self-government in 1867 through Confederation and the British North America Act; and sovereignty only later, in
1931, with the Statute of Westminster. Not only did Canada never reject
Britain, but claims to "Britishness" in literary and popular culture have
been an important cultural touchstone in the efforts Canadians have
made to explain and perform who they are. There are a great many cultural manifestations of Canadians' lauding of their British connection,
in theatre, art, literature, and music (Resnick 2005, 23–4; Berger 1970).
Canada's first attempt at a national anthem, Alexander Muir's "The
Maple Leaf Forever" (1868), is important not only because it honours
Canada's Britishness (and ignores French Canada, even as it praises
its conquerors), but also because in English Canada it was so widely
known and used for so long.

In days of yore, from Britain's shore,
Wolfe the dauntless hero came,
And planted firm Britannia's flag,
On Canada's fair domain!
Here may it wave, our boast, our pride,
And joined in love together,
The Thistle, Shamrock, Rose entwine,
The Maple Leaf forever! ...
On Merry England's far-famed land
May kind Heaven sweetly smile;
God bless old Scotland evermore,
And Ireland's Em'rald isle!
And swell the song both loud and long,
Till rocks and forests quiver,
God save our Queen and Heaven bless
The Maple Leaf forever!   (Muir 2001, 35–6)

"The Maple Leaf Forever" captured the sentiments of most English Canadians even well after the introduction of Robert Weir's English version of "O Canada" in 1908, a song that became the country's *official* anthem, although not until 1980 (Routhier, Lavallée, and Weir 2001). A clearer expression of Canadian "Britishness," "The Maple Leaf Forever" could be heard preceding professional hockey games in Toronto and Boston in the 1930s, at professional and service club meetings in the 1950s and 1960s, and in English-Canadian public school classrooms in the 1970s. For many English Canadians, Britain has been a revered "other" whose presence has been a source of celebration in Canadian literary and popular culture.

Such has not always been true with Canada's other "other" – the United States. Statesmen from Canada and the United States have for many years declared that the countries are "best of friends": close neighbours; integral trading partners; and political, military, and diplomatic allies (Thompson and Randall 1997). And in some measure, Canadian-American affinity and friendship have been expressed in literary and popular culture. Still, the relationship between these countries has not been symmetrical or equal; with ten times the population of Canada and a much more powerful economy and military, the United States is "big brother" to Canada. Canadians have developed a sibling rivalry – an occasional resentment towards big brother – that is curious in that few Americans know it exists until they visit Canada. One theme in

Canadian literary and popular culture is "anti-Americanism" – an attempt to distinguish Canadian values, norms, and character and, especially, to protect them from being altered or supplanted by those of the United States. "Anti-Americanism has been found, at differing periods and in differing intensities," historian Jack Granatstein (1996) has written, "in all segments of Canadian life" (6). In literary and popular culture, it has manifested itself especially in debates and discussions over Canadian magazines and Canadian films, and in Canadian comedy.

Comedy

For want of space, Canadian comedy will receive only brief treatment here. Canada *knows* comedy; or at least, some Canadians do. In recent years they have become ubiquitous among the comedians who work regularly in New York and Los Angeles in stand-up, "improv," television sit-coms, and feature-length movies. Though their Canadian roots might be all but unknown to American viewers, Canadian comedians are among the most prominent (and funniest) in their trade: Mike Myers, Colin Mochrie, Tom Green, Lorne Michaels, Dan Ackroyd, John Candy, Eugene Levy, Jim Carrey, Dave Foley, Rick Moranis, Catherine O'Hara, Tommy Chong, Martin Short, Dave Thomas, Rich Little, Leslie Nielsen, and Russell Peters. To this might be added the list of Canadian funny men and women who stayed to ply their trade in Canada: the casts of *SCTV*, *Codco*, *This Hour Has 22 Minutes*, and *The Royal Canadian Air Farce*, Johnny Wayne and Frank Shuster, *The Trailer Park Boys*, Rick Mercer, and Stuart McLean. The fact that Canada has produced so many successful comedians is puzzling to most students of Canada, who would be hard pressed to find anything in the country's make-up to explain it. Why are Canadians so funny? It may be perspective. Canadians are good observers and critics, especially of their southern neighbours. It makes them, as Australian Jill Kerr Conway notes in her memoir about her life in Canada, "perpetual mockers" (1995, 179; see also Pevere and Dymond 1996).

Magazines

Canadians are more than good observers, they are good consumers of other cultures too. The late nineteenth century and the early years of the twentieth saw the rise in Canada, as in other industrial nations, of mass circulation publications and, in particular, of an infant magazine industry. Magazines were an important expression of Canadian culture; cheaply produced and widely accessible, they contained a wide variety of discourses on Canadian life, from the practical to the political. Like the transcontinental railway and radio (and later television), magazines did much to integrate Canadians, symbolically and in real terms; they kept Canadians "on the same page," providing common texts and discussions for a sparsely populated country that was far flung and in transition. As early as the 1890s, periodicals such as *Maclean's*, *Canadian Home Journal*, *Saturday Night*, *Chatelaine*, *Mayfair*, and *Canadian Magazine* connected the country with news, political commentary, histories, household advice, consumer advertising, and human-interest features. They (and a host of newer incarnations of Canadian magazines) have done so ever since.

In this realm of cultural production, the American presence has been difficult to ignore. Magazine production in the United States has always dwarfed that in Canada, and Canada has been seen as a natural market. Even as early as the 1920s, American periodicals "poured into Canada," according to Mary Vipond. By the mid-1920s, 50 million copies of American magazines such as *Ladies' Home Journal*, *Saturday Evening Post*, and *McCall's* were being bought annually in Canada; for every Canadian magazine that was produced in those years, eight were imported from the United States. The disparity set off a huge public controversy in Canada, with domestic magazine publishers and their political allies demanding that the Canadian government raise tariffs on American periodical imports and establish differential postal rates for Canadian and American magazines to protect the Canadian market for Canadian magazines (Vipond, in Hillmer 1989, 237–58). Their demands were not met; the political need to maintain good trade relations with the United States trumped the fears of Canada's producers of periodical culture. What did come out of the debate was a realization that Canadians' magazine reading was not motivated by nationalism, but by a preference for the American product.

Still, Canadian magazines have hobbled along ever since, despite the competition with American publishers for Canadian readers. The issue remained a sore one into the 1970s for Canadian magazine producers, who felt a dire need for government protection in their own marketplace. The introduction of a government subsidy for the production and distribution of Canadian magazines was instituted in the 1970s, but was applied so liberally that even *Time* magazine and *Reader's Digest*, two American productions operating in Canada (though admittedly producing "Canadian editions" with some exclusive content), were granted subsidies. The easy peace was unsettled again in the 1980s, when the American magazine *Sports Illustrated* began "split runs," transmitting its weekly magazine content by satellite directly to a Canadian printing plant. The tactic enabled the magazine to recycle its content (already paid for by American advertising) and resell advertising space at discounted prices, squeezing other Canadian magazines out of the ad market. When the Canadian government passed a law to ban this practice in 1995, the United States responded quickly, challenging it (and winning) before the World Trade Organization in 1997 (Roberts 1998, 38). Nonetheless, Canadian magazines still perform their limited but useful role as vehicles for cultural nationalism. *Maclean's*, for example, remains a leading source of news and cultural criticism for Canadian readers; it also produces a popular annual guide to Canadian universities (http://www2.macleans.ca).

Film

Any discussion of film as a source and reflection of Canadian identity must be very careful to define its terms. Canadian identity can be seen through film in at least three ways – Canadians in film; Canada in film, and Canadian films. Each belongs in a broad discussion about the elements of popular culture, but each carries varying degrees of value when it comes to assessing how Canadians perform and consume Canada. Each, moreover, reflects the powerful influence of the United States in Canadian culture. First, Canadians have identified themselves in, and found connection with, the work of individuals: expatriate Canadian actors, writers, and producers ("stars in exile") who have crafted films outside Canada – in most cases, in Hollywood, at the centre of the celluloid universe. Canadians have seen themselves in Mary Pickford, David Cronenberg, Ivan Reitman, Raymond Massey, Norman Jewison, Margot Kidder, Graham Yost, Leslie Nielsen, Ellen Page, Christopher Plummer, William Shatner, Keanu Reeves, Michael J. Fox, Donald and Kiefer Sutherland, Ryan Gosling, and others. To many Canadians, their work is emblematic, regardless of the themes, settings, or storylines of their films. Canadian film workers cannot shake their *Canadianness.* "We could spot a Canadian in an instant," Pevere and Dymond assert. In short, these performers represent Canada, "no matter where [they] do it," even in if it is in Los Angeles or New York (Pevere and Dymond 1996, x, ix; see also Simpson 2000).

Second, film reflects Canadian popular culture when Canada itself has been the central setting or subject. Most often, this exercise has reflected idealized, American views of Canada and the routines and rhythms of Canadian life, which rarely capture the country (in Canadian minds, anyway) accurately or fairly. Hollywood's Canada has almost always been a grotesque caricature of its northern neighbour – an expression of what American filmmakers have preferred to see in Canada, rather than the way it really is. As Pierre Berton documented in *Hollywood's Canada*, until the 1960s Canada was painted for North American audiences as a vast, open, frozen but forested land, sparsely populated by Mounties, lumberjacks, fur traders, timber tycoons, marginal Native people, and ubiquitous Frenchmen: "happy-go-lucky rogues in toques." Canadians consumed Hollywood productions such as *The Call of the North*, *Pierre of the Plains*, *Yukon Vengeance*, *Northwest Territory*, and dozens of others voraciously and, we might assume, welcomed Hollywood's version of their country. "It was Hollywood," Berton argues, "who gave us our image of ourselves" (Berton 1997, 41; 1975). In a strange way, Canadians have embraced and appropriated (and occasionally embellished) this caricature of themselves as a nation of rustics – homespun and simple, forthright but happy. The embrace of the Hollywood image of Canada has taken humorous forms. Mocking this version of Canada is, for example, the comedic shtick of the McKenzie Brothers, the urban mythology of the ignorant American tourists, and Rick Mercer's "Talking with Americans" on the Canadian sketch comedy show *This Hour Has 22 Minutes*. There is another way in which Hollywood has depicted Canada, albeit (nearly) invisibly. In the 1980s and 1990s a lower Canadian dollar encouraged Hollywood film producers to use Canadian locations (and Canadian film crews) to shoot American pictures. Vancouver, Calgary, Toronto, and Montreal stood in, variously, for New York, Los Angeles, Chicago, and Seattle. Only a discerning eye could recognize the differences. This phenomenon hardly counts as a filmic depiction of Canadian culture; but as some critics have argued, it contributed to the stunting of the development in Canadian film in that it has co-opted Canadian film workers (Acland 1997, 285).

But the third and most important way in which film is a vehicle for expressing Canadian identity is Canadian cinema – films made in Canada, by Canadians, for a Canadian audience. Here, Canadians' efforts have been channelled into two traditions worthy of note: inward-looking and largely publicly funded documentary filmmaking and a fledgling private industry in feature films. The first of these traditions came about in 1939, when the Government of Canada established the National Film Board (NFB), whose mandate was, in the words of its first commissioner, John Grierson, "through a national use of cinema, [to] see Canada and see it whole." (The NFB's mission, as its website reveals, is "to interpret Canada to Canadians and other nations" [http://www.nfb.ca]). Since then, the NFB has produced hundreds of films documenting the sense of place and meaning of Canada for Canadians, on subjects as varied as the history of Canada, Canadian art and politics, and labour relations, with titles such as *Action: The October Crisis of 1970* (1973), *Final Offer* (1984), and *Canada at War* (2005). But the NFB has also become known for its support of avant-garde and experimental filmmaking, for animated and children's productions, and for universal subjects that focus on global issues, such as *Forbidden Love* (1992), *If You Love This Planet* (1982), and *Not a Love Story* (1981) (on the NFB generally, see Acland 1994).

In addition, a small and struggling feature film industry has grown in Canada since the 1960s, one known equally well for its quality and, ironically, its marginality. Canadian filmmakers such as Atom Egoyan, Denys Arcand, Mort Ransom, and Sandy Wilson, and film companies such as Alliance Atlantis (since 2007 called simply "Alliance"), have produced important and acclaimed films such as *Mon oncle Antoine* (1971), *The Decline of the American Empire* (1986), *Jesus of Montreal* (1989), *My American Cousin* (1985), *Gross Misconduct* (1993), *Seducing Dr. Lewis* (2002), *I've Heard the Mermaids Singing* (1987), *Atanarjuat* (2000), *The Barbarian Invasions* (2003), *Margaret's Museum* (1996), *Bon Cop, Bad Cop* (2006), and the curious (but perhaps predictable) *Score: A Hockey Musical* (2010), featuring Olivia Newton John. To help them along, the Canadian government in 1967 created the Canadian Film Development Corporation (CFDC, known as Telefilm Canada since 1984) to provide financial assistance, create infrastructure, and maintain skilled technical assistance (Smith 1994, 105–6).

Hollywood, however, is the inescapable fact that overshadows all forms of Canadian cinema. It was Hollywood's overwhelming presence in Canadian movie theatres in the 1920s and 1930s that gave rise to the need for an agency such as the NFB to balance Canadian consumption. Moreover, the dominance of American films in Canadian theatres today has continued to marginalize Canadian films, even in their own country. There are two reasons for this: distribution and taste. Canadian movie theatres are owned overwhelmingly by American theatre chains such as Cineplex, Landmark, and Empire, "branch plants" of American parent companies that decide which films will be shown, at all times and everywhere (Acland 1997, 282–3). These companies have soundly rebuffed occasional Canadian efforts (such as that of Canadian cabinet minister Flora MacDonald in 1987) to get more Canadian content into theatres in Canada (see Granatstein 1996, 242–3). The result has been that Canadian feature filmmakers have developed what critic Charles Acland calls an "Expo mentality" (Acland 1997, 290). If not in the big chain theatres, Seth Feldman writes, "their films do get shown at festivals, at odd hours on television, and for short theatrical runs in major cities" – but not widely or accessibly enough to maintain a strong domestic industry (Feldman 1993, 217). As for taste: Canadians have chosen to consume American films more than their own. Intoxicated for so long by Hollywood flash and thunder, Canadian cinema "has never truly been a part of popular cinema-going experience" for Canadians. Despite this, Canadian film has thrived, albeit modestly, "in parallel locations – the school, the film festival or retrospective, the community hall, the library, and the museum" (Acland 1997, 293, 290).

Enter the State

Canada has a "bizarre world" of cultural regulation, *New York Times* journalist Anthony DePalma argued in a 1999 editorial,

> a sometimes arbitrary, often contradictory system of rules and measures cobbled together over several decades to protect Canadian culture – not just music, but film, television, magazines and literature – from what some Canadians consider the menace of American cultural imperialism … In defending itself against brashly aggressive American culture, Canada sometimes seems like a fastidious gardener who fumes and fusses over the riot of dandelions on his neighbor's lawn while realizing that ultimately there is little he can do to keep them from encroaching on his property. But that doesn't keep him from trying. (in Thorner 2003, 507, 508)

DePalma's characterization is playful but true. Canadian literary and popular culture has never been free to thrive unassailed, in a vacuum; from its earliest expression, the producers of Canadian culture have felt themselves threatened by the twin spectres of scale and invasion. Canadian cultural production has always been fledgling and, hence, vulnerable; Canada's location next to the United States, the most powerful and extensive producer of culture for consumption, threatens to supplant Canadian culture with American forms. In response, Canadians have turned to the state. Since the 1930s, Canadians have placed their faith in their governments to nurture and protect their culture, and to deliver it to them as well. The Canadian state has become such a central player in Canadian cultural production and distribution that it is difficult to imagine the phenomenon without the government's presence. State intervention in the arts, in some measure, *is* Canadian culture. The role of the state can be seen in virtually all forms of Canadian literary and popular culture, but perhaps most especially in radio and television programming, broadcasting and its regulation.

A government mandate to nurture and protect Canadian cultural production had its roots in the 1920s, when Canadian fears about the American cultural colossus were first expressed with respect to magazines and radio broadcasting. In response to a royal commission report, the Canadian government created the Canadian Radio Broadcasting Corporation in 1932 (CBC by 1936), a publicly owned and funded broadcaster that connected Canadians through news and programs on the airwaves and combated the ubiquity of American programming (Smith 1994, 101). This agency, charged with a national mandate to connect Canadians, has remained in place ever since. In radio and, after 1952, on television, the CBC has shared the airwaves uneasily with private, commercial broadcasters in Canada. By 1950 the threat of American cultural imperialism – in all forms of cultural production – prompted the Canadian government to establish another royal commission, the Massey-Lévesque commission, known more formally as the Royal Commission on National Development in the Arts, Letters, and Sciences. Its report, published in 1951, called for massive government investment in Canadian cultural institutions to buttress "national feeling and interest" against the "forces of geography." The Massey commission "must surely be counted as one of the most influential public enquiries in the history of Canada," writes David Cameron. "It … shaped federal cultural policy for the next several decades" and confirmed the Canadian government's commitment to protect Canadian culture in the arts, heritage, and higher education (Cameron 1996, Litt 1992). In the wake of the Massey report, the Canadian government augmented its funding of the CBC and the NFB and established the Canada Council, a grants agency for the arts and universities, in 1957. In 1968 the government established the Canadian Radio-television and Telecommunications Commission (CRTC), a regulatory agency tasked with policing the structures of radio and TV transmission and, most important, the content as well. In 1970 the CRTC introduced the government's most invasive protective measure in the market of culture: content regulations. Canadian radio and television broadcasters were henceforth held to a stringent quota of Canadian content (CanCon). On AM and FM radio, 35 per cent of the songs played have to meet criteria for "Canadianness" (40 per cent, for most new stations licensed since 1999); on television, 60 per cent of programming has to be Canadian, with 50 per cent in the prime-time evening hours (Thompson and Randall 1997, 260).

It is difficult to judge what effect these "hothouse" protections have had for Canadian culture in radio and television. Except for a few years of unregulated radio transmission in the 1920s, Canadian programming has always operated within a protected environment, through the CBC before 1970, and through CanCon regulations ever since.

Within this milieu, a distinctive culture of Canadian programming has grown up, and a sort of division of leisure has emerged among Canadian consumers. Want drama? Surf the American radio and television stations. Want news? Tune in to Canadian broadcasters. For those who want *Canadian* drama, a variety of options are available. Canadian stories are told on Canadian radio and television programs: on the radio, there are *Sounds Like Canada* and *Cross Country Checkup*; on TV, *Degrassi Junior High*, *Da Vinci's Inquest*, *The Trailer Park Boys*, *Godiva's*, *SCTV*, *The Red Green Show*, *Corner Gas*, and the timely *Little Mosque on the Prairie*. But next to the flash of American programming, most Canadians have found Canadian radio and TV wanting. "In the noisy din of U.S. network programming," Pevere and Dymond write, "the Canadian stuff stuck out like a stunned moose in the middle of the trans-Canada highway" (Pevere and Dymond 1996, ix). The exceptions to this pattern have been two: the unmatchable *Hockey Night in Canada*, and Canadian news and news commentary shows, which an early start at public broadcasting nurtured and promoted among Canadians. Perhaps because of this tradition (and this market niche), Canadian broadcasters – such as Peter Mansbridge, Wendy Mesley, Lloyd Robertson, and Brian Williams in Canada; the late Peter Jennings, John Roberts, Arthur Kent, Keith Morrison, and Thalia Assuras in the United States – have had a commanding presence and an aura of authority in their reportage. If a Canadian reads the news, you had better believe it! (Simpson 2000, 330–7).

CanCon regulations in Canada have not been universally supported, however, for at least a couple of reasons. Those committed to a free market in culture (and in all things) find CanCon needlessly interventionist. In 1999, Hal Jackman told a Canadian Club audience in Toronto in a speech on "Canada's Culture": "Our preoccupation with our identity, particularly our insecurity relative to the United States, is self-defeating ... It prevents a healthy, robust culture from ever developing at all ... It is not the government or the CBC that gives us our identity. [They] should be a reflection of what we are, not someone who tells us who we should be" (in Thorner 2003, 515). Others have opposed the system because it is too clumsy and imprecise. For example, according to the CanCon formula, songs recorded by the Rolling Stones in Toronto are considered "Canadian" and qualify to be played within a radio station's quota; but a Neil Young song recorded in New York is deemed "foreign" and ineligible (Thompson and Randall 1997, 260–1). In 1992 Canadian rocker Bryan Adams won notoriety in the Canadian press when his own recording ("Everything I Do") was rejected by the CRTC as being not Canadian enough. "The Canadian government should just get out of the music business," he responded angrily on national television. "It is breeding mediocrity." But the public response was telling, too, and continued support for CanCon regulations in Canada betrays in much of the Canadian population a deeper and lasting concern about the frailty of Canadian culture and the need for national vigilance (http://cbc.ca/archives; see also Edwardson, 2008)

The French Fact

In 1945, English-Canadian writer Hugh MacLennan won the Governor General's Award for *Two Solitudes*, his novel about contemporary Montreal and Quebec. That work lamented the great divide that has rent Canadian culture to this day: language. Since the British conquest of Quebec in 1760, Canada's French and English communities have coexisted peacefully and ascribed their loyalties to a common nation-state, albeit through different symbols, ideologies, and senses of nation. Still, "two solitudes" has continued to be an apt descriptor of Canadian literary and popular culture. English Canadians have constructed one series of symbols, myths, and mottoes; French Canada has constructed a parallel (though hardly identical) literary tradition and popular culture of its own. The two rarely meet or cross over in literature, film, or theatre.

Exception are few – as in the 2006 bilingual feature film *Bon Cop, Bad Cop* about the challenges and stereotypes that emerge when a French-speaking detective from Quebec teams up with an English-speaking counterpart from Ontario to find the murderer of a man whose body is found draped over a highway sign precisely on the border between Ontario and Quebec, and in Nicolas Dickner's critically acclaimed (in both languages) novel *Nicolski*, published in French (2005) and English (2008). But these exceptions prove the rule. Cultural producers in Canada's two linguistic camps have done little to engage one another; on the whole, they have not really tried. In treating francophone literary and popular culture separately, we are not imposing an organizational separation for convenience; we are merely observing a separation that, in fact, has always existed.

Despite this separation, French-Canadian literary and popular culture has much in common with its English-Canadian counterpart. The literature and popular culture of French Canada has been shaped and informed by the same sorts of forces that have moulded English-Canadian culture. A historical construct, francophone literary and popular culture is itself fragmented, coloured by the presence of the United States (or, *Americanité*), and supported to a considerable extent by the state, in this case both the Canadian and Quebec governments. Vibrant, colourful, and lively, francophone literary and popular culture also reveals a *nation* in the making: a work in progress.

Nowhere in Canada is history a more important cultural product than it is in French Canada. French Canadians, it is fair to say, are bombarded regularly with symbols of their troubled past. The symbolism is based on a firm conviction: French Canadians, it reads, are a conquered people for whom collective identity is not merely a goal but a necessity. If English-Canadian culture has always rested on a theme of "survival," French-Canadian culture is about *survivance* – that is, a commitment to maintaining, protecting, and affirming the "island" culture of French Canada in the North American sea of menacing Englishness. In this, literary and popular culture plays a critical role; it is part of a political program for their continued existence.

Literary and popular culture in French Canada reflects this imperative, clearly and well. The weight of the past is seen in the literary constructions of writers such as Gabrielle Roy, "Ringuet," Anne Hébert, Louis Hémon, Marie-Claire Blais, and Gaston Miron; in the songs of Felix Leclerc, Robert Charlebois, and Loco Locass; in the films of Denys Arcand; in the painting of Paul-Émile Borduas, Jean-Paul Riopelle, and

Marc-Aurèle Fortin; in the theatre of Michel Tremblay and Robert Lepage; and in the poetry of Octave Crémazie and, perhaps especially, Gilles Vigneault, as in his "Mon pays":

Mon pays ce n'est pas un pays, c'est l'hiver
Mon jardin ce n'est pas un jardin, c'est la plaine
Mon chemin ce n'est pas un chemin, c'est la neige
Mon pays ce n'est pas un pays, c'est l'hiver
...
Mon pays ce n'est pas un pays, c'est l'envers
D'un pays qui n'etait ni pays ni patrie
Ma chanson ce n'est pas une chanson, c'est ma vie
C'est pour toi que je veux posséder mes hivers.

My country it's not a country, it's winter
My garden it's not a garden, it's the plain
My path it's not a path, it's the snow
My country it's not a country, it's winter
My country it's not a country, it's the opposite
Of a country that's neither country nor homeland
My song is not my song, it's my life
It's for you that I want to own my winters.

Cameron (1997, 132)

French Canadians do more than represent their history in song and prose and verse; they regularly act out their history and their place in North America in popular festivals. Carnaval, Quebec City's annual celebration of winter, reflects Quebec's historical uniqueness as a civilization that has survived and thrived in a forbidding northern climate for almost four hundred years. In Quebec (and in many French-Canadian communities across Canada and the United States), St-Jean-Baptiste Day is celebrated every year on 24 June with religious services, picnics, political speeches, sporting events, and a parade, the colourful centrepiece of the event. The celebration began in 1834, when Ludger Duvernay organized a series of national ceremonies as demonstrations against the British regime. Ever since, the day has maintained its meaning as an expression of francophone nationalism. Every year, massive parades are organized in Montreal and Quebec City, with elaborate floats and street performances in which French Canadians express their past and their aspirations for the future (MacDougall 1997; Boisvert

1990). A similar ritual is held among French Canadians every summer in New Brunswick. There, descendants of the Acadians, who were expelled by British troops during the French and Indian War in 1755, return annually to visit family homesteads and communities and to celebrate the resilience of their culture through speeches, theatre, and especially music. (Several Acadian festivals are held annually in Atlantic Canada. For example, the village of Petit-de-Grat, Nova Scotia, holds parades, barbecues, concerts, and a blessing of the fleet [http://www.lapicasse.ca/la_picasse/index.cfm?id=265].) Many Canadian-rooted Acadians attend the annual Acadian Festival in Madawaska, Maine, which features family reunions and a re-enactment of the Acadian landing in northern Maine (http://www.acadianfestival.com/Pages/default.aspx). Every five years the Congrès Mondial Acadien (Acadian World Congress) is held, an event that draws thousands of Acadian descendents from around the world to participate in a music festival, theatre productions, historical round tables, and debates. First held in Moncton, the congress took place in New Brunswick in 1994 and 2009, Louisiana in 1999, and Nova Scotia in 2004 and returned to New Brunswick in 2009 (http://www.acadian.org/congres4.html). Forgetting the past in French Canada means the sure loss of identity. "*Je me souviens*" – I remember – is the official motto of the province of Quebec, one emblazoned on its motorists' licence plates. For all French Canadians, a connection to the past *is* survival.

Yet it would be a mistake to cast French Canada as some sort of monolithic entity demographically, politically, or culturally. It does not speak with one voice, but with many – a fact that is sometimes masked by language. French Canada consists of French-origin and French-speaking Québécois, 95 per cent of the residents of that province. But it also includes Acadians (mainly in New Brunswick, Prince Edward Island, and Nova Scotia), Franco-Ontarians (largely along Ontario's Quebec border and in Northern Ontario), Métis (descendants of francophone settlers and Aboriginals who intermarried) and a smattering of francophone communities in western Canada. Literary and popular culture reflects this fragmentation. A concern about representing French voices outside Quebec has led to the founding of *Eloizes*, a journal of Acadian writing, and Éditions Acadie, an Acadian publishing house, as well as to a general recognition that important French voices – such as Acadian writers Antonine Maillet, Dyane Léger, and Melvin Gallant, and Franco-Manitoban writer Charles LeBlanc – are thriving outside Quebec (Hahn 2003, 344–8).

French-Canadian literary and popular culture is, like its English-Canadian counterpart, notably influenced by the presence of the United States. But beyond this general parallel, the similarity ends. The dynamic of American influence in French-Canadian culture is unique. French Canada does not feel threatened by Hollywood, *Time* magazine, American broadcasters, or publishing houses. A different language is its prophylactic against American cultural "imperialism." Here, the interest goes the other way. French-Canadian popular culture has borrowed significantly from American expression. Quebecers "let North America get them," in the phrasing of English-Canadian writer Morley Callaghan in 1928; had he lived longer, he might have said that *they* had got to North America (Lawrence 1928, 11). American culture in French Canada is scattered, in (translated) television shows and feature films, literature, and arts. It is present in "serious" and low culture: in the debates among the francophone intelligentsia about post-colonialism and the prospect of the Americanization of Quebec, and in the curious mimicry of American popular cultural forms, even in the unlikeliest places, such as the Festival Western de St-Tite, an annual celebration of the American West with rodeos, country dancing, cooking contests, and hauling matches with draft horses, all taking place in a small lumber town south of Shawinigan, Quebec (http://www.festivalwestern.com/en).

A final characteristic of literary and popular culture in Quebec is, as in the rest of Canada, a propensity (a perceived need) to look to the state for protection and cultivation. Quebec literature and popular culture is, in this respect, doubly blessed: it receives the support of the Canadian state, but also that of the Quebec state, a series of programs and incentives for producers of culture to represent their *nation* – that is, the French-Canadian nation – in literature, dance, theatre, painting, and other media. The CBC has a French-language counterpart, Radio Canada, which broadcasts French-Canadian cultural productions – news, sports, and drama (including *téléromans*) – on radio and television for French speakers across the country. In Quebec, literature and the arts received a boost in government support beginning in the 1960s, when the Quiet Revolution demanded better infrastructure for cultural expression. The results were impressive: large, government-funded concert halls and auditoriums, such as the Place des Arts in Montreal (1967) and the Grand Théâtre in Quebec City (1971). In Quebec the state watches culture closely, and for good reason (Dickinson and Young 1993, 331–2). A separate and thriving culture is the bellwether of French-Canadian *survivance*.

Conclusion

Defining literary and popular culture in Canada can hardly be tackled comprehensively or satisfactorily in a single essay such as this. It is too messy. One might echo the words of British historian Pamela Pilbeam who, when faced with the gargantuan task of describing and analysing the unlovely subject "the middle class in modern Europe," remarked: "What is the morphology of a quicksand?" (Pilbeam 1990, 8). Canadian literary and popular culture is like that. Still, it is not impossible to at least consider some of the central elements of this quicksand, even if we cannot hope to contain it or comprehend its whole. As this chapter has detailed, Canadian literary and popular culture is a historical construct whose manifestations can be plotted in real Canadian historical experiences. Canadian culture is, moreover, fragmentary – a jigsaw puzzle of many pieces – a series of artefacts shaped by a British colonial past and the presence, threat, and inspiration of American culture. Because of this, Canadian literary and popular culture leans on the state to a great extent, so much so that a large, interventionist, and protective government in Canada is itself a cultural product. The concern that Canadians have about their culture is, at root, the same concern they have about their country. Canada is a work in progress, and its literary and popular products reflect the energy and creativity of a people still in the throes of determining who they are. That process, painful and uncertain, is also remarkably productive, as even a visit to the National Gallery or a neighbourhood ice rink shows and a listen to a local poetry reading or a CBC broadcast reveals.

WEBSITES

Atwood, Margaret: http://www.margaretatwood.ca
Canadian Broadcasting Corporation: http://www.cbc.ca and http://archives.cbc.ca/archives
Encyclopedia of Music in Canada: http://www.thecanadianencyclopedia.com
Ferguson, Will: http://www.willferguson.ca
Hockey Hall of Fame: http://www.hhof.com
Maclean's: http://www2.macleans.ca
National Film Board of Canada: http://www.nfb.ca
National Gallery of Canada: http://www.gallery.ca/en
Online Resources for Canadian Heritage: Folk Culture and Popular Culture (Canadian Museum of Civilization): http://www.civilization.ca/splash

REFERENCES AND FURTHER READING

Acadian Festival in Madawaska, Maine. 2012. http://www.acadianfestival. com/Pages/default.aspx.

Acland, Charles R. 1994. "National Dreams, International Encounters: The Formation of Canadian Film Culture in the 1930s." *Canadian Journal of Film Studies* 3 (1): 3–26.

Acland, Charles R. 1997. "Popular Film in Canada: Revisiting the Absent Audience." In *A Passion for Identity: An Introduction to Canadian Studies*, ed. David Taras and Beverly Rasporich, 281–96. Toronto: ITP Nelson.

Atwood, Margaret. 1972. *Survival: A Thematic Guide to Canadian Literature*. Toronto: Anansi.

Barber, Jon. 2011. "Are Canadian Writers Canadian?" *Globe and Mail*, 29 October: R12.

Barenaked Ladies. 1996. "The Old Apartment." Stephen Page/Ed Robertson. Treat Baker Music SOCAN/WB Music Corp. 1996. ASCAP Ⓟ. Reprise Records.

Bemrose, John. 2003. *The Island Walkers*. New York: Metropolitan Books.

Berger, Carl. 1970. *A Sense of Power: Studies in the Ideas of Canadian Imperialism, 1867–1914*. Toronto: University of Toronto Press.

Berton, Pierre. 1975. *Hollywood's Canada: The Americanization of Our National Image*. Toronto: McClelland & Stewart.

Berton, Pierre. 1997. "Hollywood's Canada: The Americanization of Our Image." In *Canadian Culture: An Introductory Reader*, ed. Elspeth Cameron, 41. Toronto: Canadian Scholars Press.

Boisvert, Donald. 1990. "Religion and Nationalism in Quebec: The Saint-Jean-Baptiste Celebration in Sociological Perspective." PhD diss., University of Ottawa.

Bossin, Bob. 1970. "What This Country Needs Is a Sport It Can Call Its Own." *Maclean's* 88 (July): 13–14.

Boyanoski, Christine. 1989. *Permeable Border: Art of Canada and the United States, 1920–1940*. Toronto: Art Gallery of Ontario.

Brown, Craig, ed. 2002. *The Illustrated History of Canada*. 4th ed. Toronto: Key Porter.

"Bryan Adams Not Canadian?" 1992. http://archives.cbc.ca/archives. 14 January.

Cameron, David. 1996. *Taking Stock: Canadian Studies in the Nineties*. Montreal: Association for Canadian Studies.

Cameron, Elspeth. 1997. "Introduction." In *Canadian Culture: An Introductory Reader*, ed. E. Cameron. Toronto: Canadian Scholars Press.

Canadian Geographic. January/February 2006.

Careless, J.M.S. 1969. "Limited Identities in Canada." *Canadian Historical Review* 50 (March): 1–10. http://dx.doi.org/10.3138/CHR-050-01-01.

CBC. 2012. "I ... AM ... CANADIAN!" http://www.cbc.ca/player/Digital+Archives/Economy+and+Business/The+Media/ID/1747485681.

Choy, Wayson. 1995. *The Jade Peony*. Vancouver: Douglas and McIntyre.

Congrès Mondial Acadien (Acadian World Congress). 2011. http://www.acadian.org/congres4.html.

Conway, Jill Kerr. 1995. *True North: A Memoir*. New York: Vintage.

Cosentino, Frank. 1995. *A Passing Game: A History of the CFL*. Winnipeg: Bain and Cox.

Creighton, Donald. 1957. *Dominion of the North: A History*. Toronto: Macmillan of Canada.

Crummey, Michael. 2005. *The Wreckage*. Toronto: Anchor Books Canada.

Davis, Ann. 1992. *The Logic of Ecstacy: Canadian Mystical Painting, 1920–1940*. Toronto: University of Toronto Press.

Davis, Ann. 1997. "Image as Identity: Aspects of Twentieth-Century Canadian Art." In *A Passion for Identity: An Introduction to Canadian Studies*, ed. David Taras and Beverly Rasporich, 225–42. Toronto: ITP Nelson.

DePalma, Anthony. 1999. "Tough Rules Stand Guard over Canadian Culture." *New York Times*, 14 July.

Dickinson, John A., and Brian Young. 1993. *A Short History of Quebec*. 2nd ed. Toronto: Copp Clark Pittman.

Dryden, Ken. 1999 (1983). *The Game*. 3rd ed. Toronto: Macmillan.

Edwardson, Ryan. 2008. *Canadian Content: Culture and the Quest for Nationhood*. Toronto: University of Toronto Press.

Feldman, Seth. 1993. "Our House, Their House: Canadian Cinema's Coming of Age." In *The Beaver Bites Back? American Popular Culture in Canada*, ed. David H. Flaherty and Frank E. Manning, 209–21. Montreal: McGill-Queen's University Press.

Ferguson, Will, and Ian Ferguson. 2001. *How to Be a Canadian*. Vancouver: Douglas and McIntyre.

Festival Western de St-Tite. 2011. http://www.festivalwestern.com/en. 30 November.

Fisher, Donald M. 2005. "'Splendid but Undesirable Isolation': Recasting Canada's National Game as Box Lacrosse, 1931–1932." *Sport History Review* 36: 115–29.

Foran, Charles. 2000. "No More Solitudes." In *World Music: The Rough Guide, vol. 2, Latin and North America, Caribbean, India, Asia and Pacific*, ed. Simon

Broughton and Mark Ellingham with James McConnachie and Orla Duane, 350–61. Toronto: Penguin.

Francis, R. Douglas, Richard Jones, and Donald B. Smith. 2000. *Origins and Destinies*. 4th ed. Toronto: Harcourt Canada.

Frye, Northrop. 1971. *The Bush Garden*. Toronto: Anansi.

Frye, Northrop. 1982. "Sharing the Continent." In *Divisions on a Ground: Essays on Canadian Culture*, ed. James Polk., 57–70. Toronto: Anansi.

Granatstein, J.L. 1996. *Yankee Go Home? Canadians and Anti-Americanism*. Toronto: HarperCollins.

The Guess Who. 1970. "American Woman." © RCA 1970.

Hahn, Cynthia T. 2003. "French-Language Literature in Canada." In *Profiles of Canada*, 3rd ed., ed. Kenneth Pryke and Walter Soderlund, 344–8. Toronto: Canadian Scholars Press.

Harris, Eric. 2006. "I Wish I Had a River I Could Skate On." *Canadian Geographic* 126 (1): 15.

Harrison, Richard. 2004. *Hero of the Play*. 10th anniversary ed. Toronto: Wolsak and Winn.

Hawker, Ronald W. 2003. *Tale of Ghosts: First Nations Art in British Columbia, 1922– 61*. Vancouver: UBC Press.

Highway, Tomson. 1993 (1988). *Dry Lips Oughta Move to Kapuskasing*. Toronto: Fitzhenry and Whiteside.

Hill, Charles C., ed. 2006. *Emily Carr: New Perspectives on a Canadian Icon*. Vancouver: National Gallery of Canada, Vancouver Art Gallery, and Douglas and McIntyre.

Hill, Charles C., et al., eds. 1995. *The Group of Seven: Art for a Nation*. Toronto: National Gallery of Canada and McClelland & Stewart.

Hillmer, Norman, ed. 1989. *Partners Nevertheless: Canadian–American Relations in the Twentieth Century*. Toronto: Copp Clark Pittman.

Holman, Andrew C. 2009. *Canada's Game: Hockey and Identity*. Kingston, Montreal: McGill-Queen's University Press.

Keillor, Elaine. 2003. "The Canadian Soundscape." In *Profiles of Canada*, 3rd ed., ed. Kenneth Pryke and Walter Soderlund, 447–86. Toronto: Canadian Scholars Press.

Kidd, Bruce. 1996. *The Struggle for Canadian Sport*. Toronto: University of Toronto Press.

King, Thomas. 1993. "Borders." In *One Good Story, That One*, 133–47. Toronto: HarperCollins.

LaDow, Beth. 2001. *The Medicine Line: Life and Death on a North American Borderland*. New York: Routledge.

Laurence, Margaret. 1998 (1974). *The Diviners*. Toronto: New Canadian Library.

Lawrence, Margaret. 1928. "Interview with Morley Callaghan." *Saturday Night* 14 (July): 11.

Lightfoot, Gordon. 1975. "Canadian Railroad Trilogy." Gordon Lightfoot ©1975. Warner Bros. Records Inc.

Litt, Paul. 1992. *The Muses, The Masses, and the Massey Commission*. Toronto: University of Toronto Press.

Loeffler, T.A., and Natalie Beausoleil. 2004. "Crossing the Blue Line: Women's Hockey Experiences at Mid-Life." Paper presented to the conference Women's Hockey: Gender Issues on and off the Ice, St Mary's University, Halifax, 26–9 March.

Lower, Arthur. 1946. *Colony to Nation: A History of Canada*. Toronto: Longmans, Green.

Lumsden, Ian, ed. 1970. *Close the 49th Parallel etc.: The Americanization of Canada*. Toronto: University of Toronto Press.

Maclean's. 2012. University Rankings. http://www2.macleans.ca.

MacDougall, Jill. 1997. *Performing Identities on the Stages of Quebec*. New York: Peter Lang.

MacLennan, Hugh. 1945. *Two Solitudes*. New York: Collins.

MacLeod, Alistair. 2001 (1999). *No Great Mischief*. New York: Vintage Books.

Malcolm, Andrew H. 1985. *The Canadians*. New York: Times Books.

Martel, Yann. 2002. *The Life of Pi*. Toronto: Random House.

Maxwell, Doug. 2002. *Canada Curls: The Illustrated History of Curling in Canada*. Vancouver: Whitecap.

McKinley, Michael. 2000. *Putting a Roof on Winter: Hockey's Rise from Sport to Spectacle*. Vancouver: Greystone.

Metcalfe, Alan. 1987. *Canada Learns to Play: The Emergence of Organized Sport, 1807–1914*. Toronto: McClelland & Stewart.

Millard, Gregory, Sarah Riegel, and John Wright. 2002. "Here's Where We Get Canadian: English-Canadian Nationalism and Popular Culture." *American Review of Canadian Studies* 32 (1): 11–34. http://dx.doi.org/10.1080/02722010209481654.

Mistry, Rohinton. 1997. "Squatter." In *Tales from the Firozsha Baag*. Markham: Penguin Books.

Mitchell, W.O. 1997 (1947). *Who Has Seen the Wind*. Toronto: Macmillan.

Moodie, Susanna. 1967 (1852). *Roughing It in the Bush*. Toronto: McClelland & Stewart.

Moray, Gerta. 2006. *Unsettling Encounters: First Nations Imagery in the Art of Emily Carr*. Vancouver: UBC Press.

Morrow, Don, and Kevin B. Wamsley. 2005. *Sports in Canada: A History.* Don Mills, ON: Oxford University Press.

Muir, Alexander. 2001 (1868). "The Maple Leaf Forever." In *Who Speaks for Canada? Words That Shape a Nation,* ed. Desmond Morton and Morton Weinfeld, 35–6. Toronto: McClelland & Stewart.

Nemiroff, Diana, et al. 1992. *Land, Spirit, Power: First Nations at the National Gallery of Canada.* Ottawa: National Gallery of Canada.

Ondaatje, Michael. 1987. *In the Skin of a Lion.* Toronto: McClelland & Stewart.

Oxley, J. Macdonald. 1895. *My Strange Rescue and Other Stories of Sport and Adventure in Canada.* London: Nelson.

Paikowsky, Sandra. 1988. "Canadian Painting." In *Profiles of Canada,* 2nd ed., ed. Kenneth Pryke and Walter Soderlund, 369–81. Toronto: Irwin.

Petit-de-Grat Acadian Festival. 2011. http://www.lapicasse.ca/la_picasse/index.cfm?id=265.

Pevere, Geoff, and Greig Dymond. 1996. *Mondo Canuck: A Canadian Pop Culture Odyssey.* Scarborough, ON: Prentice-Hall.

Pilbeam, Pamela M. 1990. *The Middle Classes in Europe, 1789–1914: France, Germany, Italy, and Russia.* Chicago: Lyceum.

Reid, Dennis, ed. 2002. *Tom Thomson.* Vancouver: Art Gallery of Ontario, National Gallery of Canada, and Douglas and McIntyre.

Resnick, Philip. 2005. *The European Roots of Canadian Identity.* Peterborough, ON: Broadview.

Richards, David Adams. 2000. *Mercy among the Children.* Toronto: Doubleday.

Richler, Mordecai. 1959. *The Apprenticeship of Duddy Kravitz.* New York: Penguin.

Roberts, Joseph K. 1998. *In the Shadow of Empire: Canada for Americans.* New York: Monthly Review Press.

Robidoux, Michael. 2002. "Imagining a Canadian Identity through Sport: A Historical Interpretation of Lacrosse and Hockey." *Journal of American Folklore* 115 (456): 220, 221.

Rogers, Stan. 1993. "Bluenose." ©℗1993 Fogarty's Cove Music.

Routhier, Adolphe-Basile, Calixa Lavallée, and Robert Stanlet Weir. 2001. "O Canada." In *Who Speaks for Canada?: Words That Shape a Country,* ed. Desmond Morton and Morton Weinfeld, 50–1. Toronto: McClelland & Stewart.

Seiler, Robert M. 2002. "Selling Patriotism/Selling Beer: The Case of the 'I AM CANADIAN!' Commercial." *American Review of Canadian Studies* 32 (1): 45–66. http://dx.doi.org/10.1080/02722010209481657.

Shore, Marlene, ed. 2002. *The Contested Past: Reading Canada's History.* Toronto: University of Toronto Press.

Simpson, Jeffrey. 2000. *Star-Spangled Canadians: Canadians Living the American Dream*. Toronto: HarperCollins.

Smith, Allan. 1994. *Canada: An American Nation? Essays on Continentalism, Identity, and the Canadian Frame of Mind*. Montreal: McGill-Queen's University Press.

Taft, Michael. 1993. "Syncretizing Sound: The Emergence of Canadian Popular Music." In *The Beaver Bites Back? American Popular Culture in Canada*, ed. David H. Flaherty and Frank E. Manning. Montreal: McGill-Queen's University Press.

Thacker, Robert. 1980. "Canada's Mounted: The Evolution of a Legend." *Journal of Popular Culture* 14 (2): 298–312. http://dx.doi.org/10.1111/j.0022-3840.1980.1402_298.x.

Thacker, Robert. 1999. "Being on the North West Coast: Emily Carr, Cascadian." *Pacific Northwest Quarterly* 90: 182–90.

Thompson, John Herd, and Stephen Randall. 1997. *Canada and the United States: Ambivalent Allies*. Athens: University of Georgia Press.

Thompson, John Herd, and Allen Seager. 1985. *Canada 1922–1939: Decades of Discord*. Toronto: McClelland & Stewart.

Thorner, Thomas, ed. 2003. *"A Country Nourished on Self-Doubt": Documents in Post-Confederation Canadian History*. 2nd ed. Peterborough, ON: Broadview.

Traill, Catherine Parr. 1966 (1836). *The Backwoods of Canada*. Toronto: McClelland & Stewart.

Vance, Jonathan. 2009. *A History of Canadian Culture*. Toronto: Oxford University Press.

Whalen, James M. 1994. "Kings of the Ice." *Beaver* 74 (1) (February).

8   Native Peoples

MICHAEL LUSZTIG

There has been a general change in the political climate over the past
three decades: as the Canadian government has gone from a desire
to rid the country of the "Indian problem" through cultural assimilation to the imperative to compensate Aboriginal peoples for the damage done to their cultures, traditions, and values, to efforts to establish
Aboriginal self-government as a third sovereign order. The situation is
made all the more interesting by the relatively high percentage of Aboriginal people in the Canadian population (especially in Western and
Northern Canada), most notably in comparison to the United States.
Other factors that make the study of Native peoples especially interesting are their diversity in Canada (e.g., the presence of the Inuit) and a
series of seemingly intractable problems over land claims.

   This chapter outlines the history of Canada's Native policy and critically reviews its present policies. The reader will learn that there are no
easy solutions to Canada's "Indian problem." This chapter has multiple
sections. The first explores Native policy from Confederation to 1971,
a century during which the Canadian government sought (somewhat
contradictorily) to assimilate the Native population while at the same
time protecting Aboriginal land and treaty rights. The second looks at
land claims, constitutional issues, and the sovereignty of Aboriginal
peoples over the past forty years. Finally, we examine Tom Flanagan's
"second thoughts" critique of the mainstream view of Native policy in
Canada as well as Alan Cairns's understanding of Aboriginal Canadians as "citizens plus."

Protection and Assimilation

In the years after Confederation, Native policy in Canada embraced two objectives that worked at cross-purposes: protection and assimilation. Protection was provided under the Indian Act (1876), which was a means of ensuring that discrete territories were reserved for the exclusive use of Aboriginal Canadians. Administered by the Department of Indian Affairs and Northern Development (DIAND), the Indian Act is a sort of constitution that mediates the relationship between the state and those with Indian status. (Not all Aboriginal people are Status Indians – to be so designated, one's name must appear on the Indian Register.) While ultimate authority for Aboriginal matters remains with the federal government, governing band councils are elected to administer local affairs. One significant problem is that while the Indian Act reserved territory covered by treaty, Canada's treaty process was not comprehensive: large portions of Canada, including most of Quebec and British Columbia, were not covered by treaty. As a result, Aboriginal land claims in these provinces were left largely unsettled for most of the twentieth century. Land claims pertain to territories over which there is disputed ownership. As a rule, land covered by treaties has not been subject to land claims. The "historic treaty" process began as early as 1725 and continued until 1923 (subsequent treaties are known as "final agreements"). Historic treaties include peace and friendship agreements in eastern Canada, pre-Confederation treaties, and the so-called numbered treaties that covered the West but, problematically, stopped at the Rocky Mountains. Under the numbered treaties, Aboriginal peoples ceded control of traditional hunting and fishing territories to the colonial and later Canadian authorities in exchange for reserved lands – that is, lands set aside for their exclusive use. These treaties also defined hunting and fishing rights and often provided small annual grants for each band member.

The protection afforded by the Indian Act raised significant problems. For example, Indian status was often arbitrarily determined. Before 1985, because of its arcane registration process, the act failed to protect the status of many Aboriginal Canadians, even while it conferred special status on individuals who had no Indian ancestry (e.g., white women who married Native men). A 1985 amendment restored status to thousands of Indians, most prominently women (and their children) who had lost their status by virtue of marrying non-Indians; it also revoked the status of non-Indian women who married Status

Indians. And in 2010, Parliament introduced Bill C-3, which would return status to the grandchildren of Indian women who married non-Indians. While arbitrary and paternalistic, the Indian Act was vital to the protection of land rights. Also, it recognized that Status Indians constitute a different class of Canadian citizens who enjoy rights different from those who do not have Indian status.

While Aboriginal rights today are understood as protecting traditional cultural practices and perhaps the inherent right to self-government, the key issue is ownership of land. That issue generates a number of questions. Were Aboriginal peoples the original owners of the land? If so, did this make those peoples sovereign states in our contemporary understanding of the term? And if territory not covered by treaty had been appropriated by non-Aboriginals, what was the legal basis for this appropriation?

Traditional Aboriginal conceptions of land differ greatly from European ones. For Aboriginals, individual ownership of land was not conceptually relevant. The land was viewed as communal and as serving the interests of the whole people. Native people saw themselves not as the owners of the land so much as its stewards. By extension, resources were to be extracted from the land only as needed, and not with an eye to commercial gain or profit (see Fleras and Elliott 1992, esp. chap. 1).

By contrast, the traditional Anglo-American understanding is that private property is fee simple: one's land is property, and within the limits of the law, it is the owner's to use as he or she sees fit. One's property can be understood as "that sole and despotic dominion which one man claims and exercises over the external things of the world, in total exclusion of the right of any other individual in the universe" (Blackstone, in Glendon 1991, 23).

How does one come to enjoy such despotic control? Western culture's common understanding of land is that it is yours if you purchased it or inherited it. Either way, somebody owned that land before you did, and someone before that, and so forth. But how did the first owner acquire the land? At the risk of oversimplification, let us look at two prominent schools of thought and call them conservative and liberal, as they pertain to original ownership.

From the conservative perspective, the land came to be the property of the king by virtue of God's will. The king (or queen) was a servant of God, ruling by the divine authority of God. Among the king's responsibilities was to rule in the best interests of his subjects. Thus, he was imbued with a fiduciary responsibility mandated by God (and, in

Catholic Europe, mediated by the pope) over his sovereign territory. In practical terms, the principle of sovereignty was spelled out in the 1648 Treaty of Westphalia (Bueno de Mesquita 2000, 94). Among the monarch's prerogatives was to dispose of land as he or she saw fit. This prerogative was the basis of the famous 1763 royal proclamation (discussed below) under which the king reserved vast tracts of land for use by Native populations.

From the liberal perspective, property rights are one of the natural rights granted to every individual by God. This understanding of property justified settlers' intrusion into what Europeans considered common land. Since the land was not being worked productively, and there was enough and as good left for others, settlers understood the land they worked to be their property.

From either perspective, the European conception of property clashed with the established order in the New World. From the European perspective, common lands were either to be disposed of by the king at his pleasure or to be appropriated by those who would make productive use of them.

Assimilation

The logic of the Indian Act singled out Status Indians for special treatment and protection. Yet at the same time, the Canadian government maintained a long-standing commitment to assimilation, which began with a commission of inquiry culminating in the Davin report (1879) and more or less ended with the Trudeau government's white paper on Indian policy ninety years later.

Much of Canada's early history turns on the relationship between New France and British North America, an issue that was resolved with the British conquest of French North America in the Seven Years' War of the 1750s. New France's population was small, and its economy turned on the fur trade, which encompassed vast tracts of land. The interests of the French and Aboriginals ran largely parallel. Both benefited from the fur trade, which meant that both had similar uses for the lands west of Hudson Bay. French settlers, moreover, became military allies with a number of Indian nations, most prominently the Algonquians, antagonists of the Iroquois, who would later ally themselves with the British.

After the defeat of the French on the Plains of Abraham outside the walls of Quebec in 1759, and especially after the War of 1812, the settler-Native military alliance became increasingly irrelevant. With peace came the westward expansion of homesteaders, whose interest in the land no longer coincided with that of Aboriginal peoples. Indeed, Native people went from being allies to simply being inconvenient, and thus the "Indian problem" was born. After Confederation, numbered treaties solved some but by no means all of the Indian problem. Especially in British Columbia, where there were no numbered treaties, ambiguity persisted over land ownership, which gave rise to land claim disputes that continue to this day. In the nineteenth and early twentieth centuries, assimilation into Canada's social mainstream was far and away the easiest means to make the Indian problem go away. Assimilate Aboriginals, and social problems such as poverty on reserves (the Canadian term for reservations), crime, and disproportionate rates of alcoholism among the Native population would be reduced. To progressives of the nineteenth and twentieth centuries, this seemed the fairest and most sensible policy.

There is a good deal of logic to the fairness argument as it relates both to protection and to assimilation. Canada is a liberal democracy. The liberal element of that term mandates that the government ensure that all individuals are treated equally before the law and that the rights of all citizens are protected, regardless of race, national or ethnic origin, colour, religion, sex, age, or mental or physical disability.

For liberals, the good society is an integrated one, one that is blind to diversity. In such societies, a person is a person is a person. It is only when we label people that pernicious social divisions emerge. In the United States such labelling manifested itself in Jim Crow laws, in South Africa it took the form of apartheid. By contrast, it was diversity blindness that informed Prime Minister Pierre Trudeau's famous "Just Society" of the 1960s and 1970s – the ideal society to which he thought Canada should aspire.

Residential Schools

However, for many, even if the ends were admirable, the means left something to be desired. The most controversial element of the assimilation policy turned on the issue of education. Following the recommendations of the Davin report, the government sought to assimilate Native children through a system of residential schools. (The Department of Indian Affairs began to administer a small number of residential schools in 1874; Canada's last residential school closed in 1996.)

Residential schools were administered by the Department of Indian Affairs, in cooperation with various religious organizations. The mandate was clear: simply, the cultural traditionalism inherent in Native life would not be allowed to retard the development of Native children, who needed to be liberated from the pagan rituals of their ancestors and provided with an education that instilled Christian values. (Davin [1879], in keeping with the less enlightened language of the day, reviled the "influence of the wigwam" as an obstacle to civilization.) To this end, it was imperative that children be removed from their homes so that the good works of the school would not be undone in the home. To quote from the Royal Commission on Aboriginal Peoples (RCAP): "[Native children] had to be taught to see and understand the world as a European place within which only European values and beliefs had meaning; thus the wisdom of their cultures would seem to them only savage superstition. A wedge had to be driven not only physically between parent and child but also culturally and spiritually" (Canada 1996, vol. 1, chap. 10).

Of course, the goodness of these works was pretty dubious. Among the many problems (including removing children from their homes against the will of their parents) was that schools were underfunded and administered by individuals of questionable talent. Residential schools might also be condemned by a look at their social impact on those who attended them. The schools failed on two counts. First, they did a poor job of integrating young Native people into the cultural mainstream. Second, and very likely as a result, in the early and mid-1990s, Canada's Aboriginal population featured high rates of mental illness, alcoholism, fetal alcohol syndrome, family violence, injuries, diabetes, tuberculosis, human immunodeficiency virus (HIV), obesity, hypertension, and suicide (Tookenay 1996). So damaging were the effects of residential schools that the Canadian government announced in 2006 the Indian Residential Schools Settlement Agreement, under which roughly 80,000 Native people are eligible for reparations (Canada 2006).

It was to address the failure of past attempts to assimilate Native Canadians that the Trudeau government unveiled its white paper on Indian policy (1969) as a prominent part of the prime minister's quest to build the Just Society. (A white paper is an official articulation of government policy.) It proposed radical changes, including abolition of the Indian Act, the elimination of the Indian Affairs Department, and, most critically, the elimination of reserve and treaty provisions that had created a special class of citizenship for Status Indians. These recommendations made some sense. As the white paper pointed out, many so-called treaty rights were quite trivial, and where they were more substantial, they could be dealt with through existing social services or special hunting and fishing provisions.

More complicated was the issue of reserves. The white paper proposed that government trusteeship over reserve lands be ended and that a fee simple structure of ownership be developed. The white paper also sought to wash the federal government's hands of the whole mess of disputed land claims, which it deemed "so general and undefined it is not realistic to think of them as specific claims capable of remedy except through a policy and program that will end injustice to Indians as members of the Canadian community" (Canada 1969). Instead, land claims were to be negotiated with the relevant provincial governments – none of which, however, were anxious to cede their territory to Aboriginal peoples.

Elimination of special Indian status was a cornerstone of the Just Society. True justice could not prevail, Trudeau believed, when different classes of citizens enjoyed different rights, privileges, and obligations. Fairness required that all Canadians be treated equally before the law and that all be afforded the opportunity to pursue the good life as they saw fit. Separate but equal treatment of one class of citizens could not be reconciled with a just society (ibid.).

Special Status: Land Claims

Not surprisingly, the white paper was badly received in the Aboriginal community. Aboriginal leaders, meeting in the immediate aftermath of its release, rejected the proposal out of hand. Among the many problems noted were these: despite previous assurances, Aboriginal leaders had not been consulted before the proposed reform of the Indian Act; and the white paper amounted to a repudiation of special status for Native people, even though that status had apparently been affirmed as recently as the Hawthorn report of 1966. Especially troubling was that it had been difficult enough to negotiate land settlements with the federal government – dealing with the historically more recalcitrant provinces would be even more daunting (Cardinal 1969, esp. chap. 14).

For Aboriginal leaders, equality of all individuals before the law (legal equality) was a code term for the elimination of special Aboriginal status. From their perspective, equal treatment before the law could be appropriate only when the playing field was (roughly) level in the first place. Where there is pre-existing inequality between groups, legal equality merely serves to institutionalize the status quo. But the problem was not entirely socio-economic. For Native Canadians, the Indian Act was a travesty but it was still better than nothing; after all, it spelled out and protected land and treaty rights.

After taking more political heat than it could stand, the federal government withdrew the white paper in 1971, but the damage had been done. Having reneged on its promise to consult Aboriginal leaders before amending the Indian Act, the government faced a more politically mobilized movement that, instead of meekly submitting to junior-partner status in the determinations of Indian Affairs, set out to control the agenda.

The catalyst for significant change in the post–white paper era was an obscure land claim case filed by the Nisga'a band in northern British Columbia. It attracted little attention when the action was launched in 1967. Pursuit of land claims through the legal system was fraught with all sorts of difficulties. Land claims were based on the premise that Aboriginal people were the original owners of their traditional tribal lands; it followed that unless extinguished by treaty, ownership remained with them. This premise was legally shaky and was made even more problematic by the fact that the Canadian courts had a tradition of strict interpretation of constitutional law. Put differently, and as noted in chapter 3, there was a very limited tradition of judicial review (whereby the courts deem certain laws or executive actions unconstitutional). Indeed, by tradition, the courts were guided by the principle of parliamentary supremacy and intruded only where there was no alternative – for example, to determine whether or not a province or the federal government had acted beyond the scope of its constitutional authority. The constitutional basis of Indian land claims was by no means clear. In 1763 King George III had sought to clarify the territorial sovereignty of Crown lands after the conquest of French North America. And a poor job he made of it. For our purposes, the most relevant part of the royal proclamation pertained to the unsettled territories of the West: any land not already claimed or granted by the Crown was reserved for Aboriginal peoples. However, three important points must be noted. First, if the land was the king's to offer, it stands to reason that it was the Crown that enjoyed possession of this territory. Second, the proclamation did not grant this land to the Native peoples (in the same way it did, using the king's words, to the Hudson's Bay Company). It merely reserved it. Third and contrarily, the proclamation spoke of territories that had not been ceded to or purchased by the Crown. This implied that the land was something for Indians to cede or sell. If this was the case, then the king had no basis for offering land that the Crown had not acquired.

Whatever the ambiguity of the royal proclamation, the issue of Aboriginal title to the land appeared to have been disposed of in the 1888 case *St. Catherine's Milling and Lumber Co. v. The Queen*. At issue in that case was whether the federal government or the government of Ontario had the right to grant timber licences in territories covered by treaty between Indians and the federal government. The federal government's position was that it had purchased the land from the Indians and thus retained the right to regulate its use. The Judicial Committee of the Privy Council (JCPC), then Canada's highest court, ruled for the province of Ontario on the grounds that the land had never been the Indians' to sell in the first place. The royal proclamation of 1763, the JCPC ruled, granted Indians but "a personal and usufructuary right, dependent upon the good will of the Sovereign" and did not therefore constitute fee simple ownership. And it was here that legal precedent stood as the aforementioned Nisga'a case wound its way through the court system.

That case is worth closer scrutiny. In 1881, the BC government created a reserve for the Nisga'a on land that represented a fraction of the band's traditional homeland in the remote Nass Valley. The band never accepted the arbitrary reduction in the lands its members had held to be theirs from time out of memory. Decades of protest achieved little. Then, in 1963, White and Bob, two Nanaimo Indians, killed six deer on Crown land; they were arrested for it but ultimately acquitted. White and Bob argued that a document signed by the British governor in 1854 amounted to a recognition of Aboriginal hunting rights on the land in question. The BC County Court ruled that insofar as these existing (and officially recognized in 1854) rights had never been extinguished, they remained in full force. Ultimately, the Supreme Court of Canada upheld the acquittal, though its ruling was restricted to the implicit treaty of 1854 (Raunet 1984, 149).

But that ruling opened intriguing possibilities. In 1969, the *Calder* case was heard in the BC Supreme Court, with the Nisga'a arguing that they enjoyed the right to possess, use, and occupy their traditional tribal territory and that, as with White and Bob, those rights had never been lawfully extinguished. The court ruled against the plaintiff, finding that whatever title to the land the Nisga'a were claiming had been implicitly extinguished through the recognition of British Columbia's sovereign governance of the territory when that province entered Confederation in 1871. The ruling was upheld unanimously in the BC Court of Appeal.

The verdict was also upheld by the Supreme Court of Canada. In a 4–3 decision, the court ruled that the Nisga'a had no claim to the land in question. But the devil was in the details. Of the six justices who ruled on the issue of Aboriginal title (the seventh chose to dodge the thorny issue by ruling against the Nisga'a on procedural grounds alone), three determined that Aboriginal title had not been extinguished merely by the arrival of European settlers. Justice Emmett Hall's dissent was noteworthy, in that it was predicated on the notion that if you owned something, and someone had not taken it away from you, then you still owned it. In other words, it was not incumbent on the Nisga'a to prove title; rather, the onus was on the BC government to prove that title had been extinguished. It was not good enough, as the BC Supreme Court had done, to claim that title had been implicitly extinguished. Justice Hall's opinion broke ground in that his recognition of Aboriginal title was based on grounds different from the problematic royal proclamation of 1763 (Raunet 1984; Murphy 2001; Berger 2002).

Calder was heard by the Supreme Court of Canada in 1973. By the end of that year, the Trudeau government, in an attempt to regain control of a land claims process that might be subjected to a court so closely divided, had announced that the federal government would negotiate comprehensive land claims over disputed territories.

Special Status: Sovereignty

Calder did much more than create a mechanism for negotiating land claims. Its aftermath saw the emergence of a more overtly political agenda. In 1975, in the Northwest Territories, the Dene Band declared itself a nation within the broader Canadian federation. More concretely, the Inuit of the Far North proposed (and ultimately succeeded in) carving a new territorial government out of the Northwest Territories that would be controlled by the Inuit (Sanders 1983). These initiatives portended a new era in Aboriginal politics. Henceforth, Native peoples would not only seek the resolution of land claims but also demand the right to autonomy – or sovereign jurisdiction to govern their own affairs. In effect, they were seeking to add a third sovereign authority to

Canadian federalism. Indeed, the new objective was to seek constitutional recognition of Aboriginal rights.

To understand what happened next, we must digress a bit into the strange constitutional politics of the time to get a clear understanding of the process by which Aboriginal Canadians acquired special constitutional status. (Other details are available in chapter 6 on Quebec.) In 1976, a government led by the overtly separatist Parti Québécois (PQ) was elected in the largely French-speaking province of Quebec. A central component of the PQ's mandate was to complete what many believed to be the ultimate stage of Quebec's Quiet Revolution: the negotiation of "sovereignty-association" with Canada. The Quiet Revolution had started with the election of Jean Lesage in 1960. It coincided with the decline of the influence of the Roman Catholic Church and manifested itself in Quebec nationalism, the expansion of public works projects by the provincial government, and the movement of Quebec francophones into positions of economic prominence – positions that had long been held by that province's anglophone minority.

Sovereignty-association was understood as the political independence of Quebec, although the province would maintain an economic association with Canada. Pundits dubbed it divorce with bed privileges. A referendum to give the PQ a specific mandate to negotiate sovereignty-association was held in 1980. Late in the referendum campaign, with poll numbers suggesting a close vote, Prime Minister Trudeau went to Montreal and declared: "I know that I can make a most solemn commitment that following a NO vote, we will immediately take action to renew the Constitution and we will not stop until we have done that" (Trudeau 1980). Six days later, Quebecers voted overwhelmingly (roughly 60–40) to reject sovereignty-association.

Trudeau had long sought to patriate – or articulate a mechanism for amending – the BNA Act, which served as Canada's constitution. Before 1982, Canada's constitution was merely an act of the British parliament, which meant that all constitutional amendments had to take the form of changes to the BNA Act. In other words, Canada, a sovereign, independent nation, required the consent of another country's legislature to amend its constitution. Trudeau wanted to change that; he also believed strongly that Canada needed a constitutionally entrenched bill of rights.

In October 1980 the Trudeau government announced its intention to seek patriation of the constitution, with or without the support of the provincial governments. This resolution identified twelve issues that needed immediate attention. Other issues would be addressed in a second round of constitutional negotiations. Aboriginal issues were not included in the October resolution, but were on the agenda for the secondary round (Sanders 1983; Romanow, Whyte, and Leeson 1984).

Trudeau's announcement that he was willing to seek unilateral patriation if the provinces did not get on board was radical. By tradition, all changes to the BNA Act had to be approved by all provinces and the federal government. Three provincial governments (Manitoba, Newfoundland, and Quebec) sought references (or legal opinions as to the constitutionality of a proposed course of action) in their respective provincial courts of appeal. The three courts reached different opinions. The issue was thus referred to the Supreme Court of Canada, which heard the case in April 1981 and ruled at the end of September. The court's decision was a marvel of obfuscation. In *Re: The Amendment of the Constitution of Canada* (1981), the majority determined that while unilateralism did indeed violate constitutional convention, it was not illegal. In short, the court effectively punted the issue, leaving the federal and provincial governments to sort out the mess.

In the aftermath of this strange decision, Trudeau's best course of action was to move forward with the consent of the provinces. It would, after all, be undesirable to announce a new constitution for Canada, while at the same time having to admit to the unconstitutionality of the process by which it was achieved. To get provincial support, however, Trudeau had to compromise on his draft version of the amendments to the BNA Act.

For their part, Aboriginal leaders also opposed the unilateralism of the Trudeau government's October resolution. Substantively, the main problem was the proposed Charter of Rights and Freedoms. A constitutional charter of rights would provide formal equality (or equality before the law) for all Canadians. This meant, ipso facto, that no one group could enjoy special status. As such, the goal of Aboriginal sovereign self-government would be made more difficult. Indeed, the proposed charter could be seen as the 1969 white paper reborn in constitutional garb.

Procedurally, Aboriginal peoples' demands for participation in the constitutional process had largely been rebuffed. Their response was to embark on what amounted to a public relations campaign. Almost two hundred Aboriginal people travelled to England to meet with the queen and request that she not give royal assent (the final step for a bill to become a law) to any constitutional settlement that did not conform to Native demands (Romanow, Whyte, and Leeson 1984). In the fall of 1980, the public relations campaign was stepped up, both domestically and abroad, in an attempt to embarrass the government into entrenching an explicit recognition of Aboriginal rights in the proposed constitution. The strategy caught the attention of the government. Sanders (1983) quotes from an (obviously leaked) internal memorandum that highlighted the federal government's concerns: "If the Native Peoples press forward with their plans and if they succeed in gaining support and sympathy abroad, Canada's image will suffer considerably."

More revealing is the remarkable candour with which the memo acknowledged the disingenuity of the government's promise to consider Aboriginal rights in the second round of constitutional negotiations: "Native leaders realize that entrenching their rights will be enormously difficult after patriation, especially since a majority of the provinces would have to agree to changes which might benefit Native Peoples at the expense of provincial power" (1983, 312).

In January 1981 the federal government conceded by agreeing to include Aboriginal rights in the constitutional resolution. In its ultimate form, the constitutional amendment of 1982 included two important sections pertaining to Aboriginal rights. Section 25 of the Canadian Charter of Rights and Freedoms affirms that the charter "shall not be construed so as to abrogate [eliminate] or derogate [take away] from any aboriginal, treaty or other rights or freedoms that pertain to the aboriginal peoples of Canada including: (a) any rights or freedoms that have been recognized by the Royal Proclamation of October 7, 1763; and (b) any rights or freedoms that may be acquired by the aboriginal peoples of Canada by way of land claims settlement." Section 35 of the Constitution Act states that "The existing aboriginal and treaty rights of the aboriginal peoples of Canada are hereby recognized and affirmed." Ironically, the only province not to agree to the provisions in the Constitution Act was Quebec, whose people Trudeau had promised to satisfy during the 1980 referendum campaign.

When the dust settled, it appeared that the constitutional showdown between the federal government and Aboriginal leaders had ended in a draw. No new Aboriginal rights had been created, but none had been taken away, either. But this did not mean that the fight was over. By the 1980s, Canada was moving towards a new era of constitutional politics – one in which the constitution evolved at the macro level (through formal constitutional amendments) as well at the micro level (through litigation). Indeed, since the charter's entrenchment, the courts have become increasingly important to the interpretation of constitutional language (Manfredi and Lusztig 1998). And certainly this has been the case as it pertains to Aboriginal rights.

Three early post-Charter cases – *R. v. Guerin* (1984), *R. v. Simon* (1985), and *R. v. Sioui* (1990) – each dealt with the nature of treaty rights and obligations. These cases established the principle that treaties constitute agreements between sovereign nations. Sovereign nations are not sovereign states in that they are not independent countries, but neither are treaty provisions to be interpreted as rules governing the relationship between a country and its own citizens. Instead, "an Indian treaty is an agreement sui generis [unique unto itself] which is neither created nor terminated according to the rules of international law" (*R. v. Sioui* 1990; see also Canada 1996 vol. 1, chap. 7; Murphy 2001).

In *R. v. Sparrow* (1990) the Supreme Court took another step in affirming Aboriginal rights when it ruled that while the government had the sovereign power to infringe on Aboriginal rights, the onus was on the government to justify such infringement. *Sparrow* was a mixed bag. On the one hand, it suggested that Aboriginal rights could not be extinguished by mere whim of the government. On the other, it held that where the rubber hits the road, the Crown is unambiguously sovereign (Murphy 2001).

R. v. Van der Peet (1996) placed clear boundaries on the nature of Aboriginal rights. The majority held that "to be an aboriginal right an activity must be an element of a practice, custom or tradition integral to the distinctive culture of the aboriginal group claiming the right ... The practices, customs and traditions which constitute aboriginal rights are those which have continuity with the practices, customs and traditions that existed prior to contact with European society." This meant that Aboriginal rights did not include post-contact traditions and customs. Nor did they extend to customs common to all societies (e.g., the imperative to eat). Moreover, the court held that Aboriginal rights were not general, but specific to the band making the claim. In other words, the customs, traditions, and practices that give rise to rights for one band may not be relevant in the case of another.

Meanwhile, at the macro level, the government of Brian Mulroney, seeking to gain political capital in Quebec, sought to entrench amendments in the constitution that would gain Quebec's symbolic endorsement of the 1982 constitutional amendment (recall that that amendment began as a promise to Quebecers for constitutional reform if they voted against sovereignty association). The Meech Lake Accord, discussed in several other chapters of this book, unfolded over three years and culminated in failure in 1990. An agreement reached in August 1992 – the Charlottetown Accord – was negotiated by representatives of the federal and provincial governments as well as representatives from the Assembly of First Nations, the Native Council of Canada, the Inuit Tapirisat of Canada, and the Metis National Council. Moreover, instead of legislative ratification, the accord would be ratified by referendums to be held in each province.

The Charlottetown Accord would have added a whopping sixty amendments to the constitution. Perhaps most remarkable was the Canada clause, which would have altered the complexion of Canadian federalism by affirming that "the Aboriginal peoples of Canada, being the first peoples to govern this land, have the right to promote their languages, cultures and traditions and to ensure the integrity of their societies, and their governments constitute one of the three orders of government in Canada." In addition, among other provisions pertaining to Native rights, the accord would have:

- strengthened the commitment to Aboriginal rights in the Charter of Rights and Freedoms by ensuring that "nothing in the Charter abrogates or derogates from Aboriginal, treaty or other rights of Aboriginal peoples, and in particular any rights or freedoms relating to the exercise or protection of their languages, cultures or traditions;
- guaranteed Aboriginal representation in the Senate of Canada, and might have (the language is deliberately ambiguous) provided Aboriginal senators with a veto over "certain matters materially affecting Aboriginal people";
- provided for further negotiations over the relationship between Aboriginals and the Supreme Court of Canada, as well as the possibility of special representation rights in the House of Commons;
- ensured that First Ministers' conferences (meetings between the provincial premiers and the prime minister of Canada) that dealt with Aboriginal issues would require the participation of Aboriginal representatives;
- provided for a five-year time frame to negotiate the parameters of Aboriginal self-government and role in constitutional negotiations,

as well as to explore the possibility of special Aboriginal tribunals as part of the justice system;

• required that treaty rights be "interpreted in a just, broad and liberal manner"; and

• provided for Aboriginal consent to any constitutional amendment that pertained directly to Aboriginal peoples.

In all, a full one-third (in terms of the number of amendments) of the Charlottetown Accord was directly and (nearly) exclusively related to Aboriginal issues. The Charlottetown Accord, however, failed: it was rejected in Nova Scotia and the four western provinces. Canada has not since sought to entrench Aboriginal rights in the constitution.

Second Thoughts? Or Citizens Plus

There has been a significant shift in the federal government's treatment of Canada's Native population over the past two decades. In addition to the proposed amendments contained in the Charlottetown Accord, the Report of the Royal Commission on Aboriginal Peoples (1996), or RCAP, recommended a comprehensive shift in the legal status of Aboriginal nations, providing among other things for sovereignty and legal recognition of the inherent right to self-government. The Canadian people appeared ambivalent. Opinion polls found that as of 2004, 60 per cent of Canadians believed that Aboriginal peoples' right of self-government should be recognized. On the other hand, 62 per cent of Canadians did not like the idea of self-government if it "threatens the sovereign unity of Canada," while 47 per cent believed that "no Aboriginal self-government should be allowed if it gets in the way of fishing, mining and other economic development" (Compas 2001).

One prominent critic of special status for Canada's Aboriginal peoples is Thomas Flanagan (2000). His *First Nations? Second Thoughts* represents a systematic critique of what he calls the Aboriginal orthodoxy, a consensus among political, Aboriginal, and academic elites with respect to Aboriginal policy in Canada. A mythical element of the Aboriginal orthodoxy is that European immigration disrupted centuries of Native settlement in North America. In fact, Flanagan argues, land issues among Aboriginal groups were largely unsettled; through violence and conquest, they had long contested territory among themselves. Indeed, he suggests, "the standard definition of aboriginal rights is a legal fiction ... There may be specific cases where a native community has dwelled continuously upon the same territory for thousands of years (if such cases exist in Canada, they lie on the coast of British Columbia), but, in general, native peoples in Canada, like hunter-collectors around the world, moved a great deal. In many cases, the patterns of habitation upon which the land surrender agreements of the nineteenth century were based were only a few decades old" (2000, 19). In short, Flanagan argues, claims to land based on original occupation from time out of memory are specious. Control of the land over which most Indian bands lay claim was a fluid proposition long after the arrival of European settlers. Indeed, while there was a difference in how Native peoples and settlers understood property rights (at least as they pertain to land), it seems fairly clear that the means of acquisition – demonstration of greater force – were both similar and contemporaneous. The contemporary ethical and legal distinction drawn between inter-Aboriginal disputes over territory and settler-Native ones reduces to means of arrival in the New World – or, as a colleague put it, the two-if-by-sea theory of moral opprobrium.

Land claims are the foundation on which many other Native rights depend. If this prop were kicked away, there would be implications for claims that Aboriginal Canadians are qualitatively different from other Canadians and hence entitled to special rights pertaining to sovereign self-government, land use, taxation, and special representation.

Flanagan also takes issue with the idea that Indian groups were ever sovereign states in the modern sense of the term. The implications of this would affect Aboriginal peoples' demands to reconstitute Canadian federalism to accommodate a third sovereign order of government. Flanagan relies on the work of eighteenth-century international law theorists Christian von Wolff and Emerich de Vattel for the rationale that European settlers had a unique claim to sovereignty in North America.

For Wolff, "groups of men dwelling together in certain limits but without civil sovereignty are not nations" (Flanagan 2000, 55). The critical concept here is civil sovereignty. Flanagan concedes that Wolff is unclear as to whether or not North American Indians constituted nations possessed of civil sovereignty; he bases his argument here on his understanding of Aboriginal peoples' lack of "civilization." Specifically, Flanagan argues that civilization (he uses the term in its anthropological sense, not as an indicator of cultural superiority) requires a number of elements: intensive mixed agriculture in which the same territory is occupied and cultivated over a long period of time; urbanization (i.e., permanent settlement); an economic division of labour; intellectual advances such as a written language and the keeping of records; advanced technology; and "formalized, hierarchical government – that is, a state" (ibid., 33).

Vattel, employing the liberal understanding of property rights discussed above, argues that North America's Native people "cannot take to themselves more land than they have need of or can inhabit and cultivate. Their uncertain occupancy of these vast regions cannot be held as a real and lawful taking of possession … [When European nations] come upon lands which the savages have no special need of and are making no present and continuous use of, they may lawfully take possession of them and establish colonies in them" (ibid., 55). Taken together, these two streams of thought inform Flanagan's position that North American Indians never enjoyed sovereign control over land on which, at least for most bands, they were nomadic.

The Canadian and US Supreme Courts have both ruled on the issue of Aboriginal sovereignty. In the latter, the precedent was set in 1823 with *Johnson v. M'Intosh*, which Chief Justice John Marshall denied Indians the right to sell fee simple land. He based his ruling on the "Discovery Doctrine" – which in its simplest form meant that European settlers had "discovered" the New World and, as such, asserted sovereignty over it. While Aboriginal inhabitants retained right of occupancy, they did not own the land outright. Thus, while tribes were able to sell their rights of occupancy to a discovering nation, they could not sell title to land they did not own.

Sovereignty assumes importance in the contemporary Canadian context insofar as both the Charlottetown Accord and the RCAP understood Aboriginal rights to include not only an inherent right to self-government, but also a right to sovereign self-government. As noted, this would give Aboriginal bands province-like powers in areas of their own jurisdiction (whatever those might be).

It is well to examine the implications. Presumably Canada would, for the first time, create sovereign territories in which citizenship would hinge on innate characteristics (in this case, race). Currently, any Canadian can live in any political jurisdiction in Canada. There is freedom of mobility. But for Aboriginal self-government to be meaningful, citizenship in such communities would have to be limited. Otherwise, Aboriginal communities would be vulnerable to absorption by the encroachment of non-Aboriginals settling in Aboriginal communities. In addition, there would have to be some sort of criterion for establishing who was, and who was not, a full voting member of this sovereign community. If a person were only one-half Native would s/he retain citizenship? One quarter? One eighth? What if one's lineage were disputed (in the case, say, of adoption)? Would the courts be expected to rule on who is and who is not a full member of a community? The potential is for a new, more progressive type of segregation laws – Jim Crow with a happy face.

Finally, Flanagan points out that accentuating the differences between Aboriginal and settler communities simply perpetuates a sense of dependency and victimhood on the part of the minority community. This is, in many ways, the ultimate form of paternalism. Instead of encouraging independence and excellence as individuals, victimhood provides the catharsis of blaming oppressors for communal problems. It releases the individual from responsibility for his or her own performance and obligations (see McWhorter 2000). Flanagan argues that a strategy of assimilative individualism is imperative in the quest for independence and prosperity among Native Canadians.

Of course, assimilation need not, and in a liberal democracy should not, be coercive. The liberal democratic state must not take active steps to assimilate cultures – as was the mandate of the residential schools – far less seek to eradicate them. But neither is there an imperative for the state to become involved in championing or institutionalizing special privileges for certain race-based cultures (Kukathas 1995; Lusztig 2002).

As mentioned, Flanagan's position does not represent the mainstream academic viewpoint. Alan Cairns's *Citizens Plus* is more representative (2000). Cairns takes the pragmatic view that whatever happened in the past, the imperative is to deal with the present. He raises large questions: What does it mean to be a community? Does a community imply cultural homogeneity? If it does not, how do we ensure the protection of minority cultures while still maintaining bonds of unity between these cultures and the cultural mainstream?

As the title of his book suggests, Cairns's prescription is to treat Aboriginal Canadians as "citizens plus." First and foremost, Aboriginal peoples are citizens of Canada. The "plus" refers to the fact that whatever their politics, economics, and settlements, Aboriginal Canadians were here first. It is not unreasonable to argue that original possession counts for something, especially when we consider the treaty process. The Canadian authorities either believed that Aboriginal people were entitled to special consideration as original inhabitants or they didn't.

But if they didn't, why did they bother with the treaty process at all? The rights that flow from original inhabitation and treaty may not be clear or easily agreed upon, but this is not the same as saying they do not exist.

Part of the problem lies in how we understand fairness (see Chartrand 2009). Typically in liberal democratic societies we are taught to believe that each and every citizen is equal before the law. Violations of this formal equality are unfair. Put differently, we are taught that justice is the absence of injustice.

But in reality, liberal democracies do not treat everyone the same way. Poor people, for example, are entitled to state assistance – special treatment if you will – that is not available to rich people. While issues of wealth redistribution can be controversial, most citizens of liberal democracies believe that some redistribution is necessary, if only to allow people who have suffered misfortune a chance to realize their goals in life.

So most of us recognize that there is an affirmative component to fairness. Justice is more than the absence of injustice. It can entail redistribution. And if we can redistribute wealth in the name of community values and unity, we can do the same with political status. The logic of citizens plus is that unequal treatment before the law is not inherently unfair. Sometimes it is necessary merely to compensate for historical disadvantage. Sometimes it is born of rights that existed from time out of memory. And sometimes, as Cairns suggests, it is born of both.

Conclusion

Conflicting, legitimate claims to territory are never easy to sort out. In many ways, modern liberal democratic societies are hampered by their abiding mandate to seek just solutions to complex matters – something with which less progressive societies were far less concerned. Famously, in Thucydides's *History of the Peloponnesian War*, for example, it is observed that the strong do as they will and the weak do as they must. It would be easy to deem Indians a conquered people and bid them to recognize their obligation to "suffer what they must." But it would not be consistent with liberal democratic values. Much of Canada's territory was settled through either treaty or implicit extinguishment of title. The last is especially troubling. Part of the liberal democratic ethos is property rights. The state cannot take your property on a whim, and it certainly cannot do so without compensating you fairly for your loss. Aboriginal Canadians' understanding of land rights as communal strikes one as a slender reed upon which to justify whole-scale confiscation.

It is also unreasonable, by any standard of liberal democratic justice, for the dominant culture to impose its will on minority cultures (unless, of course, the minority cultures represent a threat to the safety of others). Liberal democracies practise tolerance. Indeed, the very John Locke who is cited so widely in support of private property rights, is equally explicit in the imperative to tolerate a pluralistic understanding of the good life (Locke 1689). Locke was especially concerned with religious tolerance pertaining to the means to salvation – a tolerance hardly extended to native Canadians during the assimilative era of residential schooling.

On the other hand, it is somewhat of a leap to go from recognizing the imperative not to extinguish culture to proclaiming the imperative to champion it; it is a stretch to say that a group's right to be compensated reasonably for confiscated property (where such can be established) extends to the right to be recognized as a sovereign nation with the inherent right of self-government. Aboriginal title does not imply that European settlers live in Canada on sufferance, or that they owe a debt of gratitude to Aboriginal Canadians. Nor does it imply, as does Hazel Hill of the Six Nations reclamation protest, that the "British Crown has no legal jurisdiction over our land or over us [on the grounds that w]e were here first. We never agreed to join Canada" (Six Nations 2006). To say that Thucydides's Athenians did not paint the complete moral picture is not the same as saying their words had no merit. To say that the British did not acquire land by conquest, pillaging, and violence is not to say they could not have. It was the clear intent of the British Crown to establish sovereignty over the territory that is now Canada. That it sought to do so in a (relatively) civilized way hardly weakens the legitimacy of its claim to sovereignty.

Canada's "Indian problem" has not gone away. In 2010 Amnesty International condemned Canada's treatment of its Native population. Its report focused primarily upon the twenty-year land right dispute with the Lubicon tribe of northern Alberta that, in spite of never signing away its land rights under Treaty 8, still saw its land expropriated for the purpose of natural gas extraction. Currently over two-thirds of traditional Lubicon territory is being used for resource extraction (Amnesty International 2010). On the other hand, since the Office of Land Claims was set up, Canada has successfully negotiated twenty-two land claim treaties resulting in an aggregate settlement of land owner-ship of an area roughly the size of Manitoba. As of 2010, sixty-nine land settlement or self-government treaties remain to be negotiated (Canada 2010).

As stated in the introduction, this chapter offers little by way of pre-scription. In large part this is because there is no prescription that can satisfy all sides. Such is the problem with disputes over first principles. One who accepts that Aboriginal people constitute historically sover-eign states that were never conquered and that did (or in some cases did not) enter into legally binding treaties, is likely to conclude that Aboriginal people constitute a qualitatively different form of citizen-ship. They are "citizens plus" in that they enjoy, among other things, the right to sovereign self-government. On the other hand, if one be-gins with the premise that people are people are people, and that no one class of citizens should be entitled to (or subjected to) differential treatment before the law, the idea of racially based sovereign levels of government represents, at best, a dangerous means to the progressive objective of cultural preservation.

WEBSITES

Assembly of First Nations: http://www.afn.ca
Canada, Department of Indian Affairs and Northern Development: http://
    www.ainc-inac.gc.ca
Congress of Aboriginal Peoples: http://www.abo-peoples.org
Inuit Tapirit Kanatami: http://www.itk.ca
Métis National Council: http://www.metisnation.org

REFERENCES AND FURTHER READING

Amnesty International. 2010. *Canada: 20 Years' Denial of Recommendations Made by the United Nations Human Rights Committee and the Continuing Impact on the Lubicon Cree*. London: Amnesty International Publications.
Berger, Thomas R. 2002. *One Man's Justice: A Life in the Law*. Vancouver: Doug-las and McIntyre.
Bueno de Mesquita, Bruce. 2000. "Popes, Kings and Endogenous Institutions: The Concordat of Worms and the Origins of Sovereignty." *International Studies Review* 2 (2): 93–118. http://dx.doi.org/10.1111/1521-9488.00206.

Butler, David, and Donald Stokes. 1976. *Political Change in Britain*. 2nd ed. New York: St Martin's.

Cairns, Alan C. 1991. "Citizens (Outsiders) and Governments (Insiders) in Constitution Making: The Case of Meech Lake." In *Disruptions: Constitutional Struggles from the Charter to Meech Lake*, ed. Douglas E. Williams. Toronto: McClelland & Stewart.

Cairns, Alan C. 2000. *Citizens Plus: Aboriginal Peoples and the Canadian State*. Vancouver: UBC Press.

Canada. Department of Indian and Northern Affairs. 1996. *Report of the Royal Commission on Aboriginal Peoples*. Ottawa: Department of Indian and Northern Affairs.

Canada. Indian and Northern Affairs Canada. 1969. "Statement of the Government of Canada on Indian Policy." Ottawa: Queen's Printer.

Canada. Indian and Northern Affairs Canada. 2004. *The Landscape: Public Opinion on Aboriginal and Northern Issues*. Ottawa: Department of Indian Affairs and Northern Development.

Canada. Indian and Northern Affairs Canada. 2010. "Fact Sheet: Comprehensive Land Claims." http://www.ainc-inac.gc.ca/ai/mr/is/lnd-clms-eng.asp.

Canada. Indian and Northern Affairs Canada. 2006. Indian Residential Schools Resolution Canada. "Government of Canada Approves Indian Residential Schools Settlement Agreement and Launches Advance Payment Program." Press release, 10 May.

Canada. Parliament. 1985. *The Indian Act*. R.S.C., c. I-6, s. 1.

Cardinal, Harold. 1969. *The Unjust Society: The Tragedy of Canada's Indians*. Edmonton: Hurtig.

Compas. 2001. *Big Heart, Big Impatience: Public Opinion on Aboriginal Policy*. Toronto: Public Opinion and Customer Research, Compas Inc.

Chartrand, Paul L.A.H. 2009. "Citizenship Rights and Aboriginal Rights in Canada: From 'Citizens Plus' to 'Citizens Plural.'" In *The Ties That Bind: Accommodating Diversity in Canada and the European Union*, ed. John Erik Fossum and Johanne Poirier. Brussels: P.I.E. Peter Lang.

Coulthard, Glen S. 2007. "Subjects of Empire: Indigenous Peoples and the 'Politics of Recognition' in Canada." *Contemporary Political Theory* 6 (4): 437–60. http://dx.doi.org/10.1057/palgrave.cpt.9300307.

Davin, Nicholas Flood. 1879. "Report on Industrial Schools for Indians and Half-Breeds." http://www.canadianshakespeares.ca/multimedia/pdf/davin_report.pdf.

Flanagan, Thomas. 1989. "The Agricultural Argument and Original Appropriation: Indian Lands and Political Philosophy." *Canadian Journal of Political Science* 23 (03): 589–602. http://dx.doi.org/10.1017/S0008423900010969.

Flanagan, Thomas. 2000. *First Nations? Second Thoughts*. Montreal: McGill-Queen's University Press.

Fleras, Augie, and Jean Leonard Elliott. 1992. *The Nations Within: Aboriginal–State Relations in Canada, the United States, and New Zealand*. Don Mills, ON: Oxford University Press.

Glendon, Mary Ann. 1991. *Rights Talk: The Impoverishment of Political Discourse*. New York: Free Press.

Hargrove, Eugene C. 1983. "Anglo-American Land Use Attitudes." In *Ethics and the Environment*, ed. Donald Scherer and Tom Attig. Englewood Cliffs, NJ: Prentice-Hall.

Hawthorn, H.B. 1967. *A Survey of Contemporary Indians of Canada*. Ottawa: Queen's Printer.

Kendall, Joan. 2001. "Circles of Disadvantage: Aboriginal Poverty and Underdevelopment in Canada." *American Review of Canadian Studies* 31 (1-2): 43–59. http://dx.doi.org/10.1080/02722010109481581.

Kukathas, Chandran. 1995. "Are There Any Cultural Rights?" In *The Rights of Minority Cultures*, ed. Will Kymlicka. Oxford: Oxford University Press.

Locke, John. 1689. *A Letter Concerning Toleration*, trans. Popple, William. London: A. Churchill.

Locke, John. 1974. *Two Treatises of Government*. New York: Hafner.

Lusztig, Michael. 2002. "Deeper and Deeper: Deep Diversity, Federalism, and Redistributive Politics in Canada." In *The Myth of the Sacred: The Charter, the Courts, and the Politics of the Constitution in Canada*, ed. Patrick James, Donald E. Abelson, and Michael Lusztig. Montreal: McGill-Queen's University Press.

Manfredi, Christopher P., and Michael Lusztig. 1998. "Why Do Formal Amendments Fail? An Institutional Design Analysis." *World Politics* 50 (03): 377–400. http://dx.doi.org/10.1017/S0043887100012855.

McWhorter, James. 2000. *Losing the Race: Self-Sabotage in Black America*. New York: Free Press.

Milloy, James. 1999. *A National Crime: The Canadian Government and the Residential School System 1879–1986*. Winnipeg: University of Manitoba Press.

Monahan, Patrick J. 1991. *Meech Lake: The Inside Story*. Toronto: University of Toronto Press.

Murphy, Michael. 2001. "Culture and the Courts: A New Direction in Canadian Jurisprudence on Aboriginal Rights." *Canadian Journal of Political Science* 34 (01): 109–29. http://dx.doi.org/10.1017/S0008423901777839.

Ponting, Rick, and Roger Gibbins. 1980. *Out of Irrelevance*. Scarborough, ON: Butterworths.

Raunet, Daniel. 1984. *Without Surrender, Without Consent: A History of Nishga Land Claims*. Vancouver: Douglas and McIntyre.

Romanow, Roy, John Whyte, and Howard Leeson. 1984. *Canada Notwithstanding: The Making of the Constitution, 1978–1982*. Toronto: Methuen.

Sanders, Douglas E. 1983. "The Indian Lobby." In *And No One Cheered: Federalism, Democracy, and the Constitution Act*, ed. Keith Banting and Richard Simeon. Toronto: Methuen.

Simeon, Richard. 1990. "Why Did the Meech Lake Accord Fail?" In *Canada: The State of the Federation, 1990*, ed. Ronald L. Watts and Douglas M. Brown. Kingston: Queen's University Institute of Intergovernmental Relations.

Six Nations. 2006. "Hazel's Six Nations Land Reclamation Update." 22 June. http://72.14.209.104/search?q=cache:mccxT_wqOQ8J:www.wsdp.org/six_nations.htm+Indians+%22here+first%22+canada+thank&hl=en&gl=us &ct=clnk&cd=7.

Titley, Brian E. 1992. *A Narrow Vision: Duncan Campbell Scott and the Administration of Indian Affairs in Canada*. Vancouver: UBC Press.

Tookenay, Vincent. 1996. "Improving the Health Status of Aboriginal People in Canada: New Directions, New Responsibilities." *Canadian Medical Association Journal* 155:1581–3.

Trudeau, Pierre Elliott. 1980. Speech at the Paul Sauvé Arena, Montreal. 14 May.

Waldron, Jeremy. 1992. "Minority Cultures and the Cosmopolitan Alternative." *University of Michigan Journal of Law Reform. University of Michigan. Law School* 25:751–93.

Weaver, Sally. 1981. *Making Canadian Indian Policy: The Hidden Agenda, 1968–1970*. Toronto: University of Toronto Press.

CASES CITED

Calder v. Attorney General of British Columbia (1973) S.C.R. 313.

Cherokee Nation v. Georgia (1831) 30 US 1.

Connolly v. Woolrich (1867) 11 L.C.J. 97 (Que.).

Delgamuukw v. British Columbia (1997) 3 S.C.R. 1010.

Haida Nation v. British Columbia (Minister of Forests) (2004) 3 S.C.R. 511.

Johnson v. M'Intosh (1823) 21 US 543, 5 L.Ed. 681, 8 Wheat. 543.

R. v. Guerin (1984) 2 S.C.R. 335.

R. v. Sioui (1990) 1 S.C.R. 1025.

R. v. Simon (1985) 2 S.C.R. 387.

R. v. Sparrow (1990) 1 S.C.R. 1075.

R. v. Van der Peet (1996) 2 S.C.R. 507.

R. v. White and Bob (1964) 50 DLR (2d) 613.

Re: The Amendment of the Constitution of Canada (1973) 1 S.C.R 753.

St. Catherine's Milling and Lumber Co. v. The Queen (1888) 14 App. Cas. 46.

Taku River Tlingit First Nation v. British Columbia (Project Assessment Director) (2004) 3 S.C.R. 500.

9 Women's Issues

PATRICE LECLERC

Although certainly women have been included elsewhere in this book, the present chapter stresses issues that specifically affect women in Canada, mainly in the political and social arenas. It needs to be noted that "woman" is in no way a unitary identity; there are many ways to be and experience womanhood, and this varies in particular by race and ethnicity, class, sexuality, ability, language, and region of the country. Thus, the discussion below highlights situations of a variety of women in Canada as they have struggled to achieve rights in the political and social arena. One of the key points that comes out is how government services and the expansion of the welfare state have been connected to the women's movement, most notably in the 1960s, 1970s, and 1980s.

Early Women's Rights Activities, 1850–1950

During this period, women's clubs and organizations were formed, and although they focused largely on women's traditional roles and responsibilities, they also addressed many health and educational issues. At a more explicitly political level, federal suffrage was achieved, as was provincial suffrage in all provinces but Quebec (for some women). In part because of their participation in the First World War, women were declared legally "persons," and many women entered the waged labour force, especially during the Second World War. Women generally were kept from electoral politics, but some firsts were achieved. In the United States, women gained the franchise and joined clubs and organizations. Many, however, were excluded from employment after the two world wars. There are some structural similarities between the two countries, but the cultural and political climate in which the events took place was somewhat different.

In Canada, a few women with property had been able to vote in the 1800s. The first women's suffrage group was the Toronto Women's Literary Club, founded in 1876. This group's key interests were education, property rights, and working conditions. Many early Canadian women's activities, such as in this club, may be called "maternal feminism," in that they were based on women's role as guardian of the home and viewed public participation as a woman's duty. Most of the women who participated in organizations such as this were married, heterosexual, white, middle-class, and involved in a number of social reforms. By 1890, these groups began to gain support for these issues from liberal-minded men and other women, out of interest in common betterment.

Other women who participated in activities to change the status of women did so out of a sense of religious duty and a spirit of expanded opportunities. They worked on a number of social reform issues including temperance, religious instruction, improvements in workplace conditions, better housing for single women, and state-run public health and child welfare programs. Their organizations were often denominational or auxiliaries of men's organizations. They were, of course, mainly white, abled, and middle to upper class. Through these activities, women acquired leadership and organizational skills. Social reforms and feminism were closely linked.

Women were also involved in a number of local and professional organizations. Before the First World War, one in eight women in Canada was involved in a woman's group. Typically, these groups were organized around various social, political, cultural, and economic issues. Often these women held overlapping memberships, especially in voluntary organizations.

The National Council of Women of Canada (NCW) was founded in 1893 as an umbrella organization. It performed clearing house and lobbying functions. Though its membership was mainly middle class, it provided a sense of national unity and group identity for the Canadian women participating in the affiliated organizations. Although the NCW was not a suffrage organization, some of its affiliates were, and in 1910 it endorsed female suffrage.

French-Canadian feminism (as it was then called) first became visible in Montreal over issues such as the reorganization of charitable work, equality in the workforce, and the promotion of women's rights. It became formalized with the founding of the Fédération National de Saint-Jean-Baptiste in 1907. This group coordinated women's clubs and provided a public platform for women's issues. French-Canadian feminism in Quebec was seen as an extension of Christianity; its emphasis was on home, charity, and education as expressions of nationalism. It spurred the founding of secondary schools for women and better health education. A Montreal Suffrage Association was founded in 1913 but disbanded itself when the members surmised that they were not representative of the province. The Cercles des Fermières were founded under the Ministry of Agriculture in 1915, and in 1922 a Provincial Franchise Committee was established, with both language groups represented and dual leadership from both. Its goal was to achieve provincial suffrage. In 1928 Thérèse Casgrain became its president; it then became the League of Women's Rights. Quebec women also lobbied successfully for the Commission d'Enquête sur les Droits de la Femme (Dorion commission), which in 1929 made minor improvements to the property rights of separated women, but upheld the traditional and conservative view of the family hierarchy.

The suffrage movement in Canada was organized by a relatively small, elite group of anglophones, who relied mainly on petitions and letter-writing campaigns. Tactics such as civil disobedience and destruction of property, as seen in Great Britain and the United States, were rarely resorted to. The campaign for federal suffrage was based on the premise that women's voting would reform society and that the state needed women's point of view. Between 1895 and 1910, suffrage leagues were founded in all provinces except Quebec, with branches in most urban areas. Support came from farmers' associations, labour unions, and some of the media. Additional support was provided by United States and British suffragists.

The federal vote for most women was won in English Canada just before the United States and Britain, with little contention. This was the time when most Western countries granted women suffrage: twenty-eight between 1915 and 1920. Anne Anderson Perry, an early suffragist, stated in an article in the *Grain Grower's Guide* (1920) that it was "a struggle, never a fight," and involved persuasion, not force (Cleverdon 1950). In 1917, nurses and women serving in the war received the franchise, as did the wives, widows, sisters, and mothers of servicemen. Prime Minister Robert Borden felt that they would vote for conscription, and he wanted his next campaign to be based on that issue. Despite this beginning, which seemed at least a partial victory, some women were concerned about the fact that the Wartime Election Act also disenfranchised those born in enemy countries who had been naturalized after 1902; they were being excluded because of their national origin. Japanese, Chinese, and East Indian citizens were also denied the franchise. Aboriginal people living on reserves did not receive full suffrage until 1960.

Federal suffrage for even more women was achieved in 1918 when Borden introduced an act allowing women with the same qualifications as men to vote. A subsequent act, in 1919, permitted women to be elected to the House of Commons. In 1920, the Dominion Elections Act was amended to extend suffrage to federal elections; women in all provinces were now allowed to vote at the federal level. Provincial voting rights came for most between 1916 and 1922, except in Quebec, which only granted provincial voting rights in 1960.

Between 1900 and 1925, Canadians looked to their legislatures to regulate many sectors of public life. To make an impact, it was necessary to have access to the electoral bodies. Thus, women's groups that were attempting to change society – for example, temperance groups – felt it important to obtain the vote, although they did not focus on this issue exclusively. Many Canadians feared that the franchise would alter the balance of power in families, as women would have a direct relationship with government, one that was not mediated by husbands. Family forms during this time period were primarily married and patriarchal. In urban areas, there were unmarried people, including women, working in the newly industrialized fields, but middle-class women stopped employment with marriage. Also in urban areas, fewer children were produced by middle- and upper-class families. In rural areas, and most of Quebec, larger families continued.

Other groups of women, especially on the left, worked in self-help and community organizing. For example, the Colored Women's Club of Montreal, formed in 1902, worked on immigrant women's relief issues. The "social gospel" movement of the time in many Protestant sects led church women (and men) to take up new, progressive causes. During the "club women's era," the various groups organized themselves mainly around race/ethnicity, class, and language. Many Canadian feminists in the early 1900s felt alienated from party politics, but others continued with the electoral project. The former tended to see parties as corrupt, and so little effort was made to elect women. Canadian women's groups were more moderate and less militant than those in many other democracies, partly because women in Canada already had some opportunities in education, the professions, and volunteer work, and also because some women were already being elected both federally and provincially. In addition, after the franchise, efforts for other improvements became fragmented. This was largely a consequence of the physical geography of Canada: it is a vast and sparsely populated country where communication and travel are difficult.

The *Persons* case in 1929, in which the Judicial Committee of the Privy Council (JCPC) of Great Britain declared that women were "persons" under the law, did excite support. In 1919 the Confederation of Federated Women's Institutes of Canada passed a resolution that the government should appoint a woman to the federal senate (by then, some women were holding electoral office as federal MPs and others had been appointed as provincial judges). The governments of Prime Minister Arthur Meighen and William Lyon Mackenzie King refused to appoint women as senators, stating that the British North America Act of 1867 prohibited it. In 1927 five women petitioned the government for an order-in-council to direct the Supreme Court of Canada to rule on the issue. In April 1928 the Supreme Court ruled that "qualified persons" in the BNA Act did not include women. This was appealed to the JCPC, which held that women were persons. The first woman senator, Carine Wilson, a Liberal, was appointed in 1930; she was not one of the women who had brought suit in the *Persons* case. (Today, every year a Persons Day is celebrated, on which outstanding women are honoured).

In the late 1930s, after strong pressure from the League of Women's Rights, headed by Thérèse Casgrain, the issue of provincial suffrage was raised again in Quebec. Women's suffrage was a plank in the 1938 provincial Liberal Party platform, and in 1940, despite opposition from the Catholic Church, women in Quebec obtained the provincial vote. The pace of change had been slower in Quebec because women were mainly absent from administrative and decision-making structures and because formal and informal patriarchy existed. Also, industrialization was slower in Quebec, and women's ties with the patriarchal church were strong. However, nuns made major contributions to the life of the province in administration, education, and health care.

During the 1940s, with the hardships of war, many Canadian women were preoccupied with interests other than politics. Many were employed in industries as a "temporary army of labour." After the war they lost their jobs, and many of them pressed for child care assistance to make their employment more possible. Individual women's groups worked on local issues, and efforts were made to include women in the traditional forms of politics, but at this time there were few pan-Canadian groups or national women's issues. The activities of women's organizations received little publicity, as there was a great focus on middle-class values, motherhood was seen as a virtue, and there was the expectation that middle- and upper-class married women would not work outside the home. At the same time, though, there was a proliferation of local, community-oriented women's groups.

By 1949 there had been five female members in the House of Commons (only one of these was re-elected) and two female senators. No woman had ever been appointed to the federal cabinet, but two had been appointed to a provincial cabinet, and there were twenty-three female members of provincial legislatures.

The early women's movement in Canada faced hurdles still present in Canadian life: it was a vast and sparsely settled country with many different social and ethnic groups. The decentralized federal system made it necessary to address federal and provincial issues somewhat simultaneously. Because most people were unilingual, there was a basic problem of communication. As well, a lot of feminist literature was not available to French-Canadian women; most of it was in English and had not yet been translated. And before the age of air travel and electronic media, mounting a pan-Canadian campaign of any sort verged on the impossible.

In addition, many women did not have access to organized groups, or were in situations where mainstream political activity was not possible. Aboriginal women, especially those on reserves, were active in their communities, but they were not linked to the political actions of their more privileged sisters (it should be noted that Aboriginal rights were very much absent generally). Many non-English-speaking immigrant women were isolated in their own communities by language barriers as well as by laws that impeded their education and training.

The groups that continued to exist were the bridge to the resurgent feminism of the 1960s. These continued to carry out traditional good works, but also broke new ground, identified new issues, and lobbied for change. Such groups included the YWCA, the women's auxiliaries of political parties, and peace groups. Girls were attending public schools and some were going on to university. The large majority of teachers were women, but except for that opening, women had few opportunities in the professional and cultural arenas.

Thus, between the mid-1800s and mid-1900s, Canadian women achieved suffrage and some other political rights. They formed groups to deal with specific issues of interest, primarily at the local level, but country-wide momentum for further change in women's status had generally dissipated by the late 1940s.

The Second Wave, 1950–1984

In Canada, this era was one of tremendous success for women and women's movements, as women's groups branched out from relatively narrow focuses, such as the peace movement and university issues, to deal with gender issues more broadly. The initial victory may have been persuading politicians, the media, and voters to take women's issues seriously, but more formal advances followed. A study of the condition of women in Canada was conducted, new laws about equality were passed, organizations by and for women were created within governments, and other groups received government funding; most particularly important is the National Action Committee on the Status of Women (NAC). And Anglo-Canadian women (mostly from outside Quebec) worked hard to achieve formal gender equality in the new Canadian constitution. Gender issues assumed a prominent role in Canadian culture, and affirmative action was considered an appropriate remedy. At the same time, in the United States, membership peaked in the National Organization for Women (NOW), and some electoral gains were made; on the negative side, the Equal Rights Amendment was rejected and there was growth in both organized and implicit antifeminism.

Signs of a new mobilization of women in anglophone Canada began to appear in the 1950s. The women's peace movement, women in the Co-operative Commonwealth Federation (CCF) and other left organizations, and ethnic women (especially Ukrainian, Finnish, and Jewish women), continued to organize and to make their voices heard on issues of importance to them. Governments recognized that there were important women's issues, and the Women's Bureau of the Department of Labour was established in 1954, after much lobbying by women's groups. These groups were important precursors to the more generalized activities of the 1960s, despite the overriding 1950s cultural ideal (which was far from reality for most of the population) of the suburban nuclear family, with women taking pride in their home and children and in not working for wages.

The new women's movement in anglophone Canada was chiefly university-based and left-leaning. The women involved were mainly majority women: middle-class professionals. As in the United States, there were at least two branches: those who wanted to work through the system, and the more radical groups and individuals who felt that oppression could only be overcome through social structural change.

Early political actions focused on sexuality, reproductive rights, abortion, day care, work, sexism, and peace. In addition, many groups were established to provide services for their own members; this produced a broader base for the movement and prepared the ground for political discourse. Another important factor was that the most prominent Canadian women's magazine, *Chatelaine*, under the editorship of Doris Anderson, had a strong feminist flavour for its time and focused its articles and editorials on women's changing role and gender stereotyping (this could not be said of women's general-circulation magazines in the United States).

The Voice of Women (VOW) was founded in 1960 as a women's organization for peace. In its first year it attained a membership of five thousand. Its members were mainly middle-class women, who responded to the climate of the times and the fear and uncertainties of the Cold War. Its members were from all over the country, urban and rural. From the start, VOW had a chapter in Quebec. As a pan-Canadian organization, it was one of the first groups to press for a royal commission on women (see below). Although VOW did not start out specifically as a feminist organization (it would slowly become one), it did pave the way, along with other groups, for the resurgence of the women's movement.

Besides working on their own individual issues, many women's organizations formed an ad hoc committee to press the federal government to form what would become the Royal Commission on the Status of Women. These groups included the Fédération des Femmes du Québec, an umbrella group formed in 1966 to press for legislative reform and a Council of Women, as well as mainstream groups such as the Canadian Federation of University Women and Canadian Federation of Business and Professional Women (BPW Canada). The royal commission, headed by Florence Bird, was created in 1967 with a mandate "to enquire into and report upon the status of women in Canada, and recommend what steps might be taken by the federal government to ensure for women equal opportunities with men in every aspect of Canadian society" (Bird 1974). The areas to be covered by the commission included the following: laws and practices covering women's political and labour rights and the civil service; federal taxation; marriage and divorce; criminal law; immigration and citizenship; and whatever other issues the commission thought relevant.

In the beginning the royal commission was treated by many men as a joke. The media thought it unnecessary, and many Canadians did not want to be associated with it. Some felt that women were already well treated in Canada, others that a group of mostly women could never get out such a report. There were seven commissioners – five women and two men – and they set out to ensure that the processes of this royal commission would be educational and that women would find it easy to make their presentations to its hearings. They developed an information packet, which was sent to women's organizations and made available in shopping malls and libraries, to tell women how to prepare and present a brief. It was important to the commission that women be able to express their needs in the least threatening way possible. "We sat from ten a.m. to one p.m., two to five, evenings as well. Very tiring. We heard briefs, then in the evening threw it open to individuals. We worked in shopping centres, libraries, not big hotels. We didn't sit on a dais, we sat around a table. Women were frightened, they had never done this before. I would say, 'You are with friends, ignore the people and the lights, you're talking to us as friends around a table'" (Bird 1990). The hearings themselves received a great deal of public attention. A CBC television crew was assigned to accompany the commission in its cross-country hearings so that every night the Canadian public saw "statistics become human beings" (ibid.). TV coverage changed attitudes in the media, and those of the public, by educating Canadians to the realities of women's lives. Florence Bird credits media coverage of the hearings as a major reason for the commission's success and for a change in Canadian attitudes towards women.

In December 1970, after consultations and hearings all over the country, and after 469 groups and individuals presented briefs, the report was forwarded to Prime Minister Pierre Trudeau. During the hearing process, more women and women's groups became aware of inequality and of the feminist agenda. "More women's groups became feminist, and women began to see themselves as women. This speeded up things. Most women's associations became feminist then, and still are" (Bégin 1987).

The report, issued in 1970, was favourably received by the media, the government, and Canadians generally. It became both a best-seller and the agreed-on agenda for the "second wave" of the women's movement in Canada. It also legitimated the demands and concerns of many women. "When the report came out, we got very good coverage. People were amazed that it was so good. Women's associations took it as their Bible, women carried it around" (Bird 1990).

The general principles of the report were that women should be free to choose whether to take employment outside the home; that the care of children is a responsibility to be shared by the mother, father, and society; that society has a responsibility for women because of pregnancy and childbirth; and that affirmative action is required to right past discrimination. This was very much in line with the liberal feminist agenda at the time, which dealt mainly with equality of opportunity and results. The commission did not report on (nor, according to its chair, did it receive submissions on) issues such as spousal abuse and lesbian rights.

New women's organizations oriented towards the recommendations of the report began to form. A climate was created for women to become active. In 1972 a "Strategies for Change" conference was funded by the government. This conference set the pattern of cooperation among widely diverse feminist groups; it was attended by more than five hundred people from forty groups, representing both traditional organizations and the newer, more radical ones, albeit mainly from privileged backgrounds. First-wave survivor groups were present, along with women's liberation groups and pressure groups. Many strands of feminism were included; different ideological groups worked together and cooperated over joint proposals. At this meeting the NAC was founded as an umbrella group for women's organizations to ensure that the key recommendations of the royal commission were implemented. The Canadian Advisory Council on the Status of Women (CACSW) was instituted in 1973, funded by the federal government to do research and propose legislation. It would report to Parliament through the minister responsible for the status of women.

The NAC is a unique organization. It was created and structured to manage a complex coalition of ideologies and constituencies within the women's movement. Until the late 1990s it was the focus of relations between the women's movement and the federal state (see below). Its umbrella structure – its members are groups, not individuals – allows it to function both as a focal point for a social movement and as an interest group in interacting with the government. Thus, from the first, it has consciously included groups from a broad range of ideologies, standpoints, social and economic sites, and races and ethnicities. It has forced the government to deal with women's point of view on supposedly gender-neutral issues (such as free trade). Although feminists all along the ideological spectrum have been involved in the NAC, its public face and its officers were initially middle and upper class and primarily white, abled, and heterosexual. There were, of course, lesbian women and organizations (the first lesbian conference was held in Toronto in

1973), but issues of lesbian rights did not appear on the NAC's agenda until the 1980s. There were also divisions among "groups" of women; for instance, some non-Status Aboriginal women were involved in the NAC, while traditional nationalist Aboriginal women were opposed to this kind of feminism.

Women set up services for themselves, many funded by agencies of various levels of government, particularly by the federal Women's Bureau of the Secretary of State and by all the provinces. These services included women's centres, women's health services, centres for battered women, and rape crisis centres. Throughout the 1970s, women's groups evolved from "grass-roots organizations providing direct services into a national lobbying body so far unrivalled by any other public interest group" (Kome 1983, 96). The government also acknowledged feminists, and specifically the NAC, as spokespersons for the women of Canada.

Between 1966 and 1972 the government could not ignore the demands of women. Under the Liberal government, the state was activist, centralist, and interventionist. The Trudeau government was generally receptive to the challenges presented by women's groups (the prime minister felt that women's activism would help integrate francophone and anglophone women, and thus the nation, and thereby undercut separatism). Provincial and federal services and employment for women increased.

This funding of women's services was part of an overall expansion of the federal state between the 1960s and the 1980s. Scott See (2001) writes that by the 1970s Canada had a comprehensive social network. This included unemployment insurance, the Canada Pension Plan, the Canada Assistance Act, expanded post-secondary education, and Medicare, all under the political principle of universalism.

During this time, representation of women in the policy-making process also grew. From 1972 to 1975 there were struggles among state structures to have women's interests represented, and advisers were appointed in departments and within the bureaucracy ("femocrats"). The Women's Program of the Secretary of State, which funded women's groups, was staffed by some strong feminists, and the activities during International Women's Year in 1977 (also government funded) increased general awareness. From 1976 to 1979, the relationship with the state became more professional in terms of consultations and negotiations. The status of women became a public issue. In 1976 the federal government adopted a policy that the impact of each cabinet decision had to be considered in light of the status of women, and that in each federal department or agency there should be a branch concerned with the impact of the department's activities on the status of women (this was never fully implemented). Meeting women's needs was entrenched in the Canadian bureaucracy.

The emphasis on the collective needs of women became institutionalized among governments and special agencies. Within the government there was an increase in bureaux, commissions, and committees mandated to deal with women's issues. Women became closer to the state as a result of the services extended to them. In addition, many other groups focusing on women's needs were assisted by government funding; examples are the Canadian Research Institute for the Advancement of Women, founded in 1976, and the National Association of Women and the Law (1974). International Women's Year was celebrated in 1976 (see appendix 9.1).

As a result of this attention to the needs of women, many laws were amended or enacted. In 1969 abortion became legal (though still controlled by men, as women had to appear before a hospital's Therapeutic Abortion Committee to request permission to have an abortion), and maternity leave was extended. However, many other laws and customs still worked against women. The Indian Act still discriminated against Aboriginal women as to their status and rights. Women entering Canada as immigrants were usually classified as "dependents" of husbands, which meant they were not eligible for language and vocational training; thus, they usually ended up in low-wage and dead-end jobs. African-Canadian women still experienced specific gendered racial discrimination in society and the workplace.

During this period, many women's groups, especially the NAC, were deliberately multipartisan. There were women in the movement with experience in all major political parties (including on the executive and as president). Liberal feminism prevailed, although there always existed a strong socialist element. There was some emphasis on the "electoral project": getting women elected at all levels of government. By 1980 women made up 5 per cent of the House of Commons, a few female senators had been appointed, and one woman had been appointed to the Supreme Court (see appendix 9.1). The first black woman to be elected to any Canadian legislature was Rosemary Brown in British Columbia, in 1972. Most mainstream political parties had adjusted their rules to take gender into account for attendance at conventions and for election to party executives, and this also extended women's participation in party politics.

The Status of Women in Quebec, 1950–1984

With the coming of the "Quiet Revolution" in Quebec in the 1960s, many changes took place in the province (see chapters 2 and 6). The Quebec government assumed control over many aspects of daily life that had previously been controlled or performed by the church or the family – health care, education, and pensions, for example. Changes rapidly took place in all aspects of identity, culture, and politics. These changes particularly affected women, and nationalism and feminism came to be the two major movements in the province. The two were often intertwined; at times, women who supported both nationalism and feminism found themselves conflicted.

In Quebec, women – especially francophone women – had been even more oppressed than in the rest of the country. Especially for rural women, life centred around "hearth and home," pleasing the husband, farm work, and producing many children. Little need was seen for women's education, and few women were employed outside the home. Despite this – and perhaps it is counterintuitive – Catholic nuns were powerful in education, health care, fundraising, and administration.

Before the 1960s, what higher education was available for Quebec women was mainly in convents or in "family institutes," in which women were trained to be professional wives. Education was controlled by the church until 1964. By the end of the decade, both sexes were attending in droves the new Collèges d'Enseignement Général et Professionnel (CEGEPs), which were provincially funded community colleges. The birth rate fell by half between 1959 and 1971, to 15 per 1000; by that year it was the lowest in Canada, whose rate in 1971 was 16.8 per 1000.

These societal changes and the general atmosphere of the 1960s led to the resurgence of two important social movements in Quebec: feminism and nationalism. Both these movements had existed before in the province; however, the past murmurings (and occasional uprisings) of nationalism had had little impact on the dominance, particularly economic, of the province by the English. And there had been no weakening of male dominance of the society; remember, women did not even have the vote provincially until 1940, although there were women in power in some social institutions.

The surge of reforms during the 1960s (see chapters 3 and 6) brought new vitality to the women's movement. Quebec is one of the few places where there was direct continuity between provincial suffrage and the women's movement's resurgence in the 1960s. In particular, Thérèse Casgrain, a suffrage leader, was also a leader in the Fédération des Femmes du Québec (FFQ), founded in 1966. This was a federation of a large number of women's groups, although it also had individual members. Many in this group saw it as completing the reforms begun by the first wave. Although women in Quebec lagged somewhat behind those of English Canada in founding associations, owing in part to their lack of a history of involvement in suffrage campaigns, they had been defining what they wanted at the grass-roots level. Linking with anglophone groups was accomplished mainly through contacts among individual women, particularly bilingual residents of Quebec with links to anglophones. Elite accommodation was the pattern, although there had been some joint associations such as Voice of Women.

The issues of modern feminism and the new nationalism were intertwined. The slogan of some of the early feminists in the 1960s was "Pas de libération des femmes sans Québec libre, pas de Québec libre sans libération des femmes" (No women's liberation without Quebec liberation, no Quebec liberation without liberation of women). Many say that this is still at the heart of Quebec feminism. Women's struggles were at the centre of independence politics; women's groups challenged Quebec to be more responsive to women than the federal government. In many cases they achieved their goals. However, there were also more "traditional" women's groups involved in other types of reform. For example, the more rural Association Féminine d'Éducation et Action Sociale, a Catholic group, was involved in social reforms such as the modernization of schools.

After the election of the separatist Parti Québécois, the question of the status of women came to occupy a major place in the social, political, and ideological life of Quebec. Major legislative changes were made in family law, services for women, and education. Women participated in government and business and were integrated into the policy-making process. Women were involved in the new economy and entrepreneurship and gained access to the professions and higher incomes. The Conseil de la Statut de la Femme (CSF) was founded in 1973 as a result of pressure from the FFQ. It was backed by most of the organized women's groups and was often able to translate grass-roots demands into government policies. Its major responsibilities were to advise the government on women's issues, communicate with women's groups, and do policy research. During these years it also benefited from a decentralized structure that brought the conseil directly to local groups. The CSF was strongly activist, and became integrated with progressive nationalism. It reported directly to the National Assembly and was willing to take critical stances. The Quebec government entered into areas previously left to church and patriarchy, such as health care, education, and social services. Many Franco-Quebec feminists were pleased with all that their government was able to accomplish; in most cases, Quebec was ahead of English Canada. For example, Quebec was leading the way in liberalizing abortion rules, in passing new laws relating to divorce settlements and pensions, and in removing stereotypes from school textbooks. They were supportive of the government both because of what it had accomplished for women and because of its achievements for Quebec society as a whole. It must be noted that there were many groups in Quebec whose lives still were marginal: new immigrants, Aboriginal women, and the Afro-Québécoises. And, of course, there were other points of view, including a radical antistatist movement.

As the referendum on "sovereignty-association" approached in 1980 (see chapter 6), women were torn in several directions. The PQ government had done a great deal for women, but there was fear that pronatalist policies might come into effect (due to the declining birth rate, there was discussion about promoting maternity in Quebec). Many feminists were socialists and supported the PQ for its social democratic ideology; but they also were dismayed at the slowing down of progress for women. Publicly the PQ was committed to the liberation of women, but it was still traditionally nationalist in many ways, especially in viewing women as the mothers of the nation. For a variety of complex reasons, the outcome of the referendum was 60 per cent against a change in Quebec's status.

The Charter and the Constitution, 1982–1985

One of the major differences in the status of women in Canada and the United States is that Canadian women have full constitutional legal equality; this is denied to women in the United States. This section discusses the ways in which Canadian women and women's groups mobilized to achieve this landmark; it also treats the outcomes, both positive and negative, of constitutional equality and its effects on society as a whole.

Canada's constitution is actually a series of documents, as well as unwritten conventions and traditions. The key document for more than a century was the British North America Act (BNA), an 1867 act of the British parliament, which could only be amended by the British government (at the request of the Canadian government). The documents also include a Canadian Bill of Rights, an ordinary statute passed under Prime Minister John Diefenbaker in 1960, which carried little force because it was not entrenched in the constitution and could be repealed as an ordinary act of Parliament. (Quebec also had a provincial bill of rights.) One of Pierre Trudeau's goals as prime minister (1968–79, 1980–4) was to patriate the constitution so that the final word on Canadian constitutional issues would be in Canada (see chapter 3).

A form of what was to become section 15 of the charter (for its wording, see appendix 9.2), guaranteeing equality rights, was in the proposed charter from the first. The overall principle of equality for everyone under the law was beyond debate among most Canadians. However, there was concern among women's groups that the wording, which was taken from the Canadian Bill of Rights, would not sufficiently protect women's rights. The Supreme Court cases mentioned below, as well as the *Murdoch* case, where the court held that a wife was not entitled to an equal share of her husband's property, no matter what her contribution, were evidence of this. In fact, the five major sex equality cases that had been adjudicated had been negative for women's equality. The CACSW commissioned papers and tried to alert women in Canada to the possible outcomes of section 15. Mary Eberts reminded women of two specific cases where the concept of gender equality had not been upheld. First was the case of Jeannette Lavell, in 1973, regarding the Indian Act. Lavell claimed discrimination because the act stated that an Indian man who married a non-Indian did not lose his status as an Indian, but an Indian woman who married a non-Indian did lose hers. The court ruled this was not a denial of equality before the law, as that guarantee applies only to the administration of the law, not equality in the law itself. The other case that had caught women's attention was that of Stella Bliss in 1978. Bliss was pregnant but had not been employed long enough to qualify for maternity benefits. In any case, she wanted to continue to work, and was able to. However, she was dismissed from her job for pregnancy-related reasons. When she applied for unemployment benefits, she was told she was not eligible because she should be receiving special pregnancy benefits. The court ruled that she had not been denied equality before the law, because the distinction was made because of pregnancy, not sex.

There was to be a three-year waiting period before section 15 came into force, to allow the federal and provincial governments time to re-examine and alter relevant laws and permit a process of public consultation. This was a tacit admission that the current laws were discriminatory and in need of revision, and gave the governments time to fix problems before litigation could commence.

Over the course of the constitution debate, a mass, grass-roots response developed that included women who had not been involved before in women's actions. Women injected themselves into the constitution debate, arguing for the strengthening of expansive guarantees for real change in the status of women. The charter initiative "sparked a debate about and a public awareness of rights issues which opened some space in the political opportunity structure for the mobilization of women around the question of constitutional rights" (Gotell 1990, 9). Particularly important here was the main Canadian women's magazine, *Chatelaine*, which played a major educative role for previously uninvolved women. Part of the debate concerned affirmative action for previously discriminated groups: equality as same versus equality as difference.

In the fall of 1980, justice minister Jean Chrétien introduced the constitution and the Charter of Rights and Freedoms in the House of Commons. Twenty women's groups presented coordinated briefs whose aim was to ensure that equality would be written into the charter and that it would remain there. One-quarter of the submissions to the committee concerned equality rights. Anglo-Canadian women became interested in constitutional development in part because of a recent, unsuccessful attempt by the federal government to move control over marriage and divorce laws to the provinces; their concern was that a consistent national standard be maintained. Women in Quebec, however, supported the devolution of powers to at least their province (see below).

What actually stimulated the intense interest and involvement of large numbers of women in the constitutional process was a strange series of events. (Much of what follows here is from a July 1990 interview by the author with Doris Anderson.) A women's constitutional conference had been planned by the Canadian Advisory Council on the Status of Women for September 1980. However, it was postponed because of a translators' strike in Ottawa, and the conference was rescheduled for February. Then Lloyd Axworthy, the minister responsible for the status of women, informed the president of the council, Doris Anderson, that he thought the conference should be cancelled altogether and that regional conferences should take place instead. To Anderson, it was very clear that this was a political decision – that he did not want such a conference going on while the House was debating the constitution. A meeting was called with the CACSW executive committee, Anderson, and Axworthy. Meanwhile, political pressure had been put on the executive, who agreed at the meeting with Axworthy that the conference should be cancelled. On 20 January 1981, Doris Anderson resigned and released her reasons to the press; this attracted much attention in the media and generated questions in the House of Commons every day for a week.

"I decided that I had some skills in the media, I should use them. I drafted a press release and statement to Axworthy over the weekend. It got a hell of a lot of response, the press loved this fight ... I was a well known woman, I had lots of friends in the press ... I lost that decision and became temporarily a national heroine" (Anderson 1990).

The NAC was in no position to take leadership at this time. There had been much internal debate about the need for a charter and constitutional guarantees, and in fact, the president of the NAC opposed constitutionalizing the political process. NDP women were badly divided, as were anglophones and francophones. Few socialists supported it; Quebec feminists opposed it. One week later, on 27 January, a group of women (most of them anglophones, majority, elite, able, and connected to the NAC) met in Toronto to launch a coalition of national feminist networks to put on the conference regardless of Axworthy's decision.

> Women were sitting there ready. The press called, said what are you going to do. When presented like that, you say, what do you think, I'm going to Ottawa ... I called just one person, we just talked about it. All I intended to do was have lunch with just one person to talk about this. We just started calling a couple of other women, then there were a dozen ... We then had lunch the next day, we were some twenty-odd, we decided we would go to Ottawa if we were the only ones who went. (Ryan-Nye 1990)

This turned out to be the first public conference ever held in the House of Commons. What became known as the Ad Hoc Committee was able to expand political involvement somewhat beyond elites and traditional women's groups.

Using existing networks, mailing lists, and personal contacts, the women voluntarily began to set up the conference. Individual women donated time, money, and resources; organizations donated in whatever form they could. House members, particularly women MPs, and public servants who agreed that such a conference should be held allowed their offices, phones, and photocopiers to be used by the "Ad Hocers." One week after the lunch meeting in Toronto, letters and registration materials were being sent out across the country.

In a one-month period, the Ad Hocers and the networks managed to bring together a conference of more than 1300 women from across the country, from all parties and provinces and with some francophone presence (mainly Acadian), though not from pan-Quebec women's groups. Support and resources came from ninety pan-Canadian groups and five pan-Canadian networks, as well as from political parties (the NDP did coffee and doughnuts). The conference "drew women together across regional, class, partisan and ideological lines" (Gotell 1990, 15). In particular, feminist academics and lawyers were a tremendous resource.

The consensus of the conference was that gender equality rights had to be in the charter. Specific points were made, especially by the cadre of feminist lawyers: the use of the word "persons," which was familiar in Canadian law after the *Persons* case, should be used throughout. All points in the charter were to apply equally to male and female persons. It was agreed that equality under the law must be stated as broadly as possible and that as many protections for this as necessary must be written in to cover eventualities. There was an enhanced emphasis on collective rights, on the rights of women as a group.

These resolutions were passed by the conference. They were endorsed at the February national meeting of the National Association of Women and the Law, as well as by the NAC's annual meeting in March. After initial resistance, the Department of Justice began to work with the feminist lawyers, and the resolutions eventually found their form in sections 15 and 28 of the proposed charter (see appendix 9.2 for the specific wording of these two sections).

Section 15 guarantees equality rights before and under the law and equal protection and benefit of the law to all individuals; it also allows for affirmative action programs. It covers both the content of laws and how they are administered. Section 28 guarantees all rights in the charter equally to both male and female persons.

In November, another federal-provincial conference was held. The premiers argued strongly that the provinces should control equality rights and that section 33, a provision allowing legislatures to pass laws overriding certain of the rights in the charter, should apply to section 28, the guarantee of application equally to men and women. It had already been agreed that section 15 could be overridden.

The spectre of "ten white men in suits" (the prime minister and provincial premiers) negotiating away this issue and appearing poised to scale back women's rights infuriated involved women. Angry public reaction occurred quickly and spontaneously. Women's groups sprang into action again. The NAC issued a mailing to all its member groups. There was a coordinating meeting of the Ad Hocers. Through word of mouth, established networks, and the media, women were consulted and informed. They began to contact and lobby the premiers. Influential women lobbied the premiers individually. In one week, the consent of all the premiers that section 28 would not be subject to the override was obtained, including endorsement from Quebec premier René Lévesque. This public intervention produced the final collapse of provincial opposition, and the combination of support and lobbying convinced the governments that this was a public directive.

The Constitution Act was proclaimed in the spring of 1982 (despite opposition from many in Quebec and the fact that the province had not signed on; see chapter 6 for more details), after approval by the British government and the queen. It included both clauses guaranteeing the equality of women and that section 28 could not be overridden.

The Constitution and Quebec, 1982–1985

Another view of this time, however, comes from Quebec. Here the constitution and the charter are seen by many as direct challenges to Quebec's sovereignty, and the "Night of the Long Knives" (*longs couteaux*) still lingers in the public mind. In addition, the difference in the culture has given rise to different understandings of and expectations of feminism, and the relationships with various levels of decision making and governments.

During the 1980s, women's groups in Quebec challenged the nationalist Quebec government to be more responsive than the federal one to women's demands. The FFQ supported the rights of peoples to self-determination, and there was a greater recognition than in the Rest of Canada (ROC) that "women," including their modes of organization, are not all the same. By the 1990s, however, there were many conflicts between feminists and nationalists, and a coalition of women's groups challenged the Quebec government to build "un Québec pluriel féministe" (Dumont 1992), still believing that the Quebec state was more progressive than the federal one. Despite continued goodwill at many individual levels, it was recognized that significant societal and cultural differences had produced greatly varying approaches as well as huge discrepancies in modes of organization and in relationships with the various states. In many cases there are similarities in goals and objectives; but differences in political interpretations of which government(s) (federal or provincial) should hold responsibility are divisive.

In addition, the debate over the charter, especially sections 15 and 28, forever split most Quebec-based feminist groups from the "umbrella" NAC, as the priorities and political outlooks of the two societies clashed in microcosm within this organization. The groups had already grown alienated over agendas, tactics, and the organizational status of the FFQ. Issues of federal-provincial jurisdictions and the distinct society clause combined with language, history, social change, and the links of Québécois nationalism and feminism to make permanent reconciliation impossible. In addition, Quebec women's groups felt that they had many advantages over ROC groups, in that their own government was more responsive to their needs than the federal government or those of other provinces.

Post-Charter: Social and Legal Status

The charter debates broadened the participation of rights-based groups of many kinds in the political and social life of Canada. Alan Cairns has postulated a new generation of "Charter Canadians" who feel a deep and personal connection to issues of individual and group rights. Rankin and Vickers (2001) contend that because of the charter, "many feminists outside Quebec feel a sense of proprietorship over the Charter, especially over its equality claims" (5). This was demonstrated by the rapid mobilization of new women's groups – including those for lesbians, Aboriginal women, women with disabilities, and immigrant women – and by their new visibility. The NAC's membership doubled in the 1980s, mainly due to these new organizations. As a result, the organization did a self-assessment, changed many of its procedures, and began addressing more directly issues of racism, ableism, and heterosexism in both its ideology and its structure. It was at this time that the NAC stated that antiracism was a priority feminist goal. Policy debates broadened and deepened on such issues as lesbian rights, immigrant rights, and Aboriginal women's issues. For instance, there was a more direct emphasis on "Indian Rights for Indian Women," and a deliberate attempt to understand the delicacies of collective rights versus self-government in the Aboriginal community. Although the NAC paid much attention to this issue, most Aboriginal women were connected to the NAC only indirectly, through other groups, and differences remained within the Aboriginal community among urban, non-Status women and First Nations women.

The NAC also developed its own affirmative action programs. At its 1991 annual general meeting, for instance, it resolved to set aside positions on the executive for women of colour, immigrant women of colour, women with disabilities, Aboriginal women, and francophone women. In 1993 Sunera Thobani, an immigrant woman of colour, was elected president, and in 1996 Joan Grant-Cummings, a woman of colour, was elected president.

Some outcomes of the charter have specific legal aspects (as was intended). The major players are the courts and the legal system, the Court Challenges Program, and the Women's Legal Education and Action Fund (LEAF). The Court Challenges Program was a federally funded organization that funded law cases to challenge and interpret the Charter of Rights and Freedoms. Groups and individuals sought financial support to challenge laws that might violate equality rights, or to research cases before they went to court, or to pay for the costs of the actual court proceedings. The program was established in 1978, broadened to include equality rights in 1985, defunded from 1992 to 1994, reinstated in 1994, and defunded again in 2006. In 1984 it had a budget of $200,000; in 2005 the budget was $2.75 million, 60 per cent of which went to fund cases about equality rights. The program also conducted community outreach to create test cases.

LEAF was founded in 1971 (see appendix 9.1) by feminist women lawyers, specifically to advance court cases about equality. It has been granted "intervener" status in the courts more often than any other non-governmental group and was the most frequent recipient of funds from the Court Challenges Program. Until recently its approach was to participate in interventions, including broad-based coalitions and consultations.

Litigation was increasingly used as a political tactic by rights advocacy organizations. (Of course, women have long been active in constitutional and jurisdictional issues, ever since the *Persons* case.) Some argue that the increased resort to litigation reflects a blockage of traditional partisan channels. Note also that some feminists regard legal tactics as malestream, classed, gendered, and patriarchal, and that additional disagreements arise between "expert" groups such as LEAF and the advocacy and lobbying groups.

James Kelly (2005) reviewed 353 charter decisions between 1984 and 1997. He found that 118 claims were won, 217 were lost, and 17 were inconclusive. Most successes were in the areas of Aboriginal rights (46 per cent), language and minority rights (41 per cent), legal rights (32 per cent), and equality rights (20 per cent). (Note that in many cases, a "loss" at the Supreme Court level may lead to a change in common law with a positive result overall.) Brodsky and Day's 1989 review of the 44 sex-equity cases found that 35 were brought by men.

Morton and Allen analysed 44 charter cases heard between 1982 and 1996. They found that 18 rulings (38 per cent) maintained the status quo, 30 (70 per cent) were overall "wins," and 11 (23 per cent) were losses, 3 of these policy losses for women. (In the United States over the same period, 72 per cent of such cases were wins for women.) Regarding policy fields, Canadian women have not lost any cases to do with pornography, immigration, or reproductive rights.

Sylvia Bashevkin (1998) compared legislative and judicial actions in Canada with those in the United States. She found the following: in the 1970s, before the Reagan presidency, there were 36 decisions, of which 70 per cent were favourable for women, 22.2 per cent not favourable, and 3 neutral. Under Reagan there were 29 decisions, 48.3 per cent favourable, 34.5 per cent not favourable, and 5 neutral. Under Bush 1, there were 24 decisions: 16.7 per cent favourable, 66.7 per cent not favourable, and 16.7 per cent neutral (ibid., 252–4). Data for Canada were as follows: before Mulroney, 16 decisions, with 50 per cent favourable, 37 per cent not favourable, and 13 per cent neutral; and during the Mulroney era (1984–93, after the charter came into effect), 30 decisions, with 86.8 per cent favourable, 6.7 per cent not favourable, and 6.7 per cent neutral (ibid., 254–5).

Certainly, some Supreme Court decisions have expanded legal equality rights: gays and lesbians can now marry and collect pensions; pornography has been defined as hate speech; and abortion has been removed from the Criminal Code. Many decades after Prime Minister Pierre Trudeau declared that the state had no business in the bedrooms of the nation (1960), Bill C-38, the Civil Marriage Act, passed in July 2005, defined marriage as "the lawful union of two persons to the exclusion of all others," opening marriage to all adults. This was revisited by Parliament when Prime Minister Harper presented a resolution to restore the traditional definition of marriage. This was defeated, and Harper conceded and said it would not be presented again.

Another major change came as a result of *Andrews* (1989), where the court in effect redefined equality: it ruled that section 15 should be interpreted to promote equality for those groups which are disadvantaged rather than to protect those which are privileged; more specifically, equality is to be defined as "purposive," which accepts that women are "differently situated than men and that their position of group disadvantage might require specific remedies" (Chappell 2002, 131). This, in fact, accepts definitions that have been developed in feminist jurisprudence.

However, the charter and rulings that have flowed from it remain problematic for many. Generally, that document accepts women as an unproblematic category and ignores the diversity of women's experiences and places. Also, it does not challenge the status quo, especially with regard to power. In some cases, women must fight against the charter to maintain existing rights; in other cases, some women benefit to the detriment of others.

To the Current Day

Much has changed in the past twenty years. There have been both gains and losses, politically, legally, and culturally. Women in Canada have broadened their field of political action beyond what was traditionally considered "women's concerns" and have taken part in many high-profile economic and political debates. Governments have defunded some programs, but women's and feminist issues still have a place in policy debates, and many initiatives and actions are taking place at lower or less formal levels than formerly. A major victory was the decriminalization of abortion. In the United States, antifeminism has grown, and reproductive rights are at risk.

In Canada, two things occurred simultaneously: the courts moved to establish, interpret, and legitimate certain group rights; and meanwhile, the groups that were arguing for, presenting, and forcing these rights were losing formal political power as well as social power. Women's groups, formerly at the forefront of political arguments, became more marginalized, their agendas more often dismissed. However, as a result of past actions, the courts had become more feminized. As the NAC, for instance, became more inclusive in its membership, leadership, and goals, the government moved from a consultative position vis-à-vis the organization towards a view that "special interest groups" have no business in electoral politics. At the same time, in Quebec, feminist organizations, although growing stronger, became more and more disillusioned with the government's nationalist project and began to design their own.

This has been a particularly difficult struggle for groups that focus on issues of race and ethnicity, ability, and class. Both the NAC and the FFQ have struggled with issues of racialization both within their own ranks and in society as a whole, and their marginalization seems to be concurrent with this struggle. And there is much yet to be done: despite gains, many women remain disadvantaged educationally, socially, and economically. The data show ongoing gaps between majoritarian groups and those people who are Aboriginal, non-white, immigrant, gay or lesbian, and/or living with disabilities.

Bashevkin has chronicled the change in the power of organized women's groups and the different ways in which such groups have been framed by those in power. The trend has been towards decreases in core funding for many organizations, the elimination of funding for others, and the removal of several key governmental structures that had supported women's equality in the past. Some have blamed part of this governmental "withdrawal" on women's groups', most particularly the NAC's, opposition to a variety of government measures such as free trade and constitutional reform.

And, of course, there are organized women's groups at the conservative end of the political spectrum, most obviously REAL Women (Realistic, Equal, and Active for Life), which has challenged federal funding of the NAC and which opposes abortion.

Recent decades have seen conservative governments in both Canada and the United States. "Conservative" means quite different things in the two countries, but in both it has meant downloading social responsibilities to the provinces and states, promoting free markets in the financial sector, and, in Canada especially, privatizing services that the government used to provide (see chapter 11). Of particular concern to progressive women's groups has been the change in financing formulas for social assistance programs. In 1995 these were restructured to give more power to the provinces; this led to fears that national standards in social policies would be lost.

This was part of a change in the federal government's political and social philosophy in terms of which constituent units (federal or provincial) should provide services, whether funding and services should come from the governmental or the private sector, how funding should be structured, and the meaning of universalism itself (see chapter 11).

The first of these contentious policy issues was the US-Canada Free Trade Agreement (FTA) proposed in 1987, the precursor to the NAFTA agreement of 1993. The NAC and most other women's groups opposed the FTA on the basis that it would produce unfavourable employment results for women; thus, it maintained that free trade was an important feminist issue. The Conservative government reduced funding to the NAC shortly afterwards; many maintain that was a direct result of this public opposition to what the government did not recognize as a women's issue. Shortly after this, the NAC also opposed the Meech Lake and Charlottetown Accords (see chapter 3), which were attempts to address Quebec's perennial demands. The fear was that the devolution of social powers to the provinces would threaten women, especially marginalized women. There was a concern that the loss of pan-Canadian standards for social programs could threaten women, and that the FTA could lead to a loss of service jobs in Canada, which are occupied primarily by women. (The Franco-Quebec feminist position was quite different; see above.) The NAC's president, Judy Rebick, was a prominent figure in the debates; she articulated the concerns of these women, and the NAC joined the Action Canada network, a coalition of leftist social groups, to present these arguments. Although the NAC and the FFQ developed a carefully articulated compromise position, misunderstandings continued.

The NAC "developed a 'three nations' constitutional position, based on asymmetrical federalism ... The Quebec nation and the First Nations would enjoy special status and decentralized powers, while the rest of Canada (TROC) would enjoy a centralized federation" (Vickers, Appelle, and Rankin 1993, 277). This analysis was reflected in the membership and new structuring of the NAC and its executive positions, which became more representative of the new membership and priorities of the NAC. The NAC still had a liberal wing, but was moving towards more radical and socialist feminist positions. The focus of activity was on the Ontario and British Columbia governments. An example of this is the 1996 Women's March Against Poverty, sponsored by the NAC and the Canadian Labour Congress. In Quebec, the major ideological strands are radical and socialist feminism, and many groups in that province refuse to work with Anglo groups, viewing their tactics and priorities as different. Their target is the Quebec government. Most groups in Quebec have adopted a non-partisan position and no longer involve themselves in traditional political parties.

In Quebec, day care continues to be a priority and is heavily subsidized. Prime Minister Stephen Harper has recently proposed that parents receive direct payments to defray day-care costs; this, however, would amount to a defunding of child-care spaces. Other setbacks have arisen from the perspective of progressive women's groups. In September 2006 the Harper government announced a series of spending cuts, which included eliminating the Court Challenges Program and significantly reducing Status of Women funding, as well as funding for women's groups generally. Today there is little government funding for women's groups, and some government organizations that focused on women have disappeared, including the Canadian Advisory Council on the Status of Women (in existence from 1973–95). Some provincial councils remain, however. Anglophone women's groups focus on coalition activities and networking among social activist groups. Grassroots organizing is important, as are media outreach and protest.

Some other events in Canada have focused attention on women's issues. In the "Montreal Massacre" of December 1989, Marc Lépine shot and killed fourteen female engineering students at the Université de Montréal, then killed himself. During the rampage, he shouted that he was killing the women because they were women and that he hated feminists, who he felt were taking educational opportunities from men. The reaction to his murder was overwhelming throughout the country and generated extensive media coverage. Vigils were held, and the federal government announced more funding for research into violence against women (the War Against Women Report). Men launched a "white ribbon" campaign during which those who supported the rights of women to live without violence wore white ribbons. December 6 is a day of mourning to this day.

As noted above, more women are being elected to federal, provincial, and municipal governing bodies (of particular note is the 2003 Quebec provincial election, where over 30 per cent of seats went to women – a high for Canada). Feminist women have been appointed to the Supreme Court, including a chief justice. In 2010 three of the nine justices were women, including the chief justice. Three recent governors general have been women, two of them visible-minority immigrant women (Adrienne Clarkson and Michaëlle Jean). Some political parties have altered their structure to include women at all levels and have funded efforts to recruit and elect female candidates. Despite all this, Canada is fortieth in the world in terms of female representation in the federal legislature. A new organization, Equal Voice, has been formed specifically to address this issue.

Analysis of demographic trends shows considerable gains, although some groups have gained more than others in, for example, education, life expectancy, and access to the professions and the arts. However, women's incomes have hovered around 70 per cent of men's for decades, and women are still underrepresented in most fields of power. (For an extensive discussion of demographic trends for women in Canada, see Hooks et al., chap. 5.) Some would argue that some of the agenda items of women's groups have been met – the forever promised pay-equity legislation, the decriminalization of abortion, the legalization of same-sex marriage. Others maintain that much progress was made on some generally agreed upon issues during the time of the more activist state and that the more difficult job of complex and subtle rights claiming has begun.

So what does the future hold for the relationship of women's movements to the governments of Quebec and Canada? There is no easy answer. The philosophical clash between collective and individual rights, between majority and minority concerns, between the concepts of equality and redistributive justice, will continue to form – and inform – the debate well into the next century.

As stated in CRIAW's policy paper on new policies affecting women's equality (2006):

> In 2006, the federal government made a number of important changes affecting women's equality provisions. In addition to cutbacks, the elimination of some programs and changes to other, some government equality commitments to action were stalled or reversed. The justifications for these measures were that women are strong, already equal, and don't need these policy supports. Although we have equality rights on paper, we need to do much more work to make these equality rights reality for all women in Canada.

APPENDIX 9.1 SELECTED IMPORTANT FIRSTS AND DATES FOR CANADIAN WOMEN

1917   Suffrage for some women
1921   First woman elected to House of Commons: Agnes Macphail
1929   *Persons* case
1957   First woman party leader, Thérèse Casgrain, CCF, in Quebec

1966   Founding of Fédération des femmes du Québec
1967   Royal Commission on the Status of Women formed; reports 1970
1971   National Action Committee on the Status of Women founded
1972   First black woman elected to any Canadian legislature: Rosemary
         Brown, British Columbia
1973   Canadian Advisory Council on the Status of Women / Conseil du
         statut de la femme
1974   National Association of Women and the Law founded
1975   International Women's Year
1976   Canadian Research Institute for the Advancement of Women
1977   Quebec's Charter of Rights protects against discrimination based on
         sexual orientation
1981   First lesbian pride march
1982   Charter of Rights and Freedoms
1984   Court Challenges Program established (unfunded 1992–4); NAC-spon-
         sored federal leaders' debate on women's issues televised
1988   First Aboriginal woman elected to the House of Commons: Ethel Blondin-
         Andrew; Yukon Supreme Court strikes down federal abortion law
1989   First woman federal party leader: Audrey McLaughlin, NDP
1991   First Aboriginal woman first minister and government leader, NWT:
         Nellie Cournoyea
1993   First woman prime minister of Canada: Kim Campbell, PC (note: took
         over leadership, not elected)
1993   First woman of Asian descent elected to a Canadian legislature, British
         Columbia: Jenny Kwan
2000   Nineteen visible-minority women elected to the House of Commons,
         two Aboriginal
2000   20 per cent of office holders in all legislatures are women: 34th in
         world data; Yukon premier: Pat Duncan
2003   Quebec provincial election: 30 per cent of those elected are women
2005   Gay and lesbian marriages legalized in Canada
2006   Harper budget significantly reduces social spending; Court Challenges
         Program eliminated
2008   Nunavut premier: Eva Aariak
2010   Newfoundland and Labrador premier: Kathy Dunderdale
2011   British Columbia premier: Christy Clark; Alberta premier: Alison Red-
         ford
2012   Quebec premier: Pauline Marois; 49 per cent of Canadians in prov-
         inces/territories with woman premier (Ibbitson 2012)
2013   Kathleen Wynne becomes leader of Ontario's Liberal Party and premier.
         85 per cent of Canadians now live in a province/territory with a woman leader

APPENDIX 9.2 CANADIAN CHARTER OF RIGHTS AND FREEDOMS
(EXCERPTS)

Section 15: Every individual is equal before and under the law and has
the right to the equal protection and equal benefit of the law without
discrimination and, in particular, without discrimination based on race,
national or ethnic origin, colour, religion, sex, age or mental or physical disability.

Subsection (1) does not preclude any law, program or activity that
has as its object the amelioration of conditions of disadvantaged individuals or groups including those that are disadvantaged because of
race, national or ethnic origin, colour, religion, sex, age or mental or
physical disability.

Section 28: Notwithstanding anything in this Charter, the rights and
freedoms referred to in it are guaranteed equally to male and female
persons.

Entrenched in the Canadian Constitution on 17 April 1982.

Note: The Courts have expanded the list by "reading in" other groups,
particularly in relation to sexual orientation.

WEBSITES

Canadian Research Institute for the Advancement of Women: http://www.
    criaw-icref.ca
Mapleleafweb.com: www.mapleleafweb.com
Statistics Canada: statcan.gc.ca
Status of Women Canada: http://www.swc-cfc.gc.ca
Women's Legal Education and Action Fund (LEAF). https://leaf.ca

REFERENCES AND FURTHER READING

Anderson, Doris. 1990. Interview by the author. July.
Arscott, Jane, and Linda Trimble, eds. 1997. *In the Presence of Women: Represen-
    tation in Canadian Governments*. Toronto: Harcourt Brace.
Backhouse, Constance, and David H. Flaherty, eds. 1992. *Challenging Times:
    The Women's Movement in Canada and the United States*. Montreal: McGill-
    Queen's University Press.

Bashevkin, Sylvia. 1998. *Women on the Defensive: Living through Conservative Times*. Toronto: University of Toronto Press.

Bégin, Monique. 1988. "Debates and Silences – Reflections of a Politician." *Daedalus* 117: 335–62.

Bégin, Monique. 1992. "The Royal Commission on the Status of Women: Twenty Years Later Revisited." In *Challenging Times*, ed. Constance Backhouse and David H. Flaherty, 21–38. Montreal: McGill-Queen's University Press.

Begin, Monique. 1997. Interview by the author. October.

Bilson, Janet Mancini, and Carolyn Fluehr-Lobban. 2005. *Female Well Being*. London: Zed.

Bird, Florence. 1974. *Anne Francis*. Toronto: Clarke, Irwin.

Bird, Florence. 1990. Interview by the author. July.

Black, Naomi. 1988. "The Canadian Women's Movement: The Second Wave." In *Changing Patterns*, ed. Sandra Burt, Lorraine Code, and Lindsay Dorney, 151–76. Toronto: McClelland & Stewart.

Brodsky, Gwen, and Shelagh Day. 1989. *Canadian Charter Equality Rights for Women: One Step Forward and Two Steps Back?* Ottawa: Canadian Advisory Council on the Status of Women.

Cairns, Alan. 1989. "Citizens and the Charter: Democratizing the Process of Constitutional Reform." In *The Meech Lake Primer*, ed. Michael D. Behiels, 109–24. Ottawa: University of Ottawa Press.

Canadian Advisory Council on the Status of Women. 1981. *Women and the Constitution*. Ottawa: Supply and Services Canada.

Chappell, Louise A. 2002. *Gendering Government: Feminist Engagement with the State in Australia and Canada*. Vancouver: UBC Press.

Cleverdon, Catherine Lyle. 1950. *The Woman Suffrage Movement in Canada*. Toronto: University of Toronto Press.

Clio. Le Collectif. 1982. *Histoire des femmes au Québec*. Montreal: Les Quinze.

Conseil du statut de la femme. 1978. *Pour les Québécoises: Égalité et indépendance*. Quebec: Gouvernement du Québec.

Dangenais, Hugette. 1979. "L'Évolution des Québécoises en periode de luttes féministes." *Atlantis* 4: 146–56.

de Sève, Micheline. 1992. "The Perspective of Quebec Feminists." In *Challenging Times*, ed. Constance Backhouse and David H. Flaherty, 110–19. Montreal: McGill-Queen's University Press.

Dumont, Micheline. 1992. "The Origins of the Women's Movement in Québec." In *Challenging Times*, ed. Constance Backhouse and David H. Flaherty, 72–89. Montreal: McGill-Queen's University Press.

Eberts, Mary. 1981. "Women and Constitutional Renewal." In *Women and the Constitution in Canada*, ed. Audrey Doerr and Micheline Carrier, 3–28. Ottawa: Canadian Advisory Council for the Status of Women.

Findlay, Sue. 1988. "Facing the State." In *Feminism and Political Economy*, ed. Heather Jon Maroney and Meg Luxon, 31–50. Toronto: Methuen.

Gotell, Lise. 1990. *The Canadian Women's Movement, Equality Rights, and the Charter*. Ottawa: Canadian Research Institute for the Advancement of Women.

Hooks, Tess, Patrice LeClerc, and Roderic Beaujot. 2005. "Women in Canada: A Century of Struggle." In *Female Well-Being*, ed. Janet Mancini Billson and Carolyn Fluehr-Lobban, 94–132. London: Zed Books.

Hošek, Chaviva. 1983. "Women and the Constitutional Process." In *And No One Cheered*, ed. Keith Banting and Richard Simeon, 280–300. Toronto: Methuen.

Ibbitson, John. 2012. "Rise of Women in Canadian Politics." *Globe and Mail*, 11 September.

Kealey, Linda, and Joan Sangster, eds. 1989. *Beyond the Vote*. Toronto: University of Toronto Press.

Kelly, James B. 2005. *Governing with the Charter: Legislation and Judicial Activism and Framers' Intent*. Vancouver: UBC Press.

Kome, Penney. 1983. *The Taking of Twenty-Eight*. Toronto: Women's Press.

Lamereux, Diane. 1988. "Nationalism and Feminism in Quebec: An Impossible Attraction." In *Feminism and Political Economy*, ed. Heather Jon Maroney and Meg Luxon, 51–67. Toronto: Methuen.

LeClerc, Patrice, and Lois West. 1997. "Feminist Nationalist Movements in Quebec: Resolving Contradictions." In *Feminist Nationalisms*, ed. Lois West, 220–46. New York: Routledge.

Maille, Chantal. 2000. "Quebec Women and the Constitutional Issue: A Scattered Group." *Journal of Canadian Studies/Revue d'Études Canadiennes* 35 (2): 109–27.

"Persons Case." 1930. *Edwards v. Canada* (Attorney General).

Prentice, Alison, Paula Borne, Gail Cuthbert Brandt, Beth Light, Wendy Mitchinson, and Naomi Black. 1988. *Canadian Women: A History*. Toronto: Harcourt Brace Jovanovich.

Roberts, Barbara. 1989. *Smooth Sailing or Storm Warning? Canadian and Quebec Women's Groups and the Meech Lake Accord*. Ottawa: Canadian Research Institute for the Advancement of Women.

Ryan-Nye, Linda. 1990. Interview by the author. July.

See, Scott. 2001. *The History of Canada*. Westport, CT: Greenwood Press.

Standing Committee on the Status of Women. 2005. "Gender-Based Analysis: Building Blocks for Success." Ottawa.

Status of Women Canada. 1998. "Gender Equality Indicators: Public Concerns and Public Policy." Ottawa.

Status of Women Canada. 2005. *Women in Canada: A Gender-Based Statistical Report*. 5th ed. Ottawa.

Status of Women Canada and Statistics Canada. 2003. "Women and Men in Canada: A Statistical Glance." 2nd ed. Ottawa.

Strong-Boag, Veronica, and Anita Clair Fellman, eds. 1986. *Rethinking Canada*. Toronto: Copp Clark Pitman.

Trofimenkoff, Susan Mann 1982. *Dream of a Nation*. Toronto: Macmillan of Canada.

Vickers, Jill. 1986. "Equality Seeking in a Cold Climate." In *Righting the Balance: Canada's New Equality Rights*, 16–36. Saskatoon: Canadian Human Rights Reporter.

Vickers, Jill. 2000. "Feminisms and Nationalisms in English Canada." *Journal of Canadian Studies/Revue d'Études Canadiennes* 35 (2): 149–65.

Vickers, Jill, Chris Appelle, and Pauline Rankin. 1993. *Politics As If Women Mattered: A Political Analysis of the National Action Committee on the Status of Women*. Toronto: University of Toronto Press.

10 Canadian Environmental Policy

LESLIE R. ALM AND ROSS E. BURKHART

This chapter covers several aspects of Canadian environmental policy. We examine constitutional features such as the internal federal–provincial relationship regarding the environment and the dominance of the provincial policy. The relationship between Canada and the United States also merits consideration. The dominance of the United States in its advocacy in environmental protection and Canada's supportive role and eventual adjustment to the policy priorities of the United States is emphasized. We then focus on the domestic environmental policymaking process and public opinion about the importance of the environment in relation to other public policy concerns. Then we highlight the influential international role that Canada has played in creating and supporting multinational environmental agreements. Finally, we provide some future perspective on environmental policymaking in Canada.

Constitutional Considerations and International Dimensions

Canadian environmental policy has both provincial constitutional origins and an increasingly modern, centralized political focus. Federal politicians have become more involved in environmental policymaking as international environmental treaties have become more prevalent. And Canada's environmental policy, as with much public policy, must take the United States into account.

The constitutional responsibility for environmental policymaking in Canada arises from the British North America Act of 1867 (BNA). From the BNA, different policy sectors were divided between the federal government and the provincial governments. Some of the more prominent policies given to the provinces include health care and the environment. Article 92A of the BNA states: "In each province, the legislature may exclusively make laws in relation to exploration for non-renewable natural resources in the province; development, conservation and management of non-renewable natural resources and forestry resources in the province, including laws in relation to the rate of primary production therefrom; and development, conservation and management of sites and facilities in the province for the generation and production of electrical energy." The BNA clearly established provincial authority over the environment. These policy demarcations took place during a time when the environment was not considered a prominent political issue. If anything, the environment was a place to be exploited for economic gain, not preserved as an ecosystem with intrinsic value of its own.

Yet times change, and today Canada places at least rhetorical importance on the environment as a matter of international importance. In this respect, Canada is no different from other advanced industrialized democracies. In fact, "environmental issues have become matters of central national and international concern that transcend ideology and political persuasion" (Sigmon 1996). Canadian concerns about the environment take into account global warming, melting of the polar ice caps (a particularly salient issue for Canada based on its geography encompassing the polar north), pollution from acid rain, pollution of the Great Lakes, and other issues.

Industrialized nations tie global environmental anxiety to quality-of-life issues. The post-materialist perspective put forth by Ronald Inglehart is instructive. For Inglehart (1977), a post-materialist pays special attention to matters beyond security and the pocketbook. The quality of the environment falls squarely within a post-materialist perspective. Western industrialized democracies are the location for post-materialist populations. This is due to their economic success. The linkage of the free market system that has led to economic prosperity, worries about the integrity of the global environment, and further to quality-of-life issues places the environment more closely to the centre of public policymaking than ever before. Norman Vig and Michael Kraft (2006) in *Environmental Policy: New Directions for the Twenty-First Century* state that "democracies in the twentieth century proved capable of sustaining national and international efforts to defeat enemies in war and to contain them for decades in peacetime. Sustainable development will be the challenge of the twenty-first century."

One important example of the international political economy of the environment is of Canada's role in the Commission for Environmental Cooperation (CEC), created under NAFTA. This intergovernmental organization, according to its mission statement, "facilitates cooperation and public participation to foster conservation, protection and enhancement of the North American environment, in the context of increasing economic, trade and social links among Canada, Mexico and the United States" (CEC 1997). Thus charged, the CEC could be a trailblazing organization and an exemplar of intergovernmental environmental relations because of "its provisions for public participation and for the unprecedented commitment by the three governments to account internationally for enforcement of their environmental laws" (TRAC 2004). Coordination of economic and environmental goals is established through three organs of the CEC. These include a council that consists of the highest-ranking environmental authorities in the North American countries, a secretariat that provides administrative support, technical expertise, a logistics framework to the council, and the Joint Public Advisory Committee, comprising private citizens in equal representation from the three countries who meet regularly to set an agenda for the CEC.

Canada's increasing participation in international environmental treaties and agreements puts a strain on Canadian federalism. Provincial interests in the enactment of these treaties are considerable and suggest potential rivalries with Ottawa, the signatory to international environmental agreements. Alberta, for instance, owing to its large reserves of oil and natural gas, has its own interests section in Washington, DC, through its office of International and Intergovernmental Relations. The section is in the Canadian embassy building in Washington, allowing Alberta (the only province with such an interests arrangement) to project its provincial interests on such issues as climate change legislation, and have an outsized lobbying impact on trade, business, and environmental issues (Goodman 2010). In the future, other provinces will establish interest sections at the Washington embassy.

This provincial assertion in international environmental policymaking should come as no surprise. "Since the early 1990s [both the Canadian and US] federal governments have stepped back from command and control regulations. They have devolved many of the national responsibilities for the environment to their states, provinces, and municipalities, and have increased collaborative decision-making through stakeholder groups, public private partnerships, and flexibility in enforcement" (Lovecraft 2007). Local Canada-US solutions to vexing environmental problems have the potential to be cheaper than national solutions, and the buy-in at the local level, especially regarding cross-border environmental problems, also holds promise for the degree to which agreements are honoured (as, for instance, with the longevity of the International Boundary Commission).

In fact, Canada has typically patterned its environmental policy-making after the United States, which has been long perceived as the innovator in environmental protection legislation and as the country that has placed the greater priority on the environment. Don Munton (1997) labels this "environmental dependence." John E. Carroll (1986) describes the relationship in the following way: "Both [countries] are vulnerable to each other, although the United States has a greater capacity to affect (and inflict) Canada than vice versa. Canada is much more aware of this interdependence and assigns a higher priority to it" (296). These are hardly new observations, however. The obvious asymmetry of power between Canada and the United States is expressed through the US population being nearly ten times that of Canada, the US GDP being on an order of nearly ten times greater, and the projection of US power in North America and overseas (Millard, Riegel, and Wright 2002).

Given this asymmetry, how does Canada create environmental policy that is right for Canada, yet pays attention to the United States? For one thing, it is rather fortunate that "in terms of their orientation toward environmental protection, the Canadian and American national governments ... have operated in sync with one another for much of the last two decades" (VanNijnatten 2008). The following sections explore this Canada–United States linkage and highlight the uniqueness of Canadian domestic and international environmental policymaking.

Canada and the United States: Marked Distinctions

Canada and the United States are vast and wealthy consumptive nations. For most, it is no surprise that the United States has enormous stores of natural resources. Many forget, or simply do not know, that Canada is not only richly endowed with natural resources (it possesses 24 per cent of the world's wetlands, 10 per cent of its forests, and 7 per cent of its fresh water) (Wood et al. 2010), with its cold climate it is also the world's largest per capita consumer of energy (Fox 1989). "The two countries are thoroughly intertwined" vis-à-vis energy trading: Canada supplies "20 percent of America's natural gas imports and 22 percent of its oil and refined petroleum intake" (Janigan 2005). As Hessing and Howlett (1997) propose, "the size and wealth of [Canada] alone are of global significance." The presence of the oil sands in Alberta ensures Canada's prominent position in providing global energy. In essence, both Canada and the United States possess enormous stores of natural resources and rank high among the most consumption-oriented nations in the world.

Canada and the United States are often viewed as being both indelibly linked by commonalities and as following distinctively different paths (Hillmer 2005). On the one hand, the two countries are viewed as monolithic in nature, sharing a relatively large number of common institutional linkages and common cultural characteristics (Boucher 2005). On the other hand, Canada and the United States are marked by substantial differences in population, relative wealth, and global influence (Gattinger and Hale 2010).

Canada and the United States have two distinct forms of democratic political systems (chapter 3) with differing founding values and historical experiences (chapter 2) (Adams 2003), with these differences leading to divergent domestic policy priorities (Martin 2003). Canada's parliamentary system founded in Westminster-style government is markedly different from the US presidential system of separation of powers and checks and balances (Hoberg 2002), with Canada creating a much stronger national government (Anderson and Sands 2011). Today, however, Canada is now a "model of extreme decentralization among Western democracies [where] Canadian provincial governments are more powerful, more independent, and more influential than are American state governments in most issues of environmental policy" (Rabe and Lowry 1999). The United States' system of government is fragmented, providing multiple points of access that typically result in ongoing contention and debate in the policy process. The Canadian system has limited protection of individual rights and limited access to the decision-making process, resulting in a more controlled and consultative policy process than in the United States (Allen 1997).

Canada and the United States have both set high standards for environmental protection and have displayed strong environmental leadership domestically and internationally (Benedick 1998). Americans and Canadians support environmental protection in general as a high priority (Bosso and Gruber 2006), while salience for particular environmental issues remains low (Rosenbaum 2008). Still, the Canadian environmental policymaking process is less pluralistic, less open, less adversarial, and more influential than that of the United States (Bocking 1997), with provincial governments having extensive authority over natural resources and environmental policy (Wilson, 2003).

Canadians, as a whole, are more sympathetic to environmental protection than Americans, and more supportive of environmental regulation (Steel et al. 2000), with a tendency towards seeking multilateral consensus and universally binding treaties, conventions, and norms (Ross 2006). Canadians are more socially liberal and supportive of cooperative approaches. Americans are more socially conservative and inclined towards an individualistic "survival of the fittest" view of the world (Barry 2005). Canadians are more collectivist and supportive of institutions. Americans are more individualistic and suspicious of institutions (Alston, Morris, and Vedlitz 1996).

Being members of the less populous and less powerful of the two countries, Canadians are more aware of the border and how transboundary issues affect their country (Carroll 1982). In this regard, there is a tendency on the part of Americans to take Canada for granted, whereas Canadians continue to push the United States towards recognition of the uniqueness of the Canada–United States relationship (Alm and Burkhart 2005). The asymmetry that defines the Canada–United States relationship often puts Canadian policymakers "largely at the mercy of American domestic political outcomes" (VanNijnatten 2003).

Canada and the United States: Environmental Comparisons

There appears to be a greater awareness evolving in both Canada and the United States that environmental issues have moved past the realm of local and national concern to be more and more connected to global concerns (Hessing and Howlett 1997). This evolution is characterized by the Canada–United States relationship, which is said to be representative of the problems and promise of a more integrated world (VanNijnatten and Boardman 2002), a world whose rapid ecological progress now allows for both protecting nature and maintaining a comfortable living standard (Easterbrook 1995).

The dynamics of globalization "have reduced time and distance as principal impediments to interaction between different parts of the globe" (Anderson and Sands 2011). In today's world, there exists little doubt that concern about the environment in Canada and the United States also translates into concern about global environmental problems. None have been more pointed in this assertion than Esty and Ivanova (2003), who pronounce that "the need for international cooperation to address environmental problems with transboundary or global implications is clear in both theory and practice." Their basic premise is quite straightforward: "There exists today a set of inescapably global environmental threats that require international collective action." This argument is not new. Over the past several decades, many have essentially made the same point: that in one way or another, environmental problems, being transboundary in nature, require global solutions fashioned in the international arena (Benedick 1998).

The evolution towards the grand linkage of environmental concerns and globalization has witnessed what some call "striking advances in international treaties and the establishment of new institutions and policymaking regimes" that offer "fresh, boundary-spanning approaches" to environmental decision making that cut across technologies, environmental media, socio-economic groups, and geographic boundaries (Kraft 2002). Along these lines, the slow and steady pace of ecological deterioration is forcing both Canadians and Americans to look more closely at working together in an even broader global environmental context (Kanji 1996).

However, recent research has reminded us that Canada and the United States have two distinct and different forms of democratic political systems (Kumar and Altschuld 2004), with institutional differences defining different forms of environmental politics in each country (Hale and Gattinger 2010). As noted above, Canadians are generally viewed as being more collective and supporting of institutions, while Americans are viewed as more individualistic and suspicious of institutions (Alston, Morris, and Vedlitz 1996). The Canadian environmental policymaking process is viewed as being less pluralistic, less open, less adversarial, and more informal than the United States (Bocking 1997).

A specific example highlighting the differences between Canada and the United States regarding environmental policymaking is the ability of citizens in each country to challenge administrative decisions in the courts. There is a dearth of environmental citizen suits in Canada, whereas in the United States, citizen suits are considered commonplace (Valiante 2002). Howlett (2002) documents the "general lack of citizen ability in Canada to overturn administrative decisions through recourses in the courts." He argues that limited rules of standing and restricted grounds for judicial review essentially prevent Canadian citizens from influencing environmental assessment and regulation in a meaningful way. By contrast, the National Environmental Policy Act (NEPA) provides easy access to the courts for United States citizens and guarantees the ability to pursue actions for the public good (ibid.).

Some now argue that environmental policy in the United States is in the midst of a profound transition, where the once dominant command and control structure is giving way to market considerations involving volunteerism, collaboration, and public education (Kraft 2002). Furthermore, while the Canadian environmental implementation style remains distinct from that of the United States, some believe that the United States' style is changing "somewhat towards that of Canada" (Howlett 2002).

Canada and the United States share common interests and a common geography that provide what some consider a catalyst for greater transnational interactions regarding the environment (Alper and Loucky 1996). Both nations place a high priority on environmental protection and have become "considerably more participatory in the way they formulate environmental policy" (VanNijnatten 1999).

Canadian Domestic Environmental Policy

Scholars have long noted the linkages between domestic policymaking and international relations. Schmidt (1996) goes so far as to observe that policy change at the international level occurs only at the intersection of domestic politics and international negotiations. In general terms, domestic politics are often viewed as the "dominant consideration" for nations participating in international negotiations related to the environment (Brown 1994). Along these lines, Doran (1997) posits that "the very essence of the current revolution in diplomatic discourses is the supremacy of the domestic over the foreign."

This pattern of domestic policy driving international (or cross-border) negotiations is quite prevalent in the Canada–United States environmental sphere (Allison 1999). Moreover, the dominance of US domestic policymaking (as discussed earlier) is readily apparent with respect to the Canada–United States environmental relationship (Kite and Nord 2008). Canada is often overwhelmed by the American presence and must continually fight to keep its distinctiveness from the United States (Stirrup and Roberts 2010). Along these lines, VanNijnatten (2003) notes the "political asymmetry whereby Canadian policy-makers [are] largely at the mercy of American domestic political outcomes" and Desombre directly links United States unilateralism on international environmental issues to the values of the domestic political system (Desombre 2005). Simply put, "If we want to understand what the United States has chosen to pursue or avoid internationally in terms of environmental policy, we need to look at what it has regulated or shunned domestically" (ibid.).

On the domestic side, Canada has moved towards what some call the "intergovernmentalization of environmental policy-making" (VanNijnatten and Boardman 2002), a move characterized by the federal government's efforts to harmonize environmental policymaking among the provinces through the sharing of authority and voluntary compliance (Doern 2002). Still the provinces retain the lead role in Canadian domestic environmental policymaking (McKenzie 2002). In this regard, provinces are said to be "calling the shots" (VanNijnatten and Boardman 2002) with powers over environmental matters that are considered "sweeping" (Valiante 2002).

While Canadian public support for the environment has remained fairly steady over the past several decades, some are worried that the trend is downward. McKenzie (2002) argues that "environmental issues have lain dormant in the shadow cast by continued government inaction and public apathy" and VanNijnatten and Boardman (2002) point out that despite moderate levels of concern about environmental degradation, these concerns are consistently pushed aside by concerns about the deficit, health care, and education. However, according to a Centre for Research and Information on Canada poll (CRIC 2005), more respondents said that "protecting the environment" is a "high" priority, compared to other issues.

Canadian International Environmental Policy

Canada has a long-held tradition of being a proponent and practitioner of multilateral diplomacy and it is at the international level that Canadian environmentalism appears to shine (Nord 2010). Former prime minister Paul Martin (2003) spoke of a "new politics of achievement" for Canada that "extends far beyond our relationship with the United States." He pointedly asserts that Canada's influence comes from being "at the leading edge of where the global economy is going." Along these lines, Canada's domestic environmental regime is viewed as "more than sufficient to back up its credentials as an international player" (Boardman 2002).

Despite the fact that economic globalism has seemingly diminished Canada's capacity to engage in across-the-board, proactive multilateralism, Canada continues to push an environmental agenda that reflects the pursuit of what some argue are distinctive Canadian values in the promotion of the virtues of multilateralism and international institutions (Boardman 2002). In this light, Canada has used the international stage for the germination of environmental policy ideas, de-emphasizing the "politics of shaming" (McKenzie 2002). In fact, through its advocacy of progressive solutions in both the ozone and climate negotiations, Canada has been viewed as an active policy entrepreneur (Harrison 2004).

Reflecting Lipset's general belief, Canada draws on a reservoir of "internationally recognized contributions to global environmental leadership" (Boardman 2002), with governments around the world increasingly looking to Canada as "the world's most successful pluralist state" (Ibbitson 2004). Canadians view global leadership with respect to environmental protection as a way to gain prestige within the world community and take pride in their efforts to bring about global environmental cooperation through such organizations as the United Nations. Canada pursues its domestic environmental policy goals through international means and uses its middle-power statecraft as a way to effect policy change in the international environmental arena (Boardman 2002).

The connection that Canadians feel towards the United Nations remains strong, something Canadians point to with confidence (MacDonald 2003). Canadians perceive themselves as "enthusiastic joiner[s] of international agreements" and embodied with "a strong internationalist tradition" (Toner 2008). This tendency towards multilateral relations is characterized as "an intrinsic, substantial, and growing feature of environmental policy in Canada" (Boardman 1992), one that plays directly to the values that Canadians believe are the foundation of their existence – the rule of law, liberty, democracy, equality of opportunity, and fairness (Martin 2003). Wood (2003) sums up Canada's unique view towards the world outside its borders rather nicely:

> Canada ... does not get its influence from power but from cooperation, supporting proposals, enthusiasm, forming coalitions, willingness to work with weaker nations, and contributing more than its fair share. Canada has a focus on values like understanding the social aspects of

globalization; a need for a fair process to ensure legitimization; a sharing of the burdens and the focus on legitimization.

Over the years, Canada had "gained a reputation as one of the world's most ecologically minded nations" (Schneider 1997), and has earned "a positive international image on the environmental front" (Paehlke 2000). In recent times, mostly due to the fact that Canada's economy remains natural resource–dependent, that image is under attack (Toner 2002). Smith (1998) contends that Canada's failure to provide credible leadership in the fight against climate change has tarnished its image in the international arena and Paehlke (2000) proclaims that in today's world, Canada is "losing ground in environmental protection in the face of both public opinion and international reputation." Schneider (1997) observes that economic worries are exerting pressure on environmental priorities in Canada such that Canada's image as one of the worlds "greener" industrialized countries is under attack, with Canada's focus now being on jobs, trade, and deficit fighting, at the expense of the environment.

The environmental record of the governments under Prime Minister Stephen Harper has been mixed. In January 2007, Paul Wells in *Maclean's* described the government's policy vision in these terms: "Harper doesn't believe in fancy environmental plans." In this sense, Harper's goal at the time was to fashion a winning governing majority as opposed to creating environmental policy. Since the public's interest in environmental policy has been fairly minimal, in comparison to the economy, Harper's policy calculus has been shrewd. But the tactic has come at some cost in credibility on the international stage in setting terms for long-range environmental agreements.

Stepan Wood et al. (2010) outline the decline in Canada's reputation as an environmental leader, arguing that Canada is now considered "a laggard in both policy innovation and environmental performance." In this regard, they point to Canada's record on climate change, where Canada is responsible for nearly 2 per cent of the world's greenhouse gas emissions while ranking second to last among industrialized nations with respect to addressing climate change policies. According to Wood et al., the blame belongs to both the Liberals and Conservatives. While the Liberal governments of Jean Chrétien and Paul Martin were publicly supportive of the Kyoto Protocol, they both were slow to develop climate change policies or to implement any significant measures to deal with global warming. Yet, Wood et al. reserve their harshest charge for Stephen Harper, who is said to be "overtly hostile to action on climate change." Along these lines, under Prime Minister Harper's tenure, climate change research programs have been terminated, and Environment Canada has seen a serious decline in its annual funding, with the budgets of the Environmental Monitoring and Assessment Network, the Migratory Bird Program, and the National Wildlife areas severely cut. "Canada is widely considered a climate-change miscreant. Nobody who knows the climate-change file in Canada or abroad believes the federal government's intention to reduce emissions by 17 percent by 2020 from 2005 levels" (Simpson 2011). Certainly, as Canada moves into the future, its once proud reputation as an environmental stalwart is under attack.

Future Considerations: Where Does Canada Go From Here?

We are now functioning in an era marked by great complexity and diversity, one in which environmentalism is now cast as "the most elaborate and segmented of our social issues" (Sussman, Daynes, and West 2002). There should be no doubt in anyone's mind that environmental protection is now considered one of the core values of North American society along with economic prosperity, national security, and democracy (Rosenbaum 2008). Furthermore, emphasis has turned towards the internationalization of environmental problems and policy, as issues such as climate change, acid rain, geochemical flux, and control of toxic pollution are viewed more and more from a global, rather than state, perspective (Harrison and Bryner 2004).

As illustrated above, this turn towards a global environmental perspective provides a good backdrop to view how Canada approaches the development of international environmental policies. Canada is a richly endowed country that trumpets its strong commitment for protecting the environment. With this enhanced natural resource status, for constitutional reasons Canada places its provinces front and centre in environmental policymaking. As discussed, one province, Alberta, has its own international diplomatic representation in Washington regarding the environment. While the potential for federal-provincial environmental policymaking strife remains high, viewed another way, Canada's decentralized process is innovative in seeking local buy-in on solutions to tricky issues. It also is in tune with Canada's outward focus, pushing its values through international organizations and using its reputation as a caring, multicultural country to foster conversations at the multilateral level through active participation in organizations such as the Commission for Environmental Cooperation. Seen in this light, Canadians are committed to negotiation and compromise as a way of moving towards the future protection of the global environment (Lipset 1990).

While indebted to the United States for its pioneering role in environmental policymaking, Canada continues to challenge the United States to recognize the uniqueness of the Canada–United States relationship in a way that would provide special status to Canadian views on the environment. Still, Canada is not sitting idly by, waiting for this special status to somehow appear without warning. Canada continually reaches out to the international community in ways that build upon its commitment to improving its status and influence at the global level, as well as with the United States. Canada clearly recognizes its asymmetric relationship with its powerful neighbour and looks beyond its borders for ways to foster values important to the Canadian way of life, while at the same time gaining some leverage in its bilateral relations with the United States. As pronounced by a Canadian prime minister (Martin 2003):

> Like other countries, we must come to grips with the fact that the United States has emerged as the world's lone superpower. We need a proud partnership based on mutual respect with our closest friend and nearest neighbour. Two nations with many shared values but each acting independently ... We must ensure that the global institutions of the coming decades are suffused with the values Canadians treasure – rule of law, liberty, democracy, equality of opportunity and fairness.

This view of Canadian values suggests that Canadians "have to develop new thinking about how the international community governs itself; and how sovereign nations take action together in tackling global issues" (ibid.). A central example of Canada's possible need to take action on its own is the fate of the Keystone XL pipeline (Eilperin 2011; Solomon 2011; VanderKlippe, McCarthy, and Tait 2011). President Barack Obama has requested that the pipeline route, from central Alberta to the Texas coast, be reconsidered to avoid an aquifer in central Nebraska. The request comes at the end of a three-year environmental review and public consultation process by the US State Department, the government agency in charge of assessing the international pipeline proposal from TransCanada Corporation. Environmentalists in both Canada and the United States welcomed the request from the

Obama administration, as public comment and direct protest (in early November, the White House was encircled by protestors against the Keystone project) appear to have affected the outcome. The pipeline, as proposed, is to carry approximately 700,000 barrels of Canadian crude oil daily, much of which will come from the oil sands of northern Alberta. "The pipeline would provide a bullet line from Alberta to the Gulf Coast for approximately 50 years" (Draitsch 2011).

Proponents of the pipeline claim anywhere from 5000 to 20,000 jobs will be created by the construction of the pipeline and the supply chains that will result from its presence. Opponents assert that the petroleum from the oil sands is less clean than is oil from other world regions. Oil sands producers will seek other markets, most likely in the Far East, should the US market not materialize. Yet the marketing challenges are greater than commonly believed: "The U.S. is the only export for oilsands. Less than .56% of oilsands production is exported to overseas markets" (Draitsch 2011). The proposed Northern Gateway pipeline from Bruderheim, Alberta, to Kitimat, British Columbia, for oil sands shipments to Asia "faces opposition … from native groups, whose traditional territory the pipeline would cross, and from environmentalists, who have lined up against the project for a number of reasons, including the heightened risk of oil spills" (Cummins and Welsch 2011). The Keystone pipeline issue illustrates the difficulties in coordinating environmental policymaking between Canada and the United States, as well as the importance of the consultation process in order to advance policies.

One question yet to be answered is exactly how Canada uses its sense of a more orderly, more civil, less market-driven, more collectively and socially responsible mindset to fit into the changing global dynamics and, at the same time, deal with the overwhelming influence of its southern neighbour (Segal 2004). Will the scientific projection of ecological deterioration resulting from climate change bring Canada and the United States together to work in a broader environmental context or must Canada go its own separate way? Again, this is a decision that Canadians must make, as the United States appears quite content in its relationship with Canada and has clearly indicated that such an integration with Canada in approaching global environmental concerns is not a central element of its domestic policy agenda (ibid.). In essence, while Canada does have the tools to blaze its own environmental policymaking trail, the Canadians are the ones left with the choice of joining the United States or going it on their own. The immediate decade in front of us will provide a tantalizing forum to find the answers.

REFERENCES

Adams, Michael. 2003. *Fire and Ice: The United States, Canada, and the Myth of Converging Values*, 143. Toronto: Penguin Canada.

Allen, Jennifer. 1997. "Institutions, Culture, and the Role of Scientific Information in Wetland Policy Development: A Comparative Study of the United States and Canada." Paper prepared for the biennial meeting of the Association for Canadian Studies in the United States, Minneapolis, 19–23 November, 9–11.

Allison, Juliann. 1999. "Fortuitous Consequence: The Domestic Politics of the 1991 Canada–United States Agreement on Air Quality." *Policy Studies Journal: The Journal of the Policy Studies Organization* 27 (2): 347–59. http://dx.doi.org/10.1111/j.1541-0072.1999.tb01972.x.

Alm, Leslie, and Ross Burkhart. 2005. "Canada and the United States: Approaches to Global Environmental Policymaking." *International Journal of Canadian Studies* 31: 261–79.

Alper, Donald, and James Loucky. 1996. "North American Integration: Paradoxes and Prospects." *American Review of Canadian Studies* 26 (2): 177–82. http://dx.doi.org/10.1080/02722019609480905.

Alston, Jon, Theresa Morris, and Arnold Vedlitz. 1996. "Comparing Canadian and American Values: New Evidence from National Surveys." *American Review of Canadian Studies* 26 (3): 301–14. http://dx.doi.org/10.1080/02722019609481189.

Anderson, Greg, and Christopher Sands, eds. 2011. *Forgotten Partnership Redux: Canada – U.S. Relations in the 21st Century*. Amherst, NY: Cambria Press.

Barry, Donald. 2005. "Chrétien, Bush, and the War in Iraq." *American Review of Canadian Studies* 35 (2): 215–45. http://dx.doi.org/10.1080/02722010509481371.

Benedick, Richard. 1998. *Ozone Diplomacy: New Directions in Safeguarding the Planet*, vii, 316. Cambridge, MA: Harvard University Press.

Boardman, Robert. 1992. *Canadian Environmental Policy: Ecosystems, Politics, and Process*, 224–37. Toronto: Oxford University Press.

Boardman, Robert. 2002. "Milk-and-Potatoes Environmentalism: Canada and the Turbulent World." In *Canadian Environmental Policy: Context and Cases*, 2nd ed., ed. Debora VanNijnatten and Robert Boardman, 195. Don Mills, ON: Oxford University Press.

Bocking, Stephen. 1997. *Ecologists and Environmental Politics: A History of Contemporary Ecology*, 195. New Haven: Yale University Press.

Bosso, Christopher, and Deborah Gruber. 2006. "Maintaining Presence: Environmental Advocacy and the Permanent Campaign." In *Environmental Policy: New Directions for the Twenty-First Century*, 6th ed., ed. Norman Vig and Michael Kraft, 95. Washington, DC: CQ Press.

Boucher, Christian. 2005. *Toward North American or Regional Cross-Border Communities*, 3. Ottawa: Working Paper Series 002.

Brown, Courtney. 1994. "Politics and the Environment: Nonlinear Instabilities Dominate." *American Political Science Review* 88 (2): 292. http://dx.doi.org/10.2307/2944704.

Carroll, John. 1982. *Acid Rain: An Issue in Canadian–American Relations*, 2–3. Washington, DC: National Planning Association.

Carroll, John E. 1986. *Environmental Diplomacy: An Examination and a Prospective of Canadian-US Transboundary Environmental Relations*, 296. Ann Arbor: University of Michigan Press.

Centre for Research and Information on Canada. 2005. *Portraits of Canada 2004*, 2. Ottawa: CRIC.

Commission for Environmental Cooperation. 1997. *Continental Pollutant Pathways*. Montreal: Communications and Public Outreach Department of the CEC Secretariat.

Cummins, Chip, and Edward Welsch. 2011. "Canadians push new routes for oil." *Wall Street Journal*, 25 November.

Desombre, Elizabeth R. 2005. "Understanding United States Unilateralism: Domestic Sources of U.S. International Environmental Policy." In *The Global Environment: Institutions, Law, and Policy*, ed. Regina Axelrod, David Downie, and Norman Vig, 182–3. Washington, DC: CQ Press.

Doern, G. Bruce. 2002. "Environmental Canada as a Networked Institution." In *Canadian Environmental Policy: Context and Cases*, 2nd ed., ed. Debora VanNijnatten and Robert Boardman, 107. Don Mills, ON: Oxford University Press.

Doran, Charles. 1997. "Style as a Substitute for Issue Articulation in Canada–U.S. Relations." *American Review of Canadian Studies* 27 (2): 167–78. http://dx.doi.org/10.1080/02722019709481495.

Draitsch, Danielle. 2011. *The Link between Keystone XL and Canadian Oil Sands Production*. Edmonton: Pembina Institute.

Easterbrook, Gregg. 1995. "Good news from Planet Earth." *USA Weekend*, 14–16 April: 4–6.

Eilperin, Juliet. 2011. "Obama to make decision on controversial pipeline." *Washington Post*, 1 November.

Esty, Daniel, and Maria Ivanova. 2003. "Toward a Global Environmental Mechanism." In *Worlds Apart: Globalization and the Environment*, ed. James Speth, 68. Washington, DC: Island Press.

Fox, Annette. 1989. *Canada in World Affairs*, 7. Washington, DC: The ACSUS Papers.

Gattinger, Monica, and Geoffrey Hale. 2010. *Borders and Bridges: Canada's Policy Relations in North America*, 1. New York: Oxford University Press.

Goodman, Lee-Anne. "Some in D.C. fear mixed messages from provincial presences at Canadian embassy." *The Canadian Press*, 3 September 2010.

Hale, Geoffrey, and Monica Gattinger. 2010. "Variable Geometry and Traffic Circles: Navigating Canada's Policy Relations in North America." In *Borders and Bridges: Canada's Policy Relations in North America*, ed. Monica Gattinger and Geoffrey Hale, 367. New York: Oxford University Press.

Harrison, Neil. 2004. "Political Responses to Changing Uncertainty." In *Science and Politics in the International Environment*, ed. Neil Harrison and Gary Bryner, 120. Boulder, CO: Rowman & Littlefield.

Harrison, Neil, and Gary Bryner. 2004. "Thinking about Science and Politics." In *Science and Politics in the International Environment*, ed. Neil Harrison and Gary Bryner, 1–2. Boulder: Rowman & Littlefield Publishers.

Hessing, Melody, and Michael Howlett. 1997. *Canadian Natural Resource and Environmental Policy: Political Economy and Public Policy*, 3. Vancouver: UBC Press.

Hillmer, Norman. "A Border People." *Canada World View* 24 (2005): 4.

Hoberg, George. 2002. "Canadian–American Environmental Relations: A Strategic Framework." In *Canadian Environmental Policy: Context and Cases*, 2nd ed., ed. Debora VanNijnatten and Robert Boardman, 173–80. Don Mills, ON: Oxford University Press.

Howlett, Michael. (2002) "Policy Instruments and Implementation Styles: The Evolution of Instrument Choice in Canadian Environmental Policy." In *Canadian Environmental Policy: Context and Cases*, 2nd ed., ed. Debora VanNijnatten and Robert Boardman, 32. Don Mills, ON: Oxford University Press, 2002.

Ibbitson, John. "Pluralism: The world wonders how we pulled it off." *Globe and Mail*, 6 February 2004, A21.

Inglehart, Ronald. 1977. *The Silent Revolution: Changing Values and Political Systems among Western Publics*. Princeton, NJ: Princeton University Press.

Janigan, Mary. 2005. "The Energy Payoff: Martin May Parlay Bush's Desire for Oil Security into Freer Trade across the Border." *Maclean's*, 14 Feburary, 20.

Kamieniecki, Sheldon, and Michael Kraft. 2002. "Foreword." In *Environmental Politics and Policies in Industrialized Countries*, ed. Uday Desai, ix. Cambridge, MA: MIT Press.

Kanji, Mebs. 1996. "North American Environmentalism and Political Integration." *American Review of Canadian Studies* 26 (2): 183–204. http://dx.doi.org/10.1080/02722019609480906.

Kite, Cynthia, and Douglas Nord. 2008. "Canadian Foreign Policy." In *Canadian Studies in the New Millennium*, ed. Patrick James and Mark Kasoff, 273–4. Toronto: University of Toronto Press.

Kraft, Michael. 2002. "Environmental Policy and Politics in the United States: Toward Environmental Sustainability." In *Environmental Politics and Policy in Industrialized Countries*, ed. Uday Desai, 43. Cambridge, MA: MIT Press.

Kumar, David, and James Altschuld. 2004. "Science, Technology, and Society." *American Behavioral Scientist* 47: 1360.

Lipset, Seymour. 1990. "North American Cultures." *Borderlands Monograph Series* 3: 2.

Lovecraft, Amy Lauren. 2007. "Transnational Environmental Management: U.S.-Canadian Institutions at the Interlocal Scale." *American Review of Canadian Studies* 37 (2): 218–45. http://dx.doi.org/10.1080/02722010709481856.

MacDonald, Flora. 2003. "Canada and the United Nations: Why We Must Lead the Movement for Reform." In *Canada and the United States: An Evolving Partnership*, 17. Montreal: Centre for Research and Information on Canada.

Martin, Paul. 2003. "Speech to the Liberal Leadership Convention," Ottawa, 14 November 2003.

McKenzie, Judith. 2002. *Environmental Politics in Canada: Managing the Commons into the Twenty-First Century*, 115. Don Mills, ON: Oxford University Press.

Millard, Gregory, Sarah Reigel, and John Wright. 2002. "Here's Where We Get Canadian: English-Canadian Nationalism and Popular Culture." *American Review of Canadian Studies* 32 (1): 11–34. http://dx.doi.org/10.1080/02722010209481654.

Munton, Don. 1997. "Acid Rain and Transboundary Air Quality in Canadian–American Relations." *American Review of Canadian Studies* 27 (3): 327–58. http://dx.doi.org/10.1080/02722019709481554.

Nord, Douglas C. 2010. "The North in Canadian–American Relations: Searching for Collaboration in Melting Seas." In *Borders and Bridges: Canada's Policy Relations in North America*, ed. Monica Gattinger and Geoffrey Hale, 133. New York: Oxford University Press.

Paehlke, Robert. 2000. "Environmentalism in One Country: Canadian Environmental Policy in an Era of Globalization." *Policy Studies Journal: The Journal of the Policy Studies Organization* 28 (1): 155–63. http://dx.doi.org/10.1111/j.1541-0072.2000.tb02021.x.

Rabe, Barry, and William Lowry. 1999. "Comparative Analysis of Canadian and American Environmental Policy: An Introduction to the Symposium." *Policy Studies Journal: The Journal of the Policy Studies Organization* 27 (2): 263–6. http://dx.doi.org/10.1111/j.1541-0072.1999.tb01967.x.

Rosenbaum, Walter A. 2008. *Environmental Politics and Policy*, 7th ed., 39–41. Washington, DC: CQ Press.

Ross, Douglas. 2006. "Canada, A Land of Deep Ambivalence: Understanding the Divergent Response to United States Primacy after 9/11." *Canadian-American Public Policy* 68: 4–5.

Schmidt, Robert. 1996. "International Negotiations Paralyzed by Domestic Politics: Two-Level Game Theory and the Problem of Pacific Salmon." *Environmental Law* (Northwestern School of Law) 2: 107.

Schneider, Howard. 1997. "Economy, ecology lock horns: Canada redefines relationship with the land." *Washington Post*, 27 October, A01.

Segal, Hugh. 2004. *The Politics of Enhanced Canada–U.S. Relations*. Victoria, BC: University of Victoria Centre for Global Studies.

Sigmon, John. 1996. "Saving the Environment (from Ourselves): An Editor's Perspective." *Human Dimension Quarterly* 1: 11.

Simpson, Jeffrey. 2011. "Amid dire warnings, Canada is missing in action." *Globe and Mail*, 19 November, F8.

Smith, Heather. 1998. "Stopped Cold." *Alternatives Journal* 24: 10.

Solomon, Deborah. 2011. "U.S. puts oil pipeline on hold." *Wall Street Journal*, 11 November.

Steel, Brent S., et al. 2000. "The Role of Scientists in the Natural Resource Policy Process: A Comparison of Canadian and American Publics." Prepared for the 42nd Annual Western Social Sciences Association Conference, San Diego, CA, 26–29 April, 14.

Stirrup, David, and Gillian Roberts. 2010. "Introduction to the ARCS Special Issue on Culture and the Canada-US Border." *American Review of Canadian Studies* 40 (3): 321–5. http://dx.doi.org/10.1080/02722011.2010.497008.

Sussman, Glen, Byron Daynes, and Jonathan West. 2002. *American Politics and the Environment*, 313. New York: Longman.

Ten-Year Review and Assessment Committee. 2004. *Ten Years of North American Environmental Cooperation*. Montreal: Commission for Environmental Cooperation.

Toner, Glen. 2008. "The Harper Minority Government and ISE: Second Year–Second Thoughts." In *Innovation, Science, and Environment: Canadian Policies and Performance, 2008–2009*, ed. Glen Toner, 3. Montreal: McGill-Queen's University Press.

Valiante, Marcia. 2002. "Legal Foundations of Canadian Environmental Policy." In *Canadian Environmental Policy: Context and Cases*, 2nd ed., ed. Debora VanNijnatten and Robert Boardman, 3–24. Don Mills, ON: Oxford University Press.

VanderKlippe, Nathan, Shawn McCarthy, and Carrie Tait. 2011. "Oil patch gives dire warning to the U.S." *Globe and Mail*, 3 November.

VanNijnatten, Debora. 1999. "Participation and Environmental Policy in Canada and the United States: Trend Over Time." *Policy Studies Journal: The Journal of the Policy Studies Organization* 27 (2): 267–87. http://dx.doi.org/10.1111/j.1541-0072.1999.tb01968.x.

VanNijnatten, Debora. 2003. "Analyzing the Canada–U.S. Environmental Relationship: A Multi-Faceted Approach." *American Review of Canadian Studies* 33 (1): 93–120. http://dx.doi.org/10.1080/02722010309481151.

VanNijnatten, Debora. 2008. "Environmental Policy in Canada and the United States: Climate Change and Continuing Distinctiveness." In *Canada and the United States: Differences That Count*, 3rd ed., ed. David M. Thomas and Barbara Boyle Torrey, 370. Peterborough, ON: Broadview Press.

VanNijnatten, Debora, and Robert Boardman. 2002. *Canadian Environmental Policy: Context and Cases*. 2nd ed. Don Mills, ON: Oxford University Press.

Vig, Norman J., and Michael E. Kraft. 2006. *Environmental Policy: New Directions for the Twenty-First Century*, 6th ed., 349–65, 389. Washington, DC: CQ Press.

Wilson, Jeremy. 2003. "'Internationalization' and the Conservation of Canada's Boreal Ecosystems." *Canadian-American Public Policy* 56: 6.

Wood, Duncan. 2003. Seminar discussion, Biennial meeting of the Association for Canadian Studies in the United States, Portland, OR, 23 November.

Wood, Stepan, Georgia Tanner, and Benjamin Richardson. 2010. "What Ever Happened to Canadian Environmental Law." *Ecology Law Quarterly* 37: 981–1040.

11 Civil Society and the Vibrancy of Canadian Citizens

LEA CARAGATA AND SAMMY BASU

The organizations and activities of civil society are vitally important in meeting human needs. Yet, while any consideration of the dominant forces in contemporary Western societies like the United States and Canada will readily acknowledge the roles that both government and private business or the marketplace play in providing goods and services to meet human needs, civil society is more likely to remain unseen and unacknowledged. This is true in spite of the fact that responsiveness to the needs of citizens by both the market and the state often derives from the pressures exerted and innovations modelled by actors in civil society.

The marketplace meets human needs across a breadth of sectors ranging from care for children and the elderly to restaurant meals, travel, health, and financial services, to name only a few. Governments at all levels ensure political, economic, and social security for their citizens through diplomatic relations with other nations, environmental protections, the regulation of employment and financial markets, and in extreme conditions, such as we have recently experienced, through corporate bailouts and economic stimulus plans. Together government and the marketplace are also involved in a wide range of sectors. Housing and health care provide ready examples, as private services are augmented by government funding, services, or a mix of the two, oriented to ensuring the availability of essential services. Sometimes, as in the case of health care in Canada, these public/private collaborations are population-wide, oriented to ensuring equitable access, but more frequently government-provided goods and services are directed to those without the economic means to "purchase" these in the marketplace. Sometimes governments provide services directly, often they partner – sometimes with business, sometimes with organizations from the not-for-profit sector. These latter organizations – combined with co-operatives and other types of both formal and informal organizations – constitute civil society or, as this sphere is sometimes called, the "third sector."

This "third sector" is somewhat elusive – so it may well be an apt descriptor in acknowledging its more minimal visibility compared to the state and the marketplace – but it is less apt in acknowledging its significance and describing the nature of this sphere of human activity. In fact, as of 2006, Canada's third sector comprised more than 150,000 non-profit, voluntary, community, and charitable organizations and social enterprises, which, if measured in terms of economic contribution, ranks as the second largest in the world (Hall et al. 2005; NSNVO 2006). It accounts for about 8 per cent of Canada's GDP and employs almost 10 per cent of the Canadian workforce. Neither of these estimates factor in the enormous value of the volunteer contributions that form the backbone of many organizations in this sector. Volunteer hours contributed to non-profit and cooperative organizations are estimated at 2 billion hours or an equivalent of 1 million full-time positions (Quarter et al. 2009). While most of these organizations are small – 54 per cent rely solely on volunteer labour – others rank among Canada's largest corporations (Quarter et al. 2009). Although precise numbers are not available, estimates suggest that 30 per cent of Canadians provide 85 per cent of the total volunteer hours, 78 per cent of total charitable dollars donated, and 71 per cent of civic participation contributions in Canada, in 2000 (Reed and Selbee 2000).

The "third sector," or what in Western Europe is more descriptively characterized as the "social economy," is broadly theorized as playing two important roles in shaping the state/marketplace and meeting the needs of citizens. First, it is the sphere in which members of a society come together to articulate their needs and interests and represent them to the broader society. This is especially important from the perspective of interest-group politics in that more privileged groups have greater access to the levers of the state, including at the political and bureaucratic level, but also as public discourse is shaped through media and the marketplace (Fraser 1995). Civil-society groups and organizations also enable the articulation of citizen perspectives on the activities of the marketplace – with demands for new products, demands for product improvement, and broader political demands with respect to corporate politics. Examples of these include consumer protection organizations and consumer protests, demands for government regulation, but also boycotts – such as of Nestlé over its promotion of baby formula in the developing world (Pomerantz 2001). Thus, civil society or the "third sector" plays a significant role in shaping and influencing the state and the marketplace (Powell and Geoghegan 2005; Quarter et al. 2009). Second, and beyond this role of articulating citizen needs and interests and representing them more publicly, civil society in Canada has retained its independent importance as a realm in which citizens collectively – but outside of the state and the marketplace – meet their needs. These roles are mostly strongly manifest in the Canadian cooperative movement, which spans such spheres as retail merchandising, insurance and financial services, housing, and food production and distribution – all done by collective groups of Canadians – either on a not-for-profit basis or whereby profits accrue not to stockholders but equally to the cooperative's members. These will be discussed further, but here it is important to note that this idea of mutual provisioning outside of the market and state remains central to civil society as it functions in Canada. Thus, at this broader level, civil society describes a theoretical and conceptual realm wherein the activities of citizens in this third sector meet the needs of the individuals, families, and groups who are its constituents. In so far as these associations and relationships are considered necessary for trust and cohesion within communities, they can be said to cultivate "social citizenship" and use "social capital" (Dekker and van den Broek 1998; Putnam 2000). Civil society represents and expresses communal interests and needs and acts either to meet them directly or to ensure their inclusion in the public discourse (Fraser 1995; Caragata 1999).

It might be noted at the onset that reflecting positively and prescriptively on the values and practices of social citizenship optimal to the late-modern, post-industrial, multicultural polity is itself one of the striking characteristics of both public discourse in Canada and, more so, Canadian scholarly preoccupations. Though Canada has long lacked a civil religion (Kim 1993), and one prominent strain of the national imaginary from its inception has been of "a country nourished on self-doubt," as poet Al Purdy put it in 1968 (Thorner 2003), Canada has more recently staked intellectual claims to a special degree of philosophical self-consciousness and political deliberateness about civil society (from Grant 1965 to Taylor 1989 and Resnick 2005, or similarly from Tully 1995 and Kymlicka 1995 to Adams 2007). One recent study of six influential Canadian political thinkers effectively captures in its very title a shared commitment to reflecting on the distinctive Canadian combination of *Freedom, Equality, Community* (Bickerton 2007).

Part of that early self-doubt and subsequent deliberateness may be attributable to the ways in which Canadians have sought to distinguish themselves through national identity and the operations of civil society from the United States (Thomas 2004). Lipset's (1991) argument that Canada and the United States forged distinct civil societies in the wake of the American Revolution, and that this historical momentum explains substantially divergent political cultures and civic arrangements today, has recently been renewed by Kaufman (2009). Kaufman argues that distinctive patterns in the evolution and enforcement of jurisdictional law, in structuring social relations and state institutions, notably in the areas of land ownership, relations with Indigenous populations, immigration, and voting, explain the ongoing contemporary attitudinal and practical differences between the two societies. The extent of the historical differences is open to legitimate debate, however. Grabb and Curtis (2010), for example, maintain that civic attitudes are not substantially different, and in so far as they are, the differences are neither national nor rooted in the respective national foundings, but rather arise as functions of subsequent, regional, and racialized civic processes. The further significance of regionalism emerges later in the chapter, where we see distinct and regionally based civil-society organizations that arose to meet the specific regional interests of Canada's diverse citizenry (Ornstein et al. 1980; Ornstein and Stevenson 1999).

This chapter begins with a brief theoretical framing of civil society in relation to its two roles as discussed above, namely, its engagement with the state in the political, legal, and policy spheres, and with the marketplace, but also in terms of its role independent of these spheres, wherein it may be seen as a counter-hegemonic force in which citizens articulate their shared needs and interests and collectively forge strategies and structures to address them. In the second part of the chapter, some of the major institutions and associations of civil society are described and their roles in meeting human needs, and more broadly in electoral politics, legal recognition, and policy implementation, are illustrated. The third section is concerned to disaggregate this account in order to take stock of some of the transformative effects that have resulted from the state response to globalization and to acknowledge those threadbare areas in the otherwise rich fabric of Canadian civil society. In concluding we suggest some of the possibilities and challenges that Canada's civil society will likely encounter in the future.

Overall, we hope to demonstrate the often underappreciated ways in which civil-society activities and social networks shape Canadian identity and everyday life (Tindall and Wellman 2001).

Part 1: Theoretical Framing

Arguments frequently made regarding the value of an active and expansive civil society relate to theories about citizen involvement and engagement. The democratic basis of our societies is premised on the idea that citizens should collectively decide on and shape how their society is to be governed. This includes engaged choices about electoral candidates, including considering their ideological positions and how these will shape public policy and our communities, but democratic participation can also include more directly engaging citizens in shaping the very structures by which states operate. Liberal-democratic government is often categorized as either representative or republican, distinctions seen to be important in several respects. A liberal representative democracy is usually seen as oriented primarily to protecting the private interests of its citizens – in this sense, citizens elect those they believe will best represent their interests and then go about their private lives. In this case, engagement as citizens or members of a community is more likely expected to be through the structures of civil society – through associations, clubs, groups – including political-party involvement – that reflect their own particular needs and interests. Such engagement fulfils two roles – at least theoretically: it builds social cohesion and a sense that citizens matter, and again, perhaps ideally, it creates good and responsive governance (Caragata 1999). Although republican democracies are also representative democracies, they place a greater emphasis on the expression of pluralistic views through more active citizen participation in the state. Both Canada and the United States are liberal democracies in which civil society serves a particularly important role and function. Discussions of social exclusion and citizen apathy emphasize that our communities, and ultimately the quality of our democratic structures, depend on civil society to meet the needs of citizens' diverse interests, but also to contribute to a public discourse that better enables the state to understand, recognize, and respond to this diversity of citizen needs and interests (Fraser 1991; Putnam 2000).

In Canada, civil-society organizations, movements, and actors engage with the Canadian polity, and hence have responded historically to nation building and the shaping of a distinctively Canadian federalism and, more recently, to globalization and economic restructuring and the impact of these on all aspects of Canadian life. Civil society employs three broad arenas of power and influence: on elected governance bodies, including Parliament and provincial and municipal governments, on the courts, and on the public policy process (the bureaucratic structures of the state). Through these three policy-setting spheres the interests expressed through civil society also impact the marketplace, through taxation, liberal or restrictive trade policy, consumer protection legislation, the regulation of employment, the enactment of rights to be free from discriminating practices, and the public provision of goods and services.

A critical element of civil society in Canada moves it beyond being simply a reactive sphere articulating and aggregating the interests and needs of citizens, although it is also this. Canada has a rich and enduring tradition of citizens coming together to meet their own needs collectively – but outside of the structures of the state and the marketplace. We will first explore civil society as it co-constructs and co-produces public policy (Vaillancourt 2009) and then return to discuss some of these collectivist structures that so exemplify civil society in Canada.

First, civil society generates interest-aggregating and interest-articulating input into the formal federal, provincial, and municipal representative and legislative bodies of the Canadian government through its involvement in elections, political parties, and lobbying. The effectiveness of the conventional political parties in meaningfully conveying civil-society subgroup perspectives and needs is a crucial determinant of the nature of the extra-parliamentary activism that they adopt. Similarly, the regulatory regime around lobbying, of which Canada's is of relatively moderate strength, can dramatically enable or curtail civil-society activism through such means (Chari et al. 2007).

The Canadian political system has been shifting towards a more executive-centric style of governance, concentrated in the prime minister and the cabinet, at·the expense of the democratic representativeness of Parliament, including even the elected members of the governing party. Moreover, crucially, this executive control over the broadest lineaments of the Canadian political economy has pursued a "neoliberal" or "neoconservative" market-oriented perspective of public disinvestment during the 1980s and early 1990s, followed by one of selective reinvestment through "contracting out" to the profit and non-profit sectors of civil society. Overall, this has had two unfolding implications for civil society. First, insofar as neoliberalism affirms the agency of the individual citizen as consumer or client it has been less receptive to inputs from civil society in the form of contestatory collective mobilization (Ayres 2004; Smith 2005). Instead, individuals are asked to view the associations and networks to which they belong as their own "instrumental investments" through which to meet their own needs. Second, in policy terms, political elites have sought to capitalize on globalization by enabling deeper integration at the North American level and more profitable performance on global markets while "re-scaling" and "devolving" the welfare state and privatizing the provision of services and the fulfilment of needs formerly associated in Canada with "good government" (Johnson and Mahon 2005). This has had the profound effect of moving Canada from its post-war Keynesian "welfare" system of rights and entitlements associated with "social citizenship" and administered universally to a "market citizenship" model wherein citizenship rights are tied more closely to active labour market participation (Breitkreuz 2005). This is exemplified by the adoption of a neoliberal "workfare" system oriented around private personal (or familial) responsibility that justifies more selective "social investment" (Peck 2005; Ilcan 2009). Significantly, as such, the policy outputs of the Canadian parliament, and its most representative body, the House of Commons, have not only become the subject of critical policy studies (Jenson 1997; Orsini and Smith 2007), but have also been de-centred as the object of the actual political attentions and efforts of civil-society activism (D. Smith 2007; Onishenko and Caragata 2010). This de-centring occurs too as a result of the growing significance of the 1982 Charter of Rights and Freedoms, which is being increasingly articulated through the courts as a profound shaper of public policy.

Second, then, although the parliamentary-constituency network was and remains politically pre-eminent in Canada, its importance has been somewhat diminished as the Supreme Court of Canada adjudicates on an increasingly broad range of "charter challenges," which have become commonplace in the repertoires of social-movement organizations and in the language of Canadians (Cotler 2006; Onishenko and Caragata 2010). The increasing importance of the court derives from the 1982 Constitution Act, which included passage of the above-mentioned charter in a historic moment in the Canadian parliament. Even a cursory survey of the charter's sections conveys the extent to which the nature of Canadian society and its foundational values have been substantially re-articulated, historical continuities fulfilled, and legal-constitutional lacunae addressed: voting rights (s. 3), mobility rights (s.

6), equality (s. 15), official languages (s. 16), minority-language educational rights (s. 23), multicultural heritage (s. 27), special school rights (s. 29), Aboriginal and treaty rights (s. 35), and regional equalization and disparities (s. 36). Social-movement groups within civil society have since oriented themselves as group-rights claimants around a politics of equal recognition. As a result, the Supreme Court of Canada has rapidly emerged as a conspicuous venue of final address and redress – in the form of class-action lawsuits and group-rights claims – for demands regarding social justice that originate in civil society (Macfarlane 2009). Most notable among the court's democratizing and egalitarian effects has been the 2005 sanctioning of same-sex marriage.

Perhaps no legislative change in Canada better reflects the interactions among civil-society groups, the representative political system, and the judicial system acting on the provisions and egalitarian momentum of the Charter of Rights and Freedoms than the approval of the Canadian Civil Marriage Act in 2005. An important civil-society actor behind this fundamental change to Canadian society was EGALE Canada (Equality for Gays and Lesbians Everywhere), a national volunteer organization that advances equality and justice for lesbian, gay, bisexual, trans-identified, and queer (LGBTQ) people and their families (Cotler 2006; M. Smith, 2007b). The legalization of same-sex marriage by the Parliament of Canada was a moment of significance in equality-rights history certainly in Canada but also internationally as Canada became a world leader in the formal recognition of the legitimacy of LGBTQ marriage. The Civil Marriage Act was passed after the supreme courts in several Canadian provinces had struck down marriage laws which prohibited same-sex marriage. It contained an important compromise in that no religious bodies could be forced to marry gays and lesbians if they believed that to do so violated their religion. In fact, many religious organizations and leaders have had no such qualms and Canadians proudly demonstrate high levels of acceptance of same-sex marriage in both civil and religious services for Canadians and gays and lesbians from the United States and other jurisdictions who wish to legalize their same-sex unions (M. Smith 2007b; Onishenko and Caragata 2010). The enabling charter provision, section 15, on the substantive protection of the right to equality, enumerated protections against discrimination resulting from race, national or ethnic origin, colour, religion, sex, age, or mental or physical disability, but not sexual orientation. In 1995, the Supreme Court of Canada ruled that sexual orientation was a prohibited ground of discrimination under the charter, although it had not been originally identified in the charter's equality-rights clause. The ground-breaking marriage law was preceded, as a result of the success of the 1995 charter challenge, by a number of other important LGBTQ equality provisions which prompted the federal government to pass the Modernization of Benefits and Obligations Act in 2000, altering and extending a welter of laws and benefits. Contemporarily in Canada, perhaps in part because of the presence of equality-rights issues in the public discourse, tolerance and recognition of difference, including sexual difference, are increasingly seen to be tied to a national project of self-definition (Adams 2003). Smith summarizes, capturing important Canadian/US distinctions in how rights are differentially framed:

> In Canada, the rights frame dominates public discourse and is increasingly linked in different ways with both Canadian and Quebec nationalism. In contrast, in the United States, the rights frame is highly contentious and subject to intense political competition along the partisan (red/blue) divide … Lesbian- and gay-rights claims in Canada and Quebec function within a nationalist template that defines tolerance of sexual diversity as central within the national political culture. (Smith 2007b, 7)

Other important successful Charter of Rights challenges, though not as high-profile nationally, were revisions to the Canada Elections Act elevating the status of smaller and regional political parties (Grabham 2002). The court has also upheld restrictions in the Canada Elections Act on lobby-group election campaign spending and more recently limited civil-society interest groups from financially expressing their party support through campaigns (Boatright 2009). Thus, for example, donations from trade unions were effectively severed from the New Democratic Party (NDP), though the relationship between the two persists as a result of ideological solidarity now expressed in other ways (Jansen and Young 2009).

Though the full egalitarian implications of the charter are still being discovered and defined, perhaps because the formal expression of civil rights came relatively recently to the legal structure of Canada, it has become a vivid and pervasive mode of political and civic discourse. According to Irwin Cotler (2006, 61–2), former minister of justice and attorney general of Canada, "If women, Aboriginal people, racial minorities, disabled people, refugees, and gay and lesbian people in this country are asked whether they are better off in 2005 than they were in

1982, the answer is invariably yes. Even with all of the imperfections that exist in the Charter, it has contributed to the reversal of the pattern of discrimination against vulnerable people in our country." Beyond the direct employ of the charter in court challenges, it has served to guide and shape policy and the activities of citizens' groups simply by virtue of its *anticipated* impacts. Thus, both government law and policymakers may be more collaborative in resolving policy issues rather than forcing a charter challenge.

Such collaboration occurs in this third area of civil-society influence we now describe. In the governmental bureaucratic processes of policy design, implementation, and delivery across a wide range of issue areas including banking and finance, housing, education, and health, civil-society organizations and actors have played notably significant roles in Canada (Milligan and Fyfe 2005; Phillips 2006). Many of the activities of these parallel what are described in the United States as "public interest" group lobbying, which is so formulated to contrast with the all-too-common and taken for granted lobbying by "private" interests, those representing the marketplace (Berry 1980). Organizations such as Greenpeace, the Canadian Centre for Policy Alternatives, Canada Without Poverty, Pollution Probe, and many others undertake a variety of approaches to influencing elected representatives and members of the government bureaucracy on the specific issues their organizations represent as well as in publicizing their issues to broaden public discourse and increase the level of citizen involvement. Yet other civil-society–state interactions are more fully collaborative in form. Illustrative of these are the "Toronto City Summit Alliance" or the more recent "25 in 5 Network for Poverty Reduction," coalitions that are broadly encompassing of private sector, government, and citizens' groups not only advocating for particular issues but working collaboratively with local and provincial governments to develop new approaches to important social issues (www.civicaction.ca; www.25in5.ca). In these sometimes long-standing state–society working relationships, "social networks," "social enterprises," and community groups communicate and work together with government officials and bureaucratic managers to determine and deliver government policy at the local and community level. It is important to recognize here that civil-society actors and agencies are involved not merely in the "co-production" of public policy, that is, serving in the "contracted out" or "outsourced" delivery and dissemination of state-specified goods and services, but also in "co-construction," that is, in both the delivery of policy provisions and the ongoing shaping of the relevant public policy (Vaillancourt 2009; Mendell 2010). The latter of these, the co-construction of public policy, stands to produce two positive democratic dynamics. First, policy innovation is permitted as citizens and citizen groups work directly with the state on issues wherein they are often the best arbiters of positive and innovative outcomes. Second, a further level of democratization is advanced as non-profit and cooperative organizations themselves are democratically structured and more and more diverse citizens are enabled to respond to and reflect not only their policy needs but a broader vision of a public interest – that which transcends the needs and interests of individuals.

We next discuss those elements of civil society oriented to meeting the needs of citizens outside of the state and marketplace. Interestingly, these types of arrangements developed by citizens are applauded by the libertarian right, which values the citizen autonomy and action outside of government expressed by such activity, and by the left, which sees such activities as building and reinforcing collectivist values and acting to counter the hegemony of the marketplace. These organizations include cooperatives and mutual aid organizations, credit unions, housing and other co-operatives, and mutual insurers. This discussion is followed by a sketch of the broad contours of the landscape of Canadian civil society, including some of its other most salient institutions and associations including unions, religious organizations, multicultural groups, and not-for-profit service delivery organizations. Finally, some important developments and changes to Canadian civil society are noted.

Part 2: The Broad Contours of the Landscape of Civil Society in Canada

"A cooperative is an autonomous association of persons united voluntarily to meet their common social, economic and cultural needs and aspirations through a jointly owned and democratically-controlled enterprise" (International Cooperative Alliance as cited in Quarter et al. 2009, 51). Almost 12 million Canadians belong to such an organization, a rather remarkable statistic as it means that almost half of adult Canadians are involved in a cooperative enterprise (Agriculture and Agri Foods Canada 2010; Quarter et al. 2009). This one statistic signals something important about civil society in Canada, demonstrating perhaps a continuing history of self-reliance and, in those regions where cooperatives are strongest, a continuing scepticism about absolute reliance on the marketplace. Before proceeding with our discussion of the major organizations of civil society, a brief mention must be made of Canadian nationalism and the effects on Canadians and on Canadian civil society of living on the perimeter of a country ten times larger and much more powerful. At various times over the political life of Canada there have been strong efforts oriented to nationalism and the protection of Canadian sovereignty. Often referred to as a "branch plant economy," the Canadian marketplace is strongly driven by US-based firms and the economic realities of life as a putative fifty-first state (Clarkson 1972; Hébert 2006; Geddes 2010). Reactions against these realities have shaped Canadians and Canadian civil society, as some segment of the population continues to feel committed to the expression of what are seen to be uniquely Canadian interests, including wresting some element of Canadian economic life away from US economic interests (Geddes 2010). This has taken form in state-controlled and public-sector businesses (e.g., Air Canada, Canadian Broadcasting Corporation, Via Rail, Petro-Canada), many of which have more recently been privatized or partially privatized as globalization and neoliberal-driven free trade agreements continue to re-shape Canada's economy. The cooperative sector has also been influenced by these bigger-picture globalizing shifts as mutual insurance companies have de-mutualized and farm marketing organizations have been privatized (Quarter et al. 2009). However, in many regions of the country, the commitment of Canadians to smaller-scale, democratically run cooperatives has perhaps intensified as a manifestation of commitment to locally run and member-directed enterprises that resist globalization and ever-increasing market convergence. What have been described as "New Generation Cooperatives" (NGCs) represent a younger generation of farmers and others tackling the challenges of deregulated markets and increased vertical coordination and integration in both Canada and the United States. The impact of these NGCs "goes well beyond the farm gate," as people believe "co-op fever" to be a successful local development strategy responsible for job growth and the restructuring of functional and sustainable local economies (Harris et al. 1996, 16).

A major characteristic of cooperatives is that the co-op's members design the goods or services to be provided and are then the subsequent – and only – user of these services. The profits from the enterprise – if there are any – come back to the users, usually in the form of dividends related to the value of their use or purchases. With roots in the

Rochdale pioneers in England in the mid-nineteenth century, the cooperative movement spread to Canada and the United States, Japan, and across western Europe. User co-ops include housing and food cooperatives, cooperative retail and gas outlets, and credit unions, the largest portion of the sector.

Accessibility and affordability have been the cornerstones of the development of cooperative enterprise. Mutual insurance developed because farmers needed to insure their crops, cooperative marketing boards as a way for farmers to penetrate new markets and better represent their agricultural sector in world markets, and credit unions as a way of ensuring secure credit to farmers and local communities. Housing cooperatives too developed because of the desire for housing security among those who could not afford home ownership. Here there was often an added ideological position that housing – as a fundamental human right – should not be just another market traded commodity. Whereas in northern Europe, especially Scandinavia, housing co-ops account for a significant portion of the housing stock, in Canada their numbers are relatively small, housing about 250,000 people (Cooperative Housing Federation of Canada and Rooftops Canada Foundation, n.d.). It should be noted that as a form of social housing, co-ops have many advantages over the public housing so often in the public spotlight for creating ghettos of the poor. Housing co-ops, like public housing projects, can offer subsidized rents, but do so in a context of an integrated economic mix – usually no more than 25–30 per cent of a co-op's units will be subsidized, the rest with fees set equivalent to market rents. Also differing from public housing, cooperatives contest the traditional welfare mentality in so much subsidized housing because co-op residents not only take responsibility for their actions, but they experience the direct consequences of these actions on the cost and quality of their housing (Miceli et al. 1994 and 1998). Beyond the value of housing co-ops as more effective social-housing delivery vehicles, housing cooperatives secure housing stock out of the market and become ever more affordable as mortgage financing is paid off and they build local communities as co-op members work together. In Canada, federal and provincial funding for co-ops was under increasing pressure from private-sector housing interests and at this writing there is almost no public funding available to support their development (Cooperative Housing Federation of Canada and Rooftops Canada Foundation, n.d.).

The need for affordable farm supplies provided the original impetus for user cooperative retail stores in Canada, but these soon expanded to sell a full range of retail goods. Retail co-ops have remained important in both the west and Atlantic Canada, accounting in the west for sales of more than $10 billion in 2004 excluding farm supplies. Federated Cooperatives, a western wholesale operation, was among the top one hundred largest non-financial organizations in Canada (Quarter et al. 2009). Retail co-ops have largely remained focused in regions outside of Canada's economic core, where their growth and sustenance has been preserved in part by regional disparity and alienation from the centre. In this sense these organizations are symbolically important in reflecting the structure of Canada – with Ontario as the heartland of what were perceived to be wealthy moneyed interests served by the resources-producing periphery: natural resources in British Columbia and Alberta, prairie agriculture, and fishery-dependent Atlantic Canada. Francophone Quebec requires special mention. Although Montreal was and remains an important business sector and Canada's second largest city, historically wealth remained in Anglo hands and there was – and is – a major divide between Anglo and francophone Quebecers, although this has perhaps begun to soften as the province has more powerfully asserted its francophone sovereignty. However, historically francophone Quebecers acted much like other groups that perceived themselves as peripheral to the economy of central Canada. Thus, the cooperative movement was strongly developed in Quebec and remains strong to this day (Shragge and Fontan 2000). So these minority or marginal statuses in Canada coincide with strong cooperative movements, many of which continue to be essential elements of regional histories even though the region's relative place in the economic and political power of Canada has changed over the ensuing 100-plus years.

As our discussion thus far has illustrated, this idea of mutual aid is a critical foundation of the cooperative movement. In some cases, such mutual aid was especially important because services were unavailable from the private marketplace, particularly in terms of insurance and financial services. Credit unions were important in farm communities, and through their organization in Catholic parishes in Quebec, because more conservative banks were typically unwilling to extend credit except with almost certain guarantees. Similarly then to the micro credit regimes of today such as the Grameen bank, these organizations were established on principles of a broad socialization of risk and a common bond and mutual self-interest, which helped to ensure loan repayment and ameliorate the risks identified by typical commercial lenders.

Quebec's Caisse Populaire was first established in 1900 as a cooperative savings and loan company with non-fixed capital and limited liability in Lévis, Quebec, by Alphonse Desjardin. Desjardin, whom the large financial enterprise is now named for, was a journalist and French-language stenographer in the House of Commons whose goals embraced Quebec nationalism in that he sought to support the economic emancipation of French Canadians. Using European savings and loan cooperatives as models, he encouraged working-class Quebecers to save and plan for the future and provided the credit they needed for economic development and home ownership. His vision was important in a province where the French majority was systematically locked into working-class roles with few opportunities for economic leadership. Caisses Populaires have created or acquired subsidiaries in the insurance, trust, and industrial and commercial investment sectors, as well as the funds management, securities brokerage, and banking services sectors. With some 40,000 employees, Desjardins Group is the largest cooperative financial group in Canada, with overall assets of over $173 billion, as well as Quebec's largest employer. Among civil-society organizations, especially important are these financial services organizations, as they have, as Desjardins hoped, supported the economic development of Quebec by its francophone majority. The province-wide Caisse Populaire system has 461 branches in Quebec and assets of $107 billion. Overall, Canadian credit unions hold 8 per cent of the over $3 trillion in assets of Canadian deposit-taking institutions (Quarter et al. 2009; Roby 2010).

Historically, in Canada there have been strong linkages between the cooperative sector and the trade union movement akin to the linkages between organized labour, the co-op sector, and the New Democratic Party with its social democratic ideology. Labour union–centred or union-affiliated civic mobilization has contributed to the balancing of class power in civil society through its express support of reformist parties and policymakers and its endorsation of a wide range of alternative economic models (Lee 2007).

As has been noted in many previous studies (Freeman 1998; Farber and Western as cited in Card et al. 2003), US rates of union membership have been declining since the 1950s to a current rate of less than 15 per cent of all workers. In contrast, union membership in Canada increased between 1960 and 1980, but began to decline in the 1990s. About one in three Canadian employees (31.4%) belonged to a union or were covered by a collective agreement in 2009 (HRSDC 2010; Card et al. 2003). Data from 2009 reveal that slightly more women than men belonged to a union or were covered by a collective agreement and this is likely attributable to a higher retention of unionization in public-sector organizations. Furthermore, shifts in employment patterns and job security, which unionization represents, is reflected by the fact that among younger workers (15–24) only 16 per cent are unionized, whereas almost 40 per cent of workers between 55 and 64 years of age are unionized (HRSDC). Regional difference – so much a feature of Canadian life – is also expressed in rates of unionization, highest in Quebec at almost 40 per cent and lowest in Alberta at about 25 per cent (ibid.).

Somewhat surprisingly, in Canada there was little change in wage inequality during the 1980s and 1990s, despite a moderate drop in union coverage among men. This experience suggests that other factors offset the pressures towards widening inequality associated with the decline in unionization (Card et al. 2003). Many of these equality-supporting provisions in the form of redistributive policies and pressures on wages have since begun to deteriorate as neoliberal pressures on labour markets have continued. The power of labour to use collective bargaining to improve job quality, wage share, and pay standardization has been undermined by the continued weakening of labour legislation. As a result, unionization has been made more difficult and employment standards weakened such that an increasing percentage of the labour force is outside of the provisions of the standard employment relationship (Chaykowski 2005; Peters 2008). This erosion of workplace representation through anti-union regulations and corporate practices amidst heightened expectations of contractual labour mobility and productivity might be said to be generating a new practice of "sweatshop citizenship," especially in low-status work such as janitorial services within the cleaning industry or textile manufacture (Aguiar 2006; Ng 1998). On the other hand, in the non-profit social services sector Canada has witnessed a measure of renewed unionism and collective voice, at times in collaboration with clients and even management, around labour issues and social policy (Baines 2010).

Perhaps in keeping with declining levels of attachment to formal organizations – as union membership might be seen to represent – there has also been significant decline in Canadians' participation in organized religion. According to the 2001 census, Canada is still, at least nominally, a Christian country as three out of four Canadians identify themselves as Christians: including Catholic (43%), Protestant (29%), Orthodox (1.6%), and self-identified "other" Christian faiths (2.6%). Those indicating adherence to non-Christian religions, while doubling over the previous decade, still account for only 5 per cent of the Canadian population. Religious affiliation does not speak meaningfully to the question of the centrality of organized religion or religious observance in the lives of Canadians, however, as only 32 per cent of all Canadians attend religious services at least monthly. Furthermore, an examination of these changes over time points to an increase of almost 1.5 million Canadians without any religious affiliation over the ten-year period 1991–2001 (Young and DeWiel 2009). These current statistics are rather at odds with the centrality of churches and religious institutions in Canadian life, especially in the last one hundred years. What Beyer describes as the "churching" of Canada in the latter half of the nineteenth century gave churches a major stake as dominant civil-society actors with lasting influence (Beyer 1997, 273).

The Catholic Church continues to be the largest religious organization in Canada, followed in terms of membership by the United Church, which was founded in 1925 out of a union of Methodist, Presbyterian, and Congregationalist denominations (Quarter 1992). Like most other religious organizations, these institutions have provided a range of services to their members — both oriented to meeting their spiritual and education needs as well as serving an evangelical purpose. The range of activities engaged in by religious organizations has included operating elementary and secondary schools as well as colleges and universities, foundations and charities, summer camps, international relief and missionary organizations, hospitals, children's aid organizations, and nursing homes. All of these form part of civil society and have greater or lesser roles in the direct shaping of public policy.

Amidst an increasingly diverse Canada, the services provided by religious organizations have been critical to enabling minority populations to safeguard their beliefs and religious and social practices. This was especially true of the Catholic Church and its role in Quebec. The support of religious organizations for an at risk or marginalized population was central to the development of Quebec, the second largest province, with a francophone majority that reflects Canada's earliest settlement by both English and French colonizers and the English victory over the French on the Plains of Abraham in 1759. These early residents of what was then known as Lower Canada were French and

Catholic in contrast to the more religiously diverse early anglophone settlers, who were more generally Protestant. Canada is, however, a nation of immigrants, and outside of Quebec other groups of early settlers began to create a more heterogeneous society, with a considerable variety of linguistic, religious, and social practices, all with a strong British/ anglophone overlay. This history differed in Quebec where, because French was and remains the dominant language, protected in law, a level of political and social insularity has led to important differences in the social structure, including in public policy and the role and scope of civil society. From the Second World War to the 1960s, Quebec politics and the Catholic Church were inseparable, with the state relying on the church for delivery of education and the inculcation of political and socially conservative views. Although comprising a francophone majority, Quebec was largely a branch-plant economy with Anglo business and financial leaders who lived in affluent English-speaking enclaves in Montreal, Quebec's largest city. The "Quiet Revolution" of the early 1960s was a period of dramatic social and political change that saw the decline of Anglo supremacy in the Quebec economy and of the Roman Catholic Church's influence, the nationalization of hydro-electric companies under Hydro-Québec, and the emergence of a pro-sovereignty movement under former Liberal minister René Lévesque. In the ensuing fifty years, Quebec has developed a strong national and international voice and presence and a provincial government that has remained oriented to progressive social policy and much tighter collaboration and cooperation with civil-society organizations. Quebec's significant civil-society activity deriving from the marginalization of its francophone majority population has fostered a strong nationalistic Québécois voice. Critical, too, to understanding contemporary Quebec is to see the role of the Catholic Church and its interplay with the state, where their interests became so intertwined and removed from the needs of Quebecers that it took a social movement to reclaim civil society as a space for addressing the needs of the community.

For many marginal or new immigrant groups, religious organizations have served as important advocates. B'nai Brith Canada was formed in 1875 to provide advocacy on behalf of Jewish people and was followed in 1919 by the Canadian Jewish Congress (CJC), which continued the advocacy tradition but also provided assistance to Jewish immigrants. The CJC became a powerful advocate during the Second World War in shaping government policy on providing asylum for Jews escaping Europe, and in this endeavour they worked closely with the Co-operative Commonwealth Federation party (now the New Democratic Party), where left-wing Jews played significant leadership roles. More recently, as Canadian immigration has expanded to include peoples from all over the world, other religious organizations including those representing Islamic immigrants have played important service roles, but also advocated around equality issues. Especially important in the context of the "war on terror" and a heightened awareness of its association with Islam, have been the public education roles played by these organizations as they have acted to counter negative and often sweeping media portrayals of Islam to create a more nuanced and balanced public discourse (Sharify-Funk 2009). The Canadian Islamic Congress (CIC) is a non-governmental organization that claims to represent both Sunni and Shi'ite Muslims, with offices across the country. The organization is active in public policy questions (releasing press releases on its position related to family law arbitration, for instance) and publishes a weekly online magazine, *The Friday Bulletin*, which it claims to have 300,000 subscribers around the world (Canadian Islamic Congress 2010).

Multiculturalism has become very important to the modern national and political development of Canada. Historically, of course, immigration has been a central and necessarily contentious dynamic in the colonization, settlement, and demographic expansion of Canada. In recent years, however, Canada has abided by relatively generous policies towards both migrants and refugees. Quite distinctively, moreover, Canada adopted a federal policy of multiculturalism in 1971. The Canadian Charter of Rights and Freedoms (1982) (specifically, section 27) and Canadian Multicultural Act (1985) have further institutionalized the egalitarian status of minority and cultural rights. That Canada continued to affirm itself constitutionally as a multicultural society was in no small part because of the activism of leaders of ethnocultural groups – from the Chinese Canadian National Council for Equality to the Ukrainian Canadian Committee – in the late 1970s and early 1980s. Through the Canadian Consultative Council on Multiculturalism (CCCM), an advisory body to the minister of state for multiculturalism, as well as indirectly through political parties, and quite directly in the subsequent form of submissions and demands to the Joint House of Commons and Senate Committee on the Constitution of Canada, they pressed for what became section 27 of the charter, a clause confirming Canada's multiculturalism heritage (Uberoi 2009).

Today, the multicultural cast of Canada is conspicuous. Canada is said to have "global soul" (Iyer 2000) and even to be on this account an "unlikely utopia" (Adams 2007). Toronto, Canada's largest city, regularly finds itself listed as the most "cosmopolitan city in the world" on the basis of the percentage of its foreign-born population and their multiple countries of origin. Canada's other major cities – Vancouver, Edmonton, Calgary, Winnipeg, Ottawa, and Montreal among them – are similarly diverse, some home to the largest concentrated population of a given national, racial, ethnic, or religious group outside of their home country or region. In Canada, multiculturalism involves ethnicity, recognition, and integration within civil society facilitated by the state, whereas in the United States, by contrast, it has tended to be articulated through race and civil rights discourse. As a result, Canadian immigrant identity is generally conceived in relation to national or ethnic origin, and the presumed lived cultural particularity involved (for example, one is a Pakistani-Canadian), rather than racially, as an Asian-American. Moreover, in contrast to the assimilationist "melting pot" model of the United States, with the presumption that integration will occur "naturally" in civil society and through the marketplace, Canada has adopted metaphors such as "mosaic" and "salad-bowl," suggesting that more actual cultural difference can remain intact and active in hyphenated form with one's adopted or naturalized Canadian identity and associational loyalties.

In Canada, then, and especially in urban areas, racial, ethnic, linguistic, and religious immigrant identities are readily manifest in the form of supportive community groups and networks. There are, to be sure, differences in the relationship to Canadian history and identity between multigenerational citizens and recent immigrants, in their respective emphasis on being and becoming. Still, as a recent comparative study of immigrant and non-immigrant youth attitudes in Calgary concluded, both groups can develop "complex identifications as a Canadian" (Lee and Hébert 2006, 517). In this regard, foreign-born immigrants seek naturalized citizenship (and thereby political incorporation), for which they are eligible after three years of legal residence, at notably high rates. This is due in part to the ways in which the formal Canadian citizenship regime, revolving around Citizenship and Immigration Canada (CIC), devotes resources and institutional channels towards citizenship promotion, newcomer settlement and mobilization, as well as to the facilitated involvement of the relatively informal social networks of local immigrants. That is, immigrants benefit from some measure of access to language training, host programs with volunteers, and community organizations to aid settlement and adaptation (Kunz 2005; Bloemraad 2006).

The commitment to multiculturalism is also evident in more symbolic and ritualized forms. Thus, for example, since 1958, July 1st has been a day of national celebration, commemorating the anniversary of Canadian confederation, promoted and orchestrated by the federal government to foster national unity and pride. Its evolution from "Dominion Day," when at the onset it was primarily a recollection of the British heritage of Canada with military pageantry figuring prominently, to the national performative affirmations of its Aboriginal, bilingual, and multicultural dimensions from the late 1960s through the 1970s, and to "Canada Day" (as it has been known since 1982), is striking. To some extent, more recently, the expression of cultural pluralism has been superseded by the neoliberal celebration of national achievement through exemplary individuals in art, sport, and science, but respect for diversity remains central to its symbolic tropes. Today, then, though national events are coordinated by civil servants in the Secretary of State department, there is considerable ongoing consultation with civil-society groups as part of the ongoing politics of recognition (Hayday 2010).

Similarly, in managing the sites and scripts of public commemoration, the Historic Sites and Monuments Board of Canada, which was founded in 1919, has in recent years had to accommodate contemporary social movements and political activism representing the legacy and experiences of First Nations, ethnocultural groups, women, and workers. These groups, sometimes with considerable local and grassroots vigour, have pressed for the inclusion in the collective public memory of their experiences of past injustices, violence, and invisibility within Canada (Strong-Boag 2009). At the provincial level Nova Scotia, for example, has used a citizen consultation process to create policy recommendations for heritage preservation. Such a practice of citizen engagement was positively received by the participating citizens, and added democratic legitimacy to government decision-makers (MacMillan 2010).

Many NGOs have developed in response to particular needs expressed by a particular subgroup that acts to meet these needs by forming an association or society, representing various forms of (dis)ability, child care organizations, and ethno-cultural groups among many such organizations. Many of these remain purely voluntary in form – including neighbourhood organizations, cultural groups, and sports clubs. Others become legally constituted and acquire Canadian charitable status, often hiring staff and delivering services, and sometimes contracting directly with the state for these service-delivery functions. The vast majority of these organizations are "engaged in humanistic services to improve the quality of social life" (Martin as cited in Quarter et al. 2009, 26). An extensive literature has explored the roles of NGOs, especially as they relate to the roles and responsibilities of the state including importantly, the extent to which such co-production (Vaillancourt 2009) limits the advocacy and public education roles of these important civil-society actors (Wolch 1990). As public services are cut back – as is currently the case – these organizations play increasing roles. There are an estimated 161,000 non-profit organizations, about half of which have charitable status. These non-profits contribute about 7 per cent of the Canadian GDP and employ about 2 million people. Canadians are active in these groups, as 61 per cent of Canadians reported involvement in at least one cultural, educational, or hobby organizations in 2003. In 2004, 45 per cent of Canadians aged fifteen and over volunteered approximately two billion hours in the non-profit sector, an average of seventy-six hours per person (HRSDC 2007).

Other specific features of Canada that arguably reflect values inculcated at least in part through civil society might be briefly mentioned. In more recent years, Canada has enjoyed a comparatively high standard of living and quality of life (reflected in years of sterling scores on the UN Human Development Index), the result of an expanding economy balanced by robust government-operated social welfare schemes. Canada is less wealthy but more equitable than the United States, as measured by the size of the wealth gap as well as in terms of intergenerational economic mobility.

The wealth gap is also less sticky (especially at the extremes) across generations in Canada than in the United States. It is not that Canadian values regarding the "good life" are dramatically different from the American Dream – that is, Canadians also affirm personal success achieved through individual aspiration, industry, and wealth accumulation. Furthermore, both societies regard being trapped in poverty as a problem. Where they differ somewhat is that Americans are less troubled than Canadians by the reproduction of wealth and status at the top. Where they also differ is in their attitudes towards politics. Though levels of political trust are declining in both societies, Canadians remain better disposed towards authoritative institutions, more trusting of government, than Americans. They place greater emphasis than Americans on the positive role of government institutions and policies in the framing, facilitating, and fairness of the collective outcomes of individual efforts (Heisz 2007; Corak 2009).

Perhaps corresponding to Canadians' continued belief in the value of government, Canada has traditionally enjoyed very high levels of voter participation, averaging around 75 per cent during federal elections over most of the second half of the twentieth century. Voter turnout began to decline such that only 60.5 per cent of eligible Canadians voted in the 2004 federal election. There was a moderate upswing of about 5 per cent in 2006, so that trend direction is somewhat unclear (Parkinson 2007). More general political activity in Canada appears robust: in activities which included signing a petition, searching for political information, attending a public meeting, boycotting/choosing a product for ethical reasons, contacting a newspaper or politician, participating in a demonstration or march, and volunteering for a political party, more than half of Canadians participating in a national survey reported engaging in at least one such activity in 2002. And, contrary to some reports on political activism among youth, the survey data identified that the younger the person, the more likely they were to be involved in at least one political activity, with almost two-thirds of those in the fifteen to twenty-four age group reporting participation in at least one political activity, compared to fewer than 40 per cent for those sixty-five and older (HRSDC 2007). Other findings suggest less optimistically that like youth in other OECD countries, Canadian youth seem quite disengaged from conventional political channels, and may be becoming more so. That is, electoral rates of participation, active political party involvement, and general political knowledge are all subdued, and on a level that suggests generational patterns rather than life-cycle effects (which can account for temporary low levels of political interest) (Stolle and Cruz 2005; O'Neill 2007).

Finally, some mention might be made of the ways in which some Canadian social movements have behaved influentially internationally. That is, some of Canada's civil-society organizations – notably in areas involving human rights, Indigenous rights, labour, development, and environment (e.g., Greenpeace and Friends of the Earth), are less oriented towards federal and provincial government institutions and instead interact more directly with their counterparts, as well as with affected parties, in other countries in what is referred to as the transnational "global civil society." Such civil-society collaborative action may utilize multinational mediating institutions (such as the International Labour Organization, the United Nations Environment Programme, and the United Nations Commission on Human Rights), or involve resisting them.

Part III: The Uneven Development of Civil Society

What is true about civil-society Canada in broad strokes and as national averages needs to be qualified and disaggregated spatio-temporally so that we can recognize the "changing face of Canada" (Bourne and Rose 2001). That is, while Canada remains a country with a high quality of life and demonstrable commitments to egalitarianism and pluralism across multiple domains, certain trends of uneven development affecting civil society must also be noted. "Income inequality," or the "wealth gap," measured by individual and family income, has been widening in Canada, especially during the 1990s and 2000s, and conspicuously so (alongside Germany) relative to the other thirty OECD countries (OECD 2008). Inequality has increased in Canada because of labour-market changes exacerbated by welfare-state retractions. After twenty years of continuous decline, both inequality and poverty rates have increased rapidly in the past ten years, now reaching levels above the OECD average (ibid.). Canada has among the lowest rates of corporate taxation among all G7 countries and this rate has been steadily declining since 2000 (Stanford 2005; Progressive Economics Forum 2012). Employment-insurance eligibility has been tightened and benefits levels kept low, welfare benefits have been cut so that they are now equal to where they were in the mid-1980s (Caragata and Cumming 2010), and decreases in income-tax rates have led to less and less effective income redistribution (Mahler and Jesuit 2005; Heisz 2007; Yalnizyan 2007). Canada spends less on cash benefits such as unemployment benefits and family benefits than most OECD countries. These changes, in combination with other markers of the re-commodification of social benefits (Bezanson 2007), provide a picture of increased economic inequality that translates into inequality in other life spheres. This growing polarization of family income in Canada has been caused by rising inequalities in income received from market sources (including wages, salaries, self-employment income, private pensions, and investment income), further compounded by the diminishing redistributive role of the Canadian state. Moreover, intensifying economic demands such as labour-market mobility expectations, educational-attainment expectations, longer de facto working-day norms, and the necessity of dual-income households are placing families, women, and children under greater duress (Caragata and Cumming 2010; Sager et al. 2010).

Although women and men are almost equal in their labour-market participation, there remain enormous gendered earnings inequalities. Canada sits alongside the United States – unlike many other OECD countries – in having failed to significantly reduce its gender wage gap: it is the twelfth highest among seventeen comparator countries (Conference Board of Canada 2009). Thus, while women are on par with men in labour market *participation* (Statistics Canada 2010) and their incomes strengthen well-being in two-earner families, their incomes are inadequate for women as self-sufficient earners. These issues must be appraised against Ann Shola Orloff's (2001) claim that the capacity of women to forge autonomous households is an important measure of the real extension of social rights. For many low-skilled Canadian women, especially lone mothers, economic autonomy cannot be achieved through either labour-market participation or the provisions of the welfare state.

Canada ranks high on female level of educational attainment, but women generally continue to follow traditional and gendered career paths that are associated with lower earnings levels. Policy innovation that once directed women into non-traditional spheres have been abandoned by the federal government alongside its wholesale withdrawal from significant social-welfare funding (Hughes 1995; Torjman and Battle 1995).

The UN Convention on the Rights of the Child was adopted worldwide in 1989 and came into force in Canada in 1991. Since then, Canada has made ongoing improvements and commitments in several domains such as breastfeeding rates, school nutrition policies and practices, and the mental health of children and adults. Most provinces have established independent advocates for children. Nonetheless, in a recent study, UNICEF researchers concluded that Canada is not meeting the expectations of the convention and this is of particular concern, because unlike many other countries that are also signatory to the convention, Canada has a level of affluence that makes its performance of special concern. Canada's shortcomings are most notable in four areas. These include the failure by governments to enshrine children's rights in law and to appoint a national commissioner for children. This latter recommendation is especially salient in the context of a federal government that has moved away from having a minister directly responsible for children, which affects the prominence this issue has at the cabinet table. Also at issue is the lack of a defined budget for children's benefits, which would aid in both ensuring appropriately directed spending and in accountability and oversight. The final area of critique broadly encompasses the need for an expanded public discourse and education on the rights of the child and effective multi-sectoral monitoring of Canada's implementation of the convention (Pearson and Collins 2009).

These broad shortcomings are further exacerbated by particular disparities, most notably between the status and performance of Aboriginal children and other Canadian children as reflected in various measures of well-being (Pearson and Collins 2009; Mahon 2006). On a more positive note, the Canada Child Tax Benefit, which provides child benefits to all low- and middle-income families, has been steadily improved. In 2003–4, the Government of Canada provided $5.5 billion through the base benefit of the CCTB to 3.1 million families with 5.6 million children, or approximately 82 per cent of Canadian families with children. The National Child Benefit Supplement provides low-income families with additional child benefits on top of the base benefit. For a family with an income of under $20,000 per annum the combined benefit would provide about $250 a month per child (NCB 2010). The presence of this growing benefit amidst an otherwise retracting welfare state is itself likely attributable at least in part to civil-society actors in the form of Campaign 2000, a broad national coalition whose goal was the elimination of child poverty in Canada by the year 2000. While obviously unsuccessful in absolute outcome terms, the campaign has been effective in working with politicians, policymakers, and a wide range of organizations to keep the pressure on for a child-poverty-free Canada. Less effective have been campaigns for a national day-care system, which has been planned and then withdrawn. The current Conservative government provides a meagre cash benefit in lieu of a system of affordable and licensed child care.

The Canadian feminist movement has been a driver behind many of these campaigns through its multiple associational forms. Umbrella organizations have also been crucial. It was the National Action Committee on the Status of Women (NAC) that lobbied to ensure that the status of women remained on the government's agenda and policy horizons in previous decades (Rebick 2005). At present, one of the more important coalition groups concerned with gendered justice is the Canadian Feminist Alliance for International Action (FAFIA), an alliance of some sixty Canadian women's equality-seeking and related organizations.

While the state-society co-construction and co-production of policy holds out the promise of empowered social citizenship (Bouchard et al. 2005), then, crucially, over the past two decades, the neoliberal political agenda of hollowing the reach of the state and reducing its formal functions has placed even greater responsibility, and in some quarters overwhelming demands, on civil-society structures and networks (Phillips and Hebb 2010). First, under the federal government's New Public Management ideals of project-funding, citizen organizations and self-help groups have had to compete for short-term government "contracts" with benchmarked and commodifiable performance requirements. However, such benchmarks may fail to capture the human gains of qualitative and preventative voluntary-sector activity (Mackinnon and Stephens 2010). More generally, women's voluntary organizations, which strive to meet marginal niches through collaborative practices, are not served well by competitive funding expectations (Meinhard and Foster 2003). Second, as the state dismantles physical and human infrastructure, voluntary-sector groups have to expend resources towards building their own coordinative and delivery capacity, which thereby effectively diverts resources from the clients and at-need and at-risk populations. Third, groups find that they have to downplay their critical social voice and public advocacy to be successful in obtaining contracts (Evans et al. 2005). Such a "shared governance" dynamic is evident in the negotiations between non-government AIDS organizations and Health Canada (Tsasis 2008). This muting, together with the resource constraints, curtails both their access to mainstream news media coverage (Greenberg and Walters 2004) and also the credible communicative capacity necessary to build and sustain the social networks in the first place (Gibson et al. 2007; Greenberg and Grosenick 2008). In some respects then, such policy co-construction leaves these groups compromised, and their capacities for innovation stymied (Phillips et al. 2010).

Moreover, some civil-society groups are also increasingly being left to their own devices to meet the de-politicized and privatized needs of their marginalized members. They have to depend on philanthropic funds and on wage workers willing to undertake additional unwaged work, as well as rely on extensive commitments of volunteer time. Decline in the funding of core and coordinating staff, as well as the incidental costs of volunteering undermines these organizations' overall effectiveness and creates operational uncertainties that make effective program and service delivery more difficult (Reitsma-Street et al. 2000).

Finally, viewed spatially, at the regional and local levels, the marginalized who find themselves vulnerable to one of more forms of "civil risk" and unable to fulfil the aspirational model of "responsible citizenship" by developing their own "human capital" do not always have ready access to either suitable civil-society organizations for support or the sort of orientation necessary to initiate a corrective charter claim (Ray and Kobayashi 2000; Banting 2005).

Canada's much lauded health care system, while still effective through its simple formula of private provision and public pay faces potential crises with an aging population and the increased costs of high-tech medicine. The health-care needs of some vulnerable populations are at risk and this is especially true among First Nation's people, who score significantly lower than do non-Natives across a wide range of health indicators. Several studies – examining mortality causal variables such as circulatory diseases, cancer, injury, and all-causes – also confirm that rural Canadians tend to have poorer health status and foreshortened lives relative to their urban counterparts (Pong et al. 2009). Though non-profit organizations, community support groups, and volunteer caregivers have rallied creatively, uneven geographies of health and social care across rural space leave populations vulnerable in the longer term (Cloutier-Fisher and Skinner 2006; Skinner 2008). Of course, health status is also affected by material capital considerations such as food insecurity as well as behavioural factors such as daily smoking and demographic factors such as age.

Again, women and mothers seem to have been especially adversely affected in Canada (and also in America and Mexico) by the re-scaling and contracting out of public social provision under the auspices of neoliberal continental integration (Caragata 2003; Raphael and Bryant 2004; Luccisano and Romagnoli 2007). In British Columbia, for example, insufficient public services, underfunded childcare, and inadequate social capital in the form of friend-networks and community supports noticeably impact poor and mother-led families (Bryant et al. 2009).

The actual success of Canada as a post-national, or multinational, and certainly multicultural state is also open to debate. Canada may be prone to essentializing minority cultures, thereby stereotyping and even ghettoizing their members, and postponing indefinitely all prospects of their full participation (Bissoondath 1994). It may also be going too far. into a post-national lack of consensus to sustain a shared civic culture (Resnick 2005). The idealism (and even just the aesthetic symbolism) of multiculturalism in Canada has always required the concerted effort of activist social movements and a willingness to wrestle with resistance on the ground, even in the much-vaunted cosmopolitan city and suburbs of Toronto (Caragata 1999). Still, while it is true today that it is easier to enter Canada than the United States as a skilled immigrant, migrants in Canada may find themselves poorly integrated in the short term. That is, those who enter Canada under the point system that determines economic-class entry, will sometimes struggle to find suitable employment in the face of the discounting of foreign credentials, references, and experience, and remain subject to discriminatory salary practices. By contrast, having secured employment commitments and demonstrated comparable pay levels before entering the United States, professional-class migrants (though not temporary workers) are immediately incorporated at least economically (Somerville and Walsworth 2009). It is apparent in this regard that even as the funding of co-produced immigrant settlement programs has dropped steadily since the late 1990s, concentrations of immigrant poverty in Canada's "gateway cities" are intensifying, and serving to trap populations in neighbourhoods that are sufficiently stigmatized as poverty- and crime-ridden to warrant speaking of Canadian "ghettos" (Smith and Ley 2008). It must also be acknowledged that beyond the major cities, multiculturalism lags as a visible and meaningful aspect of life (Walks 2006; Kymlicka 2003; and Harles 2004).

In this regard, and by way of closing, it might be noted that civil-society coalitional mobilization in Canada has been particularly intense, in the form of political lobbying and public demonstrations against policies of deeper socio-economic integration with the United States, to date: in the late 1980s over the Canada-US Free Trade Agreement (CUSFTA) and, subsequently, the North American Free Trade Agreement (NAFTA), and again in 2004, over the prospects and seeming inevitability of "deep integration" (Gilbert 2005; Dean and Dehejia 2006). At present, civil-society organizations such as the Canadian Centre for Policy Alternatives, an independent non-profit, non-partisan "progressive" research institute, funded by the charitable donations of its 12,000 members and beyond, work to shift the terms and agenda of public policy debates and focus attention on the ambivalent and deleterious local effects on civil society of national policies, while also mentoring civil society leadership.

Conclusion: The Future of Civil Society in Canada

What do current trends and developments portend for the future of civil society? The Canadian public stage will continue to be populated by a wide range of organized civil-society groups and plenty of social-movement activity including anti-poverty organizing; race, disability, and lesbian and gay politics; health and social movements; in addition to Aboriginal political action and the ever-present Quebec nationalism, marked to be sure by different sorts of successes and failures in affecting public discourse and public policy (M. Smith 2007a). As a result, it seems likely that Canada will experience increasing forms of contestation not only through institutions of political representation and the courts, but within civil society and at various junctures of state-mediated access to material and symbolic resources. The divergence of values across growing ethnic, gender, and age cleavage structures will generate intra-societal stress. The past and the management of collective memory will be increasingly contested. Youth activist urban subcultures – resisting and protesting the pressures of neoliberalism even as they enact their radicalism through individualized symbolic and consumerist modes and working-class styles – may prove especially important (Kanji and Doyle 2009; Kennelly 2009).

Canada will likely continue to be pressed to experiment with the notion of citizenship. The recent revitalization of Aboriginal constitutional and legal orders of self-governance to protect local political standing appears to be synthesizing, albeit in quite varied ways, Aboriginal legal traditions with the new core constitutional principles of Canada, including rights-based discourse (Alcantara and Whitfield 2010). Already, one might point to the ways in which, for example, the Nisga'a First Nation has negotiated with the provincial government of British Columbia and the Canadian federal government what might be construed as a differentiated variant on citizenship, predicated on a special relationship to the land and communal solidarity (Blackburn 2009).

NAFTA, and the deepening of continental integration, may well still have further profound effects on the Canadian political economy and civil society. In particular, insofar as government services are contracted out, and non-profit-sector service is required to meet market-based delivery standards, American service providers may begin to make inroads into the provision of social services formerly co-produced by provincial governments through local civil-society groups. It seems likely then that Canadian civil-society groups will have to press for inclusion, and strive to defend Canadian notions of caring (Trefler 2008), even as North American governance and cooperation is becoming more regional and pluralistic in its incorporation of institutional elites (Ayres and Macdonald 2006).

Finally, the media plays a considerable role in shaping the levels and forms of civic and political engagement (O'Neill 2010). As such,

Canada and its diverse civil-society actors and agencies will have to grapple with the relatively new phenomena of the political, strategic, and indeed even partisan management by the prime minister and cabinet of the media through communication strategies for electoral purposes. If government is involved both at the "front end" in setting the agenda of public discourse and at the "back end," steering perceptions about policy outcomes within civil society, it will become important that civil-society groups remain vigilant in pressing for the democratic benefits of transparency as well as for their involvement in co-construction (Nimijean 2006; Howlett et al. 2010).

As power and social control come to penetrate more deeply across a broader spectrum of the life-world, collective conflicts become increasing personal, involving the "lasting creation of new cultural practices within social movement networks" (Carroll 1997, 18) and the direct, personal practice of "innovations in daily life" (Melucci 1989, 71). These "cultural innovations" or "critical social practices" (Caulfield, as cited in Caragata 1999) not only provide individuals with alternative ideological frames and self-understandings, but in the process facilitate the development of solidarity and collective identity within the social movement. More broadly, they may also contribute to social change through what Gramsci (1992) described as counter-hegemonic actions which simply through their expression and presence challenge the socially and politically normative.

Adams (2003) suggests that Americans and Canadians are increasingly heading in different political-cultural directions, "as Americans, even those in Democratic 'blue' states, are increasingly alienated, outer-directed, deferential to authority, materialistic and socially conservative and Canadians are inner-directed, flexible, tolerant, and socially liberal" (Gidengil et al. 2005, 10). These "socially liberal views [are seen to] prevail" (ibid.). If indeed these lofty generalizations that attempt to sum up a national psyche are even partly true, credit must accrue to the actors and organizations of civil society. As they ground Canadians in collective and collaborative activities oriented to directly meeting their needs, they act to aggregate the needs and interests especially of those who are marginalized so that they may take a place in the public discourse; they work with the state in both co-producing and co-constructing public policy and programs; and, finally, they offer small and steady glimpses of life and life-worlds that operate outside of the commercial hegemony of modern capitalism.

REFERENCES

Adams, Michael. 2003. *Fire and Ice: The United States, Canada and the Myth of Converging Values*. Toronto: Penguin Canada.

Adams, Michael. 2007. *Unlikely Utopia: The Surprising Triumph of Canadian Multiculturalism*. Toronto: Viking Canada.

Agriculture and Agri Foods Canada, 2010. *Co-operatives in Canada*. Catalogue no. A80-901/1-2007.

Aguiar, Luis L. M. 2006. "Janitors and Sweatshop Citizenship in Canada." *Antipode* 38 (3): 440–61. http://dx.doi.org/10.1111/j.0066-4812.2006.00589.x.

Alcantara, C., and G. Whitfield. 2010. "Aboriginal Self-Government through Constitutional Design: A Survey of Fourteen Aboriginal Constitutions in Canada." *Journal of Canadian Studies/Revue d'Études Canadiennes* 44 (2): 122–45.

Ayres, J. 2004. "Political Economy, Civil Society, and the Deep Integration Debate in Canada." *American Review of Canadian Studies* 34 (4): 621–47. http://dx.doi.org/10.1080/02722010409481692.

Ayres, Jeffrey, and Laura Macdonald. 2006. "Deep Integration and Shallow Governance: The Limits of Civil Society Engagement across North America." *Policy and Society* 25 (3): 23–42. http://dx.doi.org/10.1016/S1449-4035(06)70081-9.

Baines, Donna. 2010. "Neoliberal Restructuring, Activism/Participation, and Social Unionism in the Nonprofit Social Services." *Nonprofit and Voluntary Sector Quarterly* 39 (1): 10–28. http://dx.doi.org/10.1177/0899764008326681.

Banting, Keith G. 2005. "Do We Know Where We Are Going? The New Social Policy in Canada." *Canadian Public Policy* 31 (4): 421–9. http://dx.doi.org/10.2307/3552361.

Berry, Jeffrey. 1980. "Public Interest vs. Party System." *Society* 17 (4): 42–8. http://dx.doi.org/10.1007/BF02694804.

Beyer, Peter. 1997. "Religious Vitality in Canada: The Complementarity of Religious, Market and Secularization Perspectives." *Journal for the Scientific Study of Religion* 36 (2): 272–88. http://dx.doi.org/10.2307/1387558.

Bezanson, Kate. 2007. *Gender, the State, and Social Reproduction: Household Insecurity in Neo-Liberal Times*. Toronto: University of Toronto Press.

Bickerton, James, ed. 2007. *Freedom, Equality, Community: The Political Philosophy of Six Influential Canadians*. Montreal: McGill-Queen's University Press.

Bissoondath, Neil Devindra. 1994. *Selling Illusions: The Cult of Multiculturalism in Canada*. Toronto: Penguin.

Blackburn, Carole. 2009. "Differentiating Indigenous Citizenship: Seeking Multiplicity in Rights, Identity, and Sovereignty in Canada." *American Ethnologist* 36 (1): 66–78.

Bloemraad, Irene. 2006. "Becoming a Citizen in the United States and Canada: Structured Mobilization and Immigrant Political Incorporation." *Social Forces* 85 (2): 667–95. http://dx.doi.org/10.1353/sof.2007.0002.

Boatright, Robert G. 2009. "Interest Group Adaptations to Campaign Finance Reform in Canada and the United States." *Canadian Journal of Political Science* 42 (1): 17–43. http://dx.doi.org/10.1017/S0008423909090027.

Bouchard, Louise, Jean-François Roy, and Solange van Kemenade. 2005. "What Impact Does Social Capital Have on the Health of Canadians?" Working paper, *Policy Research Initiative: Social Capital as a Public Policy Tool.* Ottawa.

Bourne, Larry S., and Damaris Rose. 2001. "The Changing Face of Canada: The Uneven Geographies of Population and Social Change." *Canadian Geographer* 45 (1): 105–19. http://dx.doi.org/10.1111/j.1541-0064.2001. tb01174.x.

Breitkreuz, Rhonda S. 2005. "Engendering Citizenship? A Critical Feminist Analysis of Canadian Welfare-to-Work Policies and the Employment Experiences of Lone Mothers." *Journal of Sociology and Social Welfare* 32 (2): 147–65.

Bryant, Toba, Chad Leaver, and James Dunn. 2009. "Unmet Healthcare Need, Gender, and Health Inequalities in Canada." *Health Policy* (Amsterdam) 91 (1): 24–32. http://dx.doi.org/10.1016/j.healthpol.2008.11.002. Medline:19070930.

Canadian Islamic Congress. 2010. "CIC Facts." Downloaded from http://www.canadianislamiccongress.com/cic2010.

Caragata, Lea. 1999. "The Privileged Public: Who Is Permitted Citizenship?" *Community Development Journal* 34 (4): 270–86. http://dx.doi.org/10.1093/cdj/34.4.270.

Caragata, Lea. 2003. "Neoconservative Realities: The Social and Economic Marginalization of Canadian Women." *International Sociology* 18 (3): 559–80. http://dx.doi.org/10.1177/02685809030183006.

Caragata, Lea, and Sara J. Cumming. 2011. "Lone Mother-led Families: Exemplifying the Structuring of Social Inequality." *Social Compass* 5 (5): 376–91.

Carroll, William. 1997. "Introduction." In W. Carroll, ed., *Organizing Dissent: Contemporary Social Movements in Theory and Practice.* 2nd ed. Toronto: Garamond Press.

Card, David, Thomas Lemieux, and W. Craig Riddell. 2003. *Unionization and Wage Inequality: A Comparative Study of the U.S., the U.K., and Canada.*

Working paper 9473. Cambridge, MA: National Bureau of Economic Research. http://www.nber.org/papers/w9473.

Chari, Raj, Gary Murphy, and John Hogan. 2007. "Regulating Lobbyists: A Comparative Analysis of the United States, Canada, Germany and the European Union." *Political Quarterly* 78 (3): 422–38. http://dx.doi.org/10.1111/j.1467-923X.2007.00870.x.

Chaykowski, Richard. 2005. *Non-standard Work and Economic Vulnerability: Defining Vulnerability in the Labour Market.* Ottawa: Canadian Policy Research Networks. March.

Clarkson, Stephen. 1972. "The Branch Plant Economy." *Economic and Political Weekly* 7 (36): 18.

Cloutier-Fisher, Denise, and Mark W. Skinner. 2006. "Levelling the Playing Field? Exploring the Implications of Managed Competition for Voluntary Sector Providers of Long-Term Care in Small Town Ontario." *Health & Place* 12 (1): 97–109. http://dx.doi.org/10.1016/j.healthplace.2004.10.012. Medline:16243684.

Conference Board of Canada. 2009. "Society: Gender Wage Gap." Downloaded from http://www.conferenceboard.ca/HCP/Details/society/gender-income-gap.aspx.

Co-operative Housing Federation of Canada & Rooftops Canada Foundation. N.d. "Co-operative Housing in Canada: A Model for Empowered Communities." Downloaded from http://www.unesco.org/most/usa3.htm.

Corak, Miles. 2009. "Chasing the Same Dream, Climbing Different Ladders: Economic Mobility in the United States and Canada." Economic Mobility Project. Pew Charitable Trust. Downloaded from http://www.pewtrusts.org/our_work_report_detail.aspx?id=56876&category=596.

Cotler, Hon. Irwin. 2006. "Marriage in Canada – Evolution or Revolution?" *Family Court Review* 44 (1): 60–73. http://dx.doi.org/10.1111/j.1744-1617.2006.00067.x.

Dean, James W., and Vivek H. Dehejia. 2006. "Would a Borderless North America Kill Canadian Culture?" *American Review of Canadian Studies* 36 (2): 313–27. http://dx.doi.org/10.1080/02722010609481702.

Dekker, Paul, and Andries van den Broek. 1998. "Civil Society in Comparative Perspective: Involvement in Voluntary Associations in North America and Western Europe." *Voluntas: International Journal of Voluntary and Nonprofit Organizations* 9 (1): 11–38. http://dx.doi.org/10.1023/A:1021450828183.

Evans, Bryan, Ted Richmond, and John Shields. 2005. "Structuring Neoliberal Governance: The Nonprofit Sector, Emerging New Modes of Control and the Marketisation of Service Delivery." *Policy and Society* 24 (1): 73–97. http://dx.doi.org/10.1016/S1449-4035(05)70050-3.

Fraser, Nancy. 1991. "Rethinking the Public Sphere: A Contribution to the Critique of Actually Existing Democracy." In *Habermas and the Public Sphere*, ed. Craig Calhoun, 109–42. Cambridge: MIT Press.

Fraser, Nancy. 1995. "From Redistribution to Recognition? Dilemmas of Justice in a 'Post-Socialist' Age." *New Left Review* I/212 (July/August): 1–17.

Freeman, Richard B. 1998. "Contraction and Expansion: The Divergence of Private Sector and Public Sector Unionism in the United States." *Journal of Economic Perspectives* 2 (Spring): 63–88.

Friends of the Earth Canada. 2005. *Canada's Voice in Global Governance: A Civil Society Handbook*. http://www.foecanada.org/intl/handbook.htm.

Geddes, John. 2010. "Foreign-Owned or Home-Grown Plants: As the C$ Flies High, Which Are More Apt to Flee?" *Maclean's*, 21 April. http://www2.macleans.ca/2010/04/21.

Gibson, Kerri, Susan O'Donnell, and Vanda Rideout. 2007. "The Project-Funding Regime: Complications for Community Organizations and Their Staff." *Canadian Public Administration* 50 (3): 411–36. http://dx.doi.org/10.1111/j.1754-7121.2007.tb02135.x.

Gidengil, Elizabeth, et al. 2005. "Missing the Message: Young Adults and the Election Issues." *Electoral Insight* 7 (1): 1–6.

Gilbert, Emily. 2005. "The Inevitability of Integration? Neoliberal Discourse and the Proposals for a New North American Economic Space after September 11." *Annals of the Association of American Geographers* 95 (1): 202–22. http://dx.doi.org/10.1111/j.1467-8306.2005.00456.x.

Grabb, Edward, and James Curtis. 2010. *Regions Apart: The Four Societies of Canada and the United States*. New York: Oxford University Press.

Grabham, Emily. 2002. "Law v Canada: New Directions for Equality under the Canadian Charter?" *Oxford Journal of Legal Studies* 22 (4): 641–61. http://dx.doi.org/10.1093/ojls/22.4.641.

Gramsci, Antonio. 1992. *Prison Notebooks*. Vol. 1, ed. Joseph A. Buttigieg, trans. Joseph A. Buttigieg and Antonio Callari. New York: Columbia University Press.

Grant, George. 1965. *Lament for a Nation: The Defeat of Canadian Nationalism.*. Ottawa: Carleton University Press.

Greenberg, Josh, and David Walters. 2004. "Promoting Philanthropy? News Publicity and Voluntary Organizations in Canada." *Voluntas: International Journal of Voluntary and Nonprofit Organizations* 15 (4): 383–404. http://dx.doi.org/10.1007/s11266-004-1238-6.

Greenberg, Josh, and Georgina Grosenick. 2008. "Building Communicative Capacity in the Third Sector: Research from Canada." *Third Sector Review* 14 (2): 51–75.

Hall, M., C. Barr, M. Easwaramoorthy, S. Wojciech Sokolowski, and L. Salamon. 2005. *The Canadian Non-Profit and Voluntary Sector in Comparative Perspective.* Toronto: Imagine Canada.

Harles, John C. 2004. "Immigrant Integration in Canada and the United States." *American Review of Canadian Studies* 34 (2): 223–58. http://dx.doi.org/10.1080/02722010409481199.

Harris, Andrea, Brenda Stefanson, and Murray Fulton. 1996. "New Generation Cooperatives and Cooperative Theory." *Journal of Cooperatives* 11:15–28.

Hayday, M. 2010. "Fireworks, Folk-dancing, and Fostering a National Identity: The Politics of Canada Day." *Canadian Historical Review* 91 (2): 287–314. http://dx.doi.org/10.3138/chr.91.2.287.

Hébert, Chantal. 2006. "Canada 2020, Canada sans Quebec, The 51st State." CBC News In Depth, 12 October. http://www.cbc.ca/news/background/canada2020/essay-hebert.html.

Heisz, Andrew. 2007. "Income Inequality and Redistribution in Canada: 1976 to 2004." Statistics Canada, Analytical Studies Branch Research Paper series, 2007.298. http://www.statcan.gc.ca/pub/11f0019m/11f0019m2007298-eng.pdf.

Howlett, Michael, Jonathan Craft, and Lindsay Zibrik. 2010. "Government Communication and Democratic Governance: Electoral and Policy-Related Information Campaigns in Canada." *Policy and Society* 29 (1): 13–22. http://dx.doi.org/10.1016/j.polsoc.2009.11.002.

Hughes, Karen D. 1995. "Women in Non-Traditional Occupations." In *Perspectives on Labour and Income* 7 (3): 14–19. Ottawa: Statistics Canada.

Human Resources and Skills Development Canada (HRSDC). 2007. *Indicators of Well-Being in Canada: Social Participation.* HRSDC calculations based on Statistics Canada Survey on Giving, Volunteering and Participating: Public-use micro file data, 2004. Ottawa: HRSDC.

Human Resources and Skills Development Canada. 2010. *Indicators of Well-Being in Canada: Work.* HRSDC calculations based on Statistics Canada Labour Force Historical Review, 2009, table 078. Cat. no. 71F0004XVB. Ottawa: Statistics Canada. Downloaded from http://www4.hrsdc.gc.ca/d.4m.1.3n@-eng.jsp?did=3.

Ilcan, Suzan. 2009. "Privatizing Responsibility: Public Sector Reform under Neoliberal Government." *Canadian Review of Sociology* 46 (3): 207–34. http://dx.doi.org/10.1111/j.1755-618X.2009.01212.x. Medline:20027750.

Iyer, Pico. 2000. *The Global Soul: Jet Lag, Shopping Malls, and the Search for Home.* New York: Vintage.

Jansen, H., and L. Young. 2009. "Solidarity Forever? The NDP, Organized Labour, and the Changing Face of Party Finance in Canada." *Canadian*

Journal of Political Science 42 (3): 657–78. http://dx.doi.org/10.1017/S0008423909990412.

Jenson, Jane. 1997. "Fated to Live in Interesting Times: Canada's Changing Citizenship Regimes." *Canadian Journal of Political Science* 30 (4): 627–44. http://dx.doi.org/10.1017/S0008423900016450.

Johnson, Robert, and Rianne Mahon. 2005. "NAFTA, the Redesign, and the Rescaling of Canada's Welfare State." *Studies in Political Economy* 76: 7–30.

Kanji, Mebs, and Nicki Doyle. 2009. "Value Diversity and Support for Political Authorities in Canada." *American Review of Canadian Studies* 39 (3): 191–223. http://dx.doi.org/10.1080/02722010903138743.

Kaufman, Jason. 2009. *The Origins of Canadian and American Political Differences.* Cambridge, MA: Harvard University Press.

Kennelly, Jacqueline. 2009. "Learning to Protest: Youth Activist Cultures in Contemporary Urban Canada." *Review of Education, Pedagogy & Cultural Studies* 31 (4): 293–315. http://dx.doi.org/10.1080/10714410903132865.

Kim, Andrew E. 1993. "The Absence of Pan-Canadian Civil Religion: Plurality, Duality, and Conflict in Symbols of Canadian Culture." *Sociology of Religion* 54 (3): 257–75. http://dx.doi.org/10.2307/3711721.

Kunz, Jean Lock. 2005. "Orienting Newcomers to Canadian Society: Social Capital and Settlement." In *Social Capital in Action*, 82–114. Ottawa: Policy Research Initiative.

Kymlicka, Will. 1995. *Multicultural Citizenship: A Liberal Theory of Minority Rights.* New York: Oxford University Press.

Kymlicka, Will. 2003. "Being Canadian." *Government and Opposition* 38 (3): 357–85. http://dx.doi.org/10.1111/1477-7053.t01-1-00019.

Lee, Cheol-Sung. 2007. "Labor Unions and Good Governance: A Cross-National, Comparative Analysis." *American Sociological Review* 72 (4): 585–609. http://dx.doi.org/10.1177/000312240707200405.

Lee, Jennifer Wenshya, and Yvonne M. Hébert. 2006. "The Meaning of Being Canadian: A Comparison between Youth of Immigrant and Non-Immigrant Origins." *Canadian Journal of Education* 29 (2): 497–520. http://dx.doi.org/10.2307/20054174.

Lipset, Seymour Martin. 1991. *Continental Divide: The Values and Institutions of the United States and Canada.* New York: Routledge.

Luccisano, Lucy, and Amy Romagnoli. 2007. "Comparing Public Social Provision and Citizenship in the United States, Canada, and Mexico: Are There Implications for a North American Space?" *Politics & Policy* 35 (4): 716–51. http://dx.doi.org/10.1111/j.1747-1346.2007.00082.x.

Macfarlane, Emmett. 2009. "Administration at the Supreme Court of Canada: Challenges and Change in the Charter Era." *Canadian Public Administration* 52 (1): 1–21. http://dx.doi.org/10.1111/j.1754-7121.2009.00057.x.

Mackinnon, Shauna, and Sara Stephens. 2010. "Is Participation Having an Impact? Measuring Progress in Winnipeg's Inner City through the Voices of Community-Based Program Participants." *Journal of Social Work* 10 (3): 283–300. http://dx.doi.org/10.1177/1468017310363632.

MacMillan, C. Michael. 2010. "Auditing Citizen Engagement in Heritage Planning: The Views of Citizens." *Canadian Public Administration* 53 (1): 87–107.

Mahler, Vincent A., and David K. Jesuit. 2006. "Fiscal Redistribution in the Developed Countries: New Insights from the Luxembourg Income Study." *Socio-economic Review* 4 (3): 483–511. http://dx.doi.org/10.1093/ser/mwl003.

Mahon, Rianne. 2006. "Of Scalar Hierarchies and Welfare Redesign: Child Care in Three Canadian Cities." *Transactions of the Institute of British Geographers* 31 (4): 452–66. http://dx.doi.org/10.1111/j.1475-5661.2006.00221.x.

Meinhard, Agnes G., and Mary K. Foster. 2003. "Differences in the Response of Women's Voluntary Organizations to Shifts in Canadian Public Policy." *Nonprofit and Voluntary Sector Quarterly* 32 (3): 366–96. http://dx.doi.org/10.1177/0899764003254910.

Melucci, Alberto. 1989. *Nomads of the Present: Social Movements and Individual Needs in Contemporary Society.* Philadelphia: Temple University Press.

Mendell, Marguerite. 2010. "Reflections on the Evolving Landscape of Social Enterprise in North America." *Policy and Society* 29 (3): 243–56. http://dx.doi.org/10.1016/j.polsoc.2010.07.003.

Miceli, Thomas, Gerald Sazama, and C.F. Sirmans. 1994. "The Role of Limited Equity Cooperatives in Providing Affordable Housing." *Housing Policy Debate* 5 (4): 469–90. http://dx.doi.org/10.1080/10511482.1994.9521175.

Miceli, Thomas, Gerald Sazama, and C.F. Sirmans. 1998. "Managing Externalities in Multi-Unit Housing: Limited Equity Cooperatives as an Alternative to Public Housing." *Journal of Policy Modeling* 20 (5): 649–68. http://dx.doi.org/10.1016/S0161-8938(97)00071-9.

Milligan, C., and N. Fyfe. 2005. "Preserving Space for Volunteers: Exploring the Links between Voluntary Welfare Organisations, Volunteering and Citizenship." *Urban Studies* (Edinburgh, Scotland) 42 (3): 417–33. http://dx.doi.org/10.1080/00420980500034884.

National Child Benefit (NCB). 2010. Downloaded from http://www.nationalchildbenefit.ca/eng/home.shtml.

Ng, Roxanna. 1998. "Work Restructuring and Recolonizing Third World Women: An Example from the Garment Industry in Toronto." *Canadian Woman Studies Journal* 18 (1): 21–5.

Nimijean, Richard. 2006. "The Politics of Branding Canada: The International-Domestic Nexus and the Rethinking of Canada's Place in the World." *Revista Mexicana de Estudios Canadienses* 11: 67–85.

NSNVO. 2006. *National Survey of Non-Profit and Voluntary Organizations: The Non-Profit and Voluntary Sector in Canada*. Toronto: Imagine Canada.

OECD. 2008. *Growing Unequal?: Income Distribution and Poverty in OECD Countries*. Paris: OECD Publishing. http://www.oecd-ilibrary.org/social-issues-migration-health/growing-unequal_9789264044197-en.

O'Neill, Brenda. 2007. *Indifferent or Just Different? The Political and Civic Engagement of Young People in Canada: Charting the Course for Youth Civic and Political Participation*. Ottawa: Canadian Policy Research Networks.

O'Neill, Brenda. 2010. "The Media's Role in Shaping Canadian Civic and Political Engagement." *Policy and Society* 29 (1): 37–51. http://dx.doi.org/10.1016/j.polsoc.2009.11.004.

Onishenko, D., and L. Caragata. 2010. "A Theoretically Critical Gaze on the Canadian Equal Marriage Debate: Breaking the Binaries." *Journal of Gay & Lesbian Social Services* 22 (1 & 2): 91–111. http://dx.doi.org/10.1080/10538720903332404.

Orloff, Ann Shola. 2001. "Ending the Entitlements of Poor Single Mothers: Changing Social Policies, Women's Employment Caregiving." In *Women and Welfare: Theory and Practice in the United States and Europe*, ed. Nancy Hirschmann and Ulrike Lieber, 133–59. Piscataway, NJ: Rutgers University Press.

Ornstein, Michael, and H. Michael Stevenson. 1999. *Politics and Ideology in Canada*. Montreal and Kingston: McGill-Queen's University Press.

Ornstein, M.D., H.M. Stevenson, and A.P. Williams. 1980. "Region, Class and Political Culture in Canada." *Canadian Journal of Political Science* 13 (2): 227–71. http://dx.doi.org/10.1017/S000842390003300X.

Orsini, Michael, and Miriam Smith, eds. 2007. *Critical Policy Studies*. Vancouver: UBC Press.

Parkinson, Rhonda. 2007. "Voter Turnout in Canada." Maple Leaf Web, University of Lethbridge, AB. Downloaded from http://www.mapleleafweb.com/features/voter-turnout-canada.

Pearson, Landon, and Tara M. Collins. 2009. *Not There Yet: Canada's Implementation of the General Measures of the Convention on the Rights of the Child*. Florence, Italy: UNICEF Innocenti Research Centre.

Peck, Jamie. 2005. *Workfare States*. New York: The Guilford Press.

Peters, John. 2008. "Labour Market Deregulation and the Decline of Labour Power in North America and Western Europe." *Policy and Society* 27 (1): 83–98. http://dx.doi.org/10.1016/j.polsoc.2008.07.007.

Phillips, Susan D. 2006. "The Intersection of Governance and Citizenship in Canada: Not Quite the Third Way." *IRPP Policy Matters* 4:1–31.

Phillips, Susan D., and Tessa Hebb. 2010. "Financing the Third Sector: Introduction." *Policy and Society* 29 (3): 181–7. http://dx.doi.org/10.1016/j.polsoc.2010.07.001.

Phillips, Susan D., Rachel Laforest, and Andrew Graham. 2010. "From Shopping to Social Innovation: Getting Public Financing Right in Canada." *Policy and Society* 29 (3): 189–99. http://dx.doi.org/10.1016/j.polsoc.2010.06.001.

Pomerantz, Lauren. 2001. *Death, Diarrhea and Developing Nations: Nestlé and the Ethics of Infant Formula.* http://www.teachspace.org/personal/research/nestle/title.html.

Pong, R.W., M. Desmeules, and C. Lagacé. 2009. "Rural-Urban Disparities in Health: How Does Canada Fare and How Does Canada Compare with Australia?" *Australian Journal of Rural Health* 17 (1): 58–64. http://dx.doi.org/10.1111/j.1440-1584.2008.01039.x.

Powell, F., and M. Geoghegan. 2005. "Reclaiming Civil Society: The Future of Global Social Work?" *European Journal of Social Work* 8 (2): 129–44. http://dx.doi.org/10.1080/13691450500085166.

Progressive Economics Forum. 2012. "Do Corporate Tax Cuts Really Pay for Themselves?" 13 September. http://www.progressive-economics.ca/2012/09/13/do-corporate-tax-cuts-really-pay-for-themselves.

Putnam, Robert. 2000. *Bowling Alone: The Collapse and Revival of American Community.* New York: Simon and Schuster.

Quarter, Jack. 1992. *Canada's Social Economy.* Toronto: James Lorimer.

Quarter, Jack, Laurie Mook, and Ann Armstrong. 2009. *Understanding the Social Economy: A Canadian Perspective.* Toronto: University of Toronto Press.

Raphael, Dennis, and Toba Bryant. 2004. "The Welfare State as a Determinant of Women's Health: Support for Women's Quality of Life in Canada and Four Comparison Nations." *Health Policy* (Amsterdam) 68 (1): 63–79. http://dx.doi.org/10.1016/j.healthpol.2003.08.003.

Ray, Brian, and Audrey Kobayashi. 2000. "Civil Risk and Landscapes of Marginality in Canada: A Pluralist Approach to Social Justice." *Canadian Geographer* 44 (4): 401–17.

Rebick, Judy. 2005. *Ten Thousand Roses: The Making of a Feminist Revolution.* Toronto: Penguin.

Reed, Paul B., and L. Kevin Selbee. 2000. *Patterns of Citizen Participation and the Civic Core in Canada.* Ottawa: Statistics Canada and Carleton University.

Reitsma-Street, Marge, Mechthild Maczewski, and Sheila Neysmith. 2000. "Promoting Engagement: An Organizational Study of Volunteers in Community Resource Centres for Children." *Children and Youth Services Review* 22 (8): 651–78. http://dx.doi.org/10.1016/S0190-7409(00)00106-7.

Resnick, Philip. 2005. *The European Roots of Canadian Identity.* Toronto: University of Toronto Press.

Roby, Yves (revised by Pierre Poulin and Sasha Yusufali). 2010. "Caisse Populaire." *Canadian Encyclopedia.* Downloaded from http://www.thecanadianencyclopedia.com/articles/caisse-populaire.

Sager, Eric, et al. 2010. *Families Count: Profiling Canada's Families IV*. Ottawa: Vanier Institute of the Family. Downloaded from http://www.vifamily.ca/media/webfm-uploads/Publications/Families_Count/Families_Count.pdf.

Sharify-Funk, Meena. 2009. "Representing Canadian Muslims: Media, Muslim Advocacy Organizations, and Gender in the Ontario Shari'ah Debate." *Global Media Journal* (Canadian ed.) 2 (2): 73–89.

Shragge, Eric, and Jean-Marc Fontan. 2000. *Social Economy: International Debates and Perspectives*. Montreal: Black Rose Books.

Skinner, Mark W. 2008. "Voluntarism and Long-Term Care in the Countryside: The Paradox of a Threadbare Sector." *Canadian Geographer* 52 (2): 188–203. http://dx.doi.org/10.1111/j.1541-0064.2008.00208.x.

Smith, David E. 2007. *The People's House of Commons: Theories of Democracy in Contention*. Toronto: University of Toronto Press.

Smith, Heather, and David Ley. 2008. "Even in Canada? The Multiscalar Construction and Experience of Concentrated Immigrant Poverty in Gateway Cities." *Annals of the Association of American Geographers* 98 (3): 686–713. http://dx.doi.org/10.1080/00045600802104509.

Smith, Miriam. 2005. *A Civil Society? Collective Actors in Canadian Political Life*. Toronto: University of Toronto Press.

Smith, Miriam. 2007a. *Group Politics and Social Movements in Canada*. Peterborough, ON: Broadview Press.

Smith, Miriam. 2007b. "Framing Same-Sex Marriage in Canada and the United States: Goodridge, Halpern and the National Boundaries of Political Discourse." *Social & Legal Studies* 16 (1): 5–26. http://dx.doi.org/10.1177/0964663907073444.

Somerville, K., and S. Walsworth. 2009. "Vulnerabilities of Highly Skilled Immigrants in Canada and the United States." *American Review of Canadian Studies* 39 (2): 147–61. http://dx.doi.org/10.1080/02722010902848169.

Stanford, Jim. 2005. *Protesting Too Much: The Rhetoric and Reality of Corporate Tax Cuts*. Toronto: Canadian Auto Workers.

Statistics Canada. 2010. "Labour Force and Participation Rates by Sex and Age Group." Downloaded fromhttp://www.statcan.gc.ca/tables-tableaux/sum-som/l01/cst01/labor05-eng.htm.

Stolle, Dietlind, and Cesi Cruz. 2005. "Youth Civic Engagement in Canada: Implications for Public Policy." In *Social Capital in Action*, 82–114. Ottawa: Policy Research Initiative.

Strong-Boag, Veronica. 2009. "Experts on Our Own Lives: Commemorating Canada at the Beginning of the 21st Century." *Public Historian* 31 (1): 46–68. http://dx.doi.org/10.1525/tph.2009.31.1.46.

Taylor, Charles. 1989. *Sources of the Self: The Making of the Modern Identity*. Cambridge, MA: Harvard University Press.

Thomas, David M., ed. 2004. *Canada and the United States: Differences That Count*. 2nd ed. Peterborough, ON: Broadview Press.

Thorner, Thomas, ed. 2003. *"A Country nourished on self-doubt": Documents in Post-Confederation Canadian History*. Peterborough, ON: Broadview Press.

Tindall, D.B., and Barry Wellman. 2001. "Canada as Social Structure: Social Network Analysis and Canadian Sociology." *Canadian Journal of Sociology* 26 (3): 265–308. http://dx.doi.org/10.2307/3341889.

Torjman, Sherri, and Ken Battle. 1995. *Can We Have National Standards*. Toronto: Caledon Institute of Social Policy.

Trefler, Daniel. 2008. "Innis Lecture: Canadian Policies for Broad-Based Prosperity." *Canadian Journal of Economics/Revue Canadienne d'Économie* 41 (4): 1156–84. http://dx.doi.org/10.1111/j.1540-5982.2008.00499.x.

Tsasis, Peter. 2008. "The Politics of Governance: Government–Voluntary Sector Relationships." *Canadian Public Administration* 51 (2): 265–90. http://dx.doi.org/10.1111/j.1754-7121.2008.00018.x.

Tully, James. 1995. *Strange Multiplicity: Constitutionalism in an Age of Diversity*. New York: Cambridge University Press. http://dx.doi.org/10.1017/CBO9781139170888.

Uberoi, Varun. 2009. "Multiculturalism and the Canadian Charter of Rights and Freedoms." *Political Studies* 57 (4): 805–27. http://dx.doi.org/10.1111/j.1467-9248.2008.00759.x.

Vaillancourt, Yves. 2009. "Social Economy in the Co-construction of Public Policy." *Annals of the Public and Cooperative Economies* 80 (2): 275–313. http://dx.doi.org/10.1111/j.1467-8292.2009.00387.x.

Walks, R. Alan. 2006. "The Causes of City-Suburban Political Polarization? A Canadian Case Study." *Annals of the Association of American Geographers* 96 (2): 390–414. http://dx.doi.org/10.1111/j.1467-8306.2006.00483.x.

Wolch, J.R. 1990. "The Shadow State: Government and Voluntary Sector in Transition." New York: The Foundation Center.

Yalnizyan, Armine. 2007. *The Rich and the Rest of Us: The Changing Face of Canada's Growing Gap*. Toronto: Canadian Centre for Policy Alternatives.http://www.policyalternatives.ca/publications/reports/rich-and-rest-us.

Young, John, and Boris DeWiel, eds. 2009. *Faith in Democracy? Religion and Politics in Canada*. Newcastle upon Tyne: Cambridge Scholars Publishing.

12 Canadian Foreign Policy

DOUGLAS NORD AND HEATHER SMITH

Canada's role in the international community has changed and developed over time in response to an evolving agenda of global and domestic issues and concerns. While it can be argued that there has been some degree of continuity in the manner and approach by which Canada has sought to conduct its foreign policy, it is equally clear that the country has followed a number of distinctive paths in its dealings with the world beyond its borders. Canada's international relations reflect both continuity and change. As with other global actors, Canada's foreign policy is a response to immediate needs and pressures as well as to longer-term goals and aspirations. It has also had the unique challenge of living next door to an international superpower for the past seven decades.

A historical review of Canada's interactions with the international community reveals a variety of recurring themes and issues that the country and its leaders have sought to address. These include traditional challenges relating to sovereignty and independence, peace and security, and economic growth and prosperity as well as broader concerns relating to social justice, a more harmonious natural environment, and an enhanced quality of life for Canadians and others. One can also identify distinctive periods in the development of Canadian foreign policy in which these issues and problems have been addressed. This chapter provides a focused discussion of the evolution of Canada's external relations from the era of Confederation through the coming to power of the Harper government in the first decade of the present century. It identifies major issues and concerns that have confronted Canadians and their political leaders in their dealings with the international community and the responses they have made to these challenges. We also discuss possible future directions for Canadian foreign policy over the coming decades. The discussion is organized in five sections

The first section examines the early development of Canada's external relations, focusing on the twin challenges of building a distinctive national identity both at home and abroad. It considers Canada's early foreign and defence policies in the context of its continuing commitment to the British Empire as well as Ottawa's effort to secure greater autonomy for itself in its external relations. This section also reviews Canada's post-Confederation dealings with its increasingly powerful southern neighbour, the United States, focusing on Ottawa's efforts to resolve existing trade and border disputes and to establish a new harmony in bilateral relations. Canada's contributions to the First and Second World Wars and the efforts of its politicians and diplomats to establish a meaningful peace following the cessation of hostilities are also examined.

· The second section looks at Canadian external relations from the outset of the Cold War through the era of détente some three decades later. Attention is devoted to Canada's role as a "middle power" and Ottawa's interest in building a cooperative framework of international relations in the post–Second World War era and in playing an active role in the multilateral diplomacy of the day. Consideration is also given to Canada's role as an alliance member of NATO and NORAD during the Cold War. The evolving political, defence, and economic features of the Canada–US relationship are discussed. This section recognizes the efforts of the St Laurent, Pearson, and Trudeau governments to provide a distinctive Canadian perspective and voice in and about world affairs.

The third section focuses on the particular foreign policy challenges confronted by Canada in living next to the United States. A variety of traditional economic and defence issues as well as security concerns of the post-9/11 world are considered under this heading. Special attention is devoted to the FTA and NAFTA agreements. Issues that have caused cross-border quarrels – including American access to Canadian natural resources, the sale of Canadian agricultural products across the border, and the development of common North American environmental, trade, and labour practices – are also addressed. So too is the overall question of whether there is a merging or diverging of national values in the bilateral relationship.

The fourth section considers contemporary Canadian foreign policy in a broader context. Here we examine distinctive Canadian contributions to the discussion and resolution of a number of pressing global concerns. In particular, this section considers Canada's efforts to contribute to promoting development and fighting poverty in countries of the Third World and examines Canadian initiatives on behalf of a healthier global environment, especially with respect to the challenges of global warming. We also highlight Canada's recent promotion of the idea of "human security" and the challenges of globalization. Finally, this section looks at specific initiatives of the Harper government to project a distinctive Canadian profile in the Arctic and within multilateral decision-making bodies like the G8 and G20.

The conclusion looks at future dimensions of Canadian foreign policy. It considers the various challenges the country may need to address in external relations over the coming decades, including those derived from its evolving relationship with the United States. It identifies some of the new and continuing forces that are likely to influence Canada's foreign policy choices, points to factors that may enable Canada to continue to play a significant role in the discussion and resolution of global challenges, and mentions developments that some observers worry are undermining its international influence.

The Early Development of Canada's External Relations

Canada's external relations were not uppermost in the minds of its political leaders or people during the first decades following Confederation. This was because the country was directing its attention largely inwards in an effort to establish stronger unifying bonds among the once separate British colonies of North America. Building marine and rail connections between the separate provinces – along with a broader sense of national unity and purpose – was given priority over most foreign concerns. As discussed in chapter 2, the precise division of responsibilities between Britain and Canada for foreign and defence matters was not clearly delineated at the time of Confederation. Thus, the new dominion government was hesitant to assert its new role in these areas, particularly if it might upset London or require additional scarce resources. Like many of the more recently independent states of Africa and Asia in the twentieth century, Canada was initially content in the latter half of the nineteenth century to focus on the tasks of internal development and nation building rather than on international diplomacy. Its connections to the broader world were limited and initially directed largely by British imperial interests.

The one major exception to this trend was Canada's relationship with its immediate neighbour to the south, the United States. The extent and character of the interactions between these neighbours suggested that Ottawa's diplomatic dealings with Washington could not be relegated to the back burner of national concerns, nor could they be entrusted entirely to the British. The United States then, as now, occupied a central focus of attention for the Canadian government. National unity, security, and economic prosperity were all linked to developing an appropriate modus vivendi with the Americans. Old animosities dating from the time of the American Revolution and the War of 1812 had to give way to a more palatable working relationship.

Initially the dominion government hoped this might be accomplished through a focus on economics and free trade across the border. The Reciprocity Treaty that had been accepted by both sides in 1854 seemed to have set the example of using trade and commerce to build a peaceful and mutually beneficial relationship across the border. Even when this accord was abrogated by the United States in 1866, most Canadians felt that it would soon be replaced by a new agreement once Civil War tensions had abated. Securing renewed access to the American market was to become one of the first undertakings of the new Canadian government's efforts in external relations.

Unfortunately it was not to be a successful undertaking. The United States, angered by the creation of a "new monarchical state" on its northern border and sensing that renewed free trade would be of more benefit to Canadians than to Americans, rebuffed the Canadian initiative. Not until more than a century later – with the acceptance of the Free Trade Agreement in 1989 – would the free movement of most goods and services across the US-Canadian border be restored. Absent this, in 1879 the Canadian government under Prime Minister John A. Macdonald embarked on its National Policy in order to develop the Canadian economy in an autonomous fashion from the United States. That policy became the signature theme for Canadian domestic policy for the next several decades as well as the chief feature of the nation's policy towards the United States and the rest of the international community. Allied with a continuing mistrust of Washington's expansionist behaviour, it set the foundation for Canada's spurning of a subsequent free trade agreement with the Americans in 1912.

Many of Canada's dealings with the United States over the next fifty years were to focus on the resolution of outstanding border disputes and existing claims to the associated natural resources and fisheries. Although some significant progress had been made in the early half of the nineteenth century in identifying and demilitarizing the demarcation line between British North America and the United States, a new interest arose in the last years of the century to fully delineate and pacify the international border between the new Dominion of Canada and the American republic. On the Canadian side, this interest arose, in part, from the removal of the last of Britain's military forces from the North American mainland in 1871. It was hastened, as well, by a desire to specify, with greater certainty, what rights each country could claim to valuable border resources – especially fisheries along the east coast and in the Great Lakes. It was also spurred by the mutual recognition in Canada and the United States that the frontier era of the "uncharted West" was quickly coming to an end on both sides of the border and that the further development of that region would require greater certainties of claims and enhanced cooperation.

Starting with the successful negotiation of the Treaty of Washington in 1871 and continuing through the San Juan Islands arbitration of the following year, and, finally, with the announcement of the findings of the Alaska Boundary Tribunal of 1903, the two countries completed the process of formally recognizing their shared borders and specifying their rights of access to the natural resources and fisheries associated with them. Equally significant to the future course of Canadian–American relations was the realization on the part of both parties that border issues might henceforth be resolved peacefully and in a largely cooperative and mutually beneficial manner. With this in mind, Canada and the United States agreed in 1905 to establish a bilateral Waterways Commission to regulate the use of the Great Lakes for transportation and other purposes. This was followed four years later by the creation of the International Joint Commission to jointly monitor and protect the boundary waters between the two countries. Similar initiatives designed to peacefully resolve remaining fishery disputes between the two countries and to cooperatively allocate various marine resources were undertaken in subsequent decades, including the creation of the International Joint Fisheries Commission in 1923, the Pacific Salmon Commission in 1930, and the Great Lakes Fisheries Commission in 1955.

While the early interest of the Canadian government in foreign affairs was directed primarily towards relations with the United States and their impact on national growth and internal development, Ottawa did not focus solely on questions of trade, borders, and fisheries in North America. Although securing national economic prosperity remained an important foreign policy objective for Canadian leaders in the first decades following Confederation, of nearly equal concern was their desire to establish greater autonomy and direct control over the country's foreign and defence policies. Operating as a self-governing dominion within the British Empire/Commonwealth, Canada felt an increasing need to demonstrate both its right and its ability to chart its own direction in international relations. Between 1867 and the end of the Second World War, successive Canadian prime ministers struggled to assert Canadian sovereignty in foreign affairs and to articulate the country's unique role in the international community.

Similar gradual, evolutionary steps were taken in according Canada the right to negotiate formal treaties and agreements with other international actors. As noted above, Canada was part of the 1871 diplomatic negotiations that led to the signing of the Treaty of Washington, although its primary representative, Prime Minister Macdonald, was only allocated a seat within the larger British imperial delegation. Thirty-five more years were to transpire before Canada's diplomatic status was elevated to the point where Ottawa was allowed to take the lead in the negotiations that resulted in the 1907 Canadian–French Commercial Treaty and to sign the document concurrently with the British. A further sixteen years passed before Canada was able to negotiate and sign the 1923 US–Canadian Halibut Treaty on its own.

This slow and rather protracted march towards diplomatic independence and autonomy was hastened by the Canadian government's decision in 1909 to establish its own Department of External Affairs. The creation of this small but vital unit within the Canadian bureaucracy gave the country the opportunity and means to focus its attention on what might be a distinctive role for Canada in the broader world. Similarly, Ottawa's expressed reluctance to accept continued British direction of its foreign and defence policies at a series of imperial conferences during the same decade set the foundation for a more autonomous role for Canada in its foreign affairs. However, it was on the basis of another, more important action – Canada's participation in the First World War – that the full maturation of the country's role in international relations was to be realized. Not only did Canada provide valuable war materials and supplies to the Allied cause, but it also raised a military force of some 600,000 men and women who fought across a number of fronts during the war.

This new status was greeted with pride and enthusiasm on the part of the Canadian people and their government. They saw their country emerging to play a significant role not just in the affairs of North America, but in the broader world as well. Canada joined the new League of Nations and took on a series of important responsibilities within the framework of this major postwar international organization. In 1921 it was elected to the governing body of the International Labor Organization. Three years later, a Canadian, Senator Raoul Dandurand, was elected president of the League's assembly. Three years after that, Canada secured representation on the League's council as one of its non-permanent members. Throughout the 1920s and 1930s, Canada used its position within the League of Nations to promote its developing international interests and to enlarge its international profile. Even in these early stages of its diplomatic efforts, Canada earned a growing reputation as an effective international mediator and earnest advocate for the peaceful settlement of disputes.

Yet as the storm clouds of another world war began to gather in the late 1930s, Ottawa's attention to foreign policy matters was increasingly focused on providing for its own national defence and security. Interestingly, this meant not only coordinating war preparedness with Britain and the other members of the British Empire, but also engaging in major political and defence talks with the United States. The latter were initially undertaken through a series of reciprocal visits between Prime Minister Mackenzie King and President Franklin Roosevelt, starting in Quebec City in 1936 and continuing onward to Ogdensburg, New York, in 1940. At each meeting it became increasingly apparent that the two countries would come to each other's defence in the event of invasion and that they would coordinate their defence plans and war production. For the first time in their long relationship, Canada and the United States were becoming political and military allies.

The outbreak of war in Europe in 1939 and in the Pacific in 1941 brought Canada into the global conflict as a full participant. As was the case during the First World War, Canada became a major supplier of war material and troops across several theatres of action. However, unlike 1914, Canada declared war on the Axis Powers on her own – not as an adjunct of Britain. Throughout the conflict, the Canadians made a series of significant contributions to the Allied war effort, including a prominent role in the D-Day invasion of Normandy and the liberation of the Netherlands. These and other significant undertakings were hailed by Canada's wartime allies. Prime Minister Churchill of Britain noted that throughout the conflict, Canada had served as the "essential lynchpin" between Britain and the United States. President Roosevelt praised the Canadians for their "courage and tenacity." Prime Minister King, for his part, was interested in ensuring that Canada's efforts were properly noted by his wartime allies and that the "proportionality" of Canada's contribution would be recognized in an expanded role for Canada in postwar international affairs.

From Middle Power to Multilateralism

Canada in the four decades between the end of the Second World War and the election of the Mulroney government in the mid-1980s witnessed significant changes in its foreign policy and in its position in the global community. Having achieved full status as a sovereign state during the war years, the country looked forward at the conclusion of the conflict to taking its rightful place as a significant participant in world affairs. Over the next forty years, Canada was to confront a variety of challenges connected with postwar multilateral diplomacy, the coming of the Cold War, and the eventual replacement of that international system with a more inclusive and flexible one. Throughout each of these periods, the Canadian government endeavoured to create an appropriate and distinctive role for the country within the evolving international community. Ottawa sought to balance the achievement of specific national foreign policy objectives relating to trade and defence with broader commitments to global peace, security, and economic development. In so doing, Canada was to earn a remarkably positive reputation for being both a reliable alliance partner and an innovator in international diplomacy.

The immediate challenge confronting Canada as it embarked on this journey was to find an appropriate role to play in the postwar community. One possible stance for Canada to take was that of being a "middle power." Here Canada might occupy a middle ground between the major powers of the day and the less consequential small states. Canada would use its considerable economic and political resources to play a creative role as an intermediate force in world affairs. It would champion the cause of international cooperation and seek meaningful collaboration between various countries around the world in order to address pressing problems of the day. It would encourage dialogue and consensus building across regional, economic, and emerging ideological divisions in the postwar era.

In the autumn of 1947 the country's secretary of state for external affairs – and soon-to-be prime minister – Louis St Laurent, set forth in a speech at the University of Toronto what he considered to be the basis for the country's postwar foreign policy. His talk, "The Foundations of Canadian Policy in World Affairs," became a guidebook for Canadian foreign policy over the next twenty years. In it he argued that there were five basic principles that should direct the path of Canadian diplomacy: (1) a regard for the maintenance of the country's unity; (2) a commitment to political liberty; (3) respect for the rule of law; (4) recognition of forces of good and evil; and (5) a willingness to accept international responsibilities. This latter point was particularly important, for, as St Laurent put it: "Canada's security is to be found in the development of a firm structure of international organization" (St Laurent 1947).

Having emerged from the Second World War as one of the stronger economic and military powers, Canada was eager to contribute its energies and resources to ensuring that the postwar era would operate from a foundation of international peace and cooperation. With this in mind, Ottawa became actively involved in the creation and development of the United Nations. As a founding member of this international organization, Canada soon took upon itself a number of leadership roles within the General Assembly and the UN Secretariat. During the late 1940s and early 1950s, Canada played a critical role in advancing UN initiatives in the areas of postwar economic reconstruction, refugee assistance, and the development of an international code of human rights. During this same period, Canada also played significant roles in promoting the organization's efforts to reduce the spread of nuclear weaponry and to encourage the peaceful resolution of international conflicts. It was to receive global recognition of its efforts in this latter area when Canada's minister for external affairs, Lester Pearson, earned the Nobel Peace Prize in 1957 for developing and advancing the idea of "international peacekeepers."

During the same era, Canada also helped shape the postwar international economic order. It became an active member of the International Bank for Reconstruction and Development (the World Bank), the International Monetary Fund, and the General Agreement on Tariffs and Trade – the predecessor of today's World Trade Organization (WTO). Ottawa fervently believed that the wealthier countries of the post–Second World War period had a vital role to play in stimulating global economic recovery and an expansion of trade and commerce. Later, in the 1950s and early 1960s, it led the call for expanded international responsibilities in these vital areas so as to provide needed economic aid and assistance for the newly independent countries of Asia, Africa, and the Western Hemisphere. Through these undertakings Canada earned a reputation as a country interested in the welfare and development of states throughout the international community. Its diplomats and political leaders became used to looking at global problems from a comprehensive perspective and became comfortable in addressing international needs on a multilateral basis. Such multilateral diplomatic efforts became the hallmark of Canadian foreign policy for much of this period and resulted in remarkable achievements.

Yet the coming of the Cold War and Canada's membership in the Western Alliance was to provide just as much direction for the development of the country's foreign policy in the 1950s and 1960s. The emergence of a starkly divided international system set the context for much of the country's international political, military, and economic relations during that era. Canada became a solid ally of the United States during this critical time in international affairs as well as a key participant in the Western Alliance. It was a founding member of the North Atlantic Treaty Organization (NATO), created in 1949 to provide ongoing defence and political cooperation among the North American and Western European partners. Canada played a vital role in the supply and staffing of this multilateral security organization and helped ensure that it operated more broadly than as a mere military alliance. Specifically, it pushed for the inclusion of Article II of the NATO Treaty (subsequently known as the "Canadian Article"), which envisioned economic, political, and social cooperation among the member states as well as common efforts to support democratic institutions and practices.

Cold War developments continued to influence Canadian foreign policy throughout the subsequent decade. In response to communist aggression in Korea in 1950, Canada joined a number of Western states in supplying military forces to an American-led UN command in that country. These Canadian forces fought with distinction throughout the conflict and provided visible proof of the country's ongoing military alliance with the United States. In 1958 the existing mutual defence arrangements between the two countries were further solidified with the establishment of the North American Aerospace Defense Command (NORAD). Under this arrangement Canada committed itself to the joint defence of North American airspace. This treaty, along with a series of military production agreements undertaken between the two countries during the Cold War, brought Canada fully into the military-preparedness schemes and defence planning of the United States.

Not until the 1960s did some Canadians begin to raise concerns over the loss of a certain amount of national autonomy in foreign affairs associated with such mutual defence arrangements. These fears first manifested themselves during the Cuban Missile Crisis in 1962, when Prime Minister Diefenbaker was pressed to commit Canadian military forces in support of American defence operations. The deployment of Bomarc missiles with nuclear warheads in Canada also created difficulties during the Diefenbaker years. National autonomy concerns emerged again during the Vietnam War, when Prime Minister Pearson was pressured by President Johnson to demonstrate greater support for American policy in Southeast Asia. In these situations, the burden of being closely allied to one of the Cold War's superpowers weighed heavily on Canadian political leaders and diplomats.

The 1950s and 1960s also saw a rapid growth in economic interactions between Canada and the United States. During these years there was considerable investment by each country in the neighbouring economy. In the case of the United States, this meant a major infusion of investment capital into Canada's manufacturing, natural resource, and energy sectors. The result was eventual American domination of important sectors of the Canadian economy, including automobile manufacturing, and oil and natural gas exploration and refining. This increased integration of the Canadian economy with that of its southern neighbour was furthered as well by the conclusion of a series of bilateral treaties such as the St Lawrence Seaway Agreement of 1959 and the Columbia River Treaty of 1964. Both allowed for collaborative undertakings in the areas of commercial transport and energy generation. During these years, Canada moved from being at the edge of American economic interest towards becoming a central component of it.

Towards the end of the 1960s, a new direction for Canadian foreign policy emerged. On coming to power in 1968, the new Liberal prime minister, Pierre Trudeau, announced that his government would undertake a thorough review of the country's external relations. He indicated that both he and a majority of Canadians were no longer content to see Canada continue to play the limited role of "middle power" or "American ally" and that a new position for Canada in the world would be sought. This new stance would endeavour to reflect the distinctive domestic character and values of the country as well as the reality that Canadians were living in a rapidly changing international community.

In June 1970 the results of this foreign policy review were presented to the country. Contained in a series of six booklets, *Foreign Policy for Canadians* endeavoured to set forth the Trudeau government's vision of a reinvigorated Canadian foreign policy. It was to be rooted in three major objectives: (1) maintaining Canada's security, sovereignty, and independence; (2) enlarging the country's prosperity and well-being in the broadest sense of these terms; and (3) helping Canadians make a useful contribution to the development of humanity and the global community. These broad objectives, in turn, were to be reflected in six policy themes, which would constitute the broad aims of Canadian foreign policy: (1) encouraging economic growth; (2) maintaining sovereignty and independence; (3) securing peace and security; (4) advancing social justice; (5) expanding quality of life; and (6) providing for a harmonious natural environment. The review suggested, additionally, that there should be a close link between the country's foreign policy and its domestic policies and priorities. At the same time, however, it suggested that "there is no natural, immutable or permanent role for Canada in today's world" (Department of External Affairs 1970). Canadian foreign policy was to be both principled and dynamic.

Clearly for Trudeau such a re-envisioned Canadian foreign policy would involve a variety of new initiatives and emphases. These would include new undertakings to promote nuclear arms control, the furtherance of social and economic development in the Third World, and the protection of the global environment. Such efforts could be advanced both through traditional means of multilateral diplomacy as well as more direct undertakings of Canadian political leaders and diplomats. Such an expanded vision of Canadian foreign policy would also include reaching out to new potential partners in Latin America, the Pacific, and La Francophonie. It would mean, as well, a lesser emphasis on what were seen as outmoded commitments to NATO, NORAD, and other Cold War alliances.

This was exactly the type of Canadian foreign policy that the Trudeau government pursued over the next fifteen years. During this period, Canada brought pressure to bear on the two global superpowers, the United States and the Soviet Union, to reduce their nuclear arsenals. It championed the cause of restructuring the terms of trade between the global North and South. It promoted initiatives to guard against acid rain and to protect the world's oceans. Ottawa established diplomatic relations with the People's Republic of China in 1970 and expanded its trade initiatives in the Asia-Pacific region. In 1972 it took out observer status within the Organization of American States (OAS) and expanded its diplomatic relationship with Castro's Cuba. This era also witnessed a 50 per cent force reduction on the part of Canada in NATO and a cut in Canadian forces associated with NORAD.

Perhaps surprisingly, Canada's relations with the United States were not addressed in any major detail in *Foreign Policy for Canadians* in 1970. Two years later, the Canadian minister for external affairs, Mitchell Sharp, sought to address this significant omission by authoring his own separate review of possible directions for Canada's relationship with its southern neighbour. In a paper entitled "Canada–U.S. Relations: Options for the Future" the Canadian foreign minister outlined three possible directions that Ottawa might pursue in its dealings with Washington. (Some aspects of Canadian policies are covered in chapter 4 on the economy.) The first possibility was the maintenance of the existing bilateral relationship. The second course of action might be to expand the relationship and build additional economic, political, and defence ties between the two societies. The so-called Third Option envisioned distancing Canada a bit more from the United States and allowing the country to develop its foreign and domestic policies in a manner less influenced by the United States. It was this policy that the Trudeau government adopted.

Not unexpectedly, this decision resulted in a noticeable cooling of the Canadian–American relationship during much of the Trudeau era. Rather than being treated as the normal "friendly neighbour to the north," suddenly Canada was seen as a "problem child" by successive American administrations. Ottawa had similar misgivings about its American partner. The "special relationship" that had been developed and expanded from the 1940s through most of the 1960s was starting to tarnish by the mid-1970s. As Canada's external affairs minister noted in 1975: "What we have witnessed since the early seventies has been the ending of one era and the beginning of a new period in Canada–U.S. relations" (MacEachen 1975). The US ambassador to Canada, for his part, noted simply that we are "neighbours for better or worse" (Porter 1974).

Canada's Relations with the United States – Ups and Downs in Bilateral Relations

The depth and breadth of bilateral relations between the United States and Canada can hardly be overstated. The countries cooperate both multilaterally and bilaterally in virtually every sphere of life – social, economic, political, and security. The importance of good bilateral relations for both countries is indisputable. Nonetheless, the fact that the United States is so much larger creates concerns in Canada that it may be dominated or bullied. For its part, the United States' greater size and strength often give it greater freedom and a larger number of policy options, which can lead it to behave in ways that are interpreted as insensitive or arrogant. As Charles Doran notes, while the relationship is "remarkably tranquil," there are "periods of crankiness" (Doran 2006, 389–90). The past quarter-century has been no exception, with the tone of bilateral relations being sometimes better, sometimes worse. Despite this, the overall trend has been towards increasingly closer ties and integration.

Prime Minister Brian Mulroney came to power in 1984 pledging both a new tone and new policies to "refurbish" Canadian–American relations after the coolness of the Trudeau years. Mulroney succeeded, and his election ushered in a period of warm personal relations, first between him and Ronald Reagan, then with George H. Bush. The two countries established an annual summit as a forum for discussion and exchange of views. Friendly, informal contacts between the prime minister and president were also a common feature of bilateral relations during the Mulroney years. Disagreements on matters of policy (e.g., missile defence, environmental protection, the Arctic region) were not allowed to undermine the cordiality of relations.

In matters of substance, the dominant symbol of closer bilateral relations during the Mulroney years was the free trade agreement (FTA), and it represented a fundamental policy shift. After Canadian voters rejected free trade in 1912, no government dared raise the issue again until Mulroney did so in 1985. The decision to pursue free trade unambiguously signalled the weakening of the Third Option, which had failed to reduce Canada's dependence on the United States. It had actually increased throughout the 1970s and early 1980s, as did protectionist sentiment in Congress and American use of trade remedy legislation. Mulroney argued that it was obvious that Canada needed a new strategy to secure access to the critically important American market, and he immediately began pursing it.

In Canada, the FTA proved to be a highly polarizing foreign policy initiative. Both the Liberals and New Democratic Party denounced the agreement as a sell-out of Canadian interests and as a surrendering of Canadian sovereignty. Many civil-society groups also rejected the agreement as a sell-out to the Americans (see chapter 11). Although Mulroney and Reagan signed the agreement on 2 January 1988, Parliament put off voting on it until after the Canadian elections scheduled for November. That campaign was dominated by the FTA, with both the Liberals and the NDP promising to tear up the treaty if elected. Although these parties together won a greater share of the vote than did Mulroney's Progressive Conservatives (52.3 vs 43 per cent), the Conservatives won 58 per cent of the seats in Parliament, which then passed the FTA in a vote along party lines. It came into force on 1 January 1989.

The FTA was not the only agreement that Mulroney negotiated that emphasized Canada's regional identity and role in the Americas. In January 1990 Canada became a full member of the Organization of American States (OAS). Throughout the Cold War, Canada had remained outside, in part because Canadians saw themselves as belonging more to Europe than to the Americas, but also to avoid being forced to take sides in disagreements between the United States and Latin American countries. By the late 1980s the Cold War had ended, Europe was busy deepening regional integration, and informal discussions of enhanced economic cooperation between the United States and Latin American countries were under way. These developments led the Canadian government to re-evaluate its views. An era of increased regionalization seemed to be dawning, and this helped persuade the Mulroney government that Canada should join the OAS.

Mulroney's decision to join trilateral free trade talks with the United States and Mexico was much more controversial. In February 1990, Mexican president Carlos Salinas raised the possibility of a free trade agreement between Mexico and the United States modelled on the Canada–US agreement. President Bush responded positively, and in June he and Salinas publicly announced their intention to pursue free trade negotiations. After first ruling out Canadian participation in trilateral talks, Mulroney told Bush in September 1990 that Canada wanted to be included. Canada had little genuine interest in a free trade agreement with Mexico, but worried about being left out. The government's main interest was to protect the FTA and promote multilateralism in North America rather than "hub-and-spoke" bilateralism.

The agreement was controversial in Canada, and the delay caused by newly elected president Bill Clinton meant that NAFTA also got caught up in Canadian electoral politics. Like Clinton, Jean Chrétien, leader of the opposition Liberal Party, was unenthusiastic about NAFTA, not least because there was strong domestic opposition to it, particularly among Liberal voters. Chrétien had pledged to renegotiate NAFTA if the Liberals returned to power in 1993, and he stuck with this pledge during the campaign. Nonetheless, after the Liberals won a large parliamentary majority in October, Chrétien quickly informed Clinton that the Canadian government was not interested in new negotiations. NAFTA passed both the US Congress and the Canadian parliament and came into force on 1 January 1994.

Given the Liberal Party's vociferous public opposition to the FTA and NAFTA, what explains the seemingly sudden change of heart? Liberal Party positions on the agreements were part policy (i.e., a desire in some quarters to find an alternative to it) and part politics (i.e., a response to popular opposition to free trade and to the challenge posed by the rise of the leftist New Democrats). By the time the Liberals won the 1993 election, the strength of the anti–free trade wing of the party had declined, as had the strength of the New Democrats. This, along with the realization that it was not in Canada's interest to reject a multilateral approach to North American trade, probably explains Chrétien's policy shift on NAFTA. If anything, as noted in chapter 4 on the economy, a preference for multilateralism logically resulted in Chrétien's decision to endorse NAFTA.

North American integration has not been a priority issue for either prime ministers or presidents since NAFTA was signed. It is perhaps understandable that Chrétien and Clinton, having expended considerable political capital on its passage, would practise a policy of benign neglect and let others see to the implementation of the agreement. Surprisingly, however, the conservative governments of Stephen Harper and George W. Bush that were to succeed them did relatively little more to advance the idea of a deeper and broader hemispheric trade pact. This was partly due to the effect of some of the domestic labour and environmental challenges they encountered in implementing the existing provisions of the NAFTA and partly the result of the changing international context that soon placed security concerns at a higher level of interest than trade.

In 2001 the overall framework for hemispheric trade negotiations dramatically changed. After the traumatic events of 9/11, priority was given to maintaining existing trade not necessarily to expanding it. To keep the border open and goods and people flowing quickly and easily across it has required new types of cooperation to meet American security demands. Shortly after the attacks, Canada rebuffed a Mexican suggestion that the North American partners adopt a multilateral approach to securing the borders in favour of enhanced bilateralism. The immediate result of Canadian-US efforts was the December 2001 Smart Border Agreement, a thirty-point action plan to improve the flow of traffic and security coordination between the two countries. In 2002 a Bi-National Planning Group was established and given the task of improving arrangements to defend against various perceived types of threats. In addition, five Integrated Border Enforcement Teams composed of police, immigration, and customs officers were created to improve cooperation. Such focused undertakings aimed at "securing the border" became the hallmark of Canadian–United States relations for much of the first decade of the new century. While some renewed efforts to establish a broader tripartite trade and security collaboration among Canada, the United States, and Mexico under the banner of a "Security and Prosperity Partnership" were launched at the same time, the annual rotating summit meetings for the heads of government of the three North American states have proved to be more of a convenient photo opportunity than a concrete step towards greater collective action.

Besides recasting trade relations, Brian Mulroney had come to office in the mid-1980s promising to improve bilateral security and defence relations. During the Trudeau government's last years, relations between the superpowers had deteriorated significantly. Trudeau criticized President Reagan's uncompromising anti-Soviet rhetoric, nuclear strategy (including the space-based defence initiative dubbed "Star Wars" by critics), and defence spending as contributing to renewed tensions. He had also opposed American intervention in Central America and the invasion of Grenada. When the Soviet Union shot down a Korean Airliner on its way from Alaska to Seoul, Reagan had called it a "coldblooded barbarous attack," while Trudeau had called it a "tragic accident of war" (CBC Archives 1983). Shortly thereafter, in late 1983, Trudeau launched a peace initiative. At the United Nations and in travels to Europe he called on the superpowers to negotiate comprehensive test bans on nuclear and high-altitude weapons, convene a five-power conference on nuclear arms control, and establish a consultative process between NATO and the Warsaw Pact. The initiative angered the Reagan administration and contributed to cool bilateral relations. The weakening of Canada's military since the 1970s and Trudeau's unwillingness to reverse this trend by increasing defence spending was another source of irritation in Washington. In some circles it was even interpreted as a manifestation of Canada's unwillingness to pull its weight in NATO.

Not surprisingly, Mulroney's pledge to reverse the decline of the Canadian Forces and his support for increasing Canada's presence in Europe were welcomed in Washington and contributed to improved bilateral relations. The 1987 White Paper on Defence, *Challenge and Commitment: A Defence Policy for Canada*, which emphasized the threat posed by the Soviet Union and recommended significant defence spending increases and investments, was also viewed favourably in Washington.

But external developments and budget realities soon derailed Mulroney's defence proposals. At the Reykjavik summit in October 1986, Mikhail Gorbachev indicated his willingness to abandon Brezhnev's military build-up. In 1987 he announced *glasnost* and *perestroika*, and he and Reagan signed the INF Treaty to eliminate all intermediate-range nuclear missiles by 1991. By 1989, revolutions in Eastern Europe – most symbolically the tearing down of the Berlin Wall – made it clear that the Cold War was over and the defence white paper obsolete. This, along with serious economic problems and a ballooning budget deficit, led Mulroney to abandon defence spending increases. Instead, the government cut defence spending, reduced the size of the Canadian Forces, and announced that Canadian military bases in Germany would be closed and forces withdrawn from Europe by mid-1995. Mulroney pledged that Canada would maintain forces at home that could serve with NATO, including a full battalion and fighter squadrons, thus enabling the country to continue to meet its commitments and responsibilities abroad.

Despite continued American concerns about the state of the Canadian military, bilateral relations were not really affected. In part this was due to the widespread view that defence cuts were to be expected because traditional security threats against the West had declined. It was also because Canada continued to participate actively in UN and other multilateral peacekeeping missions of importance to the United States and NATO, even when these began to change into more demanding and dangerous second-generation missions. In fact, in the early 1990s Canada's expenditures for peacekeeping increased significantly as UN peacekeeping efforts mushroomed.

Defence spending cuts continued under Prime Minister Chrétien (1993–2003), who openly acknowledged that defence was not one of his priorities. In the late 1990s several reports warned that the country's stated goals and commitments seemed incompatible with the decades-long decline in defence spending. Some in the United States and NATO also voiced concerns, but Chrétien was not persuaded, arguing as late as December 2001 that the Canadian military was well equipped and that those who said otherwise were mouthpieces for the Canadian arms industry. Nonetheless, after 2001 Chrétien did earmark more money for defence, and additional increases pledged in 2003 brought defence spending back to 1991 levels.

The marked deterioration in American–Canadian relations from the early 2000s was due to disagreements on matters other than defence spending. In a way reminiscent of the differences between Trudeau and Reagan, Chrétien and George W. Bush had very different views about how countries should act in the world, and this disagreement only deepened after 9/11. Chrétien approved of Bush's efforts to reach out to allies and build a coalition in support of action in Afghanistan, and Canada participated in it. Relations deteriorated as Bush moved towards war with Iraq and it became clear that he intended to act whether or not the UN Security Council sanctioned it. In March 2003, Chrétien informed Parliament that Canada would not be sending troops to a war against Iraq without further conditions. Washington had not been forewarned and was angered by the decision and by the manner in which it was made public. Anti-Bush rhetoric among members of Chrétien's government did not help the relationship.

When Paul Martin succeeded Chrétien as prime minister at the end of 2003 he pledged once again to improve bilateral relations. Critical public statements about the American administration by members of the Canadian government became less frequent. Martin announced that he would continue to strengthen the Canadian military, and in April 2004 his government released an official national security statement calling for a variety of new initiatives. This was followed in 2005 by an increase in defence spending and a new Defence Policy Statement, in which it was noted that the Canada-US defence partnership was very important. Despite this, Martin angered Washington in February by deciding not to cooperate with the United States on North American missile defence. The move was seen as bowing to populist anti-American sentiment and as further evidence that Canada either did not accept American views about how to make North America secure, or was unwilling to contribute to achieving this end.

The decision on ballistic missile defence also created confusion about Canadian intentions for NORAD, which was due to be renewed in

2006. The United States suggested informally in 2001 that NORAD be expanded to include both land and sea forces so that it could become the basis for integrated and broad cooperation on North American security. The Canadian decision not to participate in missile defence ruled this out, since it meant that missile defence could not be part of NORAD. Further confusing the matter, in a 2004 amendment, Canada had already agreed that NORAD would operate alongside and in support of ballistic missile defence. Faced with this unclear situation, and in light of the fact that the Americans had not yet developed ballistic missile defence capabilities that could replace NORAD, the two countries agreed in May 2006 to renew NORAD. They gave it a new responsibility for maritime warning and pledged to conduct a joint review within four years or at the request of either party. While the agreement did not resolve NORAD's future, it enabled the partners to maintain a highly successful bilateral arrangement and left open the possibility of renewing and modernizing NORAD at a more propitious time.

The ascendancy to power of the Harper government towards the end of the first decade of the new century has tended to re-establish a greater sense of common purpose between Canada and the United States on defence matters. In seeking an electoral mandate in 2006, the leader of the Conservative Party suggested that one of his highest priorities would be to rebuild the military capabilities of the Canadian Forces and to equip them to meet both Canada's existing and future defence needs and to honour the country's various alliance commitments. Upon becoming prime minister, Harper took a variety of policy and budgetary steps in support of these objectives that were greeted with enthusiasm by the government of the United States. From the vantage point of Washington, the new Canadian government was re-establishing itself as a "reliable" defence partner. Canadian participation in the global campaign against terrorism in this hemisphere – and further afield in such settings as Afghanistan and Libya – earned Ottawa new respect and admiration from both the Bush and Obama administrations.

Acid rain is a issue that has plagued Canadian–American relations for many years. The problem began in the late 1970s and was not resolved until 1991. Canadian scientists studying lakes in Ontario discovered acidification and linked it to industrial activities on both sides of the border. American officials were sceptical and refused to take immediate action, though the Carter administration agreed in 1980 to hold talks beginning in 1981. When Reagan refused to honour the agreement, Trudeau turned to other countries and to the Canadian provinces in order to raise awareness and increase support for the Canadian position, and thereby force the United States to the negotiating table. The strategy failed. In keeping with his less confrontational approach to bilateral relations, Mulroney sought to resolve the issue in private, bilateral discussions, but this also failed. When George H. Bush became president, the two sides finally succeeded in negotiating a bilateral Air Quality Control Agreement to combat acid rain.

As this brief review of relations between Canada and the United States makes clear, the bilateral relationship is broad, deep, and solid, but not without disagreements and controversies. While attending a NATO meeting in 1997, Chrétien inadvertently revealed publicly that domestic politics influences the public tone of Canada–US relations. Unaware that his microphone was open, he told Belgium's Prime Minister Dehane that anti-Americanism was popular in Canada, so he "made it his policy" to defy the United States. Interestingly, Chrétien's admission was made at a time when Clinton was president and relations between the United States and Canada were cordial. It was only after George W. Bush came to power that bilateral relations turned publicly cranky.

Over the years, other explanations for the warming or cooling of relations have been offered. One is that the temperature of relations is affected by whether the countries' policy priorities are in sync or diverging. In the 1990s, Canada promoted a foreign policy agenda that included closer ties with Cuba, support for the United Nations and multilateralism, an international ban on landmines, and the creation of the International Criminal Court. While not all of these policies were supported in Washington, they did not create significant tensions in bilateral relations under Clinton, probably because he did not have a competing policy agenda and, at least in his rhetoric, supported multilateralism. This changed when the second President Bush came to power. Moreover, the fact that the United States became preoccupied with physical security after 9/11, combined with American military superiority that allows it to act unilaterally in dealing with terrorism, exacerbated tensions between the two.

Yet another explanation for the rough patches in bilateral relations is the argument that Canadian values are different from American ones. The values-difference argument, articulated in recent years by Michael Adams (2003), is that Canadians and Americans are growing increasingly dissimilar as the latter embrace values that reflect individualism and the pursuit of survival and material gain in a hostile world, while

Canadians embrace individualism and personal fulfilment in a world they see as rather benign.

Those who think that values matter argue that they do so because they shape foreign policy priorities and the instruments used to pursue them – in the Canadian case, human security, multilateralism, the development of international institutions, and the rule of law. By contrast, American values are said to lead to unilateralism and a willingness to use pressure and military force in pursuit of power and security. Some argued that Canada should adopt a "Canadian strategy" based on multilateralism and relying on international agreements and programs to undermine terrorists. Clearly this values argument is both provocative and pessimistic. It implies that rather than simply encountering rough patches, the Canadian–US relationship can be expected to deteriorate further unless new shifts in values bring the two closer together again.

Finally, some argue that differences in interests and power contribute to the ups and downs in bilateral relations. For example, Canada's pursuit of multilateralism is at least in part a reflection of its middle-power status. Middle powers like Canada often prefer multilateral forums, treaties, and binding international institutions as a way to control superpowers and to reduce the significance of their superior economic and military resources. Superpowers tend to resist such efforts as contrary to their interest in maximizing their ability to act quickly and without "permission" from the international community.

Canada's Place in the Broader World

In his 2005 International Policy Statement (IPS), Prime Minister Paul Martin announced that his policy priorities fell "squarely within the Pearsonian tradition of an independent multilateral helpful fixer" (Government of Canada 2005). The IPS stated that Canada's "most fundamental" diplomatic objective is "the creation of a rules-based multilateral system." It identified UN peacekeeping, sustainable development, human rights, and human security as Canada's most important priorities. In short, the IPS emphasized the multilateralist and globalist thrust in Canadian foreign policy, something that all Canadian governments have promoted and protected. Canada's post–Second World War commitment to playing a constructive role in global politics is reflected in its foreign aid efforts, participation in UN peacekeeping, environmental activism, and human security initiatives.

Canada became an international aid donor in the 1950s. Levels of aid, formally known as official development assistance (ODA), measured as a percentage of GDP rose steadily until the mid-1970s to just over 0.5 per cent. They remained at that level until the early 1990s, when they began to decline. In 1970 the country adopted a target of 0.7 per cent of GNP, though the goal has never been met. Support in Canada for ODA is strong, and Canadians see it as a symbol of their solidarity and willingness to help the world's poor. As with other ODA donors, Canadian aid is motivated by a variety of factors, including humanitarian ones and self-interest, both political and economic. Aid is channelled through multilateral institutions and bilateral programs run by the Canadian International Development Agency (CIDA) and Foreign Affairs Canada (FAC).

Under Trudeau, Canada sought to raise its international profile by broadening the geographic scope of ODA. In recent years CIDA has been active in 150 countries. In 2003 about 45 per cent of bilateral aid went to Africa and the Middle East, 35 per cent to Asia, and 20 per cent to countries in the Americas (Rioux 2006). Also during the Trudeau years, there was an increased emphasis on using aid to promote commercial interests as well as on efforts to bring NGOs into ODA by channelling money through them for projects in developing countries.

ODA rose and fell during the Mulroney years. During the 1980s, Mulroney followed the international trend of using aid to support structural adjustment, but other changes in priorities were also visible. In *Sharing Our Future* the government supported a parliamentary committee report calling for a shift away from large capital and infrastructure projects towards "people-directed" efforts. In the early 1990s CIDA also began directing its efforts at promoting sustainable development and sustainable human development.

Since the 1990s, ODA has come under considerable criticism. In the early 1990s, ODA spending showed a clear downward trend. Critics argued that Canada was not a generous donor, particularly if aid were measured in terms of GNP. Another complaint was that ODA lacked focus and purpose, with the result that aid was spread among too many recipients and failed to make a significant impact anywhere. Additional criticism has been that Canadian governments have shifted focus from purely humanitarian justifications for development aid in favour of arguing that aid should also promote Canadian economic interests, values, and culture abroad.

Perhaps in part in response to domestic critics, Prime Minister Chrétien announced in late 2001 that Canada would increase ODA spending over several years, with the goal of doubling it by 2010. Chrétien also become a major champion of development aid to Africa. At the G8 summit in Genoa in 2001, African leaders presented a vision document entitled *New Partnership for African Development* (NEPAD), aimed at improving the lives of Africans and promoting development on the continent. At Genoa the G8 leaders pledged to work with African leaders to develop an action plan to implement NEPAD and to consider the action plan at the G8 summit in Kananaskis, Alberta, in June 2002.

Chrétien embraced the project and proposed a "Sherpa" process to keep the project moving forward. Under Canadian leadership, this process produced the *Action Plan for Africa* (ACA), which outlined a variety of measures to improve security against armed conflict, promote democratic governance, provide better trade access and trade enhancement measures, and promote debt relief and aid for health and education. Chrétien announced a number of Canadian initiatives at the Kananaskis summit and pledged C$400 million to implement them. He also promised to remove tariffs and quotas on most imports from thirty-four least-developed African countries.

Prime Minister Martin pledged to continue developing ODA in the directions marked out by Chrétien. In addition, aid was to be targeted towards twenty-five countries, which would receive two-thirds of Canadian bilateral ODA. Canada would be the main donor in these countries, and thus very influential. Most of the targets are African, but there are also some in Asia, the Americas, and Central and Eastern Europe. When Prime Minister Harper took office in 2006, he pledged to continue to increase ODA.

Another manifestation of Canada's commitment to playing a progressive, constructive role in the world is its long tradition of contributing to UN and other multinational peacekeeping missions. Canada became a regular participant in peacekeeping operations in the 1950s. During the Cold War the country responded positively to all UN requests for help. Between 1948 and 1990, Canada participated in seventeen peacekeeping operations, more than any other country. In the early 1990s, when Yugoslavia began to disintegrate, Prime Minister Mulroney was the first world leader to call for an international peacekeeping force.

In recent years, however, concerns have been expressed about the country's declining role in peacekeeping operations due to its military weakness caused by decades of cuts in military spending (Kilgour 2004; Cohen 2003). Canada continues to contribute to multinational missions abroad at about the same levels, but its UN commitment has declined. As Bill Robinson (2009, 6) has noted, by 2009 Canada was ranked sixty-third out of 105 contributors to UN peacekeeping missions, providing only 0.07 per cent of all total personnel.

While the decline in Canadian participation in traditional peacekeeping preceded the operation in Afghanistan, the Canadian commitment to Afghanistan has resulted in a marked increase in spending on supporting NATO efforts in that conflict as opposed to peacekeeping. The Canadian Centre for Policy Alternatives reported in 2009 that Canadian government spending was higher in 2009 than during the height of the Cold War (Robinson 2009). Yet, while spending has increased, the Canadian mission in Afghanistan is not popular with the Canadian public. The Conservative government, following a report by the Independent Panel on Canada's Future in Afghanistan, committed to a withdrawal of Canadian troops from the very dangerous south of Afghanistan in 2011. The Harper government suggests that in the post-2011 era it will focus its energies on development and diplomacy in Afghanistan.

Canada's global environmental engagement also goes back many years. Canada initially pursued environmental goals as particular issues arose, including acid rain, the threat to the Pacific salmon, and declining fishing stocks. In the 1980s, Canada's role in pushing for global environmental cooperation increased. Canada was active in efforts to promote international cooperation to protect the ozone layer. The Toronto Group, so named because the first meeting was held in that city, played an important role in the negotiations that produced the 1985 Vienna Convention for the Protection of the Ozone Layer and the subsequent protocol.

In the late 1980s Canada took a leadership role in calling for multinational cooperation on climate control. At a meeting in Toronto, Prime Minister Mulroney called for a law of the atmosphere. By 1991 attention was directed at negotiating the United Nations Framework Convention on Climate Change (UNFCCC). Canada was an active participant in meetings and negotiations, often acting as a facilitator to bring other participants closer together. The UNFCCC was the centrepiece of the 1992 UN Conference on Environment and Development, also known as the Earth Summit or Rio Conference. Canadian Maurice Strong was designated secretary general, and Canada went to the Rio conference as a recognized activist for and supporter of both the FCCC and the Biodiversity Treaty.

Canada's position on the Kyoto Protocol to the UNFCCC, negotiated in December 1997, was more ambiguous. On the one hand, Canada supported the general thrust of Kyoto and favoured legally binding measures. Along with all other wealthy industrial countries (except the United States), it signed the agreement. On the other hand, the government met strong opposition at home from the oil and gas sector and several provinces, who saw the implementation of the Kyoto Protocol as harmful to the Canadian economy. Of particular concern was Canada's being out of step with the United States. The United States, under the Bush Administration, had withdrawn from the Kyoto Protocol in 2001. However, following a very divisive domestic debate, the Liberal government under Jean Chrétien, oversaw the ratification of the Kyoto Protocol in late 2002. Unfortunately, because Canada was approximately 25 per cent over its Kyoto target, some observers wondered if Canadian ratification was anything more than a symbolic gesture (Smith 2008–9).

When the Conservative Party led by Stephen Harper was elected in 2006, Canadian federal government action to combat climate change had been minimal. There was widespread concern that Prime Minister Harper would withdraw Canada from the Kyoto Protocol, as he had long been an opponent of the international climate change agreement, regarding it as an imposition on the Canadian economy, contrary to the interests of the oil and gas sector and ineffective without the participation of the United States and large emitting states such as India and China, who did not have commitments under the protocol.

Prime Minister Harper did not withdraw Canada from the Kyoto Protocol in 2006, but did publicly declare that Canada would not meet its targets. The Conservative focus in international negotiations has been to work to secure some sort of commitments from states such as India and China and to find ways to bring the United States back in. In the North American context, and in particular since the election of President Barack Obama, the Canadian federal government has focused on the design of a North American regulatory regime. Since the international climate change meeting in Copenhagen in 2009, Canada has tied its climate change target to align with that of the United States. However, in 2011 the Conservative Party won a majority in the federal election and has since adopted policy positions that would have destabilized their previous minority governments. Consistent with the fear held by some in 2006, the Harper government withdrew from the Kyoto Protocol in December 2011.

Another global cause that Canada has been seen to champion since the mid-1990s is human security, which places individuals at the centre of efforts aimed at preserving, promoting, and spreading security. The UN's 1994 *Human Development Report* focused on human security, arguing that human security included economic well-being, secure access for all to adequate food, health security, and physical security as well as a clean environment. The Canadian government quickly became an outspoken advocate of human security as the centrepiece of what it saw as enlightened foreign policy and international cooperation.

Canada identified five human security priorities: protection of civilians, peace operations, conflict prevention, governance and accountability, and public safety. The Division of Peace Building and Human Security Agenda was created within the Department of Foreign Affairs and International Trade (DFAIT) to pursue the human security agenda. Together with Norway, Canada launched the Human Security Network, a group of thirteen like-minded countries, for the purpose of encouraging dialogue and action to promote human security.

Since the mid-1990s, Canada has pursued numerous human security initiatives. One of these was the challenge to ban antipersonnel landmines. In the early 1990s many NGOs came together to form the International Campaign to Ban Landmines (ICBL). This was a grass-roots movement organized as a coalition of independent NGOs committed to exerting political pressure on governments to negotiate a treaty banning landmines. The ICBL called on sympathetic governments to join together and identify themselves as pro-ban states. Minister of Foreign Affairs Lloyd Axworthy offered to host a government meeting of these states in Ottawa in October 1996. At this meeting he called on governments to stop talking and take action, challenging them to negotiate a simple and comprehensive treaty banning landmines by the end of 1997. This marked the start of the Ottawa Process. The governments took up the challenge. The Convention on the Prohibition of the Use, Production, Stockpiling and Transfer of Anti-personnel Mines and on Their Destruction was completed in Oslo in September 1997 and signed in Ottawa in December.

Another initiative Canada has supported as part of human security policy is the push to improve the United Nations' capacity to respond rapidly to threats to peace and security. Canada supported a 1996 Danish proposal to establish a rapid response force capable of deploying 4000 to 5000 troops within thirty days of a Security Council authorization. The Stand-By, High-Readiness Brigade (SHIRBRIG) would stay up to six months, giving larger, more permanent missions time to assemble and deploy. The first SHIRBRIG mission was to Ethiopia and Eritrea in 2000. It took the Canadian government only three days to authorize participation. Even though deployment was delayed because of equipment shortages, Canadian forces arrived twenty-eight days after Security Council authorization.

Canada has also been active in efforts to promote the norm of international responsibility to protect when governments cannot or will not provide protection for their citizens. In 2000 the *Report of the Panel on United Nations Peace Operations* (also known as the Brahimi report) called on the international community to recognize this responsibility and to take measures to implement it. Subsequent discussions of the report revealed considerable disagreement about whether and how to implement its recommendations. The United Nations' Special Committee on Peacekeeping Operations considered setting the report aside with no further action. Canadian Michel Duval, the committee's vice-chairman, played a central role in pushing the process forward: he succeeded in convincing developing states that contribute large numbers of troops to peacekeeping operations to support the Brahimi recommendations. This enabled the committee to adopt the report in March 2002.

Canada also sponsored the International Commission on Intervention and State Sovereignty, which produced the 2001 "Responsibility to Protect" document, which argues that the primary responsibility to protect lies with the state. However, when a state cannot or will not do so, the international community has a responsibility to act, and such action takes precedence over the principle of non-interference. Canada has subsequently worked to promote the report both within the United Nations and among civil-society actors.

Canada's support for the International Criminal Court (ICC) is another example of its efforts to promote human security and the international community's responsibility to act. The UN commission that completed the preparatory work on the creation of the ICC was led by Canadian Philippe Kirsch. In recognition of Canada's contribution to the establishment of the ICC, Kirsch was elected the ICC's first president.

While human security and human security–related initiatives were centrepieces of the Liberal government led by Jean Chrétien, the concept is no longer such a central theme in Canadian foreign policy. The language of human security was significantly muted in the foreign policy statement issued in 2005 under Prime Minister Paul Martin. Rather than being promoted as a broad overarching principle, as was the case with the Chrétien government, under Martin human security was strictly related to failed states. Under the Harper government, the idea of and promotion of human security is virtually non-existent, as the Harper government has rejected this vision associated with its Liberal predecessors.

The Harper government has not embraced ideas associated with past governments, claiming that previous Liberal governments were more talk than action. The Harper Conservatives have been crafting policies that bring Canada closer to the United States on various issues such as climate change, while simultaneously adopting positions that have the potential to challenge the United States. One area where the Canadian Conservative government has taken an assertive stance is on the Arctic. As climate change causes sea ice to melt and the Arctic tundra to change, governments around the world develop visions of Arctic oil, gas, and mineral wealth. However, sovereignty claims to land and sea beds are contested and the question of whether or not the Northwest Passage is a domestic or international strait is unresolved, with the United States and Canada agreeing to disagree on its status. However, the Conservative government has published two Arctic strategies, in 2009 and 2010 respectively, that foreground the importance of protecting Canadian sovereignty. The two documents indicate that the Canadian government will seek resolution, through multilateral processes, to resolve competing boundary claims and to secure recognition of Canada's continental-shelf rights.

As is clear from this discussion, Canada has long been an active, enthusiastic, and influential voice in favour of multilateral initiatives to promote international peace and security as well as new norms and ways of acting in global politics. Through support for economic openness, multilateralism, and binding international rules and processes, Canada has thus helped promote the emergence of globalization – that is, the increasing internationalization of social, economic, and political life. Many Canadians contend that globalization holds considerable promise for progress and makes it both easier and more important for Canada to act beyond its borders.

Yet globalization also poses important challenges for Canada. Economic globalization in particular has led to a significant amount of antiglobalist rhetoric in Canada. Scepticism is fuelled by economic dislocations caused by globalization and also by fears that globalization has a distinctly neoliberal bias that undermines political authority and sovereignty. Although Canadians are not alone in their scepticism, their traditional fears of being swallowed up by the United States have the potential to make them particularly sensitive to globalization. Thus, the harmonization of laws and regulations that Canadians perceive as forcing the country to abandon its own practices and traditions has generally been resisted. One of the challenges for Canadian governments is to navigate between, on the one hand, openness and robust multilateral institutions, rules, and norms and, on the other, the loss of "Canadianness."

An interesting example of this Canadian balancing act is the promotion of the international cultural-diversity agreement. In the 1990s a trade dispute with the United States over Canadian support for domestic magazines heated up. Canada argued that the legislation was designed to protect Canadian culture. The United States called it protectionism and challenged four Canadian laws in the WTO's Dispute Settlement Body (DSB). The WTO ruled against Canada. Canada responded by spearheading an international campaign to negotiate an agreement permitting states to sidestep WTO rules in the interest of protecting culture and promoting cultural diversity.

UNESCO had already produced a report on protecting culture in 1995 (*Our Creative Diversity*). At a conference on cultural policies for development in Stockholm in 1998, cultural ministers signed a declaration in support of allowing countries to treat cultural goods and services differently from other goods and services under WTO regulations. Two months later Sheila Copps, minister for Canadian heritage, convened a meeting of cultural ministers in Ottawa. They established the International Network on Cultural Policy (INCP) and appointed a steering group chaired by Canada to lead this new body. Canada also agreed to chair the Working Group on Cultural Diversity and Globalization. By the autumn of 2002 the INCP had produced a draft text on the protection of culture. In October 2005 UNESCO's General Conference adopted the Convention on the Protection and Promotion of the Diversity of Cultural Expressions.

While it is too early to tell how effective the treaty will be, it is interesting as an example of how Canada has used its traditional commitments to multinationalism and promoting international agreements – that is, a commitment to political globalization – to promote rules and principles for economic globalization. In doing so Canada has gained the support of Canadian NGOs and also shown how it is possible to make economic globalism more compatible with domestic values and priorities. Under the more recent Harper government, Canada has backed away from many of these multilateral initiatives. However, this has not tempered its desire to promote a distinctive Canadian profile in international affairs. It has spent considerable energies and resources to project a sense of Canadian leadership in the international community. Most recently it has done so by contributing to the costs of major international gatherings in Canada such as the Winter Olympics in Vancouver in 2010 and by organizing the G8 and G20 sessions in Ontario in the summer of the same year. It is unclear, however, whether such sponsorships have resulted in any greater influence for Canada in the world. On the one hand, the country received a tremendous amount of good press and exposure from hosting the Winter Olympics. On the other hand, it was quite noticeable at the G8 and G20 sessions that many of Canada's ideas on global priorities were only received with lukewarm enthusiasm by the other participants. Most recently, Canada's failure to secure one of the non-permanent seats on the Security Council of the United Nations suggests that Canadian leadership in various international arenas may be on the decline.

Conclusions

The above examination of Canadian foreign policy from the era of Confederation to our own day reveals a variety of important features that are worth our careful consideration as the country moves forward in the twenty-first century. These defining features of Canadian foreign policy over the past 140 years serve both as reminders of the important influences that have directed Canada's international relations in the past and as key indicators of some of the future directions the country might take in its foreign relations. Therefore, it is useful to take note of them again and to briefly comment on their likely consequences for Canada's future foreign policy.

One of these key features has been Canada's continuing need to integrate its foreign policy with its domestic agenda. Domestic concerns over economic prosperity, societal identity, and national unity have influenced Canadian external relations since the late nineteenth century. Canada has long linked its domestic priorities to its external policies. Foreign policy reviews undertaken by the St Laurent, Trudeau, and Chrétien governments have all emphasized the importance of domestic goals and priorities in the country's international relations. This linkage between domestic priorities and foreign policy objectives is unlikely to disappear.

An equally important determinant of Canadian foreign policy has been the influence of the United States. Canada's traditional strong links with its neighbour to the south have always had a strong impact on Canada's external relations. "For better or for worse," Canada has been drawn into an evolving partnership that has largely set the parameters of Canada's interactions on the world stage. Whether this close interaction takes the form of mutual defence agreements, joint environmental monitoring, or free trade, Canada has become increasingly linked to the United States. This close contact has had both positive and less desirable effects on the country's security, economic health, and sense of identity. This powerful pull of "American influence" will continue to shape some important contours of Canadian international behaviour over the coming years.

A third influence on the direction of Canadian foreign policy has been the country's continued need to define and redefine its specific role in the international community. At various points in its diplomatic history Canada has seen itself as a dependable alliance partner, a "middle power," a skilled practitioner of multilateral diplomacy, and a fervent advocate of new global agendas. Part of this continuing redefinition of Canada's role in world affairs has been brought about by major changes in the character of the international system over the past century. Some of it, however, can be linked directly to Canada's own ability to anticipate change and to adapt to altered circumstances. This willingness to be forward looking and flexible in its conduct of diplomacy has served Canada well over the years and will likely continue to do so in the future.

As noted at the outset, Canada is one of several "medium or smaller powers" that seem to be able to exercise influence in international affairs beyond their obvious power resources. We have seen in this survey of Canadian foreign policy that Canada has progressively expanded its participation in the international community and taken on a series of significant roles in shaping international institutions and the issues they pursue. Over the past half-century Canada has made lasting contributions the global community's ability to respond effectively to challenges in the areas of international security, human rights, and Third World development. It has helped to introduce and advance basic international practices and norms such as peacekeeping, environmental protection, and human security.

Canada's influence in international affairs is partly due to its reputation as a conscientious and considerate member of the global community. Canada has regularly emphasized the importance of international consensus building and cooperation and has made major contributions from its own national resources to the needs of the global society. It has also displayed tolerance and flexibility in its dealings with other states. Critics, most of them domestic, worry that Canada's influence in global affairs is at risk (Cohen 2003). The causes are said to be largely self-created, in particular the long-term decline in military spending and small and unfocused foreign aid budgets. The former is said to make Canada less important to the United States, less influential in NATO, and incapable of playing its traditionally strong role in peacekeeping operations. The latter limits its ability to promote development and human security.

Others point to Canada's significant contributions in Afghanistan, its efforts to focus foreign aid efforts, and its commitment to and success in promoting a progressive global agenda as evidence of Canada's continued international influence. Perhaps most significantly for future developments, Canadian identity has become connected to the country's role as a progressive state in international affairs (Byrsk 2007). Canada has become more confident of its ability to make a lasting impact on the course of human development and has sought to do so. This was the clear message that former governor general Adrienne Clarkson invoked in her speech to the Canadian people at the time of her investiture in 1999. She noted, in part: "We must not see ourselves as a small country ... We are among the healthiest, best-educated people in the world, with great natural riches. We have two of the world's great languages. We must not see ourselves as people who simply react to trends but as people who can initiate them. We must not see ourselves as people to whom things are done but as people who do things" (Clarkson 1999). This sense of creative dynamism may be the guiding force behind Canadian foreign policy over the remainder of this century.

WEBSITES

Canadian Embassy in Washington, DC: http://www.canadainternational.
   gc.ca/washington
Canadian International Council: http://www.ciia.org
Canadian International Development Agency: http://www.acdi-cida.gc.ca

Department of Foreign Affairs and International Trade: http://www.dfait-
maeci.gc.ca
Department of National Defence: http://www.forces.gc.ca
NAFTA Secretariat: http://www.nafta-sec-alena.org

REFERENCES AND FURTHER READING

Adam, Chapnick. 2008. "Canada's Aid Program: Still Struggling after Sixty
Years." *Behind the Headlines* 65 (3). http://www.opencanada.org/wp-con-
tent/uploads/2011/05/BTH_vol65_no3.pdf.

Adams, Michael. 2003. *Fire and Ice: The United States, Canada and the Myth of
Converging Values.* Toronto: Penguin Canada.

Ayres, Jeffrey M. 1998. *Defying Conventional Wisdom: Political Movements and
Popular Contention against North American Free Trade.* Toronto: University of
Toronto Press.

Beier, Marshall, and Lana Wylie, eds. 2009. *Canadian Foreign Policy in Critical
Perspective.* Toronto: Oxford University Press.

Bratt, Duane and Christopher J., eds. 2007. *Readings in Canadian Foreign Policy:
Classic Debates and New Ideas.* Toronto: Oxford University Press.

Byrsk, Alison. 2007. "The Other America: Canada as 'Global Good Samari-
tan.'" Paper presented at International Studies Association annual convention, Chicago, 28 February to 3 March.

Cameron, Maxwell A., and Brian W. Tomlin. 2000. *The Making of NAFTA: How
the Deal Was Done.* Ithaca: Cornell University Press.

Canadian Broadcasting Corporation (CBC) Archives. 1983. "Trudeau's Push
for Cold War Peace." http://www.cbc.ca/archives/categories/war-con-
flict/peacekeeping/peacekeepers-and-peacemakers-canadas-diplomatic-
contribution/trudeaus-push-for-cold-war-peace.html.

Carment, David, Fen Osler Hampson, and Norman Hillmer, eds. 2003. *Canada
among Nations 2003: Coping with the American Colossus.* Toronto: Oxford
University Press.

Clarkson, Adrienne. 1999. Installation Speech of Her Excellency the Right
Honourable Adrienne Clarkson, Governor General of Canada. 7 October.
http://archive.gg.ca/media/doc.asp?lang=e&DocID=1379.

Cohen, Andrew. 2003. *While Canada Slept: How We Lost Our Place in the World.*
Toronto: McClelland & Stewart.

Cooper, Andrew F. 1997. *Canadian Foreign Policy: Old Habits and New Directions.*
Scarborough, ON: Prentice-Hall Allyn and Bacon.

Cooper, Andrew F., and Dane Rowlands, eds. 2005. *Canada among Nations 2005: Split Images*. Montreal: McGill-Queen's University Press.

Department of External Affairs. 1970. *Foreign Policy for Canadians*. Ottawa.

Doern, G. Bruce, and Brian W. Tomlin. 1991. *Faith and Fear: The Free Trade Story*. Toronto: Stoddart Publishing.

Doran, Charles. 2006. "Canada–U.S. Relations: Personality, Pattern, and Domestic Politics." In *Handbook of Canadian Foreign Policy*, ed. Patrick James, Nelson Michaud, and Marc J. O'Reilly, 389–410. Lanham, MD: Lexington Books.

Government of Canada. 2005. *Canada's International Policy Statement: A Role of Pride and Influence in the World*. Ottawa: Canadian International Development Agency.

Griffiths, Franklyn, et al. 2008. "Canada's Arctic Interests and Responsibilities." *Behind the Headlines* 65 (4). http://www.opencanada.org/wp-content/uploads/2011/05/BTH_vol65_no4.pdf.

Hart, Michael. 1994. *Decisions at Midnight: Inside the Canada-US Free-Trade Negotiations*. Vancouver: UBC Press.

Hillmer, Norman, and J.L. Granatstein. 2007. *For Better or For Worse: Canada and the United States into the Twenty-First Century*. Toronto: Thompson Nelson.

James, Patrick, Nelson Michaud, and Marc O'Reilly, eds. 2006. *Handbook of Canadian Foreign Policy*. Lanham, MD: Lexington Books.

Keating, Tom. 2002. *Canada and World Order: The Multilateralist Tradition in Canadian Foreign Policy*. 2nd ed. Don Mills, ON: Oxford University Press.

Kilgour, David. 2004. "Canada's Peacekeeping Role: Then and Now." http://www.david-kilgour./com/mp/Peacekeeping%20U%20of%20A.htm.

Laurent, St., and S. Louis. 1947. "'The Foundation of Canadian Policy in World Affairs.' Address by the Right Honourable Louis S. St Laurent, Secretary of State for External Affairs, Inaugurating Gray Foundation Lectureship, University of Toronto." In Department of External Affairs." *Statements and Speeches* 47 (2): 3–11.

MacEachen, Allan J. 1975. "Embassy of Canada Report." Remarks by Secretary of State for External Affairs to the Winnipeg Branch of the Canadian Institute for International Affairs, Washington, DC, 23 January.

Michaud, Nelson, and Kim Richard Nossal, eds. 2001. *Diplomatic Departures: The Conservative Era in Canadian Foreign Policy, 1984–1993*. Vancouver: UBC Press.

Nord, Douglas C. 2010. "The North in Canadian–American Relations: Searching for Collaboration in Melting Seas." In *Borders and Bridges in Canada's*

Policy Relations in North America, ed. Monica Gattinger and Geoffrey Hale. Toronto: Oxford University Press.

Nossal, Kim, Stephane Roussel, and Stephane Paquin. 2010. *International Policy and Politics in Canada*. Toronto: Pearson Education.

Porter, William. 1974. *Remarks of U.S. Ambassador to Canada to the Canadian Institute of International Affairs, Winnipeg, Manitoba, 25 September 1974. News release, US Information Services*. Ottawa: US Embassy.

Potter, Evan H. 2009. *Branding Canada: Projecting Canada's Soft Power through Public Diplomacy*. Montreal, Kingston: McGill-Queen's University Press.

Rioux, Jean-Sébastien. 2006. "Canadian Official Development Assistance." In *Handbook of Canadian Foreign Policy*, ed. Patrick James, Nelson Michaud, and Marc J. O'Reilly, 209–234. Lanham, MD: Lexington Books.

Robinson, Bill. 2009. *Canadian Military Spending 2009*. Ottawa: Canadian Centre for Policy Alternatives.http://www.policyalternatives.ca/publications/reports/canadian-military-spending-2009.

Simpson, Jeffrey. 1993. *Faultlines: Struggling for a Canadian Vision*. Toronto: HarperPerennial.

Sjolander Turenne, Calire. 2010. "The Obama Charm? Canada and Afghanistan under a New US Administration." *American Review of Canadian Studies* 40 (2): 292–304. http://dx.doi.org/10.1080/02722011003734795.

Smith, Heather A. 2008–9. "Political Parties and Climate Change." (Toronto) *International Journal (Toronto, Ont.)* 64 (1): 47–66.

Smith, Heather A. 2009. "Unwilling Internationalism? Canadian Climate Policy under the Conservative Government." *Canadian Foreign Policy* 15 (2): 57–77. http://dx.doi.org/10.1080/11926422.2009.9673487.

Thompson, John Herd, and Stephen J. Randall. 2002. *Canada and the United States: Ambivalent Allies*. Montreal: McGill-Queen's University Press.

13 Future Prospects

MARK KASOFF AND PATRICK JAMES

Having studied the chapters of this book, dear reader, you now have a comprehensive introduction to Canada as compared to the United States. We started with Canada's most fundamental characteristics: its geography and history and how Canada evolved differently from the United States as a result of these forces. Additional chapters deliberately went back and forth between highly encompassing and more focused subjects to strike a balance between the conventional and more recently topical. Thus, the journey through Canada continued with a look at government institutions and politics in general, along with the economy, population, and immigration. This discussion was followed by a consideration of Quebec as a special part of Canada and an entity unto itself. The chapter on Canadian culture, cast broadly in terms of literature, the arts, and popular culture such as sports and music, revealed the contributions of the respective founding peoples and told the story of a nation still in the making. The struggles of women and Aboriginals came next. These stories of overcoming adversity were followed by an account of Canada's environmental stewardship of its vast landscape. We finished up by looking at characteristics of Canada from the inside and outside – its civil society and foreign policy.

This has been a necessarily brief introduction, but probably the most that can be conveyed in a single comprehensive overview such as this book. In finishing, we will identify several themes for reflection that transcend individual disciplines or topical areas. The goal is to suggest some interesting directions for further study and to identify challenges that Canada will likely face in the years to come.

One enduring theme in the study of Canada is reference to Canada as beset by challenges. (Dimensions of this theme relate to both internal and external levels of interaction.) Examples of this point of emphasis include survival in Canada's foreboding geography, proximity to the sometimes overwhelming United States, the persistence of ethno-linguistic divisions (such as francophone language and culture), the status of Aboriginal peoples, and cultural survival in the face of fragmentation. Ideas about "what to do" are not in short supply regarding how Canada should respond to these challenges. Consensus about the best path to take, in either an overall sense or with regard to special issues, is another matter.

Besides the enduring challenge of Canada's geography, the future brings the need to anticipate the effects of global climate change. Canada will have to do its fair share in reducing greenhouse gases. At a more local level, this changing picture will include growing competition over Canada's Arctic waters, which are likely to become navigable within a few decades. Precursors to land disputes in the North include incidents already on record between Canada and Denmark over an island off the coast of Greenland. Tensions with the United States over Arctic sovereignty may occur, posing a potential threat to hemispheric solidarity regarding matters of security. Besides territorial concerns, a key economic issue will be control of oil and natural gas reserves, which are substantial. Thus, Canada will need to find practical ways to assert its authority. Multilateral diplomatic initiatives will be vital to ensure that Canada will receive its perceived fair share when resources are commercially developed. A unilateral component of response will involve the acquisition of enough cold-weather ships to represent the country's interests.

Canadians will struggle to define their national identity in the coming decades. The usual Canadian starting point in defining the country's identity is *negative*. "We are not Americans" is the standard refrain. After working through the pages of this book, the reader knows that much, at least, to be true. What, then, *is* a Canadian? The preceding chapters provide at least six clear, if not mutually exclusive, signposts. First, the history of Canada reveals a long-standing struggle to resolve a basic divide between significant francophone and anglophone legacies, with the mixed results to be expected from such a great challenge. Second, Canadians are federalists in their politics, but with varying perceptions of the optimal division of power between the central and provincial governments and with especially sharp divisions between many residents of Quebec and other citizens. A third characteristic is Canadians' commitment to managing the concerns expressed by

Aboriginal people, women, and other marginalized groups, which led to the Charter of Rights and Freedoms in 1982. Fourth, cultural diversity, with Canada's ideal as a "salad bowl" rather than an American-style melting pot, comes to the fore in shaping Canadian identity. Fifth, Canadians are committed to an extensive range of social programs – perhaps closer in scope to those of Europe – and take pride in their national health care system. Financial constraints will challenge the tradition of universal access and increase calls for movement towards a two-tier system. Sixth and finally, Canadians prefer a multilateral approach when it comes to foreign policy, perhaps in response to the frequently unilateral emphasis seen south of the border and the country's smaller population and economic base. Still, Canada will have to keep devising ways to strengthen bilateral relations with the United States.

The capacity of existing political and governmental institutions to meet the future challenges of economic, military, and personal security will be severely tested. The Charter of Rights and Freedoms, along with movement towards a stronger judiciary, will erode the parliamentary supremacy that has been in place since Confederation. With greater influence from the West, pressure will increase for a more effective senate and for a devolution of political power from Ottawa to the provinces. Even the nominal connection of the Canadian state to the British Crown will receive greater attention.

Beyond the pressures noted above vis-à-vis the performance of Canadian institutions are those created by the neighbouring United States – the world's leading and most active state over the past century. The preservation of a distinct Canadian culture in the face of American-centred globalization is a challenge that every Canadian government must meet, even if this involves sometimes recognizing that citizens will prefer excellence regardless of its point of origin. Certainly, hemispheric integration is well along in economic terms, so Canada's ability to preserve an independent stance arises as a source of concern. Multilateral versus American-centred bilateral liberalization of economic exchange, including both capital and labour, has emerged as a preferred strategy, with specific tactics pursued according to context. This multilateral theme also arises in terms of national security. Canadians, for the most part, do not want their foreign policy dictated by Washington, but they do generally accept the ongoing presence of the United States as leader of a coalition that is seeking to manage and even eradicate the problems created by global terrorism, the extremes of religious fundamentalism, and the proliferation of weapons of mass destruction.

Much as Canada favours multilateral approaches to address policy issues with the United States, bilateral cooperation will also be required. Examples include the continued joint stewardship of the Great Lakes, the Devils Lake dispute between North Dakota and Manitoba, and especially border management cooperation. Since Canada will remain heavily dependent on the United States for economic growth, it will have to ensure that border measures do not create an implicit tax for private business. This can only hurt Canada by reducing trade with the United States and dampening inward foreign direct investment.

Canada and the United States should continue exploring joint security-perimeter measures to minimize the costs of enforcing homeland security at existing borders. The reader should understand that this is a very modest proposal and a *long* way from economic and political union European-style; we are not even proposing a customs union where member countries levy the same external tariffs. For the foreseeable future, Canada's commerce with the Americans will be governed by NAFTA. The *joint perimeter concept* outlined here will ensure that the current border does not become an impediment to free trade.

In closing, we can say that Canada remains a young country, at least in terms of political sovereignty, but one already boasting many accomplishments in a wide range of areas. Some might even say that keeping together such a diverse civil society, spread across an entire continent, for well over a century and in a generally peaceful way, is the greatest accomplishment of all. The goal of this book has been to introduce rather than finish the story of this fascinating country and thus, it is hoped, create interest in further study.

Contributors

Leslie R. Alm is a professor with the Department of Public Policy and Administration and the Department of Political Science at Boise State University. His research interests are environmental policymaking and US–Canada relations (with a focus on the environment). He has recently published articles in *Journal of Environmental Systems* and *Canadian-American Public Policy*. His latest (co-authored) book is *Turmoil in American Public Policy: Science, Democracy, and the Environment* (Praeger/Greenwood, 2010).

Sammy Basu is an associate professor in politics, chair of American Ethnic Studies, and coordinator of College Colloquium at Willamette University in Salem, Oregon. Trained in political philosophy, his research interests centre on deliberative democracy from historical and comparative perspectives. He teaches courses in political philosophy and ethics and public policy, on topics ranging from death to humour, and Nazi Germany to Canada. He has taught a Canadian Studies course for several years combining wide-ranging readings with a pedagogy of "digital field-work."

Roderic Beaujot is professor emeritus of sociology, member of the Centre for Population, Aging and Health, and director of the Research Data Centre at the University of Western Ontario. He is also principal investigator for Population Change and Lifecourse, a Strategic Knowledge Cluster funded by the Social Sciences and Humanities Research Council, and chair of the Statistics Canada Advisory Committee on Demographic Statistics and Studies. He is author of *Earning and Caring in*

Canadian Families (Broadview, 2000) and co-author with Don Kerr of *Population Change in Canada* (Oxford, 2004).

Louis Bélanger is a professor of international relations in the Department of Political Science at Université Laval, Quebec City. He is the author of numerous publications on North American integration, Canadian foreign policy, Quebec's international activities, and secessionist movements. Professor Bélanger held visiting positions at Duke University, Sciences Po-Paris, the Woodrow Wilson International Center for Scholars, the Paul H. Nitze School of Advanced International Studies, and Sciences Po-Grenoble. He recently completed a four-year mandate as a member of the Military Police Complaints Commission of Canada.

Michael J. Broadway is professor of geography and dean of the College of Arts and Sciences at Northern Michigan University. He is a co-author of *Slaughterhouse Blues: The Meat and Poultry Industry in North America*, 2nd edition (Cengage, 2013) and co-editor of *Any Way You Cut It: Meat-processing and the Transformation of Rural America* (Kansas, 1995). In 2006 he was a visiting Fulbright Research Chair in the Department of Rural Economy at the University of Alberta, where he studied the impact of "mad cow disease" on a rural community, and the social changes accompanying the expansion of a meat-packing plant in Brooks, Alberta. Recently, he published articles dealing with urban agriculture in Milwaukee and Vancouver, British Columbia. From 2002 to 2006 he served on the executive council of the Association for Canadian Studies in the United States, and currently serves on the editorial board of the *American Review of Canadian Studies*.

Ross E. Burkhart is associate professor of political science and co-director of the Canadian Studies Program at Boise State University. He is also the executive director of the Pacific Northwest Canadian Studies Consortium. His research interests are the political economy of democratization, Canadian-US environmental policy and Canada-US borderlands. He has recently co-authored, with Leslie R. Alm and Marc V. Simon, *Turmoil in American Public Policy: Science, Democracy and the Environment* (Praeger, 2010), and has published articles in the *American Political Science Review*, *International Journal of Canadian Studies*, and the *Social Science Journal*.

Lea Caragata is professor of social policy and community development at Wilfrid Laurier University in Kitchener, Ontario. Her recent research includes a multi-site interdisciplinary longitudinal study of single mothers in three Canadian cities examining the effects of labour market change and workfare programs on these families. Other research has focused on citizenship, social movements, gender, social exclusion, and considerations of space and place. Her academic career followed almost twenty years of work in government and the non-profit sector, including more than ten years as executive director of a social housing organization.

Charles F. Doran is Andrew W. Mellon Professor of International Relations and director of the Center for Canadian Studies, Johns Hopkins University, School of Advanced International Studies (SAIS), Washington, DC. The author of many articles and books on Canada, he is the recipient of both the Donner Medal (1991) and the Governor General's International Award (1999) for distinguished scholarship on Canada. A past president of the Association for Canadian Studies in the United States, he is also a senior associate at the Center for International and Strategic Studies and a member of the Council on Foreign Relations.

Munroe Eagles is a professor of political science and director of the Canadian studies academic program at the University at Buffalo–State University of New York. He is also team leader of the "Parliament and Parties" research group for Samara.org, a research unit dedicated to strengthening Canadian democracy. He is currently working on a book exploring the constituency foundations of Canadian politics.

Andrew Holman is professor of history and Canadian studies at Bridgewater State University in Massachusetts, where he teaches a variety of courses on Canada and the United States. He is author of *A Sense of Their Duty: Middle-class Formation in Victorian Ontario Towns* (McGill-Queen's, 2000), editor of *Canada's Game: Hockey and Identity* (McGill-Queen's, 2009) and co-author (with Robert Kristofferson) of *More of a Man: Diaries of a Scottish Craftsman in Mid-nineteenth-century North America* (Toronto, 2013).

Patrick James is Dornsife Dean's Professor of International Relations and director of the Center for International Studies at the University of Southern California. He is the author or editor of over 20 books and more than 120 articles and chapters. James has served as editor of *International Studies Quarterly*, vice-president of the International Studies Association, and president of the Association for Canadian Studies in the United States. He currently serves as president of the International Council for Canadian Studies.

Mark Kasoff served as founding director of Bowling Green State University's Canadian studies program. He recently retired as professor of economics and Canadian studies emeritus and remains active in the Canadian studies community. From 2002–6 Kasoff was editor of the *American Review of Canadian Studies*. He has published articles and book chapters on Canadian international trade and direct investment.

Patrice LeClerc is associate professor of sociology at St Lawrence University. She writes and teaches about social movements, especially women's movements and nationalisms. Her most recent publication is "The Big Smoke Screen: Toronto's G20 Protests," in *Socialist Studies Journal* 5 (7) (with Ian Hussey). She is also a regular contributor to *Choices*. Her current research is on the development of nationalism in Canada and the United States.

Michael Lusztig is professor of political science at Southern Methodist University. In addition to numerous scholarly articles on Canadian politics and international trade, Lusztig is author of two books: *Risking Free Trade* (Pittsburgh, 1996) and *The Limits of Protectionism* (Pittsburgh, 2004) He is currently completing a book manuscript entitled "Liberal Republics and the Challenge of Multiculturalism."

Sharon A. Manna is a professor of government at North Lake College in Irving, TX. She spends her working days convincing her students to be active participants in their government. The struggle continues.

Douglas Nord is professor of political science at Western Washington University in Bellingham, Washington. He has written widely in the areas of Canadian foreign policy and Canadian–American relations. He also works in the fields of comparative public policy and regional development. He is currently looking at the different approaches that Canada and the United States have taken towards the North and their roles on the Arctic Council.

Muhammad Munib Raza is a PhD candidate at the Department of Sociology, University of Western Ontario. He is also enrolled in the Migration and Ethnic Relations Program in the Faculty of Social Sciences. He is currently teaching "Minority Groups in Canada" at King's University College and "International Migration in a Globalized World" at the Department of Sociology, University of Western Ontario.

Mark Paul Richard is associate professor of history and Canadian studies at the State University of New York, Plattsburgh, where he coordinated the Canadian studies program from 2005 to 2011. He is the author of *Loyal but French: The Negotiation of Identity by French-Canadian Descendants in the United States* (Michigan State, 2008.) At present, he is writing a monograph on the activities of the Ku Klux Klan in French-Canadian population centres of the northeastern United States during the 1920s.

Heather Smith is professor of international studies at the University of Northern British Columbia. Her areas of expertise include Canadian climate change policy, gender and Canadian foreign policy, and indigenous perspectives on climate change. Recent publications include "Choosing Not to See: Canada, Climate Change and the Arctic" in *International Journal* (Autumn 2010); "Unwilling Internationalism or Strategic Internationalism? Canadian Climate Policy under the Conservative Government" in *Canadian Foreign Policy* (Summer 2009), and "Disciplining Nature of the Discipline" in Marshall Beier and Lana Wylie, eds, *Canadian Foreign Policy in Critical Perspective* (Oxford, 2009).

Paul Storer is professor of economics at Western Washington University, where he teaches courses on the Canadian economy and Canadian business environment. In Canada, he served as a staff economist for the Bank of Canada and a faculty member at the University of Quebec at Montreal. His current research interests include North American economic integration. He has published in scholarly journals such as the *American Review of Canadian Studies* and *Canadian Public Policy* and is also a coauthor on the 13th US edition of the introductory economics textbook by Lipsey, Ragan, and Storer.

Robert Thacker is Charles A. Dana Professor of Canadian Studies and English and associate dean, Academic, at St Lawrence University. His book *The Great Prairie Fact and Literary Imagination* (New Mexico, 1989) is a critical examination of the literature of the prairie-plains region in its binational context. His *Alice Munro: Writing Her Lives: A Biography* (2005), written with the cooperation of Munro, was updated and published by Emblem Books, Toronto, in 2011. *Reading Alice Munro,*

1983–2012, his selected essays, is in preparation. From 1994–2002, Thacker was the editor of the *American Review of Canadian Studies*.

John Herd Thompson is professor emeritus of history and taught North American history at Duke University. A fifth edition of his *Canada and the United States: Ambivalent Allies* (co-authored with Stephen J. Randall) is in progress, and he is at work on *The Globe through the Diamond: Baseball and Nation in North America, the Caribbean, and Asia*.

Index